If you're wondering why you should buy this new edition of *Terrorism and Counterterrorism*, here are five good reasons!

1. Chapter 1, "The Perennial Debate: What Is Terrorism?" brings you up-to-date on the recent **terrorist attacks in Mumbai** and examines how they affect the study of terrorism.

2. Chapter 5, "Religious Terrorism: Political Violence in the Name of God" now includes an expanded discussion of **religious extremism and Jihadi terrorism.**

3. Chapter 10, "Terrorism and America's Post—9/11 National Security Strategy" is a new chapter that will help you understand **American counterterrorism strategies**, ranging from the Bush Doctrine to what we can expect from the Obama administration.

4. Chapter 11, "The Utility of Hard and Soft Power in Counterterrorism" fully explains different responses to terrorist threats, including both **military and nonmilitary responses.**

5. Chapter 12, "Balancing Security, Liberty, and Human Rights" includes new examples that will show you **how terrorism affects individuals.**

D1367645

PEARSON

PRAISE *for*
TERRORISM AND COUNTERTERRORISM
By Brigitte L. Nacos

In this book Brigitte Nacos skillfully surveys the landscape of terrorism in the contemporary world. As she notes, there are few studies of much relevance on our shelves after 9/11. *Terrorism and Counterterrorism* begins to provide us with an understanding of the enormous variety and scale of what we need to understand.

> —Charles B. Strozier, Director, Center on Terrorism, John Jay College, CUNY, and author, "Apocalypse: On the Psychology of Christian Fundamentalism."

Professor Nacos demonstrates how a skilled educator can guide her students on a clear path through the noisy jungle of terrorism studies. Her work synthesizes a complex and growing field of research, illuminating important concepts and issues with clarity and precision. From beginning to end, this book will certainly enhance any reader's understanding of terrorism and the counterterrorism challenges of the 21st century. While written primarily for students and scholars, it will also be useful to policymakers, national security professionals and local emergency responders, and is accessible to a broad, general audience.

> —James JF Forest, Ph.D., Director of Terrorism Studies, U.S. Military Academy, West Point

This text addresses both the basics and the advanced aspects of terrorism in a thorough manner. The text then moves forward into other critical and timely events that are at the core of the study of terrorism, and the author's perspective is real world and realistic.... [It is] an accurate, realistic, encompassing text that addresses the most salient aspects of terrorism in an easy reading manner.

> —Peter A. Barone, National Lecturer/Consultant, HIDTA Assistance Group, and Director of the Criminal Justice Program, Teikyo Post University

This book is fair, balanced, scholarly, and easily accessible because it is jargon-free. It possesses depth and breadth simultaneously while engaging the reader in its content. This book is a most useful teaching and learning tool in addition to being a "good read" for the general public.

> —Dean A. Minix, Department of Political Science and Criminal Justice, Northern Kentucky University

PENGUIN ACADEMICS

TERRORISM AND COUNTERTERRORISM

UNDERSTANDING THREATS AND RESPONSES IN THE POST—9/11 WORLD

THIRD EDITION

BRIGITTE L. NACOS

Columbia University

Longman

Boston   Columbus   Indianapolis   New York   San Francisco   Upper Saddle River
Amsterdam   Cape Town   Dubai   London   Madrid   Milan   Munich   Paris   Montreal   Toronto
Delhi   Mexico City   Sao Paulo   Sydney   Hong Kong   Seoul   Singapore   Taipei   Tokyo

Acquisitions Editor: Vikram Mukhija
Editorial Assistant: Toni Magyar
Marketing Manager: Lindsey Prudhomme
Production Manager: Wanda Rockwell
Manager, Rights and Permissions: Zina Arabia
Manager, Cover Visual Research & Permissions: Karen Sanatar
Image Permission Coordinator: Kathy Gavilanes
Project Coordination, Text Design, and Electronic Page Makeup: Saraswathi Muralidhar, GGS Higher Education Resources, A Division of PreMedia Global Inc.
Creative Director: Jayne Conte
Cover Designer: Bruce Kenselaar
Cover Illustration/Photo: George Logan/zefa/Corbis
Cover Printer and Binder: Courier Companies, Inc.

For more information about the Penguin Academics series, please contact us by mail at Pearson Education, attn. Marketing Department, 51 Madison Avenue, 29th Floor, New York, NY 10010, or visit us online at www.pearsonhighered.com

Library of Congress Cataloging-in-Publication Data

Nacos, Brigitte Lebens.
   Terrorism and counterterrorism: understanding threats and responses in the post–9/11 world/Brigitte L. Nacos.—3rd ed.
   . p. cm.—(Penguin academics)
   Includes bibliographical references and index.
   ISBN-13: 978-0-205-74327-8
   ISBN-10: 0-205-74327-7
1. Terrorism.   2. Terrorism—Prevention.   I. Title.

   HV6431.N34 2010
   363.325—dc22

                                                    2009025465

Page 2: Daniel Hulshizer/AP Wide World Photos; page 18: Getty Images, Inc. AFP; page 35: © Bettmann/CORBIS All Rights Reserved; page 54: Jason Turner/The Journal/AP Wide World Photos; page 77 left: Peter Cosgrove/AP Wide World Photos; page 77 center: State of Florida DMV/AP Wide World Photos; page 77 right: str/ZOOM/AP Wide World Photos; page 96 left and center: Getty Images; page 96 right: Getty Images, Inc. AFP; page 116: AP Wide World Photos; page 130: David Ake/Getty Images, Inc. AFP; page 154: Anja Niedringhaus/AP Wide World Photos; page 170: Getty Images; page 183: Getty Images; page 206: Ted S. Warren/AP Wide World Photos; page 229: Getty Images; page 252: AP Wide World Photos; page 270:Getty Images; page 286: Pablo Martinez Monsivais/AP Wide World Photos; page 300: Cartoon by Nicholson from The Australian.

1 2 3 4 5 6 7 8 9 10—CRS—12 11 10 09

Longman
is an imprint of

www.pearsonhighered.com

ISBN-13: 978-0-205-74327-8
ISBN-10:   0-205-74327-7

brief contents

detailed contents

Delivering the intelligence community's annual threat assessment in early 2009, the new Director of National Intelligence Dennis C. Blair told the U.S. Senate Select Committee on Intelligence, "The primary near-term security concern of the United States is the global economic crisis and its geopolitical implications." While this was the first time since 9/11 that terrorism was not highest on the threat list, there was no reason to celebrate an easing of the terrorist threat. Blair warned of a proliferation of instability and high levels of extremism in a deepening economic crisis around the world and thus of the very conditions that tend to breed political violence, including terrorism.

Regardless of the consequences of a worsening economic crisis, domestic and transnational terrorism remain high on threat lists around the globe. As I write this preface to the third edition of *Terrorism and Counterterrorism*, the news is grim. Within the last 24 hours, a female suicide bomber attacked Iraqi women and children on a pilgrimage to the Shi'ite holy city of Kabala, killing 40 people and injuring 60 others. Hamas fired rockets into southern Israel. Afghanistan's capital Kabul is trying to recover from yesterday's simultaneous strikes against three government buildings by gunmen and suicide bombers that killed 20 and injured 57 persons. These and similar incidents continue to impact the domestic and foreign policies of many countries and, consequently, international relations.

Sixteen years ago, when I put together the syllabus for the very first terrorism course I taught, it was difficult to find good articles and chapters—forget textbooks—that covered the whole range of what I considered important aspects of transnational and domestic terrorism and counterterrorism. After September 11, 2001, there was a flood of new publications that dealt mostly or exclusively with 9/11; the perpetrators of that horrific event; the motives of bin Laden, Al Qaeda, and like-minded individuals and groups; the implications for American domestic and foreign policy; and the impact on U.S. foreign policy and/or international relations, and so on.

Fine textbooks by single authors are often written for readers with special interests, for example, students in criminal justice courses or members of the emergency response community; others cover all conceivable topics in too short sections; and still others are exclusively devoted to transnational terrorism. Even the best among edited volumes seem less suited to serve as basic texts than as valuable supplements to a basic textbook written by one author.

The students in my terrorism/counterterrorism class were in the past and are today predominantly political science majors, mostly concentrating on the study of international relations, American government, and comparative politics. I have also had students who majored in sociology, history, urban studies, and psychology. I wrote this textbook with these undergraduate students in mind, but even graduate students who have a good basic knowledge of the topic will find here the background and tools with which to study terrorism and counterterrorism at an advanced level. Teaching graduate courses on media and politics, for example, I learned that many students did not study this area as undergraduates but could be brought up to speed for more advanced studies by working their way through a good textbook.

Features

This book provides a detailed description, analysis, and discussion of political violence carried out by non-state actors and of the counterterrorist responses of governments. In a departure from most other textbooks in the field, I have chosen to concentrate on what I believe are the most important topics and to cover them comprehensively, rather than summarize all conceivable themes. Thus, comprehensive chapters are devoted to homegrown terrorism of the past and present in the United States and to the various waves of international terrorism throughout history, including the contemporary threats posed by the new catastrophic type of terrorism. Building on these early parts of the volume, the following chapters explore the most important questions and issues surrounding terrorism, such as the making of terrorists in terms of external conditions and personal traits, the role of nation-states as sponsors or involuntary hosts of terrorists, the organization of terrorist groups and how they finance their activities, and the rationale behind the selection of terrorist targets and methods. Similarly, whole chapters deal with the most important aspects of counterterrorism, namely, military and nonmilitary responses, measures to prevent terrorist strikes, and the need to provide homeland security and preserve civil liberties. Finally, several chapters explain the role of propaganda in the terrorist scheme, the importance of the Internet for terrorist and hate groups, and the centrality of the media in the politics of counterterrorism.

New to this Edition

A successful textbook is a work in progress. While the first edition of *Terrorism and Counterterrorism* was well received, comments and suggestions by instructors and students who used the volume were instrumental in extended revisions, additions, and changes for the much improved second edition. This third edition, too, is not simply an updated version of the previous one but offers important additions and improvements.

Part 1 which features comprehensive chapters on domestic and international terrorism and the motives and operations of terrorist groups, individuals, and state sponsors, has now a significantly expanded Chapter 5. In addition to exploring the similarities among religiously motivated terrorists from major world religions, the new, second section is devoted to Muslim extremists and explains how radical Salafi thinkers, past and present, and contemporary jihadi leaders justify and urge the use of political violence against "infidels" inside and outside their own religion.

Part 2, which deals with counterterrorism, underwent the most significant changes. It now begins with a new Chapter 10 about the predominant role of terrorism and counterterrorism in the post–9/11 national security strategy of the United States with the controversial "war on terror" as centerpiece. Chapter 11 discusses the utility of hard and soft power in counterterrorism and is a heavily revised and expanded version of the chapter on military and nonmilitary responses in the earlier editions. Chapter 12, on security versus civil liberties, also is not simply an update from the second edition but expands on controversies surrounding the legal status and treatment of "enemy combatants." Finally, I reorganized and added to and wrote a more accessible Chapter 13 on the state of homeland security and the institutions charged with terrorism prevention and preparedness.

Acknowledgments

The topics introduced and discussed in my seminars on terrorism and the notes prepared for lecture courses on terrorism and on the media in American politics informed the organization and the content of this volume, as did the thoughtful input by my students at Columbia University and Barnard College during our lively but always civil class discussions. I owe debts to these students—they inspired me to write this volume. I am also grateful to Richard Goldberg for doing a great job in retrieving and categorizing opinion polls on terrorism, and to my son, James Nacos, for once again putting together graphs and tables for his mother.

Most of all, I thank Eric Stano, editor-in-chief of Longman, whose skillful guidance and patience helped me all along to keep my focus on what kind of book we had envisioned at the outset. Eric selected reviewers whose expertise was instrumental in helping me to improve, change, and add to literally all parts of this volume. I am very grateful to the following reviewers for their detailed comments, suggestions, and constructive criticism:

Sean K. Anderson, Idaho State University

Victor Asal, SUNY-Albany

Vincent Auger, Western Illinois University

Shaheen Ayubi, Rutgers University–Camden

Peter A. Barone, University of Bridgeport

Timothy A. Capron, California State University, Sacramento

Lamont Colucci, Ripon College

Michael V. Deaver, Sierra College

Larry Elowitz, Georgia College and State University

John Fielding, Mount Wachusett Community College

James L. Freed, University of Maryland University College

Hasan Kosebalaban, University of Utah

Jecek Lubecki, University of Arkansas, Little Rock

C. Augustus Martin, California State University, Dominguez Hills

Dean A. Minix, Northern Kentucky University

Tricia Mulligan, Iona College

Thomas R. O'Connor, North Carolina Wesleyan College

William Rose, Connecticut College

Stanley E. Spangler, Bentley College

George C. Thomas, Marquette University

Carlos Yordan, Drew University

The encouragement, guidance, and cooperation I received from Vikram Mukhija and Toni Magyar made my work on the additions and updates for the third edition far more pleasant than I had imagined.

Finally, I owe thanks to Saraswathi Muralidhar of GGS Higher Education Resources, the project editor in charge of the editing and production process for the third edition. Her professionalism and the excellent copyediting by Pamela Rockwell made the revision process smooth and painless.

The author posts her observations and comments about terrorism, counterterrorism, the mass media, and current events on her blog, reflectivepundit (http://www.reflectivepundit.com). Readers are invited to visit her blog, comment on posts, or e-mail questions and comments.

BRIGITTE L. NACOS, a long-time U.S. correspondent for newspapers in Germany, received a Ph.D. in political science from Columbia University, where for more than fifteen years she has taught and continues to teach courses in American politics and government. Her research concentrates on the links between the media, public opinion, and decision-making and on domestic and international terrorism and counterterrorism. Besides publishing many articles and several book chapters, she is the author of *The Press, Presidents, and Crises* (Columbia University Press, 1990); *Terrorism and the Media: From the Iran Hostage Crisis to the World Trade Center Bombing* (Columbia University Press, 1994); *Terrorism and the Media: From the Iran Hostage Crisis to the Oklahoma City Bombing* (Columbia University Press, 1996); *Mass-Mediated Terrorism: The Central Role of the Media in Terrorism and Counterterrorism* (Rowman & Littlefield, 2002); and (with Oscar Torres-Reyna) *Fueling Our Fears: Stereotyping, Media Coverage, and Public Opinion of Muslim Americans* (Rowman & Littlefield, 2006). She is also the coauthor of *From Bonn to Berlin: German Politics in Transition* (Columbia University Press, 1998) with Lewis J. Edinger, and the coeditor of *Decisionmaking in a Glass House* (Rowman & Littlefield, 2000) with Robert Y. Shapiro and Pierangelo Isernia.

Apart from teaching, researching, and writing, Brigitte Nacos loves cooking and barbecuing for her family and friends as well as tending to her indoor and outdoor flowers. She and her husband, Jim, love to play golf. Most importantly, however, they are blessed with two wonderful sons, John and James, two lovely daughters-in-law, Julie and Helen, and five most delightful grandchildren, Theodore, William, Emelia, India, and Peter.

CHAPTER 1

Introduction: The Terrorist Threat

ON NOVEMBER 26, 2008, COORDINATED TERRORIST ATTACKS targeted ten sites in Mumbai (formerly Bombay), India's largest city and financial capital. Among them was a train terminal, a movie house, a hospital, and a café. By moving quickly from one site to another and randomly killing as many civilians as possible before shooting their way into and taking over two large hotels (the Taj Mahal and the Oberoi Trident) and the orthodox Jewish Narriman House, the ten terrorists left the impression that they were part of a far larger group of attackers. By the time security forces gained complete control of the Taj Mahal hotel three days later, 164 persons had been killed and many more injured. Nine of the ten terrorists had died as well as they fought police officers and soldiers. Identified as members of Lashkar-e-Taiba, a Pakistani terrorist organization that is particularly active in the Indian–Pakistani conflict over Kashmir, the ten young men had traveled from Pakistan aboard a fishing trawler and come ashore in speedboats with knapsacks full of arms and ammunition. Because of the large number of targeted sites, the combination of facility attacks, hostage-takings, firefights with security forces, and the high number of victims, the Mumbai attacks were dubbed by the news media and perceived by many in the country as India's 9/11—just as the horrific Madrid train bombings on March 11, 2004 were considered Spain's 9/11 and the July 7, 2005 suicide bombings of London's commuter system the United Kingdom's.[1]

After the attacks of September 11, 2001, when hijackers flew commercial airliners into the twin towers of the World Trade Center in New York and into the Pentagon (the distinct building housing the headquarters of the U.S. Department of Defense) just outside of Washington, D.C., the meaning of the term *terrorism* no doubt changed for most Americans and for most people around the globe. From that day on, 9/11 became and remained the benchmark for the severity and scope of terrorist strikes. The terror of "Black Tuesday," referred to since then as "9/11," transformed most people's perception of terrorism from fictional scenes in disaster movies to images of real-life horror. Never before had so many people—about 3,000—died in one terrorist operation. Never before had a terrorist coup inflicted so much grief, so much devastation, and so much fear of further, and more lethal, attacks. It was a most painful conclusion to the first World Trade Center bombing in 1993. The terrorism of the past had turned into something much more catastrophic, much more threatening—into what has been called the "new terrorism," "superterrorism," or "postmodern terrorism."

Just as important, never before had one terrorist attack reshaped the priorities and the actual policy agenda of a victimized state as drastically, and impact international relations as severely, as the assault on targets in New York and Washington. In response to 9/11, U.S. President George W. Bush, backed by most members of the U.S. Congress and a vast majority of the American people, declared war, not against a conventional enemy, a foreign country, but rather against a violent activity—a war against terrorism. Less than four weeks after 9/11, military actions by an American-led, international coalition commenced in Afghanistan against the assumed masterminds of the terror on American soil, Osama bin Laden and his close associates in the Al Qaeda ("The Base") terror organization, and against the ruling Taliban that had harbored Al Qaeda terrorists and their Afghan training camps for many years. According to President Bush, Afghanistan was merely the first battleground in a long and difficult campaign against a web of terrorist cells and organizations scattered around the globe and against states actively supporting terrorist activities. Furthermore, the president, in a speech at West Point on June 1, 2002, and the White House in a comprehensive follow-up "National Strategy to Combat Weapons of Mass Destruction," formulated a new doctrine of preventive wars that justified preemptive military actions against "emerging threats before they are fully formed."[2] By citing evidence of existing weapons of mass destruction (WMD) in Iraq and the threat that the country's ruler, Saddam Hussein, might place such weapons into the hands of terrorists, the Bush administration followed the new doctrine when it decided to invade the country and force a regime change.[3]

Even before the dust had settled around the totally destroyed World Trade Center and the partially demolished Pentagon, people in the United States and abroad began to recognize that this terrorist assault pushed the United States and much of the world

Manhattan's Darkened Skyline on September 11, 2001

Except for the unshaken Statue of Liberty in New York Harbor, downtown Manhattan was darkened by thick clouds of smoke shortly after terrorists flew two hijacked airliners into the two towers of the World Trade Center and shortly before the towers collapsed as a result of the most deadly case of catastrophic terrorism to date.

into a crisis that seemed just as dangerous as, or perhaps more explosive than, the Cold War conflict between the Soviet Union and the United States and their respective allies in the decades following the end of World War II. In some quarters, the end of the Cold War had fueled expectations for an era of greater international understanding and cooperation and a "peace dividend" that would better the economic conditions in the underdeveloped world and bring improvements in the industrialized nations. But during the 1990s, such dreams did not come true. Instead, there was a troubling wave of conflicts in many parts of the world.

Instant commentary in the media compared the events of 9/11 with the Japanese attack on Pearl Harbor sixty years earlier, claiming that both incidents had been as unexpected as bolts of lightning from a blue sky. Indeed, two months before the kamikaze flights crashed into the World Trade Center and the Pentagon, a former counterterrorism specialist in the U.S. Department of State wrote in an op-ed article in the *New York Times*, "Judging from news reports and the portrayal of villains in our popular entertainment, Americans are bedeviled by fantasies about terrorism. They seem to believe that terrorism is the greatest threat to the United States and that it is becoming more widespread and lethal. . . . Nothing of these beliefs are based on facts."[4] But others had warned for years that the United States and other Western countries should brace for catastrophic terrorism that would result in mass disruption and mass destruction.[5] For example, Walter Laqueur, a leading terrorism expert who had characterized terrorism in the past as an irritant rather than a major threat, came to a different judgment at the end of the 1990s, when he concluded,

> *Terrorism has been with us for centuries, and it has always attracted inordinate attention because of its dramatic character and its sudden, often wholly unexpected occurrence. It has been a tragedy for the victims, but seen in historical perspective it seldom has been more than a nuisance. . . . This is no longer true today, and may be even less so in the future. Yesterday's nuisance has become one of the gravest dangers facing mankind.*[6]

Several horrific incidents in the 1990s and certainly the events of 9/11 proved the pessimists right and ended the threat debate. One could argue that the age of catastrophic terrorism began in December 1988 with the downing of Pan Am Flight 103 over Lockerbie, Scotland, caused by a terrorist bomb that killed a total of 270 civilians on board (most of them Americans) and on the ground (all of them Scots). This was, at the time, the single most devastating act of terrorism in terms of the number of victims. Actually, nearly as many Americans were killed when extremists of the Lebanese Hezbollah drove an explosive-laden truck into the U.S. Marine barracks near the Beirut airport in 1983. But while the victims were deployed as peacekeepers and thus were not combatants in the sense of fighting a war, they nevertheless were not civilians like the passengers and crew aboard Pan Am Flight 103 and the people who died on the ground in Lockerbie. As the next chapter explains, whether civilians or members of the military are targets and victims figures prominently in the discussions of what kinds of violent acts constitute terrorism. The fate of Pan Am Flight 103 in 1988 along with the Oklahoma City bombing in 1995 that caused the deaths of 168 persons represented turning points in the lethality of terrorism. Until these events, the widely held supposition was that "terrorists want a lot of people watching and a lot of people listening and not a lot of people dead."[7] But after Pan Am Flight 103 and the terror in Oklahoma City, this assumption was no longer valid. Another terrorist incident fueled fears of even more deadly terrorist strikes and changed intentions on the part of terrorists: In 1995, members of a Japanese doomsday cult named Aum Shinrikyo (meaning "supreme truth") released poison gas in the Tokyo subway system, killing twelve persons and sickening thousands of commuters. As devastating as the consequences were, experts concluded that the release of the nerve gas sarin could have killed far more people had members of the Aum cult handled the poison differently. Pointing to the Japanese group's ability to develop nerve gas and to acquire toxic materials and know-how from sources in Australia, the United States, Russia, and elsewhere, U.S. Senator Sam Nunn concluded that the Japanese case signaled the beginning of "a new era" in terrorism. He warned that weapons of mass destruction could spread indiscriminately and fall into the hands of terrorists.[8]

For Americans, the threat of a major bioterrorist catastrophe hit close to home three weeks after the terror of 9/11, when letters containing anthrax spores were delivered to several media organizations and members of the U.S. Congress. Although in this case "only" five persons died and a dozen or so fell sick as a result of inhaling the finely powdered biological agent, an anthrax attack designed to kill as many people as possible could have easily caused a much more lethal catastrophe. Even before the anthrax case frightened the American public, *New York Times* reporters Judith Miller, Stephen Engelberg, and William Broad published a book in which they called germ weapons "the poor man's atom bomb" and warned that

> the threat of germ weapons is real and rising, driven by scientific discoveries and political upheavals around the world. As Aum Shinrikyo's failed efforts [to inflict far more harm than planned] suggest, the crucial ingredient in a successful biological attack is not advanced laboratory equipment or virulent microbes alone, but knowledge. Such expertise is increasingly available.[9]

Several months after 9/11, high officials in the U.S. administration warned that terrorists would inevitably acquire weapons of mass destruction. Testifying before a Senate committee, U.S. Defense Secretary Donald H. Rumsfeld said terrorists "would seek to obtain nuclear, chemical, and biological weapons, and ultimately would succeed despite U.S. efforts to prevent them [from doing so]."[10] Worse yet, in June 2002 the U.S. government announced the arrest of Abdullah Al Mujahir, an American citizen who years earlier had been a Chicago street gang member named Jose Padilla. The Brooklyn-born Muslim convert, who had allegedly trained in Al Qaeda camps in Afghanistan, was accused of conspiring with fellow terrorists to acquire and detonate a so-called dirty bomb in Washington, D.C., or elsewhere in the United States. Although this would not trigger a nuclear explosion and would not be as lethal as sophisticated nuclear weapons, a dirty bomb would nevertheless release enough radioactive material over several city blocks to harm many people and contaminate the affected area. As it turned out, there was no evidence that Mr. Padilla had planned to get his hand on a dirty bomb but the news of such a threat contributed to the American people's worries.

Even though no further terrorist attacks occurred within U.S. borders in the years following the events of 9/11, there were many devastating strikes abroad. Thus, many hundreds of innocent victims were killed and thousands injured when multiple bomb explosions hit crowded commuter trains, subways, and buses during rush hours in Madrid in 2004, London in 2005, and Mumbai in 2006. There were especially deadly bombings in Morocco, Indonesia, Pakistan, Egypt, and many other places in different parts of the world. And while Iraqi insurgents and foreign terrorists targeted initially members of the coalition forces and workers for foreign contractors during Iraq's occupation, they eventually attacked mostly Iraqi civilians. By 2006, when the deadly sectarian conflict between Shias and Sunnis seemed to have expanded into a civil war, terrorism was the preferred method of attack. All of these developments supported the notion that terrorism—and counterterrorism—had entered into a new, most dangerous phase.

But although the faces of terrorists and their brand of violence change over time, the calculus of terrorism remains basically the same. This terrorist calculus, or scheme, is driven by a set of assumptions:

- Groups that are too weak to fight nation-states openly in conventional civil or foreign wars will realize some and perhaps all of their objectives by striking against civilian or noncombatant targets or by merely threatening to do so.
- States and governments are ill prepared to react to the type of psychological warfare that terrorists wage against their citizens. While capable of fighting and winning conventional wars against other nation-states, the military forces of even the mightiest states are not suited to fight against elusive enemies who strike at unpredictable times, places, and targets by equally unpredictable means.
- Because of their openness and far-reaching civil liberties—especially press freedom—liberal democracies are far more susceptible to terrorist activities and propaganda than authoritarian systems. By striking seemingly at random, terrorists transmit the false message that everyone in their target societies is a potential victim.
- In reaction to serious acts of terror, decision-makers in constitutional democracies are likely to overreact in efforts to prevent and counter terrorism, at the expense of their country's fundamental values and civil liberties. Such overreactions will motivate citizens in democracies, or at least part of them, to oppose their own governments.

The basic rationale for political violence of this sort guides unsophisticated amateurs and sophisticated professionals, lone wolves and formidable organizations, the arsonists inspired by the Earth Liberation Front and the 9/11 kamikaze terrorists dispatched by Al Qaeda. This volume describes and analyzes, in the first place, the most important facets of the terrorist scheme and, second, how the governments of targeted countries and other institutions (e.g., the news media and international organizations) react—and how they should react—to actual terrorism and threats thereof.

Terrorism Trends Over the Last Three Decades

David C. Rapoport concluded that "September 11 marks the most important date in the long and bloody history of terrorism. No other terrorist attack used passenger planes as bombs [and] produced such staggering casualty figures."[11] But while at the time unparalleled in scope, the terrorist assaults of 9/11 came on the heels of more than a quarter century of consequential international terrorist incidents that targeted Americans, mostly abroad but also, beginning with the first World Trade Center bombing in 1993, at home. Although Americans were certainly not the only victims, the United States was the target of "approximately one third of all international terrorist attacks over the last 30 years."[12]

Apart from their venues, the nationality of the targets, and their domestic or international nature, individual acts of terrorism have caused more deaths and injuries in the last several years of the twentieth and the first years of the twenty-first centuries than in several of the preceding decades combined. Whereas the number of incidents with respect to both international and domestic terrorism decreased markedly, the total number of casualties increased significantly. Thus, as Figure 1.1 shows, in the five-year period from 1988 through 1992, a total of 2,345 international terrorist incidents were recorded that caused 4,325 casualties (persons killed and injured). The number of incidents decreased by 552 during the following five years (1993 through 1997) to 1,793, but there were 8,767 more casualties, or a total of 13,092 killed or injured victims. Finally, the next five years (1998 through 2002) witnessed a further decline of terrorist deeds to a total of 1,649 and yet another jump in casualties to a total of 16,807.[13] This first set of trend statistics presented here ends with the year 2002 because of a controversy that arose after the initial release of the numbers for 2003 by the U.S. Department of State. These numbers reflected a rather sharp decline in international terrorist incidents and casualties, encouraging a State Department official to tell the press, "You will find in these pages clear evidence that we are prevailing in the fight [against terrorism]."[14] But it turned out that not all relevant international incidents were counted and that the true numbers in the revised report represented increases in both casualties and incidents. These and other problems led to the suspicion that the numbers had been massaged to support the claim of progress in the war against terrorism. Whereas the State Department had prepared the "Patterns of Global Terrorism" report for years, the newly established Terrorist Threat Integration Center, a creature of the Department of Homeland Security, FBI, and Department of Defense, was in charge of the 2003 issue.

Up to 2002, then, the statistics showed increases in major terrorist incidents, or what have been called "terrorist spectaculars," and a decline in less dramatic acts of political violence by nonstate actors. In fact, the tendency toward fewer but more spectacular and more lethal incidents had already begun during the 1980s. The change coincided with the growth of what is commonly called "religious terrorism"—the use of violence for

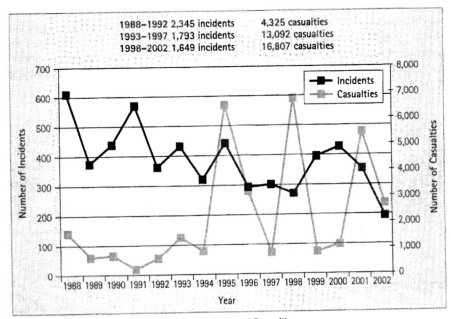

FIGURE 1.1 Trends in International Terrorist Incidents and Casualties

Source: U.S. State Department, "Patterns of Global Terrorism."

political ends by groups whose motivations and justifications are couched in religious convictions, terms, and symbols. However, the 1980s were in this respect only a prelude to the far more pronounced developments in the post–Cold War era, when religious and pseudoreligious terrorism became significantly more prevalent than the secular variety. The total number of significant incidents of domestic and international terrorism around the world increased from 74 in the 1970s to 122 in the 1980s and 157 in the 1990s. Here, too, the number of killed and injured victims jumped from about 2,000 in the 1970s to more than 3,000 in the 1980s and to over 15,000 in the 1990s.[15] Of course, all of these numbers were far surpassed in the first decade of the new millennium.

In comparison to other countries and regions, the United States had not experienced a large number of terrorist incidents in the past. That was particularly true for international terrorism. Figure 1.2 shows that in the regional breakdown for the seven-year period from 1996 through 2002, Latin America had by far the largest number of international terrorist incidents (1,032), followed by Asia (418), Western Europe (362), the Middle East (217), Africa (189), Eurasia (156), and North America (19). This trend followed the patterns recorded in the pre-1996 years as well. At first, the terrorist attacks of 9/11 did not change these distinct regional differences with respect to the frequency of international terrorist strikes: North America was and remained the region with fewer incidents of international terrorism than all other regions. However, while North America had by far the lowest number of casualties caused by international terrorism in the years preceding 9/11, the grim toll of the attacks on the World Trade Center and the Pentagon moved the region into third place for the seven-year period from 1996 through 2002 with 4,091 persons killed and injured, behind Asia (6,006) and Africa (5,936) and ahead of the Middle East (3,039), Western Europe (971), Eurasia (785), and Latin America (311).[16]

It is noteworthy that Latin America, where more international terrorist incidents were recorded than in any other geographic region, suffered consistently fewer casualties than all other areas. The fact that such incidents were quite common but resulted in relatively few casualties explains, perhaps, why most of these cases did not

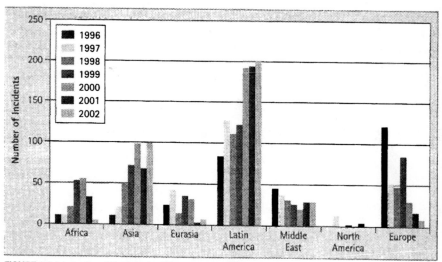

FIGURE 1.2 International Terrorist Incidents by Region, 1996–2002
Source: U.S. State Department, "Patterns of Global Terrorism," 2001 and 2002.

make the news outside of Latin America—except for those countries whose nationals were the victims of terrorism in the region. Typical cases in Colombia, for example, involved (and continue to involve) violence against foreign nationals or foreign business interests by the Revolutionary Armed Forces of Colombia (FARC). In many instances foreigners, mostly representatives of corporations or international organizations, are kidnapped and released in exchange for ransom. Frequently, FARC members have bombed oil pipelines and derailed trains in order to damage the economic interests of foreign corporations. But in the absence of compelling visuals, dramatic human interest stories, and, in the big picture, large numbers of North American victims compared to native targets, these sorts of incidents did not receive in the past a great deal of news coverage abroad—and they do not today.

NEW TERRORISM STATISTICS DO NOT ALLOW COMPARISONS WITH OLD DATA

The Department of State's international terrorism trend data up to the end of 2002 are revealing, but they do not allow comparisons with subsequently compiled government information. Following the above-mentioned controversy about the statistics published in the State Department's "Patterns of Global Terrorism" for 2003, the yearly report was renamed ("Country Report on Terrorism") and restricted to narrative descriptions. The data for 2004 and 2005 were compiled and publicized by the National Counterterrorism Center (NCTC) and based on different criteria than those used for decades by the State Department. Indeed, the NCTC's "Report on Incidents of Terrorism 2005" cautioned that the figures in this report were comparable neither to the compilations published for decades in "Patterns of Global Terrorism" nor to the agency's incident report for the previous year. Obviously recognizing that it is not always possible to distinguish between domestic and international terrorism, the agency began in 2005 to compile all terrorist acts—not only international incidents.[17]

Starting with the compiled world-wide statistics of both domestic and transnational terrorist incidents, comparisons are once again possible starting with the 2005 data.

The number of terrorist incidents around the globe increased from 2005 through 2007, but it is the increase in the lethality of terrorist strikes that was far more striking (see Figure 1.3). Considering that the official statistics cannot reflect all such incidents and their consequences, the available numbers are mind-boggling. However, in 2008 there was an 18 percent decrease in the number of incidents world-wide and a 30 percent decrease in the number of victims killed as the result of terrorist attacks.

FIGURE 1.3

Worldwide Terrorist Incidents and Fatalities

	Number of Incidents	Number of Deaths
2005	11, 156	14,616
2006	14, 570	20,872
2007	14, 499	22,685
2008	11,770	15,765

Source: National Counterterrorism Center.

As depicted in Figure 1.2, Latin America used to be the region with the greatest number of terrorist incidents although not the highest numbers of victims killed or injured in such attacks. This, however, changed in the last several years. While the National Counterterrorism Center's regional categories differ from those used earlier by the Department of State and lump Latin America into a new "western hemisphere" region, statistics since 2005 reveal that the Near East, South Asia, and the East Asia/Pacific areas ranked significantly higher in terms of terrorist incidents and fatalities (see Figure 1.4). According to the 2005 and 2006 statistics, Africa had the lowest number of terrorist incidents but ranked higher in terms of victims killed in terrorist acts. By 2007, though, Africa was in fourth place in number of terrorist attacks and in third place based on the number of deaths. It is very likely that the number of incidents in Africa is actually significantly higher but underreported both by the authorities and the media.

Iraq experienced more terrorism than any other country. In 2005, it accounted for 30% of terrorist attacks worldwide; in the following two years, the number jumped up so that in 2006 45% and in 2007 43% of all terrorist incidents around the globe occurred in Iraq. Moreover, terrorism in Iraq was more lethal than elsewhere. In 2005, 2006, and 2007, Iraq's share of worldwide fatalities from terrorism was 60%, 65%, and 60%, respectively.

Bombings used to be the most frequent method of terrorist attack, but in 2005 there were more armed attacks (41% of total terrorist incidents worldwide) than bombings (37%)—including suicide bombings. It seemed that this was an exception, because in the next two years, bombings became once again the most widely used mode of terrorist attack with suicide terrorism comprising typically one-third of all bombings. But in 2008, there were once again more armed attacks than bombings.

As one would expect, acts of international and domestic terrorism have significant impact on target societies when they are particularly lethal. But in the past, there were also many incidents that did not result in large numbers of casualties, or that resulted in none at all, but that still achieved the status of terrorist spectacular because political leaders perceived such incidents as acute crises and reacted accordingly. In early 1975, for example, members of the Baader-Meinhof group kidnapped Peter Lorenz, a Christian-Democratic candidate for mayor of West Berlin. Four days later and after the

FIGURE 1.4

Terrorist Incidents and Fatalities by Region

	2005		2006		2007		2008	
	Attacks	Dead	Attacks	Dead	Attacks	Dead	Attacks	Dead
Near East	4,222	8,708	7,755	13,691	7,540	14,010	4,594	5,528
South Asia	4,022	3,046	3,654	3,609	3,807	4,737	4,354	5,826
East Asia/Pacific	1,005	758	1,036	854	1,429	1,119	978	762
Western Hemisphere	868	854	826	556	482	405	352	370
Europe Eurasia	780	373	659	220	606	227	774	292
Africa	256	879	422	1,643	835	2,187	718	2,987

Source: National Counterterrorism Center.

West German government released five jailed terrorists and paid $50,000 in ransom, Lorenz was released unharmed. This was not the first time the authorities in the Federal Republic of Germany had given in to terrorists' demands. But, according to Peter Katzenstein, "Two months later the government stood firm when West German terrorists seized eleven hostages in the West German embassy in Stockholm. It refused to make any concessions in 1977 when terrorists kidnapped and eventually murdered Martin Schleyer, one of the most prominent business leaders of the Federal Republic."[18] The boldness of Lorenz's kidnapping and the fact that, for the first time, a politician had been targeted elevated the Lorenz case in the minds of the West German public and government to the level of a major crisis—even though no one had been killed or injured. As a result, the West German authorities altered their response to terrorism, decided to make no more concessions to terrorists, and stuck to their new policy of toughness. The kidnapping and murder of former Italian Prime Minister Aldo Moro in 1978 by the Red Brigade had a similar effect on the Italian government and public. In this case, the terrorists killed their immediate victim (the well-liked Moro) and, during the kidnapping, five of his bodyguards; the incident was quickly perceived as a major crisis. This was not simply because of the number of casualties—after all, Europe had witnessed far more lethal terrorism before the Moro case—but because the Red Brigade had laid bare the vulnerability and impotence of the Italian authorities to protect even a former head of government. As a result, as Jeffrey Simon observed, "The subsequent crackdown on the Red Brigade by the Italian police and security forces was not seen as repressive by the public, but as a welcome response."[19] More recently, in the summer of 2006, when members of the Lebanese Hezbollah crossed into Israel and abducted two Israeli soldiers, this kidnapping triggered massive retaliation by Israel and a major military conflict between Israel and Hezbollah.

Over the last twenty-five years or so, anti-American terrorism incidents had significant impact on American decision-makers, U.S. politics and policies, and, just as importantly, the public at large regardless of whether the immediate victims of terrorism survived their ordeal. Thus, although none of the Americans held as hostages died during the 444 days of the Iran hostage crisis (1979–1981), this incident had tremendous effects on Jimmy Carter's presidency and on U.S. policies and politics during this period and beyond. By demonstrating that the American superpower—short of military action—was impotent, a bunch of young Iranians held the United States hostage, as the media reminded Americans day in and day out. We enhance our understanding of many aspects of terrorism in general if we know the most pertinent details of those terrorist incidents with outstanding characteristics and effects. But younger generations do not know about many incidents of anti-American terrorism abroad that older Americans remember very well. Younger Americans certainly have no personal recollection of the Iran hostage crisis or the long ordeal of American hostages in Lebanon in the 1980s. For this reason, the appendix ("Major Terrorist Incidents Since the Early 1970s") provides readers with a number of both extensive and brief summaries of terrorist events in three categories: (1) major international and domestic incidents that targeted Americans, (2) major international terrorist strikes in which Americans were among the victims, and (3) major international incidents without American targets and victims.

Following this introduction, the rest of this book is divided into three distinct sections: "Part I: Terrorism;" "Part II: Counterterrorism;" and "Part III: Media and Public." Chapter 2 addresses the definitional disagreements surrounding the terms *terrorism* and *terrorist*. When people disagree with the causes of those who commit political violence against civilians or noncombatants, they tend to call them terrorists;

when people share or sympathize with the grievances of the perpetrators, they tend to speak of revolutionaries, rebels, freedom fighters, militants, warriors, and the like. Because the "t" word (for *terrorism*) has negative connotations, what one calls the perpetrators of political violence and their deeds matters a great deal to their friends and foes. Among the key questions that will be addressed in Chapter 2 are the following: What is terrorism? In what cases should we define political violence as terrorism? Should there be a definitional distinction between political violence against civilians that is committed by individuals or groups on the one hand and by states or governments on the other? Who determines whether perpetrators of political violence are labeled terrorists rather than guerrillas, revolutionaries, or freedom fighters? Is terrorism ever justified and, if so, under what circumstances? This book proposes a working definition that limits the meaning of the term *terrorism* to political violence when committed by groups or individuals and a different label, *state terror*, for political violence deliberately committed by governments against civilians.

Although in the past it was rarely as serious a threat as it is today, terrorism in one form or another has existed in every time and was typically committed by groups who were too weak to fight for their causes in open conflicts. Drawing on the past in the context of terrorism will often illuminate recent and present developments, events, and issues and can help us to make comparisons and find similarities and differences. Chapters 3 and 4 are designed to accomplish this by providing the reader with a historical and geographic perspective on terrorism in the global setting—in the past and up to the present time (Chapter 3)—and with an examination of terrorism in the American setting (Chapter 4).

The significantly expanded Chapter 5 is devoted to discussing religious terrorism—political violence undertaken in the name of God. The examination of three distinct cases of terrorism perpetrated by Christian, Muslim, and Jewish extremists demonstrates that so-called religious terrorists have distinct political objectives and justify their violence along the same lines—regardless of their religious affiliation. But considering that the most serious terrorist threat in the early twenty-first century comes from Muslim extremists, the second and added part of this chapter deals specifically with the history, motivations, and goals of Jihadi terrorists, namely, Al Qaeda and like-minded groups. Chapter 6 explores the making of terrorists: what conditions and personal characteristics draw a person to join a terrorist group. To what extent are the socioeconomic background, psychological makeup, social contacts, or other markers and influences decisive factors here? One section deals with female terrorists and both the reality and the stereotypical perceptions of female terrorists. Finally, the stages in the emergence of terrorist groups are described. Chapter 7 is devoted to the state sponsors of terrorism and what state sponsors and terrorist groups get out of their symbiotic relationship. Even though they may be discreet in their relationship to terrorists, state supporters can be of enormous benefit in the financing, training, and recruitment of terrorists. Finally, attention is paid to what one might call "involuntary hosts of terrorists," that is, countries—namely, those in the West—that are the new breeding and staging grounds for terror cells which are part of either Al Qaeda or autonomous groups inspired by Osama bin Laden. Chapter 8 describes how ideology and cultural traditions affect the goals of terrorist groups, the selection of targets, and the choice of tactics. The centerpiece is a discussion of the multitude of terror methods available to modern-day terrorists, with more attention to the history and utility of suicide bombings than in the first edition. Chapter 9 takes a look inside terrorist organizations in terms of their structure (e.g., the value of leaderless cells and the emergence of global networks). What causes terrorist groups to go out of business? What happens when a terrorist movement loses its leadership? These questions are discussed, as are the origins of terrorists' financial resources.

Chapter 10, the first chapter of Part II, "Counterterrorism," is new to this edition and deals with the centrality of counterterrorism to America's post–9/11 national security strategy, the so-called "Bush Doctrine," and the critique of the "war on terrorism" that focused primarily on defeating terrorism abroad. The extensively revised Chapter 11 examines hard-power and soft-power approaches to dealing with and defeating terrorism. As the immediate post–9/11 years during the Bush administration showed once again, military superiority alone cannot defeat even the weakest of terrorist movements or mere groups. So, what are the prospects for governments of utilizing both hard power (military and economic) and soft power (diplomacy and public diplomacy) to weaken and defeat terrorists?

The following chapter on the need for security and for upholding civil liberties (Chapter 12) explores the difficulties inherent in this balancing act—especially when democracies are faced with serious terrorist threats. While the main focus is on the United States, attention is also paid to developments in the United Kingdom and Germany in this respect. An important component of the terrorist calculus is the determination of terrorists to force liberal democracies into curbing their most esteemed individual rights and values so that citizens sooner or later direct their anger and frustration against their own governments. The chapter explores the difficult trade-off between the need for security against terrorism and the protection of fundamental liberties in general (and after 9/11 in particular). Of course, the issue of whether or not to torture terrorists and suspected terrorists is addressed in this chapter as well. Chapter 13, the last in Part II, examines first the successes and failures surrounding governmental efforts to prevent and prepare for terrorist attacks and describes and evaluates the fundamental reorganization of the homeland security sectors and the intelligence community as a result of the 9/11 attacks. There is a discussion of the crucial importance of good intelligence and the ability of the domestic intelligence community to share and analyze information in an expert and timely manner. International cooperation in the areas of intelligence and law enforcement is equally crucial in fighting transnational terrorism, the most serious threat today, and especially the global Al Qaeda net and its affiliates and like-minded cells. This chapter describes the post–9/11 initiatives and improvements in bilateral and multilateral cooperation and new efforts of international organizations (e.g., the United Nations and INTERPOL) and regional bodies (e.g., Europol of the European Union) to combat terrorism.

Chapter 14, the first chapter of Part III, "Media and Public," is devoted to the central role of publicity in the terrorist scheme. Even before the printing press was invented, terrorists knew intuitively that their deeds would not have any effects beyond their immediate victims unless the largest possible number of eyewitnesses spread the word about their violence. In more recent times, terrorists were eager to embrace each advance in communication technology for their publicity purposes. As this chapter details, the modern mass media's appetite for sensational and shocking news plays a major role in satisfying terrorists' need for publicity or propaganda. Chapter 15 focuses on the Internet because the World Wide Web opened a host of new opportunities for terrorist organizations and for hate groups with the propensity to motivate individuals to commit political violence. For these circles, the Internet is a vehicle for spreading propaganda, for intraorganizational communication, for planning terrorist acts, for recruitment, and for fund-raising. Moreover, the prospect of so-called cyberterrorism—attacks on computer systems that control important parts of the infrastructure, such as electric power grids, oil and gas pipelines, dams, and air traffic—threatens mass disruption and mass destruction. Chapter 16 examines how major news organization cover military and non-military responses to terrorist attacks. Before and after 9/11, the same news media that tend to over-cover even minor terrorist incidents showed little interest in reporting domestic policies to prevent terrorism and to prepare the emergency response community for catastrophic terrorist strikes. In contrast, military responses to major terrorist incidents—from the bombing of Libya in 1986 to the invasion of Iraq in 2003 and its aftermath—received extensive news coverage.

Finally, the short concluding chapter discusses the reality that terrorism is here to stay and raises the question of how societies can manage to live with the threat of terrorism—even catastrophic terrorism caused by weapons of mass destruction.

Notes

1. According to reports, the terrorist team planned to kill at least 5,000 persons. Had they succeeded, they would have set a new terrible record and trumped the number of victims of the 9/11 attacks by about 2,000. As it was, the number of dead and injured victims was not a record for the Mumbai area because it was lower than the 209 killed and more than 700 injured in seven simultaneous bomb explosions on commuter trains in Mumbai on July 11, 2006. Yet, the multipronged method of attack moved this case into a new realm of catastrophic terrorism in the minds of those who watched in Mumbai and on television and computer screens around the world.

2. Stated in a letter that accompanied the *National Strategy to Combat Weapons of Mass Destruction* (Washington, D.C.: 2002), ii. For an analysis of the doctrine of preemptive wars, see Robert Jervis, "Understanding the Bush Doctrine," in Demetrios James Caraley, ed., *American Hegemony: Preventing War, Iraq, and Imposing Democracy* (New York: Academy of Political Science, 2004), 3–26.

3. In January 2005, the White House announced that the United States had ended the search for weapons of mass destruction in Iraq without finding any evidence of banned weapons. The 1,200 specialists of the Iraq Survey Group had spent nearly two years searching many sites, such as laboratories, factories, and military installations.

4. Larry C. Johnson, "The Declining Threat of Terrorism," *New York Times*, July 10, 2002, A19.

5. Especially alarming were the scenarios described by Robert Kupperman and Jeff Kamen, *Final Warning: Averting Disaster in the New Age of Terrorism* (New York: Doubleday, 1989).

6. The quote is from Walter Laqueur, *The New Terrorism: Fanaticism and the Arms of Mass Destruction* (New York: Oxford University Press, 1999), 3–4. In an earlier book, Laqueur had called terrorism "a sideshow" in comparison to far greater problems. See Walter Laqueur, *The Age of Terrorism* (Boston: Little, Brown, 1984).

7. Brian Jenkins is quoted in Bruce Hoffman, *Inside Terrorism* (New York: Columbia University Press, 1998), 198.

8. Christopher Drew, "Japanese Sect Tried to Buy U.S. Arms Technology, Senator Says," *New York Times*, October 31, 1995.

9. Judith Miller, Stephen Engelberg, and William Broad, *Germs: Biological Weapons and America's Secret War* (New York: Simon & Schuster, 2001), 315–16.

10. According to the *Washington Post*. See Bill Miller and Christine Haughney, "Nation Left Jittery by Latest Series of Terror Warnings," *Washington Post*, May 22, 2002, A1.

11. David C. Rapoport, "The Fourth Wave: September 11 in the History of Terrorism," *Current History* (December 2001): 419.

12. Martha Crenshaw, "Why America? The Globalization of Civil War," *Current History* (December 2001): 424.

13. The incident/casualty numbers were compiled from statistical data published by the Department of State in its yearly editions of "Patterns of Global Terrorism."

14. Deputy Secretary of State Richard Armitage was cited by Paul Krugman, "Errors in Terror," *New York Times*, June 25, 2004, A23.

15. The data on major terrorist incidents and the casualties they caused were compiled by using the data of the Centre for Defence and International Security Studies (CDISS). Because the data for 1999 were not available in the database and were therefore not included in the numbers for the 1990s, the real increase in major incidents and casualties was still more pronounced. I made some adjustments in the data compiled by the CDISS. Thus, a few entries were eliminated because they did not fit the terrorist incident criteria. For example, in September 1996 raids by the British police were said to have thwarted an IRA bombing campaign in London and netted weapons and explosives. This incident and similar cases were scratched from the major incident data. Also, in a few cases the casualty numbers were not specific enough. When it was said that more than 100 persons were injured, the most conservative number was assumed—in this case, 100.

16. The numbers for terrorist incidents and casualties by regions were taken from the Department of State's "Patterns of Global Terrorism 2001."

17. For example, if non-Iraqi terrorists attacked Iraqi civilians, it constituted an international incident, but if terrorist strikes were carried out by Iraqi groups, they were acts of domestic terrorism. The National Counterterrorism Center's full statistical data are available at www. nctc. gov.

18. Peter Katzenstein, "West Germany's Internal Security Policy: State and Violence in the 1970s and 1980s," Western Societies Program, Occasional Paper no. 28, Center for International Studies (Ithaca, NY: Cornell University, 1990), 31.

19. Jeffrey D. Simon, The Terrorist Trap: America's Experience with Terrorism (Bloomington: Indiana University Press, 1994), 322.

PART 1

Terrorism

CHAPTER 2

The Perennial Debate: What Is Terrorism?

IN 2001, BEFORE THE ATTACKS ON THE WORLD TRADE CENTER and the Pentagon, the FBI's list of the "Ten Most Wanted Fugitives" included three men sought for their involvement in acts of political violence: Osama bin Laden, the mastermind of lethal attacks on the American battleship USS *Cole* in the fall of 2000 and on the American embassies in Kenya and Tanzania two years earlier; Eric Robert Rudolph, who was sought for the deadly bombing of an abortion clinic in Alabama, the fatal explosion in Atlanta during the 1996 Olympic Games, and similar attacks on other facilities; and James Charles Kopp, who was charged with the assassination of Dr. Barnet Slepian, a provider of legal abortions. At the time, bin Laden was called a "terrorist" in the United States—by U.S. government officials, the media, and the public. However, with the exception of activists in the pro-choice movement, hardly anyone characterized Rudolph and Kopp publicly as "terrorists"; each was described as a "criminal," "murderer," or "extremist." After Slepian's violent death, President Bill Clinton said, "I am outraged by the murder of Dr. Barnett Slepian in his home last night in Armherst, NY."[1] Yet, neither Kopp nor Rudolph was an ordinary murderer. Both were antiabortion extremists who killed in the name of an elusive "Army of God" and single-issue politics as pursued by the most violent wing in the pro-life movement. Just like bin Laden, they acted to publicize, dramatize, and further their political and religious agenda. Why, then, did public officials, the media, and Americans in general choose different terms to explain the same types of deeds and the same types of perpetrators?

At first sight, one might guess that the severity of an act of violence, the damage inflicted, and especially the number of victims influence the language that described the deeds and their perpetrators. After all, even before the attacks of 9/11, bin Laden and his associates had caused the deaths of hundreds of innocent victims, whereas

Kopp had shot "just" one person and Rudolph had killed two people while injuring more than one hundred others. But the number of killed and injured victims does not determine whether an act of political violence is labeled "terrorism" or "crime." To this day, for example, the Iran hostage crisis (1979–1981) is widely perceived as a major terrorist incident, although none of the forty-nine Americans who were held for 444 days in the U.S. embassy in Tehran was physically harmed, nor were the three U.S. embassy officials who were stuck in Iran's foreign ministry. The Lebanese men who in 1985 hijacked a TWA airliner en route from Athens to Rome, brutally killed a young U.S. Navy diver, and held other passengers hostage were also considered "terrorists" in the United States.

One plausible explanation is the likelihood that government officials and reporters are more inclined to call political violence "terrorism" when it is committed abroad and "crime" when perpetrated at home. But this speculation does not solve the definitional puzzle either, as a review of pertinent domestic cases reveals. Timothy McVeigh, the man responsible for the 1995 Oklahoma City bombing and the death of 168 innocent people, was considered a terrorist and still is.[2] In the past, the FBI and news organizations described homegrown arsonists from the radical environmental groups Earth Liberation Front and Animal Liberation Front as "terrorists" and their deeds as "terrorism," although the perpetrators did not kill or injure people but were content to damage buildings and research projects. Similarly, Europeans have been more inclined to characterize political violence as terrorism when it is committed in their own country or in their neighborhood. In the past, the German government and media, for example, tended to call politically motivated violence *Terrorismus* (terrorism) when it was committed by indigenous groups, such as the Red Army Faction and its successor groups and cells, or by organizations in other Western European countries, such as the Basque separatist organization *Euskadi ta Askatasuna* (ETA) in Spain. But the same officials and media organizations characterized the Abu Sayyaf separatists in the distant Philippines as *militante Moslemrebellen* (militant Muslim rebels), *Rebellengruppe* (a rebel group), or *Separatisten* (separatists)—even at a time when the

Yes, I Am a Terrorist, and I Am Proud of It!

Unlike other modern terrorists who consider themselves freedom fighters, Ramzi Yousef (left), the mastermind of the first World Trade Center bombing in 1993, told Judge Kevin Duffy (right) during the sentencing phase of his trial that he was proud to be a terrorist. Yousef was sentenced to 240 years in prison without parole.

Filipino group held three Germans hostage. Public officials, the news media, and the public in England called acts of violence by the IRA and by splinter groups thereof terrorism but avoided the controversial "t" word when reporting on politically motivated violence abroad. However, the attacks on the World Trade Center and the Pentagon, although occurring on another continent, were condemned as terrorism in both countries in the days and weeks after 9/11.

All of this begs one conclusion: When public officials, the news media, and experts in the growing field of terrorism studies (what one observer has called "terrorology") make definitional choices, the severity and the venues of violent deeds are not unequivocal guides.[3] Nor is the nationality of the victims. While research has shown that the U.S. media have been more inclined to characterize political violence as terrorism when it is committed against Americans rather than against other nationals, this has not been a consistent determinant either.[4] The ambiguity about what constitutes terrorism—and what does not—deserves attention because the choice of language determines, or at least influences, how politically motivated violence is perceived inside and outside a targeted society: If violent acts for political ends are described as criminal activity, the perpetrators are readily seen as social misfits and compared to other dangerous criminals that every society must deal with; if, however, political violence is labeled "terrorism," the perpetrators are easily perceived as threats to the political, social, and/or economic fabric of the societies they terrorize. In the first case, the problem is simply seen as one of the criminal justice system; in the second case, it is more likely to be seen in the larger context of national security. As one leading terrorism scholar observed,

> It is clear from surveying the literature of terrorism, as well as the public debate, that what one calls things matters. There are few neutral terms in politics, because political language affects the perceptions of protagonists and audiences, and such effect acquires a greater urgency in the drama of terrorism. Similarly, the meanings of the terms change to fit a changing context.[5]

Even when there is agreement that the perpetrators of violence are not ordinary criminals but are politically motivated, the definitional ambiguities remain. The greatest difficulty is rooted in the tendency of different people to perceive one and the same act as either a despicable or a justifiable means to political ends, as either an evil deed carried out by terrorists or a courageous act committed by warriors or revolutionaries in pursuit of just causes. The slogan that "one person's terrorist is another person's freedom fighter" captures these contrasting value judgments. There is no doubt that the terms *terrorism* and *terrorist(s)* have negative connotations. As one terrorism expert recognized, "[T]o call an act of political violence terrorist is not merely to describe it but to judge it," because "[n]obody wants to be called a terrorist; terrorism is what the *other* side is up to."[6]

Before he was sentenced to 240 years in prison, Ramzi Yousef, the mastermind of the first World Trade Center bombing in 1993, stood in a New York courtroom and declared defiantly, "Yes, I am a terrorist, and I'm proud of it."[7] Anarchists in the second half of the nineteenth century did not reject the "t" word either. On the contrary, some of them called themselves terrorists and their violence terrorism. However, a Jewish terrorist group that was active in the 1940s and known as the Stern Gang is believed to be among the last of such groups to describe themselves as a terrorist organization.[8] Most contemporary perpetrators of political violence reject the "t" word. In the mid-1990s, when members of the Peruvian Tupac Amaru group occupied the Japanese Embassy in Lima and held scores of people hostage, then-Peruvian President Alberto Fujimori repeatedly called the hostage-holders terrorists and their actions terrorism, while the captors inside the embassy insisted that they were commandos of a revolutionary movement and that their violent takeover was a military occupation. Like the Tupac Amaru leaders, most contemporary perpetrators of political violence understand well that the choice of words and the invocation of metaphors affect how friends and foes perceive them and their actions.

The Meaning of *Terrorism* Over Time

The usage of the term *terrorism* has changed a great deal over time. In its original definition in the eighteenth century, it described violent actions by those in control of a state or, in other words, political violence "from above," as exercised during the Reign of Terror in the wake of the French Revolution, when *terrorism* meant the mass guillotining of the aristocracy and other real or perceived enemies of the state. During the nineteenth century, the meaning of *terrorism* expanded to include violence against those in power from those not in control of a state or government, and thus stood also for violence "from below," such as the assassinations of leaders and other politicians.[9] By the end of the century, mostly because of bombings and assassinations by anarchists, *terrorism* was predominantly associated with antistate, antigovernment violence. In the twentieth century, *terrorism* even more so came to mean political violence "from below" both in domestic and international settings. This latest shift in the definitional evolvement worked in favor of governments in that officials were quite successful in rejecting the terrorist label for their government's or friendly countries' violent actions.

Even when applied to political violence committed by groups, not all nonstate actors are treated equally in this respect either; rather, small groups are more often called terrorists than large groups, and the latter are more frequently identified as guerrillas or revolutionaries. According to Richard E. Rubenstein,

> Descriptively "terrorism" suggests violent action by individuals or small groups. Judgmentally, it implies illegitimacy. These meanings are closely related, since there are very few situations in which assassinations, bombings, kidnappings, or bank robberies seem justified. By contrast, wars and revolutions are frequently considered not only justified but holy.[10]

Similarly, Martha Crenshaw has argued,

> Terrorism is not mass or collective violence but rather the direct activity of small groups, however authentically popular these groups may be: even if supported by a larger organization or political party, the number of active militants who engage in terrorism is small.[11]

Precisely because an act of political violence is more likely to be seen as illegitimate, as an ordinary crime, or as an act of terrorism when carried out by individuals or small factions, most groups, regardless of their true size, describe themselves as large organizations with significant popular support; they also invoke metaphors of war, revolution, and liberation. These linguistic tactics are reflected in the names they choose for themselves, as the following examples demonstrate: Tupac Amaru Revolutionary Movement, Irish Republican Army, Red Army Brigade, Red Army Faction, Armed Islamic Group, Popular Front for the Liberation of Palestine, and Revolutionary Armed Forces of Colombia.

Members of such organizations call themselves and want to be perceived as commandos, fighters, soldiers, warriors, guerrillas, or revolutionaries.

The case of Richard C. Reid, a self-proclaimed disciple of Osama bin Laden and member of the Al Qaeda organization, was a case in point. Sentenced to life for his attempt to blow up an American airliner with explosives hidden in his shoes, the would-be shoe bomber told Judge William G. Young of the Federal District Court in Boston, "I am at war with your country." But the judge rejected vehemently the assertion that Reid was a soldier, telling him, "You are not an enemy combatant, you are a terrorist. You are not a soldier in any army, you are a terrorist."[12]

The Definitional Potpourri

Government officials are in a more advantageous position than other political actors to confer the "t" word on groups or withhold it and thereby affect public perceptions, because most of the time the mass media cover officialdom far more frequently than other sources. Indeed, this is true not simply in authoritarian systems where the government controls the media but also in liberal democracies.[13] It has been argued that during the Cold War era, government officials, terrorism experts, and the news media in the West, especially in the United States, denounced violent left-wing groups and movements inside and outside the United States as terrorists because these organizations were hostile to the economic and political arrangement in Western liberal democracies, and that the same Western establishment supported equally or more violent right-wing perpetrators of political violence as freedom fighters because of their anticommunist pedigree.[14] But to whatever degree this criticism was valid, these lines of demarcation faded away once the Cold War was over. In a 2002 review of domestic terrorism, for example, the Federal Bureau of Investigation (FBI) stated,

> During the past decade we have witnessed dramatic changes in the nature of the terrorist threat. In the 1990s, right-wing extremism overtook left-wing terrorism as the most dangerous domestic threat to the country.[15]

Contrary to the suggestion that "individual governments have been swift to ratify their own definitions" of terrorism and that the continuing "definitional haze" remains simply a dilemma for the international community, individual governments have not solved this definitional problem either; if they managed to streamline their terminology, they did not apply their own definitions in consistent ways.[16] The United States was, for a long time, a case in point in that the executive departments and agencies of the federal government did not adopt a standard definition. The Federal Emergency Management Agency (FEMA), for example, defined terrorism as violence "for purposes of intimidation, coercion, or ransom" without including the provision that it must be politically motivated; this definition covered many ordinary crimes.[17] It was only in the aftermath of 9/11, when the press reported and a congressional committee complained about the lack of a uniform definition within the government, that FEMA adopted the general definition of terrorism that was used by the FBI, namely, that terrorism is the "unlawful use of force or violence against persons and property to intimidate or coerce a government, the civilian population, or any segment thereof, in furtherance of political or social objectives."[18]

As the law enforcement agency that is charged with preventing terrorism and with investigating terrorist incidents once they occur, the FBI developed the following working definitions that distinguish between domestic and international terrorism

and, not surprisingly, focus heavily on the unlawful nature of terrorism and the violation of criminal laws by the perpetrators of political violence:

- Domestic terrorism is the unlawful use, or threatened use, of violence by a
  group or individual based and operating entirely within the United States or
  its territories, without foreign direction, committed against persons or property, to intimidate or coerce a government, the civilian population, or any segment thereof, in furtherance of political or social objectives.
- International terrorism involves violent acts dangerous to human life that are
  a violation of the criminal laws of the United States or any state, or that would
  be a criminal violation if committed within the jurisdiction of the United
  States or any state. Acts of international terrorism are intended to intimidate
  or coerce a civilian population, influence the policy of the government, or
  affect the conduct of a government. These acts transcend national boundaries
  in terms of the means by which they are accomplished, the persons they are
  intended to intimidate, or the locale in which perpetrators operate.[19]

The Department of State, with jurisdictions in the area of international terrorism
but not in the domestic realm, adopted a terminology that was closest to an official
U.S. government definition because it was contained in Title 22 of the *United States
Code*, Section 2656f(d), a federal statute, which requires the State Department to provide Congress with annual reports on terrorist groups and countries that sponsor terrorism. According to this statute's and the Department of State's definitions,

- "Terrorism" means premeditated, politically motivated violence perpetrated
  against noncombatant targets by subnational groups or clandestine agents,
  and is usually intended to influence an audience.
- "International terrorism" means terrorism involving citizens or the territory
  of more than one country.
- "Terrorist group" means any group practicing, or that has significant subgroups that practice, international terrorism.

This definition and particularly its first part delineate the most important, but
also the most contested, attributes assigned to terrorism:

FIRST, THE MOTIVES ARE POLITICAL. Unlike the term *crime*, which implies that
perpetrators act for personal gain and satisfaction, material and otherwise, *terrorism* is
understood as politically motivated. There is no disagreement on this characteristic
regardless of whether the perpetrators are guided by secular or religious beliefs.
However, while it is not difficult to differentiate between criminal and political
motivations most of the time, sometimes the lines are blurred—especially during
ongoing incidents. In the fall of 2002, for example, when a pair of snipers terrorized
millions of people in Washington, D.C., and the surrounding areas of Virginia and
Maryland for twenty-one long days, killing ten and seriously injuring three persons,
law enforcement specialists had no clue about the nature of these attacks, that is,
whether they were criminal or terrorist acts. Even in the face of threats that the
random killings would continue unless a large sum of money was paid, nobody was
sure whether the crime-or-terrorism mystery was completely solved. In the past,
politically motivated groups frequently committed violent crimes, such as attacks on
armored cars, bank robberies, and kidnappings for ransom, in order to support

themselves and their terror operations. As for the Washington snipers, even after their arrest, it was not clear whether their motives were purely criminal or were influenced by political grievances as well. After all, as terrorism expert Jessica Stern pointed out, one of the pair, John Allen Muhammad, "reportedly told a friend that he endorsed the September 11 attacks and disapproved of U.S. policy toward Muslim states."[20]

SECOND, THE TARGETS ARE CIVILIANS OR NONCOMBATANTS. In declared or undeclared wars and other military conflicts, the warring sides target members of each other's armed forces; terrorists intentionally and randomly target civilians and what one might call innocent bystanders. However, terrorists are also known to single out the citizens of one or more countries or the members of particular religious, racial, or ethnic groups. In the 1970s and 1980s, for example, some Palestinian groups and the Lebanese-based Hezbollah (or Party of God) targeted U.S. citizens and especially Jewish Americans. Terrorists would typically force the passengers of a hijacked plane to surrender their passports to identify Americans and, based on their names, single out those who they believed to be Jews. Domestic terrorists as well have targeted innocent bystanders randomly but sought out members of particular groups. Over the July Fourth weekend of 1999, for example, a young adherent of the white supremacy hate group World Church of the Creator went on a killing spree in Illinois and Indiana that left an African American basketball coach and a Korean graduate student dead and six orthodox Jews injured. There was no doubt that Benjamin Nathaniel Smith, the perpetrator, encountered all of the victims by chance but chose to harm them because he could identify them as black, Asian, and Jewish.

It is noteworthy that the most authoritative definition used by the U.S. government does not characterize the deliberate targets of terrorism as "civilian" but as "noncombatant" and thus puts civilians, government officials, and military personnel into the same category of targets and victims as long as public officials and members of the armed forces are not engaged in combat. If one embraces the "noncombatant" definition, the Iranian hostage crisis (1979–1981) was a terrorist incident because the American captives, although members of the U.S. embassy staff, were not involved in an armed conflict. The U.S. Marines in the embassy compound were there to protect the embassy. Similarly, the 2001 attack on the USS *Cole* in the Yemeni port of Aden during a refueling stop that resulted in the death of 17 crew members would qualify as an act of terrorism, as was a truck bombing of the U.S. Marine barracks outside Beirut in 1983 that killed 241 Americans. If one subscribes to the "civilian" definition, these three incidents do not qualify as terrorism. In the Beirut case, the supporters of the lethal truck bombing and some Muslim clerics justified the so-called suicide bombing by rejecting the "noncombatant" definition; instead, they explicitly called the targets and victims of the attack members of a hostile military. The U.S. Marines had been dispatched to Lebanon as peacekeepers, but they did get involved in the country's civil strife.[21] In the case of the strike against the USS *Cole* and other Al Qaeda–related incidents, bin Laden and his associates did not even bother to justify these terrorist acts as directed against U.S. military personnel. After all, several years earlier, bin Laden had called on all Muslims to kill Americans everywhere—civilians and members of the armed forces.

THIRD, THE PERPETRATORS ARE NONSTATE ACTORS. Neither the Department of State's nor the FBI's definitions leave doubt that in their understanding, political violence is terrorism only when carried out by groups, subgroups (State Department definition), or individuals (FBI definition) who intentionally target noncombatants. Unlike some scholars, among them Crenshaw and Rubenstein, U.S. government agencies and departments do not distinguish between small and large groups, but the FBI's definition does include political violence by individuals without the requirement that they be members of or directed by a group. Conversely, Bruce Hoffman seems to exclude politically motivated violence by lone wolves when he states that "terrorism is conducted by an organization with an identifiable chain of command or conspiratorial cell structure."[22] Following this definitional element, one would not categorize individuals such as the Oklahoma City bomber Timothy McVeigh or Benjamin Smith, the white supremacist mentioned earlier, as terrorists. This book reflects the view that one individual or several persons can commit terrorist acts if they have political motives and goals—regardless of whether they are members of a group. McVeigh, for example, was not a formal member of one of the organizations in the right-wing, antigovernment movement, but he moved in these circles and was familiar with and embraced the extremist ideas and grievances common in this milieu.

More importantly, because they do not include governments or states and their agents as possible perpetrators of terrorism, the United States and other parties have been accused of applying a double standard. Thus, Edward Herman and Gerry O'Sullivan explained these definitional choices with the ideological Cold War biases of Western governments, Western terrorism experts, and the Western media, accusing them of looking upon the West as the sole victim of terrorist activities. They argued in particular that "the Western establishment has defined terrorism so as to exclude governments, which allows it to attend closely to the Baader-Meinhof gang and the Red Brigades and to play down the more severely intimidating actions of governments that they support."[23] Actually, the long-standing definition of the U.S. Department of Defense was in this respect more useful to critics, who insisted all along on the inclusion of states or governments in any explanation of terrorism. The Defense Department's terminology was broader than the definitions embraced by the FBI and the U.S. Department of State, and not explicit as to the characteristics of the perpetrators of terrorism. For the Defense Department, terrorism meant

> the unlawful use of—or threatened use of—force or violence against individuals or property to coerce or intimidate governments or societies, often to achieve political, ideological, or religious objectives.[24]

However, the FBI's and the U.S. Department of State's more specific versions that single out nonstate actors as the perpetrators of terrorism, not the Department of Defense's less specific definition, have been the preferred models for other executive agencies in the U.S. administration. There is no disagreement on one important point: Terrorism is committed in order to intimidate and terrorize a target audience. Therefore, the target society is far more important in the terrorist calculus than the immediate victims, in that terrorists are after a targeted public's and government's psychological mindsets in order "to make them act in a way which the attackers desire."[25] Michael Stohl has explained terrorism as a three-step process that consists of the "act or threat of violence, the emotional reaction to such an act or threat, and the social effects resultant from the acts and reaction."[26] With this process model in mind, Stohl concluded that "terrorists are primarily interested in the audience and not the victims" and that the "act or threat of violence is but the first step [in the three-part process]."[27]

Obviously aware of the definitional difficulties, the European Convention to Combat Terrorism that was adopted in 1977 by the member states of the European

Union did not contain a definition of terrorism and listed instead a number of crimes that made perpetrators of such criminal acts liable to be extradited from one European country to another. Agreement on the definition of terrorism was never achieved in the larger setting of the United Nations, although there were many efforts to embrace a single definition as the precondition for a truly international convention to have all member states agree to condemn and fight terrorism. The efforts to agree on one understanding of terrorism began between World War I and World War II and continued throughout the rest of the twentieth and into the twenty-first centuries. In 1937, the League of Nations Convention made the first attempt to embrace an internationally accepted definition of terrorism that would allow the unconditional condemnation of terrorism. This first effort identified as terrorism

> [a]ll criminal acts directed against a state and intended or calculated to create a state of terror in the minds of particular persons or a group of persons or the general public.[28]

Sixty-two years later, in 1999, a resolution of the United Nations (UN) General Assembly suggested that

> criminal acts intended or calculated to provoke a state of terror in the general public, a group of persons, or particular persons for political purposes are in any circumstance unjustifiable, whatever the considerations of a political, philosophical, racial, ethnic, religious or other nature that may be invoked to justify them.[29]

But the member states of the UN have not agreed to this or any other proposal and have adopted instead a dozen conventions and protocols over the last several decades that prohibit specific acts of terrorism, such as hijacking, hostage-taking, attacks on diplomats, and nuclear terror. Even after the events of September 11, 2001, renewed efforts to agree on a definition of terrorism and adopt a comprehensive agreement to combat this kind of violence failed. While the United States, the European Union, and many other countries agreed to focus on the victims of terrorism and condemn the targeting of civilians, a bloc of nations led by the Organization of the Islamic Conference insisted on the exclusion of national liberation movements and resistance to foreign occupation.[30] In 2002, Islamic nations adopted an agreement that obliged them to support a definition of terrorism that made a distinction between terrorism and legitimate struggle against foreign occupation. The delegates declared specifically, "We reject any attempt to link terrorism to the struggle of the Palestinian people in their exercise of their inalienable right to establish their independent state."[31]

Given these difficulties, one prominent terrorism expert, Walter Laqueur, has suggested that it is even less likely now than it was in the past to formulate and agree upon one definition, and that therefore new approaches are needed to solve the increasingly more complex problem. According to Laqueur,

> Today there are more varieties [of political violence] than existed thirty years ago, and many are so different from those of the past and from each other that the term terrorism no longer fits some of them. In the future, new terms will probably be found for the new varieties of terrorism.[32]

In the search for a value-free definition of the term terrorism, it has been suggested that the focus must be on the acts of political violence and not on the motives and justifications of those who commit them. Terrorism expert Brian Jenkins, for example, has proposed that political violence needs to be defined "by the nature of the act, not by the identity of the perpetrators or the nature of their cause."[33] Many news organizations have made this choice in that they use the term *terrorism* sparingly or forget about it altogether. Instead, they describe the methods of violence as bombing, hijacking, kidnapping, and so on, and the perpetrators as bombers, hijackers, hostage-takers, and the like. The news media are particularly influential in shaping the public's perception of what political violence qualifies as terrorism. A content analysis of leading American newspapers found that stories about political violence contained the terms *hijacker(s)*, *gunman(men)*, and *guerrilla(s)* far more often than *terrorist(s)* and refrained from characterizing the acts as terrorism but described them rather as hijackings, killings, bombings, explosions, attacks, blasts, shootings, seizures, and so on.[34] Just as revealing was the study's finding that more than 94% of these characterizations were chosen by the media in headlines and journalistic descriptions, compared to less than 6% that were attributed to the way that government officials, witnesses, and other sources defined acts of political violence.

Following the events of 9/11, some news organizations came under attack for avoiding the term *terrorism* in reporting about the strikes against the World Trade Center and the Pentagon. The news agency Reuters in particular prohibited its reporters and editors from using the "t" word even in the context of 9/11 because, as members of the management explained in memos to the staff and in interviews,

> We all know that one man's terrorist is another man's freedom fighter and that
> Reuters upholds the principle that we do not use the word terrorist. . . .
> We're trying to treat everyone on a level playing field, however tragic it's
> been and however awful and cataclysmic for the American people.[35]

As it turned out, the news agency's decision was not simply motivated by the determination to appear even-handed but by practical considerations as well. One of the organization's news executives explained, "We don't want to jeopardize the safety of our staff . . . in Gaza, the West Bank, and Afghanistan."[36]

Other news organizations were accused of applying a double standard in deciding when to use and not to use the "t" word. The *Star Tribune* in Minneapolis, for example, defended its practice of avoiding the term *terrorism* in reports about the Israeli–Palestinian conflict and explained that this was decided "because of the emotional and heated nature of the dispute." The newspaper stated furthermore, "In the case of the term 'terrorist,' other words—'gunman,' 'separatist,' and 'rebel,' for example—may be more precise and less likely to be viewed as judgmental. Because of that we often prefer these more specific words." However, after 9/11 the *Star Tribune* did describe Al Qaeda as a terrorist network, explaining that the term is permitted in some circumstances. In the case of Al Qaeda, the exception was made because, as the newspaper's assistant managing editor explained, the network had been identified by the U.S. government and other countries as a terrorist organization; furthermore, the argument was that some of its members had been convicted as terrorists.[37]

More than two years after 9/11, *Washington Post* ombudsman Michael Getler defended the newspaper's choices with respect to the language of terrorism in response to readers' complaints about bias in the *Post*'s coverage of the Israeli–Palestinian conflict. Getler argued, "Terrorism and terrorist can be useful words, but they are labels. Like all labels, they do not convey much hard information. We should rely first on specific facts, not characterization."[38] He also explained what the *Post* considered differences between different organizations according to their activities and goals as he rejected attempts to equate the "U.S. battle against Al Qaeda with the Israeli battle against Hamas."[39] As Getler put it,

> Hamas conducts terrorism but also has territorial ambitions, is a nationalist movement and conducts some social work. As far as we know, Al Qaeda exists only as a terrorist network. It is composed of radicals from several Islamic countries. The Palestinian resistance is indigenous. Al Qaeda launched a devastating surprise attack on the United States. Israelis and Palestinians have been at war for a long time. Palestinians have been resisting a substantial and, to Palestinians, humiliating, Israeli occupation of the West Bank and Gaza since they were seized in the 1967 war. That resistance has now bred suicide bombers.[40]

Of the four letters to the editor that the *Post* published in response to Getler's op-ed piece, three were critical and one was supportive of Getler's position, a fact that underlined the vast disagreements in this debate. Most Western news organizations avoided the "t" word and called nonstate actors that deliberately commit violence against civilians "militants" or "militant groups" or the like and characterized their actions according to the methods used—bombing, rocket attack, kidnapping. But even this did not satisfy all critics who wanted a distinction between organizations that besides perpetrating terrorist acts have other, even legitimate roles and those exclusively involved in violence. In the midst of the Israeli–Hamas confrontation of late 2008 and early 2009, one critic wrote:

> At present, American papers' reflexive use of the words "militant organization," or some variation thereof, closely mirrors the U.S. government's political stance on Hamas, which is that it's a "terrorist organization." But the phraseology is simply too stark, given the complexity of forces at play in this decades-old conflict.[41]

Is Terrorism Ever Justified?

Timothy Garton Ash noted that one needs to look beyond the nature of a violent act in order to decide whether it is committed by a "good terrorist" or not. While endorsing the adoption of a universal definition of terrorism, Ash suggests "four things to look at in deciding whether someone is a terrorist, and, if they are, what kind of terrorist: Biography, Goals, Methods, and Context. Only a combination of the four will yield an answer."[42] But even if political violence by groups or individuals were to be judged along those lines, Ash himself foresees difficulties in finding common ground because "the content in each case will be very different and there will be no universal guidelines for judging the combination."[43]

Nevertheless, one school of thought sees merit in adding normative approaches to the value-neutral understanding of the terrorist phenomenon. Thus, Martha Crenshaw would first "establish a neutral descriptive definition" that is general enough to be applicable to different circumstances in different countries, and then "make value judgments about different cases."[44] Her general definition identifies the most important attributes of terrorism as premeditated "systematic use of unorthodox political violence by small conspiratorial groups with the purpose of manipulating political attitudes rather than physically defeating the enemy." Her normative approach examines both the "morality of the ends and the morality of the means."[45] This allows different evaluations of different types of political violence: If terrorists fight for fundamental civil liberties and civil rights or the survival of a community, their violence is more justifiable than if their goals are nondemocratic or not for the sake of basic human rights.

Conor Cruise O'Brien, too, rejects the proposition of a value-free definition as a starting point, because for him, "the words 'terrorism' and 'terrorist' are not terms of scientific classification. They are imprecise and emotive."[46] Depending on whether political violence is directed against a democratic society that is based on consent or against a nondemocratic regime, O'Brien would use the pejorative term *terrorism* in the first instance but withhold the epithet and rather speak of *revolt* in the second case. In this evaluative framework, the violence committed by the Red Army Faction in the Federal Republic of Germany, a liberal democracy, was unjustifiable terrorism, but a violent uprising of the Jews in Hitler's Third Reich, a fascist regime, would have been justified as revolt.

In addition to suggesting an evaluation of terrorist objectives, Crenshaw deems it also necessary to compare terrorists' choice of violence to the conditions that breed terrorism. In her view, "Terrorism must not, as far as the terrorists can foresee, result in worse injustice than the condition the terrorists oppose."[47] In comparing their grievances with the violence they planned or actually committed, terrorists try in effect to rationalize their deeds as proportional or less violent than the violence inflicted on them and/or those they claim to represent. Thus, the would-be shoe bomber Richard Reid refused to apologize in court for trying to blow up an American airliner and thereby cause the deaths of 197 persons aboard, among them more than 20 children. Reid explained that what he had tried to do was not equal to the evil the U.S. government was guilty of. "Your government has killed two million children in Iraq," he said; "your government has sponsored the rape and torture of Muslims in prisons in Egypt and Turkey and Syria and Jordan."[48]

In his communications before and after 9/11, bin Laden, too, time and again justified violence against all Americans as reaction to the evils that the American government, military, and public perpetrated directly or indirectly against Arabs and Muslims. Addressing the United States more than a year after 9/11, bin Laden posed the question, "Why are we fighting and opposing you?" His answer: "Because you attacked us and continue to attack us."[49] The long list of U.S. transgressions that followed was one more attempt to portray the terrorism against Americans as just and justified—even before God. To that end, bin Laden used the following quote from the Qu'ran: "Permission to fight (against disbelievers) is given to those (believers) who are fought against, because they have been wronged and surely, Allah is Able to give them (believers) victory."[50]

Achin Vanaik recognizes a "genuine merit in the view that the goodness or worth of the ends achieved bears some significant relationship to the integrity of means used in the pursuit of those ends." But he also cautions that the "idea that means must prefigure ends has to be handled carefully."[51] Yet, after discussing Barrington Moore's "calculus of suffering" and Malcolm X's "by any means necessary" principle as exemplifying the notion that if the ends are just, there must not be—in advance—a curtailment of the violent means, he rejects the notion of extreme suffering and oppression as justification for all means of violence. Using a different rationale, he concludes,

> Any judgment of the possible indefensibility of the use of certain means is connected not so much to the concrete effect of those means on the form in which the just cause is realized, but on the ground of other general principles, namely ethical principles concerning individual human rights. This is the basis of the well-known and very important distinction between the justice of war and the justice of the conduct of war.[52]

For Vanaik, then, just as one can agree on certain ethical rules of warfare—regardless of whether there is consent on whether the war itself is just—one can agree on certain ethical rules of terrorism, especially with respect to what targets are attacked and how, regardless of whether there is consent on the morality of the terrorist cause itself.[53]

Ultimately, whether with or without a value-neutral definition as a starting point, the idea of judging the roots and objectives of political violence returns the debate inevitably to the perennial "terrorist or freedom fighter" and "nonstate actors versus nation-states" issues. But whether one concludes that terrorism is never justified or justifiable in certain cases, any discussion of the ethics of terrorism gains by considering nonviolent movements and nonviolent actions as alternatives to violent movements and violent actions. The most obvious cases here are, of course, Mahatma Gandhi's nonviolent Indian independence movement and Martin Luther King's nonviolent American civil rights movement as well as the ultimately nonviolent end of South Africa's apartheid system.

State Terror(ism) and State-Sponsored Terrorism

By suggesting a focus on terrorism by nonstate actors, this book does not minimize or excuse the violence perpetrated by governments and their agents against civilians and noncombatants—more often than not in covert ways. Acknowledging that "governments and their agents can practice terrorism" inside their countries or abroad, Crenshaw points out that such "use is usually carefully concealed in order to avoid public attribution of responsibility."[54] Moreover, when committed by governments, violence against civilians and noncombatants can be and has been in many instances equally as brutal and lethal as the actions of nonstate actors and, in fact, far more cruel and deadly. But when governments commit this type of violence, there are a number of appropriate pejorative terms, such as *war crimes, crimes against humanity, human rights violations, genocide, atrocities*—and *terror*. As the linguist Geoffrey Nunberg has noted, "Unlike 'terrorism,' 'terror' can be applied to states as well as to insurgent groups."[55] Bruce Hoffman, too, points to the distinction between *terror* to characterize state violence "mostly against domestic populations" and *terrorism* to describe violence by "non-state entities."[56]

Post–World War I Germany can serve as an example here. Beginning in the 1920s, well-organized, violent groups of Adolf Hitler's followers attacked political opponents and stirred the political instability that brought him to power in 1933. Clearly, the terrorist tactic (i.e., political violence against civilians by nonstate actors) was successful in this case, as it was in the coming to power of another fascist ruler, Hitler's contemporary Benito Mussolini in Italy. The state of violence during the Hitler years was primarily directed against Jews, who were the victims of genocide, and also against other "undesirable elements," such as Communists, socialists, and gypsies. During Hitler's reign of terror, more than 10 million innocent civilians were brutally tortured and killed according to government policies. This was unspeakable state terror, as were the imprisonment and killing of many millions of people in the Soviet Union during Joseph Stalin's rule. More recently, totalitarian regimes in various parts of the world oppressed, persecuted, tortured, and killed thousands, hundreds of thousands, and millions of people within their borders—in Argentina, Cambodia, Uganda, Iraq, Sudan, and many other places. No case of nonstate political violence comes even close to the enormity of these atrocities. To characterize this kind of political violence committed by the power-holders in states as "terrorism" would actually minimize the enormity of systematic political violence and mass killings of civilians by those in control of states.

In his extensive documentation, explanation, and discussion of "death by government," R. J. Rummel, too, does not include state terrorism or government terrorism as definitional concepts, but distinguishes between genocide (the killing of people because of their ethnic, racial, religious, and/or linguistic group membership), "politicide" (the killing of persons because of their "politics or for political purposes"), mass murder or massacre (the indiscriminate killing of persons), and terror (defined as "extrajudicial execution, slaying, assassination, abduction or disappearance forever of targeted individuals").[57] More important, Rummel comes up with a useful definition of illegitimate state violence—"democide"—that includes genocide, politicide, mass murder, terror, and, in addition, what each of these four categories excludes. Thus, the author explains democide as

> the intentional killing of an unarmed or disarmed person by government agents acting in their authoritative capacity and pursuant to government policy or high command (as in the Nazi gassing of Jews). . . .
>
> It is democide if governments promoted or turned a blind eye to these deaths even though they were murders carried out "unofficially" or by private groups (as by death squads in Guatemala or El Salvador). And these deaths also may be democide if high government officials purposely allowed conditions to continue that were causing mass deaths and issued no public warning (as in the Ethiopian famines of the 1970s). All extra-judicial executions or summary executions comprise democide. Even judicial executions may be democide, as in the Soviet show trials of the late 1930s.[58]

So, choosing different definitions is a way to mark the distinction between different perpetrators of deliberate political violence against civilians and noncombatants—one when governments commit this sort of violence (democide, terror), and another when groups or individuals are the perpetrators (terrorism). The decision to use the same word or different terms in itself does not make value judgments and minimize or maximize the seriousness and scope of either state or nonstate political violence. Conceptual differentiation in this particular case offers the opportunity of dealing separately with terrorism (the topic of this book) and state terror or democide (not the topic of this book).

State Sponsors of Terrorism

When states support groups whose political violence is directed against civilians in a foreign country, they are sponsoring terrorism. Governments support terrorist groups in order to further their own foreign policy goals. Most of the time, governments do not admit this sort of support but, indeed, deny it. During the Cold War, both the Soviet-led Eastern bloc and the U.S.-led Western world supported groups that committed terrorism against the other side. East Germany, Czechoslovakia, and Bulgaria, for example, provided safe haven, explosives, and logistic support to left-wing terrorist groups in Western Europe, while the United States provided substantial support to the Nicaraguan Contras in their fights against the leftist Sandinista government and its supporters. During those years, these countries were state sponsors of terrorism.

The Meaning of *Terrorism* in This Volume

I agree with Walter Laqueur's suggestion that new and multiple definitions are needed to get a better handle on the distinctive features of different kinds of political violence committed by different types of actors. For the time being, I prefer the distinction between *terror* and *terrorism*, as discussed above. This, then, is my definition of terrorism in the context of this volume:

> **TERRORISM IS POLITICAL VIOLENCE OR THE THREAT OF VIOLENCE BY GROUPS OR INDIVIDUALS WHO DELIBERATELY TARGET CIVILIANS OR NONCOMBATANTS IN ORDER TO INFLUENCE THE BEHAVIOR AND ACTIONS OF TARGETED PUBLICS AND GOVERNMENTS.**

Notes

1. From "The Public Papers of the President, Administration of William J. Clinton," 1998, 2124.
2. For the most authoritative book on McVeigh, see Lou Michel and Dan Herbeck, *American Terrorist: Timothy McVeigh and the Oklahoma City Bombing* (New York: Regan Books, 2001).
3. Alex Houen, *Terrorism and Modern Literature: From Joseph Conrad to Ciaran Carson* (New York: Oxford University Press, 2002), 9.
4. A. Odasuo Alali and Konoye Kelvin Eke, eds., *Media Coverage of Terrorism: Methods of Diffusion* (Newbury Park, CA: Sage, 1991), 30.
5. Martha Crenshaw, ed., *Terrorism in Context* (University Park: Pennsylvania State University Press, 1995), 7.
6. Richard E. Rubenstein, *Alchemists of Revolution* (New York: Basic Books, 1987), 17, 18.
7. The words were part of Yousef's statement before he was sentenced by Judge Kevin Thomas Duffy of the Federal District Court in Manhattan on January 8, 1998. See, "Excerpts from Statements in Court," *New York Times*, January 8, 1998, B4.
8. Bruce Hoffman, *Inside Terrorism* (New York: Columbia University Press, 1998), 28–29.
9. The distinction between terrorism "from above" and "from below" is made in Walter Laqueur, *A History of Terrorism* (New Brunswick, NJ: Transaction Publishers, 2002), ch. 1; and Walter Laqueur, *The Age of Terrorism* (Boston: Little, Brown, 1987), ch. 1.
10. Rubenstein, 17.
11. Crenshaw, 4.
12. Shoe bomber Reid and Judge Young were quoted in Pam Belluck, "Threats and Responses: The Shoe Plot; Unrepentant Shoe Bomber Sentenced to Life," *New York Times*, January 31, 2003, A13; and Thanassis Cambanis, "Sentenced to Life, Reid Denounces US," *Boston Globe*, January 31, 2003, A1.
13. See, for example, W. Lance Bennett, *News: The Politics of Illusion* (New York: Longman, 2001); and Brigitte L. Nacos, *Mass-Mediated Terrorism: The Centrality of the Media in Terrorism and Counterterrorism* (Lanham, MD: Rowman & Littlefield, 2002), especially ch. 5.
14. Edward Herman and Gerry O'Sullivan, *The Terrorism Industry: The Experts and Institutions That Shape Our View of Terror* (New York: Pantheon Books, 1989).
15. "Statement for the Record of Dale L. Watson Executive Assistant Director Counterterrorism and Counterintelligence Federal Bureau of Investigation on the Terrorist Threat Confronting the United States before the Senate Select Committee on Intelligence Washington D.C.," February 6, 2002.
16. Houen, 7–8. Houen writes that individual governments have been "swift to ratify their own definitions" but that the international dimensions of 9/11 kept the definitional problem alive. But disagreements over the definition of political violence continue to exist with respect to both domestic and international terrorism.
17. This definition was mentioned in Oliver Libaw, "Defining Terrorism: Little Agreement on Where to Draw the Line," abcnews.go.com/sections/world/dailynews/stratforo01117.html, October 11, 2001.
18. This new definition of terrorism in general and FEMA's definitions of domestic and international terrorism were available on FEMA's web site, www.fema.gov./hazards/terrorism/terror.shtm (retrieved January 12, 2003).

19. The definitions are contained in many FBI documents and statements; see, for example, "Statement for the Record of Dale L. Watson."

20. Jessica Stern, "The Protean Enemy," *Foreign Affairs* (July–August 2003): 34.

21. For details on the U.S. military's involvement in Lebanon, see David C. Martin and John Walcott, *Best Laid Plans* (New York: Harper & Row, 1988), chs. 5 and 6.

22. Hoffman, 43.

23. Herman and O'Sullivan, 214.

24. The definition is quoted by Hoffman, 38.

25. C. J. M. Drake, "The Role of Ideology in Terrorists' Target Selection," *Terrorism and Political Violence* 10:2 (Summer 1998): 53.

26. Michael Stohl, "Characteristics of Contemporary International Terrorism," in Charles W. Kegley Jr., ed., *International Terrorism: Characteristics, Causes, Controls* (New York: St. Martin's, 1990), 83.

27. Ibid.

28. The definition was quoted by the United Nations Office on Drug and Crime on its web site, www.unodc.org (retrieved January 7, 2003).

29. Contained in GA Res. 51/210, "Measures to Eliminate International Terrorism," as excerpted by www.unodc.org.

30. For more on the failure to reach an agreement at the UN after 9/11, see Michael Jordan, "Terrorism's Slippery Definition Eludes UN Diplomats," *Christian Science Monitor* (February 4, 2002), 7.

31. Associated Press, "Muslim Meeting Won't Define Terror," *New York Times*, April 3, 2002.

32. Walter Laqueur, *The New Terrorism* (New York: Oxford University Press, 1999), 6.

33. Hoffman, 33.

34. Robert G. Picard and Paul D. Adams, "Characterizations of Acts and Perpetrators of Political Violence in Three Elite U.S. Daily Newspapers," in Alali and Eke, 12–21. The content analysis covered pertinent news coverage from 1980 through 1985.

35. Cited by John O'Sullivan, "Retracting Required," *National Review*, September 25, 2001, www.nationalreview.com/jos/jos092501.shtml (retrieved January 12, 2002); and Norman Solomon, "Media Spin Revolved around the Word 'Terrorist,'" *Media Beat*, October 4, 2001, www.fair.org/media-beat/011004.html (retrieved January 9, 2003).

36. Cited by O'Sullivan.

37. Lou Gelfand, "Newspaper Careful in Use of Label 'Terrorist,'" *Star Tribune*, February 3, 2002, 27A. See also "'Terrorism' Is a Term that Requires Consistency: Newspaper and Its Critics Both Show a Double Standard on 'Terror,'" *Fairness and Accuracy in Reporting*, April 8, 2002, www.fair.org/press-release/terrorism.html (retrieved January 4, 2003).

38. Michael Getler, "The Language of Terrorism," *Washington Post*, September 21, 2003, B6.

39. Ibid.

40. Ibid.

41. Katia Bachko, "War of Words." *Columbia Journalism Review* (Online), January 8, 2009. See http://www.cjr.org/campaign_desk/war_of_the_words.php (accessed January 11, 2009).

42. Timothy Gorton Ash, "Is There a Good Terrorist?" *New York Review of Books*, November 29, 2001, www.nybooks.bom/articles/14860 (retrieved April 2, 2003).

43. Ibid.

44. Martha Crenshaw, "Reflections on the Effects of Terrorism," in Martha Crenshaw, ed., *Terrorism, Legitimacy, and Power* (Middletown, CT: Wesleyan University Press, 1983), 2.

45. Ibid., 2–3.

46. Conor Cruise O'Brien, "Terrorism under Democratic Conditions: The Case of the IRA," in Crenshaw, 91.

47. Crenshaw, "Reflections," 4.

48. Quoted in Belluck, A13.

49. "Full Text: bin Laden's 'Letter to America,'" *Observer*, November 24, 2002, www.observer.co.uk/worldview/story/0,11581,845725,00.html (retrieved June 5, 2003).

50. Ibid.

51. Achin Vanaik, "The Ethics and Efficacy of Political Terrorism," in Eric Hershberg and Kevin W. Moore, eds., *Critical Views of September 11: Analysis from Around the World* (New York: New Press, 2002), 37, 38.

52. Ibid., 39.
53. In his essay, Vanaik details two such rules that he considers pertinent.
54. Crenshaw, *Terrorism in Context*, 4.
55. Geoffrey Nunberg, "How Much Wallop Can a Simple Word Pack?" *New York Times*, July 11, 2004, sec. 4, 7.
56. Hoffman, 25.
57. R. J. Rummel, *Death by Government*, ch. 2, www.hawaii.edu/powerkills/welcome.html. Rummel's web site offers a great deal of information about cases in which governments systematically and intentionally killed large numbers of people inside and outside their own borders.
58. Ibid.

3 CHAPTER

Terrorism in the Global Context

TERRORISM HAS BEEN USED AS A WEAPON OF THE WEAK AGAINST militarily, politically, and economically stronger rulers and governments for a long time and in many parts of the world. The earliest cases of terrorism had religious and political overtones and date back to biblical times. The Sicariis, a distinct group, were involved in the Zealots' struggle against the Roman occupiers of Palestine and fellow Jews who collaborated with the Romans. The Sicariis attacked their targets typically on holidays and in the midst of large crowds with a "sica," a small sword that was hidden beneath their coats until they were close enough to stab their victims. Although fighting in the name of God, whom they considered their only legitimate ruler, they had immediate political motives—most of all the burning desire to remove the secular foreign rulers from power. However, the terror campaign ended in 73 A.D., when hundreds of Zealots committed mass suicide rather than surrender to the victorious Romans.

Far more enduring than the Sicariis were the Assassins (eleventh to thirteenth centuries), an extremist offshoot of the Ismaili branch of Shi'ite Islam, who were active in Persia (now Iran) and Syria. Hassan-i-Sabbah, the founder of this fiercely anti-Sunni sect, was poised to spread his brand of Ismaili Islam throughout the Middle East and defeat the Sunni rulers. He convinced his fanatically devoted followers that actively fighting for their cause would assure them a place in paradise. Recognizing that their membership was too small to fight their enemies openly, the Assassins operated clandestinely until the assigned member or members attacked a prominent leader—typically in front of large crowds. They assaulted their targets with daggers and made no attempt to escape but seemed content, even eager, to be caught and killed after they had accomplished their lethal missions. Thus, in today's parlance, the Assassins practiced a form of "suicide terrorism."

Rumor had it that the Assassins were under the influence of hashish when they envisioned paradise, when they attacked their targets, and when they went eagerly to their death. Indeed, because of the myth of their wide use of hashish, the members of the sect were called *hashishin* in Arabic; this name turned into "assassin" in the vocabulary of the

Carlos, the Jackal, During Joint-Venture Terrorism Coup

German and Palestinian terrorists and the legendary Venezuelan Carlos, the Jackal, attacked a meeting of OPEC ministers in Vienna, Austria, in December 1975, killing three persons and taking many hostages. After lengthy negotiations, the Austrian government agreed to fly the Jackal (left, in trench coat), his accomplices, and forty-two of their hostages to Libya. Once the terrorists were sure that millions of dollars in ransom had been deposited in a bank in South Yemen, they released their captives.

Christian Crusaders and eventually came to mean political murder in many Western languages. The Assassins did not realize their religious and political goals but were wiped out when the Mongols conquered Iran and Syria in the middle of the thirteenth century. Nevertheless, as one terrorism expert pointed out, the Assassins "demonstrated a basic principle of contemporary terrorism: the ability of small groups to wage effective campaigns of terror against much stronger opponents."[1]

The Thugs, who organized in the eleventh century, terrorized India for hundreds of years before the British destroyed them in the nineteenth century. Group members targeted travelers and strangled their victims with a silk tie before robbing them. According to rumors, the Thugs worshiped the goddess Kali and killed so that they could nourish her with the blood of their victims. But it is not clear whether the Thugs practiced religious terrorism or were simply bandits out for material gains. One way or the other, today the term *thug* characterizes a hoodlum, crook, thief—in other words, a criminal.

Beginning in the Middle Ages, Christian sects as well resorted to violence. Typically following a charismatic leader or prophet, they claimed to fight for the purification of the Christian religion and Christian life. Their targets were Jews and whoever they considered Christians in name only. Following the Reformation, for example, the Anabaptists, a millennial sect, emerged in Germany. Members of the group considered the city of Muenster as the true Jerusalem and themselves as God's chosen instruments in the violent campaign against the anti-Christ—sinful Catholics and Protestants who stood in the way of the millennium.

No doubt, then, that terrorism originated with religious and pseudoreligious sects and that the adherents of the major religions, among them the Christians, Muslims, Jews, Buddhists, Hindus, and Sikhs, resorted to political violence in the name of God.

Different Types of Groups

Besides religious terrorism, which will be discussed in Chapter 5, several other major types of both international and domestic terrorism emerged in more recent times. The majority of groups that resort to political violence fit the following categories: nationalist/separatist, left and/or revolutionary, right and/or reactionary, antiglobalization, and extreme environmentalist. As the name suggests, nationalists/ separatists strive for statehood or more autonomy; good examples here are Palestinian organizations, such as the Palestinian Liberation Front (PLO), and the Basque group Euzkadi Ta Askatasuna (ETA). The former demand an independent Palestinian state, the latter greater autonomy within Spain, if not independence. Left/revolutionary groups like the Revolutionary Armed Forces of Colombia (FARC) want to establish a Marxist regime in Colombia and cooperate with other Latin American left-revolutionary groups. In Venezuela, the right-wing United Self-Defense Forces of Venezuela (AUV) fight to remove the leftist government of Hugo Chavez, are hostile to Chavez supporters in neighboring countries, and work closely with the right-wing Self-Defense Forces of Colombia (AUC). Antiglobalization groups, such as the Mexican Fuerzas Armadas Revolucionarias del Pueblo (FARP), are often also left-leaning and even Marxist. Others fit both the profile of anarchists and extreme globalization foes. Thus, the self-proclaimed anarchists, who provoked what came to be known as "The Battle of Seattle" during the World Trade Organization's summit in 1999, staged violence to express their opposition to globalization and thereby energized the antiglobalization movement abroad. Finally, environmental extremists like Earth First and the Earth Liberation Front resort to violent means in North America and in Europe, especially the United Kingdom, in the name of protecting the environment.

The Roots of Modern Terrorism

The origins of modern terrorism "from below"—or political violence directed against the forces of power in society, namely, political leaders—go back to the second half of the nineteenth century. In the first stage, radical socialists and anarchists contributed to the theoretical underpinnings of a philosophy of violence as a means to fight and destroy oppressive leaders and governments. In 1849, a journal in Switzerland that was edited by political refugees from Germany published a radical tract under the headline "Der Mord" (Murder), in which its author, Karl Heintzen, laid out the rationale for terrorist action against "reactionaries" and "the mass party of the barbarians." Accusing the people in power of "mass murder, organized murder, or war, as it is called," Heintzen concluded,

> Even if we have to blow up half a continent or spill a sea of blood, in order to finish off the barbarian party, we should have no scruples about doing it. The man who would not joyfully give up his own life for the satisfaction of putting a million barbarians into their coffins carries no Republican heart within his breast.[2]

Heintzen advocated murder for political ends, or what soon thereafter was defined as terrorism, even if that meant death for members of what he called "the party of freedom." Heintzen anticipated the development of weapons that would make political violence "from below" far more lethal and effective when he wrote, "The greatest benefactor of mankind will be he who makes it possible for a few men to wipe out thousands."[3] One hundred and fifty years later, Osama bin Laden and the Al Qaeda organization embraced the same idea when they searched for weapons of mass destruction.

In Russia, Sergey Nechaev, Nikolai Morozov, and Pyotr Kropotkin were among the radical leaders who justified terrorist means in their writings and prescribed rules of conduct for the true revolutionary to follow. The terms *revolutionary* and *terrorist* were used interchangeably. Although living for most of his political life in Switzerland, Mikhail Bakunin, who advocated his own brand of anarchism, had devoted followers in Russia. During this era, the most influential terrorist-revolutionary organization in Russia was the Narodnaya Volga (The People's Will) because it made the step from radical rhetoric to actual terrorist acts, which included the assassination of Czar Alexander II in 1881.

The anarchist movement was not limited to Russia but was truly international and became associated with political violence during the 1880s and 1890s and, to a lesser extent, in the first decade of the twentieth century. During that period, anarchists and social revolutionaries were responsible for a wave of political assassinations in several countries, among them Russia, France, Spain, and Italy. The United States was not immune either because European immigrants, among them Karl Heintzen and John Most, advocated anarchist ideas and deeds in their new homeland. The anarchists of this era did not strike randomly but targeted high-ranking political figures, among them French President Sadi Carnot, Spanish Prime Minister Antonio Canovas, King Umberto of Italy, and Empress Elisabeth of Austria and U.S. Presidents James Garfield and William McKinley. Sometimes, anarchists aborted their assassination plans because they did not want to harm innocent bystanders. Attempts on the lives of other prominent figures, among them the German Chancellor Otto von Bismarck and the German emperor William II, failed. But, as Laqueur has pointed out, "Inasmuch as the assassins were anarchists—and quite a few were not—they all acted on their own initiative without the knowledge and support of the groups to which they belonged."[4]

Although left-wing movements occupy a dominant place in the annals of terrorism for the years between about 1850 and World War I, a variety of very different groups resorted to political violence during this period—among them Irish nationalists fighting against the British and Armenians struggling against Turkish oppression. But the leading figures in the anarchist and social reform movements were the ones who provided the theoretical underpinnings for political violence and thereby have influenced terrorists of all ideological colors ever since.

Between World War I and World War II, right-wing movements in particular embraced the "propaganda by the deed" maxim, but it was especially the emerging fascist camps that used political violence in their push for power. Italian dictator Benito Mussolini made no secret of his sympathy for violence, and Joseph Goebbels, Adolf Hitler's propagandist-in-chief, considered terror and brutality in the streets as sure means for rather obscure groups to become widely known and win the support of the masses. Extremists at the right and left were very similar in that they recognized the efficacy of political violence as a tool to undermine the legitimacy of the political systems they opposed. And although in some instances terrorist theory preceded terrorist actions, as in the case of the anarchists, it was the other way around in at least as many cases. According to Walter Laqueur's astute observation,

> In short, it has been possible since time immemorial to make love and to cook without the help of textbooks; the same applied to terrorism. In some cases the decision to adopt a terrorist strategy was taken on the basis of a detailed political analysis. But usually the mood came first, and ideological rationalization only after. On occasion this led to the emergence of a systematic strategy of terrorism and to bitter debates between proponents and opponents. But terrorism also took place without precise doctrine and systematic strategy.[5]

The Post–World War II Wave

Terrorism did not disappear with the outbreak of World War II but flared up regularly—from the anti-British bombings in the United Kingdom by the IRA to political violence by both Jews and Arabs in the British mandate of Palestine. For David Rapoport, the "principal stimulus was a major war aim of the victorious allies in both world wars: national self-determination. The ambivalence of colonial powers about their own legitimacy made them ideal targets for a politics of atrocity."[6] But it was the post–World War II era that experienced the most powerful outburst of political violence "from below" in many parts of the world, as people struggled for decolonization and national liberation as well as for revolutionary social change.

Developments like the retreats of the British, French, Dutch, and Americans from Aden, Cyprus, Palestine, Algeria, Indonesia, the Philippines, and other places were often preceded and accompanied by terrorist violence. In Latin America, the revolutionary ferment was directed against American interference on behalf of the ruling class and aimed at a new social order that challenged the capitalist model. In Africa and Asia, European powers were the targets. Frantz Fanon and Regis Debray provided the theoretical justifications for violent actions for the sake of national liberation and fundamental social change. Using the case of Algeria to indict the inhumanity of the Western model in general and colonialism in particular, Fanon endorsed all-out violence not only as a means to an end—national liberation—but also as an end in itself that would free the liberated individuals from their marks of oppression and empower them. In *The Wretched of the Earth* he wrote,

> At the level of the individuals, violence is a cleansing force. It frees the native from his inferiority complex and from his despair and inaction; it makes him fearless and restores his self-respect.[7]

He also called for a new, just, and humane social and political model that was applicable beyond the special cases of Algeria and Africa to the Third World in general and to the struggle of minorities for self-determination in the First World as well. As Fanon put it in the conclusion of his treatise,

> Let us decide not to imitate Europe; let us combine our muscles and our brains in a new direction. Let us create the whole man, whom Europe has been incapable of bringing to triumphant birth.
>
> Two centuries ago, a former European colony decided to catch up with Europe. It succeeded so well that the United States of America became a monster, in which

the taints, the sickness, and the inhumanity of Europe have grown to appalling dimensions.

Comrades, have we not other work to do than to create a third Europe?[8]

In *Revolution in the Revolution*, Debray provided the rationale for the anti-imperialist, anticapitalist revolutionary uprisings in Latin America in particular. Unlike Fanon, who recognized the usefulness of terrorist action, Debray did not subscribe to the efficacy of terrorism but recommended larger-scale guerrilla warfare.

Fanon (a native of Martinique) and Debray (a Frenchman) were outsider theorists focusing on Africa and Latin America; the Brazilian Communist Carlos Marighella was a homegrown Latin American revolutionary whose *Handbook of Urban Guerrilla Warfare* provided hands-on instructions for violent struggle "from below." Besides physical fitness and absolute dedication to the cause, Marighella recommended technical expertise, especially with respect to arms, such as machine guns, revolvers, shotguns, mortars, and bazookas. In one passage of his manual, he gave the following advice:

> *A knowledge of various types of ammunition and explosives is another aspect to consider. Among the explosives, dynamite must be well understood. The use of incendiary bombs, of smoke bombs, and other types is indispensable knowledge.*
>
> *To know how to make and repair arms, prepare Molotov cocktails, grenades, mines, homemade destructive devices, how to blow up bridges, tear up and put out of service rails and sleepers, these are the requisites in the technical preparation of the urban guerilla that can never be considered unimportant.*[9]

In the 1960s and 1970s in particular, Fanon, Debray, and Marighella, for their theoretical contributions, and Ernesto "Che" Guevara, for his influence on and participation in Fidel Castro's Cuban Revolution, affected radicals far beyond the Third World. In Western Europe and, albeit to a lesser extent, in the United States, breakaway groups from the New Left's student movements decided to fight the symbols of American imperialism and the ruling establishments in their respective countries. Whether the Red Army Faction (RAF), better known as the Baader-Meinhof group, in Germany; the Red Brigades in Italy; or the Weather Underground in the United States, members of these groups considered themselves Marxist urban guerrillas fighting a class war against the existing order and its capitalist arrangement.

Although providing the theoretical context for their violent deeds in frequent communications, groups like the RAF insisted that it was time for terrorist action, not just terrorist doctrine. In "Stadtguerrilla und Klassenkampf" ("Urban Guerrilla and Class Struggle"), the RAF stated, "In this stage of history nobody can deny that an armed group, however small it may be, has a better chance to grow into a people's army than a group that limits itself to proclaim revolutionary principles."[10] The authors of the RAF's "Das Konzept Stadtguerrilla" ("The Concept of Urban Guerrilla") acknowledged that the idea of the urban guerrilla originated in Latin America and that Marighella's primer on the subject was used as their model.

Although the RAF initially committed violence inside West Germany, the group became part of a "terrorist international" that was responsible for major terrorist acts abroad beginning in the mid-1970s. However, it was not Ulrike Meinhof, Andreas Baader, and their German comrades, but the PLO under Yassir Arafat's leadership that pioneered international cooperation among terrorists by instructing radicals from abroad in training camps in Jordan. Among these early trainees were Baader and Meinhof, who, upon their return to Germany, established the RAF. The German trainees and their Palestinian hosts had parted on a sour note in the late 1960s, but by the mid-1970s members of the RAF and its offshoots teamed with their Palestinian colleagues to carry out terrorist attacks.

German leftists, inspired by Baader and Meinhof, and Palestinian nationalists, motivated by the PLO's Arafat and Abu Abbas, seemed strange bedfellows at first sight. But there was a meeting of the minds in that the Palestinians shared the RAF's anti-American sentiments because of the United States' strong support for Israel.

1968: The Advent of Modern-Day Terrorism

Many students of terrorism consider 1968 as the beginning of modern-day terrorism because this year marked the start of a period of ever more spectacular terrorism dramas both internationally and domestically. According to Jeffrey D. Simon,

> The significant breaking point was the launching of a sustained campaign of airline hijackings and sabotage by Palestinian guerrillas that was on a scale of violence and intensity never before seen by the international community. The Popular Front for the Liberation of Palestine (PFLP), under the command of a Palestinian physician named George Habash, dramatically publicized its struggle against Israel by hijacking an El Al plane in June 1968 on a flight from Rome to Tel Aviv and diverting it to Algeria. Then, in December, they attacked an El Al plane at the Athens airport, killing one passenger.[11]

From then on, the scope of the hijacking coups grew rapidly and soon targeted Americans and U.S. interests abroad. Nothing illustrated this better than the quadruple hijacking of four New York–bound airplanes in September 1970 by members of the PFLP. While security guards aboard the El Al plane overwhelmed this group of hijackers and killed one of them, other terrorists forced a Trans World Airways plane, a Pan American World Airways plane, and a Swissair jet to land in a remote area of Jordan. Hundreds of passengers, most of them Americans, others Europeans, were held hostage. Some of the hostages were released fairly soon, but others were detained for about three weeks. Eventually, when the United Kingdom, West Germany, and Switzerland agreed to release Palestinian prisoners, all hostages were freed. These terrorist spectaculars were designed to get the world to pay attention to the Palestinian cause. Explaining this rationale, one of the Palestinians, Dr. Habash, said, "We force people to ask what is going on."[12] Pointing to the massive publicity in the wake of terrorist strikes, another Palestinian terrorist remarked, "We would throw roses if it would work."[13]

What was the cause that motivated these terrorists? Palestinian terrorism was and still is rooted in the fate of more than a million Palestinians who fled or were displaced when the Jewish state of Israel was established and by Israel's territorial gains in the 1967 Six-Day War. The result of Israel's victory over the armies of Jordan, Syria, and Egypt was the lasting occupation of the non-Israeli part of Palestine—the West Bank and Gaza—and the Syrian Golan Heights. With the hope for a military victory over Israel crushed, some Palestinians turned to international terrorism in order to force governments and peoples outside the Middle East to take notice of their plight.

By the time the Palestinian "Black September" group attacked and brutally killed members of the Israeli Olympic team during the 1972 Olympic Games in Munich, the links between West Germany's Red Army Faction and its Palestinian counterparts were so close that the RAF provided logistical support for the terror attack.

In the following years, Germans and Palestinians planned and carried out numerous joint ventures, such as the terrorist attack during the 1975 OPEC meeting in Vienna; the 1976 hijacking of an El Al plane to Entebbe, Uganda; and the 1977 hijacking of a Lufthansa plane to Mogadishu, Somalia.

Some leftist groups in Europe were more inwardly oriented and less interested in and dependent on international cooperation. One commander of the Italian Red Brigades, for example, revealed in the early 1990s,

> Put simply and clearly, at the time [when the Red Brigades were still a factor] our approach excluded any contacts with foreign groups except contacts for materiel or those related to solidarity among revolutionary movements. We had one contact with a Palestinian faction for an arms shipment which we transported to our country and shared with three other Italian armed groups. Besides this, we adhered to the Maoist theory of "counting on one's own strength," both for weapons and for money.[14]

But, as the same Red Brigades commander pointed out, the RAF considered itself and acted as "the European fifth column of an 'Anti-imperialist Front'" that reached into the Eastern Bloc and revolutionary movements in the Third World.[15] Not surprisingly, in the 1980s, German terrorists tried to forge a Euro-terrorist alliance, an attempt that was inspired by the example of their Palestinian friends. According to Bruce Hoffman,

> The profound influence exercised by the Palestinians over the Germans was perhaps never clearer than in 1985, when the RAF joined forces with the French left-wing terrorist organization, Direct Action (in French, Action Directe, thus AD), in hopes of creating a PLO-like umbrella "anti-imperialist front of Western European guerrillas" that would include Italy's Red Brigades (RB) and the Belgium Communist Combatant Cells (CCC) as well.[16]

The ambitious plan did not succeed because many terrorists in various Western European countries were arrested or forced to flee to safe havens in the waning years of the Cold War. It has been argued that the RAF and related organizations could not have survived as long as they did without Palestinian support.[17] But this argument ignores or minimizes the significant support that these groups and individuals received from the Eastern side of the Iron Curtain.

In fact, much of the terrorism that plagued the West during the 1970s and 1980s related in one respect or another to the Cold War confrontation between the two superpowers and their respective spheres of influence. And the Israeli–Palestinian conflict, too, was fought in this context. While communist countries were supportive of leftist groups in Europe, Latin America, and elsewhere, some governments with friendly ties to Moscow supported religiously motivated groups as well. For example, the Lebanese Hezbollah, which was created in 1982 and financially sustained by the Islamic Republic of Iran, was tolerated and at times backed by Syria, which shared Hezbollah's anti-Israeli stance.

IRA and ETA: Groups That Transcend the Average Life Span of Terrorist Groups

David C. Rapoport has documented four waves of distinct terrorist movements beginning with the anarchist wave in the late nineteenth century, with an average span of 40 to 45 years for each of these distinct periods. He concluded that this "pattern suggests a human life cycle pattern, where dreams that inspire fathers lose their attractiveness for the sons."[18] Many groups had, in fact, far shorter lives than the waves they were part of. But there have also been some groups that survived the demise of their particular waves and the average life span of these types of groups.

A good example is the Irish Republican Army (IRA), whose roots go back to the end of the eighteenth century. The organization was founded in 1919 to fight for Ireland's independence from the United Kingdom. In 1921, when moderate nationalists agreed to the establishment of an independent Irish state in the predominantly Catholic south and to continued British control over six counties in the north, radical nationalists opposed this solution. They wanted all of Ireland to be independent. The result was a civil war in which the extreme nationalists were defeated by the newly independent Irish state. Although the majority of the IRA denounced violence in the late 1920s, remnants of the group continued to fight for Northern Ireland's independence. This was not the end of divisions within the IRA. In 1969, after paramilitary Protestants brutally interfered with a peaceful demonstration by Catholics in Northern Ireland, a militant IRA faction broke away and took the name "Provisional IRA." In the decades since then, the Provisional Irish Republican Army (also simply called the "IRA") was most instrumental and most violent in pushing the nationalist cause in Northern Ireland. At the same time, terrorism was also the weapon of choice of Protestant Loyalist groups, such as the Ulster Defense Association and the Ulster Vanguard Movement. In protest against a peace process that resulted in the Belfast Agreement of 1998 and in the hope of ending the violent conflict over the status of Northern Ireland once and for all, some IRA members formed the Real IRA. In the following years, members of this group carried out dozens of bombings and other terror attacks in Northern Ireland, Dublin, London, Birmingham, and elsewhere. In July 2005, the Provisional IRA declared an end to its armed struggle and announced that the organization would work within the democratic political process to achieve its goal. In the following three months, the group decommissioned its arms under the supervision of an Independent International Commission on Decommissioning.

Another example of an enduring terror organization is the Basque ETA, the separatist movement that was founded in 1959 when the wave of self-determination swept around the globe. The terrorist organization continued its deadly terrorist attacks during the 1990s. There was a short cease-fire at the end of the decade, but the group resumed its lethal terror in the first years of the twenty-first century, even while losing popular support inside and outside the Basque region in the last few years.

The Decline of Left-Wing Terrorism

When the Iron Curtain faded and the Cold War ended, many observers expected a dramatic decline in international terrorism. In April 1992, the RAF announced that it was laying down its arms. In a series of communiques, the RAF admitted the failure of its armed struggle up to the fall of the Berlin Wall and of its subsequent efforts to refocus its revolutionary activities in the wake of Germany's reunification. But even in defeat, the RAF reaffirmed its support for its past actions and for active liberation movements around the world.[19] Except for some groups and cells in Greece, Spain, and Turkey, these last communications were understood as obituaries for the Marxist groups that had terrorized Western Europe since the late 1960s. But even a decade later, when nineteen members of the Greek terrorist organization November 17 were arrested and tried, there were some signs that remnants of the Red Brigades were attempting a comeback in Italy.

In Latin America, many terrorist groups along with similar groups elsewhere disintegrated, but others survived and remained very active. Probably the best-known Latin American movement, the Tupamaros, or National Liberation Movement, in Uruguay, founded in 1962, became the model for urban terrorism or what proponents called "urban guerrilla warfare" across Latin America and elsewhere. While they provided the dominant model for Marxist groups, the Tupamaros also affected the organizational forms and terrorist methods of right-wing organizations. Aiming at overthrowing the existing domestic order and establishing a fairer system, the mostly middle- and upper-class members of the Tupamaros established an effective terror network across their country that fought foreign diplomats as well as domestic police and military forces. Ultimately, however, the Tupamaros lost their earlier public support and became the targets of an effective counteroffensive by Uruguay's security forces. By the 1980s the organization, once the poster child for terrorism, "totally abandoned the armed struggle, preferring instead to re-enter democratic politics."[20]

Other groups, such as the Revolutionary Armed Forces of Colombia (FARC) and the National Liberation Army (ELN) in Colombia, both established in the early 1960s, continued their struggle against foreign influence and their own governments into the twenty-first century. The leftist FARC is believed to be the best-trained, best-organized, and best-financed terror organization in Latin America. In the past, the left-wing ELN, an ecoterrorist group that specializes in sabotaging the pipelines of foreign oil corporations, had priests among its active members.

In sum, then, at the end of the twentieth and the beginning of the twenty-first centuries, Marxist terrorists were no longer the threat they had been in the preceding decades. Instead, a far more dangerous and deadly form of terrorism surfaced during the 1990s.

The Rise of Catastrophic Terrorism

Just as 1968 is considered the beginning of modern terrorism, 1995 can be seen as the advent of catastrophic terrorism. There had been plenty of warnings in advance. During the 1980s, some experts in the field cautioned that the United States and the world should brace for the most violent chapter in the history of terrorism. Robert Kupperman and Jeff Kamen, for example, described eerie scenarios of major acts of terrorism that would cause mass disruption and mass destruction. But other well-regarded experts, Walter Laqueur among them, looked upon the terrorist reality at that time as merely a nuisance for the United States and other Western democracies. The events of the 1990s, starting with the first World Trade Center bombing in 1993 and the Oklahoma City bombing in 1995, proved the pessimists right. But it was the 1995 nerve gas attack on subway riders in Tokyo, which killed a dozen and wounded more than 5,000 people, that became the definitive turning point. Addressing the fact that members of the Aum Shinrikyo sect, who were responsible for the incident in Japan, had been able to acquire and develop highly toxic materials, U.S. Senator Sam Nunn identified the sarin gas strike as the onset of "a new era" in terrorism with the possibility, if not likelihood, of terrorists deploying weapons of mass destruction and committing catastrophic terror.[21]

Why did terrorism blossom in the post–Cold War era? Four developments in particular are relevant here:

1. The collapse of communism, the disintegration of the Soviet Union, and the end of the bipolar world dismantled what one might call a mechanism of restraint that had been part of the old balance-of-power arrangement.
2. The dissolution of the Soviet Union into independent republics, the disappearance of Soviet-style communism as an alternative ideology, the changes in what had been the Eastern Bloc, and the new geopolitical realities that cast the United States in the role of the only remaining superpower unleashed ethnic, religious, and pseudoreligious fervor and led to the emergence and strengthening of movements and groups that were willing to resort to catastrophic terrorism for their purposes.
3. The growing opposition to certain aspects of modernity and globalization was at least one factor in the emergence and radicalization of religious and ethnic groups. These sentiments had found expression in the rule of the Taliban in Afghanistan after the retreat of the Russian troops a decade later. To be sure, other root causes existed as well. In the case of Iran, it was the oppressive and U.S.-supported regime of the Shah that the revolution overthrew.
4. The expansion of air traffic and the advances in communication technology allowed terrorist organizations to dispatch their operatives to strike in distant places and to exploit global communication nets and media for intragroup communications and for the dissemination of their propaganda.

Unrestrained Terrorism and Counterterrorism After the Cold War

In the early 1980s, journalist Claire Sterling pointed to state sponsors of anti-American and anti-Western terrorism involving Soviet states in Eastern Europe, Africa, Latin America, and the Middle East.[22] Details about the insidious roles of East Germany, Czechoslovakia, Bulgaria, and other states in the Soviet orbit were only revealed after the collapse of the Soviet Empire. But in a strange way, these relationships between state supporters and terrorist groups provided also a safety valve against catastrophic terrorism: The Soviet Union and its client states did not want unrestrained terrorism that could have risked retaliation and perhaps a superpower confrontation. Similarly, the United States supported organizations that fought against socialist regimes with terrorist tactics, such as the Contras in Nicaragua or the National Union for the Total Independence of Angola (UNITA).

This bipolar geopolitical order limited also the likelihood of disproportionate counterterrorist strikes by major Western target states, most of all the United States. During the 444 days of the Iranian hostage crisis, when dozens of American citizens were held hostage in the U.S. embassy in Tehran with the blessing of the Iranian authorities, President Jimmy Carter and his advisors discussed possible punitive military strikes against Iran, if only to demonstrate American power and determination. But once the Soviet Union had invaded Afghanistan, even Carter's hawkish National Security Advisor, Zbigniew Brzezinski, abandoned his push for military actions because of fears that these measures "would simply give additional opportunities to the Soviets in their drive toward the Persian Gulf and the Indian Ocean."[23] And although Iran was seen in the West as a far more flagrant sponsor of anti-American terrorism than Libya during the 1980s, the Reagan administration chose Libya to demonstrate the United States' counterterrorist muscle—certainly in recognition that the North African country was far less important in Moscow's geopolitical design than was Iran. To this end, the Reagan administration launched a massive diplomatic and public relations campaign that branded Libya as the "chief culprit" among the sponsors of anti-American terrorism.[24] In April 1986, Washington was able to blame Libya for the terrorist bombing of a disco in Berlin that was known to Libyan agents as the favorite hangout for American GIs. The Reagan administration retaliated with air strikes on Tripoli and Benghazi—but only after tipping off the Soviet government in advance so that it could warn its advisors in Libya.

After the end of the Cold War, no such checks were in place. The expected "New World Order" became more of a "New World Disorder" with respect to terrorism. And counterterrorist considerations were no longer harnessed as they were during the bipolar realities of the Cold War period. This was clear after the terror attacks of September 11, 2001, when the United States launched extensive military actions against Al Qaeda and the Taliban in Afghanistan and even more so when Iraq was invaded by U.S.-led forces. President George W. Bush and his advisors did not have the balance-of-power/spheres-of-interest concerns of earlier presidents, namely, Jimmy Carter and Ronald Reagan.

The Old and New Terrorism in the Post–Cold War Era

After the Cold War was over, a number of movements, groups, and individuals that had committed terrorism during the Cold War stayed on course. Besides the already mentioned IRA, offshoots thereof, and the Loyalists in Northern Ireland, the Basque ETA in Spain, the FARC and similar groups in Colombia and other Latin American countries, Palestinian secular groups like the PFLP, and religious organizations like the Hezbollah in Lebanon continued on. But after the Cold War ended, new movements and groups embraced terrorism as their political weapon of choice.

The dissolution of the communist bloc laid bare the deep-seated animosities in the territories it had spanned. The breakup of the Soviet Union into more than a dozen independent countries did not end once and for all the historic ethnic conflicts within and between these states. But it was the rapid rise of Islamic militancy and radical teachings in the overwhelmingly Muslim Central Asian republics of Kazakhstan, Kyrgyzstan, Tajikistan, Turkmenistan, and Uzbekistan that destabilized the whole region. Trained by Al Qaeda and the Taliban in Afghanistan, and financially supported by governments and wealthy individuals in the Middle East, Islamic radicals used terrorist methods to fight for the spread and dominance of Islam. As one expert described these developments that came after seven decades of Soviet rule,

> The penetration of radical Islamic ideologies from Afghanistan, Pakistan, Jordan, Egypt, and Turkey; the financing of mosques and Islamic schools (madrassahs) by Iran and Saudi Arabia; and charities that give money to Islamic schools and mosques have contributed to the de-russification and Islamization of Central Asians.[25]

Similar developments took place in the Russian Federation itself, where roughly one of six citizens was not a Russian, and in the ethnically and religiously diverse Balkans.

The Russian–Chechen conflict was and still is a case in point. In the Chechen struggle for independence, the weaker party resorted to terrorism against Russians inside and outside the Chechen territory. For many observers, this was in response to the brutality with which the Russian military prosecuted the war against Chechen rebels. By taking over and occupying hospitals and other public facilities, the Chechens staged dramatic hostage situations. Chechen leaders threatened repeatedly that they would target the Moscow subway system and nuclear power plants in Russia. Shortly before he was assassinated in 1996, Andrei Dudayev, a Chechen separatist leader, threatened even Western Europe with terrorism because, as he explained, Europeans supported Russia's aggression against Chechnya.

With the end of the Cold War, ethnic conflicts broke out in the Balkans as well, most of all in Yugoslavia. And just as Muslim Chechen separatists were supported by Muslim fighters from abroad, the Muslim regions of the Balkans witnessed an influx of Muslim militants with expertise in terrorism. This was most obvious in Bosnia, where Iranian Revolutionary Guards and equally militant groups from a host of Arab countries fought on the side of Bosnian Muslims during the bloody civil war of the early 1990s. When the Dayton Peace Accord was signed, these Muslim fighters did not leave the region as required by the agreement. Instead, terrorism became an additional threat to American and other NATO soldiers trying to keep peace among the various factions. To be sure, Muslims from abroad were not the first to promote terrorism at the time. In fact, Serbs were the first party to actually perpetrate an act of international terrorism in the Bosnian conflict, when they seized United Nations peacekeepers as hostages in 1995 in order to prevent further NATO strikes. But the bloody clash between Muslims and Serbs and, as Bosnian Muslims felt, the West's indifference to the genocide perpetrated against them stirred anti-Western and anti-American sentiments far beyond the Muslim communities in Bosnia. Sefir Halilovich, then commander of the Bosnian Army, threatened at one point that terrorists would put "European capitals ablaze" unless the West would come to the aid of Bosnian Muslims.[26] His anger was shared by fellow Muslims all over Europe as well as in Asia and Africa.

A large number of the fighters who helped their Muslim brethren in Bosnia were veterans of the war in Afghanistan during most of the 1980s, when they had fought side by side with Afghans against the Soviet military after the Soviets invaded Afghanistan in 1979. Financed by oil-rich Arab states, especially Saudi Arabia, the Arab *mujahideen* had forged a close relationship with representatives of the U.S. government, who supported them with sophisticated weapons. One of these Arab fighters was Osama bin Laden, the offspring of a wealthy Saudi family, who had found his calling in Afghanistan and in the jihad against the Soviet intruders. Once the Soviet forces had withdrawn, Washington had achieved its goal and was no longer interested in Afghanistan and unwilling to contribute to the reconstruction of the country. Realizing that they had been Washington's pawn in the Cold War, the one-time allies—many *mujahideens*, Osama bin Laden among them—turned their ire against the United States.

Modernization, Globalization, and the Proliferation of Religious Violence

In the fall of 1999, a few hundred self-proclaimed anarchists disrupted a summit meeting of the World Trade Organization (WTO) in Seattle by detonating M-80 firecrackers and vandalizing brand-name stores like Starbucks, Nike, and Old Navy.

Subsequent meetings of the WTO, the World Bank, the International Monetary Fund, and other international organizations were plagued by more serious antiglobalization violence. American and European left-leaning environmentalists and opponents of Western-style industrial modernization, postmodern developments, and U.S.-dominated globalization and consumerism were and are the driving forces in the antiglobalization movement. But the opposition to these developments has proven strongest amongst all kinds of religious fundamentalists.

In his book *Jihad vs. McWorld*, Benjamin Barber examines the resentment against the reach of mass production, mass consumption, mass entertainment, and mass information that transcends national borders. He characterizes the extreme reactions to these developments as "jihad."[27] But *jihad* (holy war) does not simply stand here for what fundamentalist Muslims say and do to counter the McWorld universe and Hollywood-dominated entertainment. Rather, in this context, *jihad* is a metaphor for the extreme reactions of distinct groups that see their traditional religious, ethnic, political, and economic values under attack. To be sure, the religious zealots of the Al Qaeda terrorism network would qualify on the jihad side, but so would right-wing Christian or pseudo-Christian groups in the United States. Mark Juergensmeyer, an expert on religious violence, comes to similar conclusions when he writes,

> Activists such as bin Laden might be regarded as guerilla antiglobalists. . . . The era of globalization and postmodernity creates a context in which authority is undercut and local forces have been unleashed. I do not mean to imply that only globalization causes religious violence. But it may be one reason why so many instances of religious violence in such diverse places around the world are occurring at the present time.[28]

Furthermore, Juergensmeyer points out that the "perception of an international conspiracy and an oppressive economic 'new world order' has been explicitly mentioned by Osama bin Laden, the Aum Shinrikyo, and Christian militia groups [in the United States]."[29]

But while antiglobalization sentiments have fueled the hate of all kinds of religious and ethnic groups, the events of 9/11 and subsequent bombings in Indonesia, Morocco, Spain, Saudi Arabia, and elsewhere have drawn most attention to Muslim extremists who strike in the name of God and their religion. Nobody has justified violence in reaction to U.S. dominance in and exploitation of Arab and Muslim countries as well as U.S. support for oppressive regimes in the Middle East as categorically and frequently as Osama bin Laden, the founder of Al Qaeda. In his 1996 *fatwa*, he wrote about the predicament of Muslims in general and of Saudi Arabia in particular:

> From here, today we begin the work, talking and discussing the ways of correcting what had happened to the Islamic world in general, and the land of the two Holy Places in particular. We wish to study the means that we could follow to return the situation to its normal path. And to return to the people their own rights, particularly after the large damages and the great aggression on the life and the religion of the people. An injustice that had affected every section and group of the people, the civilians, military and security men, government officials and merchants, the young and the old people as well as school and university students. Hundreds of thousands of the unemployed graduates, who became the widest sections of society, were also affected.[30]

Addressing the situation of Saudi Arabians, he complained,

> *More than three hundred forty billions of Riyal owed by the government to the people in addition to the daily accumulated interest, let alone the foreign debt. People wonder whether we are the largest oil exporting country?! They even believe that this situation is a curse put on them by Allah for not objecting to the oppressive and illegitimate behavior and measures of the ruling regime.*[31]

He blamed the "American crusader forces" for a great deal of the catastrophic policies "imposed on the country, especially in the field of oil industry where production is restricted or expanded and prices are fixed to suit the American economy ignoring the economy of the country."[32]

Years before the terror in New York and Washington, D.C., political scientist Samuel Huntington predicted that the greatest dangers in the post–Cold War era would arise from conflicts between nations and groups of different civilizations, of different cultural backgrounds.[33] Several weeks after the events of 9/11, while rejecting the notion that these attacks signaled such a collision, Huntington was sure that "bin Laden wants it to be a clash of civilizations between Islam and the West."[34] Bin Laden's statements validated this conclusion all along. In his 1998 declaration of war against "Jews and Crusaders," he listed the wrongdoings of the "crusader-Zionist alliance" and reminded all Muslims that the "jihad is an individual duty if the enemy destroys the Muslim countries" and that "[n]othing is more sacred than belief except repulsing an enemy who is attacking religion and life." He then called on all Muslims "to kill the Americans and their allies—civilians and military . . . in any country in which it is possible to do." In October 2001, when the U.S. military commenced military strikes against Al Qaeda camps and Taliban strongholds in Afghanistan, bin Laden declared,

> *The events have divided the whole world into two sides. The side of believers and the side of infidels, may God keep you away from them. Every Muslim has to rush to make his religion victorious. The winds of faith have come. The winds of change have come to eradicate oppression from the island of Muhammad, peace be upon him.*[35]

Since Muslims did not rise in a massive united front to fight the Christian and Jewish infidels in the holy war that bin Laden had declared, the Al Qaeda leader and his supporters did not realize their most ambitious objective. On the contrary, they lost their safe haven, headquarters, training facilities, and weapon arsenals in Afghanistan. In this respect, bin Laden and his comrades in arms underestimated, perhaps, the resolve of the United States and the willingness of other governments to cooperate with Washington. But one must also doubt that the Al Qaeda leadership expected to provoke the existential clash of civilizations simply as a result of the 9/11 operation and the anticipated military response. It is far more likely that the plan was to move with each additional terror attack closer toward a confrontation between "the side of believers" and "the side of infidels."

Certainly, the events of 9/11 increased the tensions between Muslim minorities and Christian majorities in many Western countries—in Europe more so than in the United States. Although it had singled out Muslim immigrants in the past because of their different cultural and religious preferences, the xenophobic right in France, Austria, Belgium, Denmark, Germany, and elsewhere became far more popular when people feared that Muslims within their borders could commit violence along the lines of 9/11. These fears were fueled by reports that terrorist "sleeper cells," ready to be awakened any time to commit violent acts, existed in many Western countries. In this atmosphere, populist leaders made Muslims the scapegoats for all kinds of ills in their societies. In capturing this trend, one observer wrote,

> In her best-known campaign poster, Pia Kjaersgaard, the leader of Denmark's People's Party, showed a pretty little blond child with the caption: "By the time you retire, Denmark will be a majority Muslim-nation." Yet in Denmark just 1 person in 15 is of foreign origin and most of these are thoroughly assimilated.[36]

As new antiterrorism laws and profiling criteria in Western democracies targeted Muslims and Arabs in particular, the gap between Muslim minorities and non-Muslim majorities widened. Although far from moving rapidly toward the cataclysmic clash of civilizations that Huntington warned of and bin Laden wished for, there was certainly increased hostility between "infidels" and "believers" in many Western countries and perhaps more fertile ground among the Muslim diaspora for bin Laden's divisive agenda and his final goal. In the United States, post-9/11 opinion polls revealed that 44% of the public believed that American Muslims were not doing enough to help authorities track down Islamic terrorist cells in the United States, 32% were not sure, and only 24% thought that Muslim Americans cooperated in this respect.[37]

David Rapoport has suggested that the current wave of religious terrorism got its most important impulses from the Islamic revolution of 1979 in Iran and, a decade later, from the defeat of the Soviet Union in Afghanistan. His point does not contradict the influence of antiglobalization and clash-of-civilization sentiments on the rise of religious terrorism—especially of the Muslim variety. The Iranian revolution, too, was at least partially a reaction to American and Western influence and support of the regime of the Shah. Moreover, the developments in Iran and later in Afghanistan "gave evidence that religion now provided more hope than the prevailing revolutionary ethos did."[38] In both cases, formidable terror organizations emerged that had ties to the fundamentalist Muslim regimes in Iran and Afghanistan: Hezbollah and Al Qaeda.

Founded in 1982 by Lebanese followers of Iran's Ayatollah Khomeini, members of Hezbollah were trained in the Bekaa Valley by Iranian Revolutionary Guards and otherwise supported by the government in Tehran. This relationship was an important step forward for Iran, because, as Adam Shatz concluded, "Hezbollah provided a means" [for Iran] of "spread[ing] the Islamic revolution to the Arab world" and "gaining a foothold in Middle East politics."[39] But besides fighting Israel and the foreign military presence and influence in Lebanon, Hezbollah did not have a grander anti-Western and antiglobalization design. Hezbollah's focus was on Lebanon and the Israeli–Palestinian problem—not on a united Muslim front against the West.

While this was foremost on Al Qaeda's agenda, bin Laden, his associates, and his supporters were not just opposed to Western-driven and U.S.-dominated globalization; they also despised the regimes in the region that cooperated with the United States and the West. Indeed, bin Laden expressed as much contempt for Saudi Arabia's rulers as for the U.S. government. When he returned from Afghanistan to Saudi Arabia in 1990, he was offended by the presence and influence of Westerners in his homeland. After the Saudi rulers and other governments in the region supported the U.S.-led military coalition against Iraq in the early 1990s, he was particularly disturbed by the lasting presence of the U.S. military on the Arabian Peninsula. Bin Laden turned so vehemently against Saudi Arabia's government because of this issue that he lost his citizenship.

While originally serving bin Laden as a vehicle for financing and managing all kinds of pet projects during the Afghanistan war against the Soviet Union, the Al Qaeda organization developed into a management group for the indoctrination, training, and financing of an unprecedented network of global terrorists. After losing his Saudi citizenship, bin Laden and his associates found a new base of operation in Sudan, also an Islamic republic. Here the group established businesses and plotted violent actions against the United States and the Saudi rulers. Under pressure by the United States, the Saudis, and other countries in the region, the Sudanese government asked Al Qaeda to leave the country. In the spring of 1996, accompanied by family members and supporters, bin Laden flew to Afghanistan, where he found agreeable surroundings. According to Reeve,

> He had chosen Afghanistan, where he knew he could rely on the support of his old comrades [with whom he had fought against the Soviet invaders of Afghanistan in the 1980s]. Many of them had now reorganized into the fundamentalist Islamic militia known to the West as the Taliban, which was imposing harsh Sharia law in the country: forcing men into mosques at gunpoint five times a day, banning music and alcohol, and preventing women from working.[40]

In this environment, cut off from what he considered the evils of Western influence, bin Laden and his associates refined their doctrine and trained "holy warriors" for the envisioned clash with the infidel West. To advance this goal, Al Qaeda, like other terrorist organizations, embraced modernity and globalization by using the latest technological advances.

Technological Advances and Global Communication

Terrorists at all times have embraced the newest technologies to serve their purposes. Thus, after Alfred Nobel invented dynamite from a mixture of nitroglycerin in 1866, the anarchists embraced the highly explosive material eagerly as their weapon of choice, as the preferred component of their potent bombs. More recent terrorists (e.g., the Japanese sect Aum Shinrikyo and Al Qaeda) tried to get their hands on nuclear material. Vast advances in the field of aviation in the post–World War II period and declining ticket prices made air travel affordable and allowed terrorists to travel long distances to train with their comrades and strike in faraway places. But nothing was more helpful to terrorists everywhere than the advances in those technologies that were the basis for the establishment of global satellite television networks such as CNN and Al Jazeera, national and international cellular phone connections, and, most importantly, the Internet. To be sure, a few hate groups in the United States and Europe began to utilize the Internet in the 1980s, but it took several more years before terrorists everywhere were able to exploit the Internet, cell phones, and global TV networks for their purposes.

One example will suffice here: Soon after heavily armed Chechen separatists seized a theater in Moscow in late October 2002, accomplices outside delivered videotaped material to the Moscow bureau of the Arab TV network Al Jazeera in which they proclaimed to have chosen to die on "the path of struggling for the freedom of the Chechen."[41] Soon thereafter, the videotape was played by TV networks and stations around the world. As many of the hundreds of hostages inside used their cell phones to communicate with families and friends, some of them conveyed the chilling messages of their captors to the Russian public and especially to President Vladimir V. Putin. The Chechens left no doubt that they would blow up the building and kill themselves and hundreds of innocent people unless the Putin government ordered the withdrawal of Russian troops from Chechnya. At the height of the siege, one of the captors grabbed the cellular phone of one of the hostages, who was speaking to a local radio station, and delivered a tirade against Russia's war against Chechnya. The hostage holders got their messages across—not only to Russians but also to governments and the general public around the globe.

In the past, the neat distinction between international and domestic terrorism was a useful tool for examining the complexities of the terrorist phenomenon. But this differentiation is no longer meaningful, if only because the news about indigenous terrorism transcends national borders. Take the Oklahoma City bombing, which at first sight seemed utterly domestic in nature because Americans, Timothy McVeigh and his accomplice Terry Nichols, struck in the American heartland against fellow Americans. Although no formal ties were proven, both men shared the ideas of white supremacy hate groups in the United States, which are seemingly an indigenous phenomenon. But the leaders of these groups and their followers do embrace international conspiracy theories and cultivate ties to similar hate organizations. Ingo Hasselbach, the founder of a neo-Nazi party in eastern Germany who eventually quit the hate group scene, revealed after the Oklahoma City bombing,

> Virtually all of our propaganda and training manuals came from the right-wing extremist groups in Nebraska and California. . . . We also received illegal materials from our friends in Nebraska . . . like a U.S. Army manual called Explosives and Demolitions, which has since been copied and circulated (still with the top-secret stamp across the title page) to thousands of right-wing extremists all over Europe.[42]

To sum up, a number of factors favored the proliferation of post–Cold War terrorism, among them the disintegration of the Soviet Empire, the collapse of the bipolar Cold War world order, growing opposition to the effects of modernization and globalization, and advances in global communication and air travel.

Notes

1. Jeffrey D. Simon, *The Terrorist Trap: America's Experience with Terrorism* (Bloomington: Indiana University Press, 1994), 27.
2. Heintzen's treatise is reprinted in Walter Laqueur and Yonah Alexander, *The Terrorism Reader: The Essential Source Book on Political Violence Both Past and Present* (New York: Penguin Books, 1987), 59.
3. Ibid., 59.
4. Walter Laqueur, *A History of Terrorism* (New Brunswick, NJ: Transaction Publisher), 14.
5. Ibid., 77.
6. David C. Rapoport, "The Fourth Wave: September 11 in the History of Terrorism." *Current History* (December 2001): 420.
7. Frantz Fanon, *The Wretched of the Earth* (New York: Grove Weidenfeld, 1963), 94.
8. Ibid., 313.
9. From excerpts of Carlos Marighella, *Handbook of Urban Guerrilla Warfare*, in Laqueur and Alexander, 163.
10. For "Stadtguerrilla und Klassenkampf" and other RAF documents, see www.baader-meinhof.com.
11. Simon, 97, 98.
12. Martha Crenshaw, "The Logic of Terrorism: Terrorist Behavior as a Product of Rational Choice," in Walter Reich, ed., *Origins of Terrorism* (New York: Cambridge University Press, 1990), 18.

13. Donna M. Schlagheck, *International Terrorism* (Lexington, MA: Lexington Books, 1988), 69.
14. Xavier Raufer, "The Red Brigades: Farewell to Arms," *Studies in Conflict and Terrorism* 16:4 (1993): 315–25.
15. Ibid., 323.
16. Bruce Hoffman, *Inside Terrorism* (New York: Columbia University, 1998), 83.
17. Hoffman, in *Inside Terrorism*, 83, cites David Schiller, a German-Israeli counterterrorism analyst, who argued that "without assistance provided by the Palestinians to their German counterparts the latter could not have survived."
18. David C. Rapoport, "The Four Waves of Rebel Terror and September 11," p. 2, http://www.anthropoetics.ucla.edu/apo801/terror.htm.
19. The communiques of April and June 1992 are reprinted in the appendix of Dennis A. Pluchinsky, "Germany's Red Army Faction: An Obituary," *Studies in Conflict and Terrorism* 16:2 (1993): 135–57.
20. Peter Calvert, "Terrorism in Uruguay," in Martha Crenshaw and John Pimlott, eds., *Encyclopedia of World Terrorism*, vol. 2 (Armonk, NY: M. E. Sharpe, 1997), 454.
21. Senator Nunn made the remarks during a Senate hearing. See Christopher Drew, "Japanese Sect Tried to Buy U.S. Arms Technology," *New York Times*, October 31, 1995, 5.
22. Claire Sterling, *The Terror Network* (New York: Berkeley, 1982).
23. Zbigniew Brzezinski, *Power and Principle* (New York: Farrar, Strauss and Giroux, 1983), 489.
24. Ronald H. Hinckley, *People, Polls, and Policy Makers: American Public Opinion and National Security* (New York: Lexington Books, 1992).
25. Rohan Gunaratna, "Central Asian Republics," in Frank Shanty and Raymond Picquet, eds., *Encyclopedia of World Terrorism, 1996–2002* (Armonk, NY: M. E. Sharpe, 2003), 357–61.
26. Magnus Ranstorp and Gus Xhudo, "A Threat to Europe? Middle East Ties to the Balkans and the Impact upon Terrorist Activity throughout the Region," *Terrorism and Political Violence* 6:3 (1994): 210.
27. Benjamin R. Barber, *Jihad vs. McWorld* (New York: Ballantine Books, 1996).
28. Mark Juergensmeyer, *Terror in the Mind of God* (Berkeley: University of California Press, 2000), xii.
29. Ibid.
30. Unless otherwise indicated, quotes from and references to bin Laden's communications are from his 1996 "Ladenese Epistle: Declaration of War" and his 1998 "Jihad against Jews and Crusaders." The documents are available on a number of web sites, among them www.washingtonpost.com.
31. Ibid.
32. Ibid.
33. Samuel P. Huntington, *The Clash of Civilizations and the Remaking of World Order* (New York: Simon & Schuster, 1996).
34. "Q&A: A Head-on Collision of Alien Cultures," *New York Times*, October 20, 2001, A13.
35. "'Text: bin Laden statement,'" www/guardian.co.uk/waronterror/story/0,1361,565069,00html (retrieved April 7, 2002).
36. For more on the European far right's antiforeigner and anti-immigration stands, see Tony Judt, "America's Restive Partners," *New York Times*, April 28, 2002, sec. 4, 15.
37. Survey was conducted by Fox News, April 2–3, 2002.
38. Rapoport, "The Fourth Wave," 421.
39. Adam Shatz, "In Search of Hezbollah," *New York Review of Books*, April 29, 2004, 41.
40. Simon Reeve, *The New Jackals* (Boston: Northeastern University Press, 1999), 186.
41. Michael Wines, "Hostage Drama in Moscow: The Moscow Front; Chechens Kill Hostage in Siege at Russian Hall," *New York Times*, October 25, 2002, A1.
42. Ingo Hasselbach, "Extremism: A Global Network," *New York Times*, April 26, 1995.

CHAPTER 4

Terrorism in the American Context

THE UNITED STATES HAS EXPERIENCED DIFFERENT TYPES OF homegrown terrorism, most of it being of either the right-wing or left-wing variety. In addition, there has been a hodgepodge of other kinds of terrorism in the United States that has not fallen into either of these categories, for example, political violence by exile groups aiming for regime change in or national independence for their native countries (e.g., Cuban anti-Castro militants or Croatian nationalists). This chapter provides an overview of the various types of terrorist activities inside the United States in the past and the present involving groups and individuals who have resorted to violence themselves or who have encouraged others to commit such acts, if only by preaching their gospel of hate.

Right-Wing Terrorism

"Right wing" here refers to an ideology that is further right, and far more extreme, than mainstream conservatism. Although groups that are commonly lumped into this category have differed in their belief systems, they share some common characteristics—namely, opposition to progress, to changes in political, economic, and social arrangements. The contemporary right wing believes that the U.S. constitutional system no longer reflects the design of the Founding Fathers, that the federal government has taken too many rights away from the states, and that the United Nations and other international entities control U.S. politics. Not all of these groups are racist, as Martin Durham has pointed out, but most oppose equal religious, ethnic, racial, and gender rights, which in their view upset the old social, political, economic, and moral order of the white-male-supremacy era.[1] In the first decade of the twenty-first century, right-wing extremism rose significantly in the United States. According to the Southern Poverty Law Center (SPLC), at the end of 2008 there were 926 known right-wing groups that promote hate in words and deeds against entire classes of people—50 percent more than in 2000.[2] Moreover, the election of President Barack

KKK: The Most Durable Domestic Terrorist and Hate Organization

Masked and in white robes, contemporary Ku Klux Klan members uphold the tradition of their organization by staging marches and displaying the Confederate flag as a symbol of the pre–Civil War "order" for which their forefathers fought in southern slave states. The Klan of today has far fewer members than in earlier periods; nevertheless it has survived for more than 130 years.

Obama in November 2004 and the economic crisis resulted in a membership surge for these types of groups. Thus, Don Black, a former Ku Klux Klan leader and the founder of the neo-Nazi, white supremacy "Stormfront" organization, claimed that "on the day after Obama's election, more than 2,000 people joined his Web site, a remarkable increase from the approximately 80 new members a day he was getting . . ."[3]

The Ku Klux Klan

In the history of indigenous political violence in the United States, the Ku Klux Klan has the distinction of being the most enduring organization—albeit with periods of dormancy. Founded in 1865 to resist the consequences of the Civil War and in particular the adoption of the Thirteenth Amendment to the U.S. Constitution, which abolished slavery and thus slave labor, the Ku Klux Klan targeted black freedmen and whites supportive of African Americans' rights. Wearing white robes and masks, members of the KKK terrorized by beating and lynching their targets under the cover of night with the goal of upholding white supremacy in the defeated South. There is no doubt that the original Klan (as well as its successors in the twentieth century) was a terrorist organization under the definition put forth in Chapter 2: Klan groups and individual members were nonstate actors who committed violence against civilians for political (and economic) ends. Within a few years, the Klan perpetrated thousands of violent acts. In reaction, the federal government adopted laws that made "nightriding" a crime and allowed the president to deploy troops to end civil disturbances and even suspend habeas corpus for a time. As a result, President Ulysses S. Grant moved troops into the South, and many Klansmen were arrested. But by 1872, when the first KKK dissolved voluntarily, southern states began legislating measures that assured white dominance and racial segregation. Even though segregation was achieved and maintained by official policies in the South, white lynch mobs continued to kill many blacks.

The second Ku Klux Klan emerged after the release of D. W. Griffith's motion picture *Birth of a Nation*, which glorified the first Klan and the southern power structure and racial discrimination it stood for. At the peak of the second Klan period in the mid-1920s, the organization had a total membership of 3–4 million. This forceful revival came about for other reasons as well: (1) the perennial fear of Southern whites that blacks could finally achieve equality and challenge white supremacy once again—sentiments that were fueled by *Birth of a Nation;* (2) the uneasiness of northern whites over black migration from the South to the North; and (3) Protestant objections to immigration because many of the newcomers were Catholics and Jews—groups that were hated by the Klan as well. Moreover, newcomers were typically willing to work for lower wages than the existing workforce and thus threatened the economic status quo of the latter. All of these factors drove people in all parts of the country into the arms of the Klan. By casting themselves as the protectors of patriotism and moral values, the Klan recruited a large number of fundamentalist preachers—often by promising that the Klan would boost attendance in their churches.

In the 1920s, the Ku Klux Klan foreshadowed the organizational structure of more recent and contemporary terrorist organizations in that it worked both within the legitimate political process and at the same time had members who engaged in illegal political violence. As a powerful interest group, the Klan influenced politics and policies on the local, state, and federal levels and was especially successful in affecting election outcomes. A day after the 1924 election, the *New York Times* reported under the headline "Victories by Klan Feature Election: Order Elects Senators in Oklahoma and Colorado, Governors in Kansas, Indiana, Colorado" that "the candidates endorsed by the masked organization have apparently scored sweeping victories in Indiana, Kansas, Colorado, and Oklahoma, and later returns may add Montana to the list."[4] Moreover, the Klan had its hand in splitting "the Democratic presidential convention, mainly because the Catholic Al Smith was a strong contender."[5] During the 1924 campaign, Smith, the governor of New York, attacked the Klan and President Calvin Coolidge, the Republican candidate, for keeping mum about the organization. Reporting on one of Smith's speeches, the *Times* wrote,

> The Governor vigorously assailed the Ku Klux Klan, not only characterizing it as an unpatriotic and un-American organization, created for the dissemination of hate and religious bigotry, but accusing the Republican Party of using it for political capital and President Coolidge of countenancing a policy of silence toward it.[6]

While the Ku Klux Klan made strides in working within the political system, the organization did nothing to stop the violence committed by its members in the southern states, where "Klansmen tarred and feathered, tortured, and lynched blacks suspected of being involved with white women. Prosperous African Americans and immigrants who jeopardized white economic power found their businesses burned and their possessions stolen."[7] But as the press reported extensively on the Klan's terrorism and states adopted "anti-masking" laws, the opposition to the KKK strengthened. By the end of the 1920s, the organization was only a shadow of its peak in

1924–1925 in that its membership declined from a record high of 3–4 million to about 40,000.

The U.S. Supreme Court's milestone rulings in favor of desegregation in the 1950s (especially *Brown v. Board of Education*, 1954) and the activism of a strong civil rights movement in the early 1960s were met by yet another revival of the Ku Klux Klan in the 1960s and a wave of political violence against African Americans and whites who insisted on desegregation, the free exercise of voting rights by blacks, and the end of all discrimination. As James Ridgeway observed, the election of John F. Kennedy, the first Catholic president, "revived the Klan's old papist hatred, but that soon gave way to a new sense of desperation and dread as Greyhound buses filled with white and black kamikaze college students calling themselves Freedom Riders descended upon the South."[8] The result was a reign of terror by Klansmen against Freedom Riders and against southern blacks and Jews. According to one account, "[The Klan] burned and bombed houses and churches and synagogues. The Klan acted with relative impunity. Its torchlight ceremonies and cross-burnings, attended by men camouflaged in robes and hoods, gave it a powerful image."[9] Christopher Hewitt found that from 1955, when this wave of violence began, to 1971, when it subsided, a total of 588 incidents were reported, with the peak in a three-year period from 1963 though 1965.[10] According to opinion polls, only a tiny minority of Southerners had a positive view of the Klan at the time, but the hate organization's messages and deeds played nevertheless into white Southerners' support for segregation and opposition to change. As Kenneth S. Stern concluded,

> By encouraging that shared perception of the white populace, and by scapegoating groups that seemed to threaten "the way things were," the Klan became an alternative social structure that gave many people a feeling of power.[11]

Following the brutal murder of civil rights advocates in the South, the FBI began to crack down on the Klan and eventually reduced this sort of violence significantly. Infiltrated by FBI agents and informers, the Klan either abandoned violence or risked swift indictments. In this situation, Klan leaders split into factions, including one that insisted on violent tactics and another in favor of a "mediagenic call to non-violence."[12] But those who presented themselves and their organization as nonviolent and legitimate players did not shed the tradition of hate. Instead, underneath the more benign public image, the hard-core racism of the Klan remained intact. One of the leaders who typified the change from an openly racist demeanor to a less threatening public face was David Duke. Before he formed his own KKK organization in the 1970s, Duke wrote,

> The plain truth is our race is losing. We're losing our schools to Black savagery, losing our hard-earned pay to Black welfare, losing our lives to No-Win-Red treason and Black crime, losing our culture to Jewish and Black degeneracy, and we are losing our most precious possession, our white racial heritage, to race-mixing.[13]

While recognizing the value of the soft sell as Grand Wizard of the Klan and, even more so, as a member of the Louisiana state legislature, Duke's message never changed during his years as Klan leader and as founder of his own hate organizations. In 2003, for example, the web site of Duke's latest organizational vehicle, the European–American Unity and Rights Organization (EURO), carried the following message: "Unless European-Americans organize and act soon, America will become a 'Third World' country—that is, European-Americans will become outnumbered and

> Summer 1998: James Byrd Jr., a forty-nine-year-old black man, walks down Martin Luther King Boulevard in Jasper, Texas. Suddenly, he is grabbed by three white men who had spotted him from their pickup truck. According to what is revealed later, one of the threesome says, "We are starting *The Turner Diaries* early." This is a reference to a novel about whites in the United States fighting a race war against blacks. Byrd is chained by the ankles to the rear of the vehicle and dragged several miles along a dirt road. The next morning, "Byrd's head, with his face spray-painted black, is found along with other body parts strewn along the pavement."[14] When arrested, two of the killers are found to have white supremacy tattoos on their bodies.

totally vulnerable to the political control of Blacks and other non-Whites."[15] While a bit more carefully worded, the message was typical of those in white supremacy circles at the end of the twentieth and the beginning of the twenty-first centuries, as were calls for "affirmative action" on behalf of the white race and the constant drumbeat against an alleged Jewish conspiracy for "supremacy" in the United States and the world.

Although the Klan declined dramatically by the late 1980s and early 1990s, it did not completely disappear. In fact, new, aggressive KKK groups were founded during this period. For example, according to the Anti-Defamation League, the Church of the American Knights of the Ku Klux Klan was formed in 1995 by Jeff Berry of Butler, Indiana, whose organization followed

> the traditional Klan model, with its crudely racist literature, its use of vile epithets at public rallies and its combative stance. At an October 1998 rally in Jasper, Texas, Berry told the crowd, "We hate Jews. We hate niggers. . . . I'm a Yankee and I have never heard of thank you in the nigger vocabulary. . . . We don't like you niggers. . . . Tell me one thing your race has accomplished."[16]

In 2001, the Southern Poverty Law Center identified 110 Klan groups across the country in its list of hate organizations.[17] But the declining trends since the beginning of the decade was reversed in 2008, when Klan groups increased significantly to 186 from 155 in 2007.[18] Like other racist groups, Klan organizations were poised to mobilize their membership and recruit new members in the wake of President Obama's election. This is what the Imperial Wizard of the National Knights of the Ku Klux Klan posted on its web site, "America has been lost today and officially died November 4, 2008. To express protest, all members are requested to wear black Armbands on January 20th and 21st, 2009, and if any of you do possess yankee flags, please fly them upside down. Fly the confederate flag." And there was also the invitation to "join the kkk today."[19] But the KKK was only one among several so-called radical right-wing movements in the United States. Jeffrey Kaplan identified the Ku Klux Klan, Christian Identity groups, neo-Nazi organizations, single-issue groups—what he labeled "Reconstructed Traditions, Ideosyncratic sectarians," and "the inchoate hope seeking a means of fulfillment (or less elegantly, the young toughs or knuckle draggers of the movement)"—as major components of the radical right wing. In fact, these groupings had, and still have, far more similarities than differences.[20] All of them subscribe to one or another aspect of the so-called Christian Identity movement, especially its insistence on the supremacy of the white race. Publicly, most of these groups do not promote political violence, but by stirring the hate of their followers and sympathizers against members of other races, religions, and nationalities, indirectly they have encouraged terrorist acts.

The Christian Identity Movement

Christian Identity originated in nineteenth-century Great Britain as "British Israelism" and over the years developed the most elaborate theory of white supremacy. At the heart of Christian Identity's original gospel is the claim that white Christians are the true Israelites of the Old Testament and therefore God's chosen people. When Christian Identity made its way to the United States in the 1940s, it developed an even more divisive and hateful pseudoreligious twist. British Identity teachings were clearly anti-Semitic, but American adherents added a distinct racist element. As James Ridgeway described it, modern American Christian Identity teaches in particular that

> *nonwhite races are "pre-Adamic"—that is, part of the creation finished before God created Adam and Eve. In this wisdom, they say, God fashioned the subhuman non-whites and sent them to live outside the Garden of Eden before the Fall. When Eve broke God's original commandment, she was implanted with two seeds. From Adam's seed sprang Abel and the white race. From the serpent Satan's seed came the lazy, wicked Cain. Angered, God cast Adam, Eve, and the serpent out of the Garden of Eden and decreed eternal racial conflict. Cain killed Abel, then ran off into the jungle to join the pre-Adamic nonwhites. It is almost too neatly done: Identity theology provides both a religious base for racism and anti-Semitism, and an ideological rationale for violence against minorities and their white allies.*[21]

For many years, the Church of Jesus Christ/Aryan Nations and its founder and head, Richard Butler—Pastor Butler to his followers—were the centers of Christian Identity activity. Every year, adherents of Butler's gospel of hate as well as leaders and members of like-minded groups descended on the Aryan Nations' compound at Hayden Lake, Idaho, to participate in survivalist training and indoctrination reinforcement. According to Kaplan, Butler's "Church" was also instrumental in the establishment of the Aryan Brotherhood movement among white prisoners.[22] There were close contacts with members of the Ku Klux Klan, neo-Nazi groups, and skinheads. Writing about the Aryan Nations, the Anti-Defamation League characterized the hate organization as the "once most infamous Neo-Nazi group in the United States"—a testament to the shared prejudices of these groupings.[23] As he advanced in age, Butler's influence declined, especially after he lost the Idaho compound in 2001 following legal action by the victims of an assault by Butler's guards. While some tried to revitalize the Aryan Nations, others established their own groups, such as the new Church of the Sons of Yahweh. According to one observer of the radical right, "Factional infighting . . . increased the risk of violence and even terrorism."[24] In 2009, former Butler associates tried to enlist support for the reestablishment of a Butler-like group in Idaho and promised to revive their idol's annual national conventions.[25]

Although fragmenting further without Butler and his "Church" as rallying mechanisms, Christian Identity ideas remained alive and well in many of the most extreme right-wing hate movements with violent tendencies. Take, for example, Tom Metzger, who was active in the Ku Klux Klan, ordained as a minister in the Christian Identity milieu, and in 1983 founded his own organization, White Aryan Resistance (WAR). Even after a jury returned a $12.5 million judgment against him and his son for inciting the murder of an African immigrant by skinheads in 1990, Metzger continued to preach hate of nonwhites in ways that were especially tailored to appeal to skinheads and prison inmates. Commenting on other racists' reactions to the events of 9/11, Metzger wrote in 2002, "Recently the crazy idea of meeting and marching with nonwhite mid easterners [sic] has been promoted by some right-wing racists. Understanding their gripes is one thing. Tying our cause to theirs is stupid and dangerous. Moslems are no less an enemy than the Jews."[26]

Robert Mathews, who founded The Order in the early 1980s as an offshoot of Richard Butler's Aryan Nations, was also closely aligned with the neo-Nazi organization National Alliance and its founder, William Pierce. Mathews's group was the most violent of the right-wing variety in the 1980s. In 1984, members of the group killed Denver talk show host Alan Berg, who had been very critical of white supremacists on the air. Later that year, Mathews was killed in a shootout with police in the state of Washington. Even when it was assumed that The Order was defunct, the group remained attractive as a right-wing model. In 1998, law enforcement authorities discovered a plot to bomb the offices of the Anti-Defamation League by a group that called itself The New Order and modeled itself after Mathews's original The Order.

William Pierce, once a physics professor, was a member of the American Nazi Party before he founded his own organization, the National Alliance, in 1974 and formulated an ideology as hateful as that of his idol, Adolf Hitler. But it was especially his novel The Turner Diaries (published under the pseudonym Andrew MacDonald) that influenced a whole generation of extremists in radical right-wing circles, from Christian Identity adherents to neo-Nazis, Klansmen, militia, and survivalist activists. The book describes a civil war in the United States in which white Aryans fight what the author and other right-wing extremists call the Zionist Occupation Government (ZOG), killing blacks and Jews indiscriminately. The dramatic highlights are the ruthless destruction of American cities to pave the way for the dream come true of a white United States and a white world. Pierce died in 2002, but in spite of bitter infighting over his succession, the National Alliance continued its operations. Even before Pierce's death, Kaplan wrote that the founder of the National Alliance "will be best remembered" as the author of "The Turner Diaries and perhaps its successor Hunter."[27] These books continue to be popular among right-wing extremists. The Turner Diaries served as a blueprint for Timothy McVeigh as he planned the bombing of the Alfred Murrah Federal Building in Oklahoma City in 1995.

McVeigh, who had fought in the Persian Gulf War in 1991, moved in militia circles when he prepared his terror attack in Oklahoma City. The militia movement emerged in the early 1990s as something of a marriage between adherents of Christian Identity ideas and right-to-bear-arms proponents. Like other and earlier extremist movements, the militia movement centers around the claim that the U.S. government has been hijacked by dangerous forces that are determined to enslave Americans. It was no coincidence that the movement was born after the Cold War had ended. The vision of a "new world order" that was enunciated by President George H. W. Bush and others as the beginning of a peaceful era of international cooperation was seen as proof of Americans losing control over their own affairs. Militia circles reported the sighting of UN or Russian tanks and helicopters and of UN storm troopers or American GIs under UN command. In response, militia leaders and members were to defend the U.S. Constitution against the government and its agents. The result was many violent confrontations between these defenders of "the rights of the people" and federal agents as well as local and state officials. Describing the tactics of the militia of Montana, for example, Kenneth S. Stern wrote, "Many of its [Montana's] most dedicated public servants had gone from worrying about losing elections to wondering whether doing their job could cost them their lives."[28]

According to Kaplan's categories of radical right-wing groupings, the Church of the Creator, also called World Church of the Creator, fits what he calls "idiosyncratic sectarians." Although denying the existence of God and hostile to literally all religions, Creator had all the appearances of a religious sect. The teachings of this group resembled the hateful white supremacy ideas of the Christian Identity movement. Led at the end of the twentieth and the beginning of the twenty-first centuries by a young lawyer, Matthew Hale, who called himself Reverend and Pontifax Maximus, the group utilized the Internet as a propaganda organ and vehicle for recruitment. The following principles were summarized in the group's Sixteen Commandments of the "White Man's Bible" that was on the group's web site:

1. It is the avowed duty and holy responsibility of each generation to assure and secure for all time the existence of the White Race upon the face of this planet.
2. Be fruitful and multiply. Do your part in helping to populate the world with your own kind. It is our sacred goal to populate the lands of this earth with White people exclusively.
3. Remember that the inferior colored races are our deadly enemies, and the most dangerous of all is the Jewish race. It is our immediate objective to relentlessly expand the White Race, and keep shrinking our enemies.
4. The guiding principle of all your actions shall be: What is best for the White Race?
5. You shall keep your race pure. Pollution of the White Race is a heinous crime against Nature and against your own race.
6. Your first loyalty belongs to the White Race.
7. Show preferential treatment in business dealings with members of your own race. Phase out all dealings with Jews as soon as possible. Do not employ niggers or other coloreds. Have social contacts only with members of your own racial family.
8. Destroy and banish all Jewish thought and influence from society. Work hard to bring about a White world as soon as possible.
9. Work and creativity are our genius. We regard work as a noble pursuit and our willingness to work a blessing to our race.
10. Decide in early youth that during your lifetime you will make at least one major lasting contribution to the White Race.
11. Uphold the honor of your race at all times.
12. It is our duty and our privilege to further Nature's plan by striving towards the advancement and improvement of our future generations.
13. You shall honor, protect and venerate the sanctity of the family unit, and hold it sacred. It is the present link in the long golden chain of our White Race.
14. Throughout your life you shall faithfully uphold our pivotal creed of Blood, Soil and Honor. Practice it diligently, for it is the heart of our faith.
15. As a proud member of the White Race, think and act positively. Be courageous, confident and aggressive. Utilize constructively your creative ability.

16. We, the Racial Comrades of the White Race, are determined to regain complete and unconditional control of our own destiny.

Although the group did not openly call for violence against other races, some of the group's members and former members did exactly that. For example, over the July Fourth weekend in 1999, twenty-one-year-old Benjamin Nathaniel Smith went on a killing spree, murdering two men and injuring nine others. As victims he sought out a group of Orthodox Jews, an African American, and an Asian graduate student. As it turned out, Smith had been indoctrinated in the World Church of the Creator. Asked whether he felt sorry for the victims of Smith's shooting spree, the group's leader, Matthew Hale, answered that he did not and added,

> We can have compassion for animals, but animals aren't a threat to us. The blacks and the non-whites are taking this country right from under us. We are becoming a niggerfied, Jewified, Mongolfied country, and it's disgusting. We have to stop it.[29]

In these four short sentences, Hale, who has a law degree but was denied admittance to the Illinois bar because of his racist views, summarized the essence of his and other white supremacists' pseudoreligious agenda. Smith expressed the same prejudices before he acted on his hateful sentiments. During an interview with a PBS station in Indiana, Smith said, for example, "The Jews and the blacks and all the mud races are trying to destroy our people, and that is why we hate them."[30] Matt Hale was convicted of trying to solicit the murder of U.S. District Judge Joan Lefkow. The Chicago judge had ordered Hale's World Church of the Creator to change its name because of a trademark violation. Hale's bodyguard, who was supposed to kill Judge Lefkow, turned out to be an undercover FBI informer. In April 2005, Hale was sentenced to forty years in prison.

By 2003, the leading neo-Nazi, white supremacy, and Christian Identity groups had suffered severe setbacks. But nobody could assume that their problems signaled the demise of right-wing hate groups. Moreover, in reaction to the terrorist attacks of September 11, 2001, right-wing anti-immigrant groups became stronger—especially in the Southwest, where their members took it into their own hands to round up and mistreat illegal immigrants before calling the police. These activities coincided with the brutal murder of several Mexicans as they tried to enter the United States—certainly another variety of terrorism. In a report on armed vigilantes who roam the Arizona–Mexico border, the Southern Poverty Law Center described a number of cases like the following one:

> January 19, 2003 Rodrigo Quiroz Acosta, a migrant from Navajoa Sonora, was approaching Highway 80 when a truck pulled over. A tall man dressed like a rancher got out of the vehicle and began to punch and kick Quiroz, who said he was also hit on the head with a flashlight and bitten by one of the man's dogs. After a woman emerged from the truck and intervened to stop the beating, Quiroz jumped a nearby barbed-wire fence but was caught by the man's dogs and soon arrested by border agents.[31]

The Surge of the Black Supremacist Movement

In a 1999 FBI report, the FBI warned of extremists in the Black Hebrew Israelite (BHI) movement who believe that they are God's chosen people and consider whites and Jews to be the manifestations of evil. As the report noted, "[s]uch beliefs bear a striking resemblance to the Christian Identity theology practiced by many white supremacists." In fact,

Tom Metzger, renowned white supremacist, once remarked, "They're the black counterpart of us."[32] Nine years later, it was reported that extremist Hebrew Israelite churches operated in cities of many states, namely Florida, Maryland, Minnesota, Missouri, Nebraska, New Jersey, North Carolina, Pennsylvania, Oklahoma, and Oregon, and had thousands of members.[33] And according to the Southern Poverty Law Center's "The Year in Hate" report for 2008, like their white counterparts black supremacists, too, tried to exploit the political divisions and economic crisis to pursue their radical agenda and expand their membership. To that end, they attacked Barack Obama as a "house nigger" and a "puppet of Israel" and blamed the economic ills on Jews.[34]

The BHI movement was founded by Ben Carter of Chicago who took the name Ben Ami Ben Israel and, in 1969, moved with a group of supporters to Israel based on a voice telling him that African Americans were the descendants of biblical Israelites and should move to the holy land. While the BHI movement in Israel is peaceful, its branches in the United States are more militant and extreme. According to the FBI, extremist BHI followers are prone to commit violence and "have been observed in public donning primarily black clothing, with emblems and/or patches bearing the 'Star of David' symbol. Some BHI members practice paramilitary operations and wear web belts and shoulder holsters."[35]

Left-Wing Terrorism

Just as certain aspects of right-wing ideologies and causes changed over time, the belief systems of left-wing groups did as well. But they have always stood for fundamental changes in the existing political, economic, and social arrangements—whether in a monarchy or a democracy—by violent means, if needed. In more recent times, these groups have resorted to violence in opposition to globalization, which they consider another form of exploiting less developed countries—economic imperialism. Like the mainstream left, the extremists insist on de facto, not only legal, equality (e.g., race, ethnic, and gender equality)—by affirmative action, if needed. The left-wing groups in the United States that turned to terrorism in the 1960s and 1970s as a result of the Vietnam War and the civil rights struggles were inspired by Marxist ideology, but at the beginning of the twenty-first century, these kinds of "extreme-left" terrorist groups did not exist in the United States.

The First Anarchists in the United States

On September 6, 1901, while visiting the Pan-American Exposition in Buffalo, New York, President William McKinley was shot by an assassin and so severely wounded that he died soon thereafter. The perpetrator was caught at the scene of the attack and identified as Leon Czolgosz of Cleveland, a self-described anarchist and disciple of Emma Goldman, whose writings and speeches were well known in anarchist circles and who Czolgosz had met once. Although Goldman was arrested in Chicago as a suspected accomplice, she was soon released and never charged. However, John Most, the founder of the anarchist newspaper *Freiheit*, was charged and convicted for publishing an anarchist article and thereby committing "an act endangering the peace and outraging public decency."[36] The article was a reprint of Karl Heinzen's fifty-year-old essay "Murder," which justified terrorism and had appeared in the September 7 issue of the *Freiheit*—just one day after Czolgosz shot the president.

Although the defense claimed that no copy had been sold, the judge ruled against Most and stated in his opinion,

> It is in the power of words that is the potent force to commit crimes and offenses in certain cases. No more striking illustration of the criminal power of words could be given, if we are to believe the murderer of our President, than that event presents. The assassin declares that he was instigated and stimulated to consummate his foul deed by the teachings of Emma Goldman.
>
> It is impossible to read the whole article [authored by Heinzen] without deducting from it the doctrine that all rulers are enemies of mankind, and are to be hunted and destroyed through "blood and iron, poison and dynamite."
>
> It [the article] shows a deliberate intent to inculcate and promulgate the doctrine of the article. This we hold to be a criminal act.[37]

This was a remarkable ruling in that it made a direct connection between inflammatory words and illegal actions. Years before McKinley's violent death, Most and Goldman had coauthored an article that gave a nod of approval to violence; they wrote: "It cannot and it shall not be denied that most Anarchists feel convinced that 'violence' is not any more reprehensible toward carrying out their designs than it is when used by an oppressed people to obtain freedom."[38] However, after McKinley's death, Goldman insisted that "Anarchy did not teach men to do the act for which Czolgosz is under arrest."[39]

In the decades preceding McKinley's assassination, labor union members were involved in violent clashes with plant managers over wages and working conditions. In many of these bitter conflicts, mine operators and foremen were killed by workers and workers were murdered by company-hired guards and soldiers. The Molly Maguires, allegedly an Irish terrorist group, fought employers during bitter disputes in the coal mines of Pennsylvania. At times, anarchists got involved in this kind of violence. In 1892, for example, Alexander Berkman, a young anarchist, attempted to kill Henry C. Frick of the Carnegie Company because of Frick's position on striking workers. Berkman's deed divided the anarchist movement in that "[John] Most, in *Freiheit*, denounced him, while Emma Goldman in the *Anarchist* came to his defense."[40]

Although anarchists were far from popular before President McKinley's death, they became the targets of public outrage, threats, and violence afterward. In this climate, "Mobs forced dozens of anarchists to flee their homes and tried to wreck, in one case successfully, the offices of anarchist publications. Without warrant the police arrested scores, perhaps hundreds."[41] The "war on anarchists" continued for years. During this period, President Theodore Roosevelt ordered the establishment of a federal detective agency that became the forerunner of the Federal Bureau of Investigation. Roosevelt pressed for increasingly tough measures in the fight against the anarchist danger. Addressing both chambers of Congress in 1908, he said,

> When compared with the suppression of anarchy, every other question sinks into insignificance. The anarchist is the enemy of humanity, the enemy of all mankind, and his is a deeper degree of criminality than any other. No immigrant is allowed to our shores if he is an anarchist, and no paper published here or abroad should be permitted circulation in this country if it propagates anarchist propaganda.[42]

Given these strong sentiments, anarchists were suspected and accused of violent deeds they had not committed. Thus, in 1910, when dynamite exploded in the building of the *Los Angeles Times*, killing twenty-one unorganized workers, newspaper owner Harrison Otis published an editorial that blamed "anarchist scum" for the act of terrorism.[43] Eventually, John McNamara, a labor union official, and his brother James were indicted, tried, and sentenced for the bombing of the *Times*.

In the United States, as Jeffrey D. Simon concluded, "The anarchist movement failed to achieve its goal of uprisings and revolution."[44]

The Weather Underground

It was not until the 1960s and 1970s that leftists in the United States once again embraced terrorist methods to further their political ends. Just like the groups in Latin America, Europe, and Asia, mostly young Americans organized, as they explained, to bring about revolution and the defeat of imperialism. In the late nineteenth and early twentieth centuries, the original anarchists and social reformers in the United States were long on terrorist theory and short on actual violence, and to the extent that terrorism was traced to anarchism, the perpetrators were typically individuals not directly associated with organized groups. In sharp contrast, the self-declared revolutionary groups of the 1960s and 1970s practiced what they preached. The Weathermen, later renamed the Weather Underground to signify the prominent roles of women in the organization, were the best known among the white terrorist groups of this era. An offshoot of the radical New Left organization Students for a Democratic Society (SDS), the founders took their name and the title of their first manifesto, "You don't need a weatherman to tell you which way the wind blows," from the lyrics of a Bob Dylan song. Their radicalism was fueled by opposition to the Vietnam War and to racial and social inequality in the United States. Shortly after organizing themselves in early 1969, the Weathermen began a campaign of agitation in Chicago during what they called "Days of Rage," causing riots and clashes with the police. By 1970, disappointed that they had been unsuccessful in winning over the working class to their cause, the core of the group went underground as a revolutionary vanguard and began a terrorist campaign against public and private institutional cornerstones of the existing political and economic order. The Pentagon and other military symbols, police facilities, banks, and multinational corporations were the particular targets. In the 1974 manifesto "Prairie Fire," the last communication by the group, the Weather Underground claimed responsibility for nineteen major acts of terrorism and warned of more violence. Missing from the detailed list was an explosion in a Greenwich Village townhouse in March 1970 in which three members of the group blew themselves up as they were constructing a bomb.

Soon thereafter, the Weather Underground broke apart; some members joined or established new groups, and others surrendered after a time to the authorities and were tried and sentenced. Unlike their European soulmates, the Weather Underground never managed to terrorize the whole country by spreading massive fear and anxiety. Concluding that the Weather Underground was a failure, Ehud Sprinzak noted that the group had "never more than four hundred members and followers, and most of the time its inexperienced leaders and recruits worried not about the revolution but about their hideouts, survival logistics, and internal group relations."[45]

In "Prairie Fire," the Weather Underground expressed its admiration for black revolutionary groups, noting that the "Black Liberation Army—fighting for three years under ruthless attack by the state—the fighters in prison, and recently the Symbionese Liberation Army are leading forces in the development of the armed struggle and political consciousness, respected by ourselves and other revolutionaries."[46] Eventually, some members of the Weather Underground plotted joint terrorism ventures with the Black Liberation Army and similar groups. In the fall of 1981, a group of heavily armed men and women in dark ski masks ambushed a Brink's armored car in a shopping mall in Rockland County, New York, near New York City, killing one of the guards and injuring two others. Two police officers were killed when state troopers and detectives stopped the perpetrators' cars at a hastily established roadblock. The perpetrators were identified as members of the Weather Underground, the Black Panther Party, the Black Liberation Front, and the Republic of New Africa, a separatist group with the goal of establishing an independent black state in the American South. Contrary to the fears of observers at the time, this incident was not a sign of renewed strength in leftist terrorist circles but an act of desperation.

The Black Panther Party

The Black Panther Party for Self Defense was founded in the fall of 1966 by Bobby Seale and Huey P. Newton in Oakland, California, as an organization that was to protect the black community from police brutality. But the party's platform contained more ambitious goals and left-wing ideological fervor. In a speech in Oakland, Bobby Seale revealed the ten points of the Black Panther Party's platform, which demanded above all the freedom to determine the destiny of the black community, full employment, housing fit for human beings, education "which teaches us our true history and our role in the present day American society," exemption from military service for all black men, and the release of all black men from federal, state, county, and city jails and penitentiaries.[47] The Black Panthers were not racist but condemned the oppression of both blacks and whites by the capitalists and their corporate power structure. To this end, they cooperated with the Weathermen for a short period. For white radicals, the "Black Panthers, who armed themselves heavily and fought the police fiercely, provided an attractive model to follow."[48] But, as Sprinzak noted, white radicals felt guilty because they were not treated as brutally as their black counterparts by the police.[49]

The Panthers' tough rhetoric and perhaps their uniforms, black leather jackets and black berets, attracted young black men to their ranks. Their membership was never higher than a few thousand, but the organization had chapters in inner cities across the country and published its own newspaper. But the group's militancy also attracted criminal elements that made it easier for law enforcement to justify the brutal treatment of the Panthers in general. In 1969 alone, twenty-seven members of the organization were killed in clashes with the police and more than seven hundred members were arrested. On December 4, 1969, when the organization was no longer a factor because most of its leaders were either in prison or in exile, Fred Hampton, the twenty-one-year-old chairman of the Panthers in Illinois, and Mark Clark, a twenty-two-year-old member, were killed during a police raid on their apartment in Chicago. Five months later, a federal grand jury in Chicago decided that "the police had grossly exaggerated Black Panthers' resistance" and that "the police had riddled the Panthers' apartment with at least 82 shots, while only one shot was apparently fired from inside."[50] In reaction to and in memory of Hampton and Clark's violent deaths, surviving Panthers formed the December 4 Movement, but it disappeared nearly as quickly as it had emerged.

Although involved in violent actions but often the target of unprovoked police violence, the Black Panther Party did not understand itself as a terrorist organization. As the full name indicated, the Panthers perceived themselves as the black community's defense against an overly aggressive police force, a rationale vindicated by incidents like the deadly raid on Hampton and Clark's apartment.

The Symbionese Liberation Army

Founded in 1972 in Oakland, California, by community activists and graduate students, most of them with comfortable family backgrounds, the Symbionese Liberation Army (SLA) emphasized from the outset its interracial character and also the black and minority leadership of the group. In its 1973 Manifesto, the organization explained its revolutionary character:

> *We of the Symbionese Federation and the S.L.A. DO NOT under the rights of human beings submit to the murder, oppression and exploitation of our children and people and do under the rights granted to the people under The Declaration of Independence of The United States, do now by the rights of our children and people and by Force of Arms and with every drop of our blood, Declare Revolutionary War against the Fascist Capitalist Class, and all their agents of murder, oppression and exploitation. We support by Force of Arms the just struggle of all oppressed people for self-determination and independence within the United States and The World.*[51]

With its first violent action, the murder of Dr. Marcus Foster, the superintendent of Oakland's public school system, the SLA alienated black community activists, who were furious that Foster, one of the few African Americans in a high public office, had been targeted. But it was the 1974 kidnapping of Patricia Hearst, the granddaughter of press tycoon William Randolph Hearst, that drew national, even worldwide, attention to the SLA. The group exploited the sudden wave of publicity to present itself as a modern-day Robin Hood, in that it insisted on the establishment of a free food program in return for the release of the kidnap victim. Strangely, however, after Patricia Hearst's father agreed to put up a total of $4 million to feed the poor, his daughter decided to stay with her kidnappers and participated in a bank robbery. Although the SLA claimed that Hearst acted out of free will, once captured and indicted, Patricia Hearst insisted that she had been brainwashed.

There is no doubt that criminal elements were among the hard-core members of this group, among them its leader, Donald DeFreeze. Five member of the group, including DeFreeze, died in a 1974 shootout with police in Los Angeles; others fought on for a short while before becoming fugitives. But eventually all of the surviving SLA members were caught. In early 2003, the last chapter of the SLA was written in a courtroom in Sacramento, California, when two women (Sara Jane Olson and Emily Montague) and two men (William Harris and Michael Bortin), all in their mid-fifties, were sentenced to prison terms of six to eight years for participating in a 1975 bank robbery and the killing of a young wife and mother, Myrna Opsahl. Soon thereafter, a fifth onetime SLA member, James Kilgore, was sentenced under a similar plea bargain agreement as his old colleagues. All five had lived quite normal lives for more than twenty-five years before being brought to justice.

Single-Issue Terrorism

Embracing specific agendas, groups with vastly different motivations pursue a range of goals fitting their overall belief systems. Single-issue or special-interest groups, on the other hand, are narrowly focused on one particular political point or a package of closely related issues. And here, too, groups and individuals tend to fit either the conservative/right or the liberal/left side of the political spectrum, as the examples of conservative antiabortion extremists and the liberal pro-environment extremists demonstrate.

Antiabortion Violence

In 1973, the U.S. Supreme Court ruled in *Roe v. Wade* that the U.S. Constitution grants women the right to abortion. In the wake of the controversial decision, antiabortion or pro-life organizations emerged with the explicit goal of overturning the *Roe v. Wade* decision and legalized abortion. The overwhelming number of pro-life activists and the groups they joined were and are distinctly nonviolent and willing to work within the legitimate political process. However, some individuals and factions were not content with bringing legal actions to the courts, lobbying members of Congress, organizing demonstrations, harassing abortion providers and seekers, and staging acts of civil disobedience; instead, they called for and/or committed violence—against abortion clinics and their personnel. In the early 1990s, two physicians who worked in abortion clinics in Pensacola, Florida, were shot by followers of extremist antiabortion groups, namely, Rescue America and Defense Action. But clinics and personnel in other parts of the United States were also targeted by bombings and assassinations. These violent actions intimidated many physicians enough so that they stopped working in abortion clinics. Those who carried on were not even safe away from their workplaces. Thus, in 1998, Dr. Barnett A. Slepian was shot and killed in the kitchen of his private residence in Amherst in western New York State by James C. Kopp, a longtime antiabortion radical. Kopp, who had never met his victim, claimed later on that "[m]any abortion clinics are like fortresses with no windows" and that therefore the best chance to attack a doctor was during his walk from the car to the clinic. But, according to Kopp, this approach could have endangered innocent bystanders.[52]

From 1977 through 2002, the National Abortion Federation, one of the pro-choice groups that track violence against abortion providers and clinics, documented more than 4,000 acts of violence and more than 75,000 incidents of intimidation, harassment, threats, and picketing.[53] Mere threats to attack abortion clinics and kill abortion doctors can have devastating effects on the psyche of clinic personnel. Perhaps this was best understood after September 11, 2001, when the attacks on New York and Washington were followed up with a serious anthrax scare after news organizations and members of Congress received letters containing anthrax powder. Well before this scare, abortion clinics had received hundreds of anthrax threats and letters claiming to contain the lethal material. Although no anthrax was found in any of the mailings, the mere threat frightened the recipients.

The self-proclaimed Army of God, one of the most extreme antiabortion groups, did not hide its violent agenda, as the following excerpt from the Army of God's *Manual* reveals:

> *Beginning officially with the passage of the Freedom of Choice Act—we, the remnant of God-fearing men and women of the United States of Amerika [sic], do officially*

declare war on the entire child-killing industry. After praying, fasting, and making continual supplication to God for your pagan, heathen, infidel souls, we then peacefully, passively presented our bodies in front of your death camps, begging you to stop the mass murder of infants. Yet you hardened your already blackened, jaded hearts. We quietly accepted the resulting imprisonment and suffering of our passive resistance. Yet you mocked God and continued the holocaust.

No longer! All of the options have expired. Our Most Dread Sovereign Lord God requires that whoever sheds man's blood, by man shall his blood be shed. Not out of hatred for you, but out of love for the persons you exterminate, we are forced to take arms against you. Our life [sic] for yours—a simple equation. Dreadful. Sad. Reality, nonetheless. You shall not be tortured by our hands. Vengeance belongs to God only. However, execution is rarely gentle.[54]

A number of white supremacy and antigovernment groups have traditionally condemned abortion, at least as far as the procedure concerned Aryan women. Some individuals from this milieu have committed antiabortion terror as well. According to law enforcement officials, Eric Robert Rudolph, a white supremacist and survivalist, is such an individual. After detonating a bomb at the Olympic Games in Atlanta in 1996 and a gay nightclub in the region, he bombed two abortion clinics. When he was finally arrested in the spring of 2003, many people in and around Murphy, North Carolina, where he had hidden for years, expressed strong support for the man whose terrorist blasts had killed 2 and injured 111 persons. A mother of four said, "Rudolph's a Christian and I'm a Christian and he dedicated his life to fighting abortion. Those are our values. These are our woods. I don't see what he did as a terrorist act."[55]

The Animal and Earth Liberation Fronts

On the left side of the political spectrum, the Animal Liberation Front (ALF) and the Earth Liberation Front (ELF) have also advocated political violence to draw attention to their causes—the preservation of all animal life and the protection of the environment against exploitation by "the capitalist society [that] is destroying all life on this planet."[56] In the United States, the Animal Liberation Front was established in the late 1970s along the line of the British ALF model. Growing increasingly more action oriented, the ALF has claimed responsibility for attacks on and destruction of fur companies, mink farms, animal research laboratories, and restaurants. The Earth Liberation Front, established in the United States in 1994, also took its cue from the ELF in Great Britain, an extremist offshoot of the Earth First! environmental group, which had left the mainstream environmental movement to engage in highly visible protests and a civil disobedience campaign. According to the FBI, which has characterized the activities of ELF and ALF in North America as ecoterrorism,

The ELF advocates "monkeywrenching," a euphemism for acts of sabotage and property destruction against industries and other entities perceived to be damaging to the natural environment. "Monkeywrenching" includes tree spiking, arson, sabotage of logging or construction equipment, and other types of property destruction.[57]

The ELF has also damaged or destroyed large numbers of sports utility vehicles (SUVs) in order to dramatize its supporters' opposition to "gas-guzzling" automobiles and their negative impact on the environment.

The followers of ALF and ELF do not formally become members of these organizations and do not pay dues; they organize in small, autonomous underground cells that plan and execute violent acts to achieve social and political change. ALF and ELF work closely together and may have overlapping followers. The FBI estimated that from 1996 to early 2002, followers of ALF and ELF were responsible for more than 600 acts of ecoterrorism causing damages of more than $43 million. These numbers do not reflect the consequences of threats against individuals and groups of people working in particular areas of the private sector. During a *Washington Post* online forum on ecoterrorism with FBI Special Agent James F. Jarboe, one participant described the tactics of ecoterrorists this way:

> I work for an industry that has been targeted by ecoterrorism—and in the past have been personally threatened by an animal rights activist who said he knew my address and was planning to come into my home one evening and slash my face to ribbons with a razor blade. Perhaps some of the people viewing this discussion don't feel that ecoterrorism is very real—but I can assure them that I was terrified and was very grateful that the FBI took the threat seriously. The group targeting me (they got my name off of a website) have been known to blow up boats, break into homes and offices and shut down computer systems. To me, that's terrorism.[58]

In spite of the growing aggressiveness of ecoterrorists in recent years, they have not killed or injured human beings. However, their rhetoric has become increasingly militant and threatening. The ELF web site proclaimed in early 2003 that "[t]he only way, at this point in time, to stop that continued destruction of life [on this planet] is to by any means necessary take the profit motive out of killing."[59] Placed above this text was an advertisement for ELF's free "Guide to Setting Fires with Electric Timers," which contained do-it-yourself material about "devices, fuel requirements, timers, security, and more." Visitors to the site were invited to print or download the manual. A similar ALF do-it-yourself guide ("Arson-Around with Auntie ALF: Your Guide for Putting the Heat on Animal Abusers Everywhere") was available on both the ELF and ALF web sites. "Auntie ALF, Uncle ELF and the Anti-Copyright gang" advised readers explicitly not to injure or kill "animals, human or otherwise" when resorting to arson, but by describing in detail the preparation of incendiary devices, these guidelines read like invitations to join ALF's and ELF's arson activists.[60]

People for the Ethical Treatment of Animals (PETA), a large aboveground organization with 750,000 members, has not resorted to violence but seems comfortable with the violent approaches of ALF and ELF. Indeed, one PETA official seemed to endorse violence when he stated, "I think it would be a great thing if, you know, all these fast food outlets and these slaughterhouses, and the banks that fund them exploded tomorrow."[61]

The Jewish Defense League

JDL (Jewish Defense League) upholds the principle of Barzel—iron—the need to both move to help Jews everywhere and to change the Jewish image through sacrifice and all necessary means—even strength, force, and *violence* [emphasis added].[62] This sentence, contained in the "The Five Principles of the Jewish Defense League," reveals the organization's endorsement of violence in the service of a cause first articulated by Rabbi Meir Kahane. In 1968, Kahane founded the JDL in New York for the purpose of protecting Jews in what he characterized as a hostile, anti-Semitic environment in the

United States. The next year, after more than two dozen helmeted JDL members, clubs in their hands, appeared as "protectors" in front of a New York synagogue because James Forman, a radical African American, planned to present the congregation with reparation demands, one rabbi called them "Batmen" and "no different from whites, carrying robes and hoods, standing in front of burning crosses."[63] For many years, the JDL staged protests against and took over the offices of mainstream Jewish organizations. But its violent activities, mostly bombings, were directed against Arabs and Soviet nationals in New York, Washington, and other parts of the country. Although Kahane moved to Israel in the early 1970s, the JDL remained active in the United States. According to the Jewish Anti-Defamation League, "Kahane consistently preached a radical form of Jewish nationalism which reflected racism, violence and political extremism."[64]

Preaching in favor of a territorially greater Israel, Meir Kahane established a new, JDL-like organization, Kach (Thus), in Israel. After he was killed by an Arab extremist during one of his appearances in New York in November 1990, his son Binyahim Kahane founded Kahane Chai (Kahane Lives) to carry on the legacy of his father. Because of their violence against Palestinians, both Kach and Kahane Chai were included on the U.S. Department of State's list of terrorist organizations. The most lethal act of terrorism by a follower of Meir Kahane and a member of Kach was carried out in 1994, when Brooklyn-born Dr. Baruch Goldstein killed twenty-nine Palestinians as they prayed at a Hebron, Israel, mosque before he was overwhelmed and killed by survivors of his terrorist attack.

Puerto Rican Nationalist Groups

On November 2, 1950, the New York Times published a front-page story about an assassination attempt on President Harry Truman by Puerto Rican nationalists the previous day.[65] One of the Puerto Ricans, Grisello Torresola, was killed during a shootout with White House police officers that left one policeman dead and two others injured. The second would-be assassin, Oscar Collazo, was eventually sentenced to death, but President Truman commuted the death sentence to imprisonment for life. On March 2, 1954, a small group of Puerto Rican nationalists fired shots from the visitors' gallery of the U.S. House of Representatives onto the floor of the chamber, injuring five members before they were arrested. Rafael Miranda, Andres Cordero, and Irvin Flores were sentenced to seventy-five-year prison terms; the only female member of the team, Lolita Lebron, received a fifty-year sentence. Neither the assassination attempt on President Truman nor the attack on U.S. representatives alarmed decision- and opinion-makers inside and outside of government. This was reflected in an editorial in the New York Times that called the terrorists "fanatics," compared them to "the Nihilist assassins of Czarist Russia," and assured a nervous public that "we have to consider a deed of that sort as an aberration."[66]

Although the two attacks in the U.S. capital were the first acts of terrorism by Puerto Rican extremists on the American mainland, the movement had committed many acts of violence on the Caribbean island in the preceding years. Following a respite after the Washington incidents, several new groups were established in the late 1960s and early 1970s, some of them by Latinos of Puerto Rican descent born in Chicago and New York, others by Puerto Ricans born on the island. Some of these groups operated exclusively on the U.S. mainland; others struck in Puerto Rico and on the mainland. Founded in 1974 by William Morales and Rosado Ayala, both born in

Chicago, the organization Armed Forces for National Liberation (FALN) put itself on the map of public awareness in January 1975 when it bombed the historic Fraunces Tavern in downtown Manhattan, killing four and injuring forty-four persons. In a communique that was found in a telephone booth near the site, the group claimed responsibility for the attack on the restaurant and "reactionary corporate executives inside." The message stated, furthermore,

> The Yanki [sic] government is trying to terrorize and kill our people to intimidate us
> from seeking our rightful independence from colonialism. They do this in the same
> way they did it in Viet Nam [sic], Guatemala, Chile, Argentina, Mexico, the Congo,
> and in many other places including the United States itself. . . .
> You have unleashed a storm from which you Yankis [sic] cannot escape.[67]

In the following weeks, months, and years, the FALN was responsible for several dozen bombings across the United States that killed six people and injured many more. The organization was also responsible for strikes against military and mostly civilian facilities in Puerto Rico. A major terrorist attack claimed by Los Macheteros (The Cane Cutters, or "machete wielders"), another extremist group, occurred in 1981 and destroyed several U.S. military planes at an Air Force base in Puerto Rico. In a follow-up, members of the group attacked American sailors in San Juan, killing one and injuring three of the soldiers. But the group operated on the U.S. mainland as well. In 1983, Los Macheteros pulled off a robbery at a Wells Fargo terminal in Hartford, Connecticut, which netted the group more than $7 million. But what at first sight seemed a successful coup turned into the group's most costly misstep: The robbery provided the FBI with enough evidence to trace and arrest key members of the group. Two years thereafter, law enforcement caught up with several FALN members as well.

A core of radical Puerto Rican nationalists continued to fight violently for the island's independence. Thus, of the five cases that the FBI categorized as domestic terrorism in 1998, three occurred in Puerto Rico: the bombings of an aqueduct project in Arecibo and of two banks in Rio Piedras and Santa Isabel.

After Left-Wing and Right-Wing Waves: What Next?

Whereas left-wing political violence by groups and individuals dominated the domestic scene of the 1960s, 1970s, and early 1980s, and right-wing terrorism posed the greatest problem in this respect in the 1990s, during these periods other brands of terrorism existed side by side with the two predominant varieties. Looking back at some four decades of fighting domestic terrorism at the end of the twentieth century, the Federal Bureau of Investigation concluded,

> Waves of domestic terrorist activity are not absolute or all encompassing. During the
> 1970s and early 1980s, at the heights of the violent antiwar/left-wing activism, there
> were dozens of terrorist attacks carried out by Jewish extremist groups (such as the
> Jewish Defense League and the United Jewish Underground) and other extremist eth-
> nic groups (such as the Justice Commandos of the Armenian Genocide). There were
> also sporadic incidents involving special interest groups supporting nuclear disarma-
> ment and other causes. During the 1990s, when antigovernment right-wing groups
> became a primary counterterrorism focus, left-wing extremist Puerto Rican separatists

continued to conduct the majority of successful terrorist attacks in the United States—primarily on the island of Puerto Rico.

Today, right-wing terrorists—most notably loosely affiliated extremists—continue to represent a formidable challenge to law enforcement agencies around the country, even as animal rights and environmental extremism takes on a higher profile.[68]

During the twenty years from 1980 to 1999, left-wing terrorists were responsible for over 40% of all domestic terrorist incidents inside the United States and for plots to commit terrorism that were foiled by law enforcement. In close to 30% of these cases, right-wing terrorists were identified as perpetrators or plotters; in more than 20%, special-interest terrorists; and in close to 5%, lone wolves like the Unabomber, Theodore Kaczynski. The perpetrators or plotters in the rest of the cases were not identified.

The perpetrators' ideological markers were different in the years following the 9/11 attacks. According to the Federal Bureau of Investigation, there were only 23 actual domestic terrorist incidents in the United States during the four-year period from the beginning of 2002 through the end of 2005. With the exception of the firebombing of a synagogue by a white supremacist, all other attacks by domestic perpetrators were carried out by single-issue extremists of the environment and animal rights milieu. Up to the end of 2008, attacks by the Earth Liberation Front, the Animal Liberation Front, and similar groups did not kill or injure a single person but caused significant property damages. Arson was typically the method of attack. There was an additional, transnational act of terrorism, when an Egyptian citizen, Hesham Hedayet, fatally shot two people at the El Al ticket counter at Los Angeles International Airport in July 2002. During the 2002–2005 period, the FBI prevented fourteen acts of terrorism, of which eight were plotted by right-wing extremists. Besides the two victims killed during the incident at the airport in Los Angeles, no other persons were killed or injured during these years.

According to the FBI statistics of the last 25 years (see Figure 4.1), there was hardly ever a "wave" of terrorism in this country. The low number of terrorist incidents inside the United States is comforting at first sight, but these statistics seem to omit far more violent attacks that have all the characteristics of terrorism but are categorized as hate crimes. As mentioned, the terrorism report includes one attack against a Jewish house of worship within the four-year period; it was probably included because the perpetrator was active in right-extremist circles. But the same or similar attacks or threats against Jews, Muslims, African Americans, Hispanics, gays and/or their facilities are very frequent but not reflected in the statistics of terrorist incidents. The FBI's annual statistics of hate crimes include typically several thousand. For 2007, for example, there were 7,624 reported hate crimes nationwide with the following breakdown by motive:

- Racial Bias: 50.8%;
- Religious Prejudice: 18.4%
- Sexual Orientation Bias: 16.6%
- Ethnic/Nationality Hate: 13.2%
- Disability Bias: 1.0%

More than 63% of all racial bias violence was committed against African Americans; more than 18% against whites. Jews were the targets of more than 68% of all religiously motivated attacks, 9% were Muslims, 4% each Catholics and Protestants. Nearly 62% of ethnic/nationality violence was perpetrated against Latinos; more than 59% of sexual orientation violence was directed against gay males, close to 13%

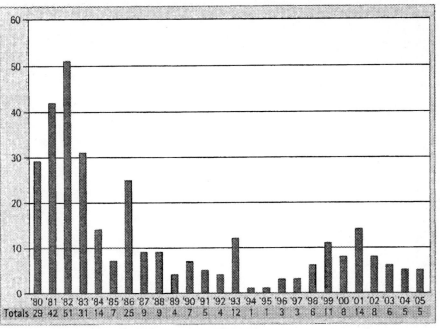

FIGURE 4.1 Terrorist Incidents in the United States (1980–2005)

Source: FBI report "Terrorism 2002–2005."

against lesbians, and 27% against all homosexuals and bisexuals. Since the biases that motivate this sort of violence are fueled by political and social issues and policy preferences, many, if not most of these deeds are as much acts of terrorism as the antiabortion terrorism and ecoterrorism.

Notes

1. Martin Durham, "The American Far Right and 9/11," *Terrorism and Political Violence* 15:2 (Summer 2003), 97.
2. David Holthouse, "Number of Hate Groups Tops 900" Intelligence Report: The Year in Hate (Spring 2009), available at http://www.splcenter.org/intel/intelreport/article.jsp?aid=1027, accessed May 4, 2009.
3. This war reported by CNN at http://www.cnn.com/2009/US/02/26/hate.groups.report/index.html?eref=rss_crime, accessed May 4, 2009.
4. "Victory by Klan Feature Election," *New York Times*, November 5, 1924 (retrieved from ProQuest Historical News).
5. Allison J. Gough, "Ku Klux Klan Terror," in Martha Crenshaw and John Pimlott, eds., *Encyclopedia of World Terrorism* (Armonk, NY: M. E. Sharpe, 1997), 527–29.
6. "Smith Denounces Coolidge's Silence on Ku Klux Klan," *New York Times*, October 19, 1924 (retrieved from ProQuest Historical News).
7. Gough, 527.
8. James Ridgeway, *Blood in the Face: The Ku Klux Klan, Aryan Nation, Nazi Skin Heads, and the Rise of a New White Culture* (New York: Thunder Mouth Press, 1995), 68.
9. Kenneth S. Stern, *A Force upon the Plain: The American Militia Movement and the Politics of Hate* (New York: Simon & Schuster, 1996), 43.

10. Christopher Hewitt, "The Political Context of Terrorism in America: Ignoring Extremists or Pandering to Them?" *Terrorism and Political Violence* 12:3–4 (2000): 323–44.

11. Ibid., 44.

12. Jeffrey Kaplan, "Right Wing Violence in North America," *Terrorism and Political Violence* 7:1 (1995): 44–95.

13. Duke was quoted by Ridgeway, 146.

14. This is the Southern Poverty Law Center's description in "The Toll of Hate," www.splcenter.org (retrieved March 12, 2003).

15. From the web site of the European-American Unity and Rights Organization, www.whitecivilrights. com (retrieved March 10, 2003).

16. "ADL Backgrounder: Church of the American Knights of the Ku Klux Klan," www. adl.org/ backgrounders/american_knights_kkk.asp (retrieved March 17, 2003).

17. www.splcenter.org/centerinfo/ci-index.html (retrieved March 14, 2003).

18. Holthouse, "Number of Hate Groups Tops 900."

19. Posted on the group's web site: http://www.cnkkkk.com/upcomingevents.htm, accessed May 4, 2009/

20. Kaplan, 46.

21. Ridgeway, 54.

22. Kaplan, 53.

23. "Breakup of Aryan Nations Leads to the Formation of Successor Groups," www.adl.org (retrieved March 17, 2003).

24. Ibid.

25. "Aryan Nations reappears in North Idaho." http://www.ktvb.com/news/localnews/stories/ktvbn-apr2509-aryan_nations.10ea62923.html, accessed May 4, 2009.

26. Cited by the Anti-Defamation League, "Tom Metzger/White Aryan Resistance: Update," August 1, 2002, www.adl.org/learn/ext%5Fus/metzger%5Fup.asp (retrieved March 18, 2003).

27. Kaplan, 58.

28. Stern, 95.

29. Ibid.

30. Smith was quoted in Richard Roeper "Hatemongers 'Church' Unites Paranoid Losers," *Chicago-Sun Times* (July 7, 1999). No—I cannot find the page number.

31. Bob Moser, "Open Season: As Extremists Peddle Their Anti-Immigrant Rhetoric along the Troubled Arizona Border, a Storm Gathers," *Southern Poverty Law Center's Intelligence Report* (Spring 2003): 6–19.

32. FBI, "Project Megiddo," 1999, 23, available at http://permanent.access.gpo.gov/lps3578/www.fbi. gov/library/megiddo/megiddo.pdf, accessed May 4, 2009.

33. "Ready for War." *Intelligence Report* (Fall 2008), published by the Southern Poverty Law Center. Available at http://www.splcenter.org/intel/intelreport/article.jsp?aid=941, accessed March 4, 2009.

34. Holthouse, "The Year in Hate."

35. FBI, "Project Megiddo," 23.

36. Quote is taken from "Anarchy at the Turn of the Century," University Libraries, Pan-American Exposition Exhibit Group, University of Buffalo, http://ublib.buffalo.edu/libraries/exhibits/panam/ copyright.html (retrieved March 27, 2003).

37. Ibid.

38. John Most and Emma Goldman, "Anarchy Defended by Anarchists," *Metropolitan Magazine* 4:3 (October 1896).

39. "Emma Goldman Is Arrested in Chicago," *New York Times* (September 11, 1901) (retrieved from ProQuest Historical News).

40. Walter Laqueur, *A History of Terrorism* (New Brunswick, NJ: Transaction Publishers, 2002).

41. Richard Bach Jensen, "The United States, International Policing and the War against Anarchist Terrorism, 1900–1914," *Terrorism and Political Violence* 13:1 (Spring 2001): 15–46.

42. Ibid., 32.

43. The quote is from Jeffrey D. Simon, *The Terrorist Trap: America's Experience with Terrorism* (Bloomington: Indiana University Press, 1994), 41.

44. Ibid., 38.

45. Ehud Sprinzak, "Extreme Left Terrorism in a Democracy," in Walter Reich, ed., *Origins of Terrorism: Psychologies, Ideologies, Theologies, States of Mind* (New York: Cambridge University Press, 1990), 77.

46. "Prairie Fire—Political Statement of the Weather Underground," in Walter Laqueur and Yonah Alexander, eds., *The Terrorism Reader* (New York: Penguin, 1987), 173.

47. The quote is from the Ten-Point Party Platform of the Black Panther Party, www.pbs.org/hueynewton (retrieved May 12, 2003).

48. Sprinzak, 77.

49. Ibid.

50. Reported by Fred P. Graham, "U.S. Jury Assails Police In Chicago on Panther Raid," *New York Times*, May 15, 1970, 1, 14.

51. The quote is from "Symbionese Liberation Army Manifesto (1973)," in Frank Shanty and Raymond Picquet, eds., *Encyclopedia of World Terrorism: Documents* (Armonk, NY: Sharpe Reference, 2003), 960.

52. Ibid.

53. "2001 Year-end Analysis of Trends of Violence and Disruption Against Reproductive Health Care Clinics" published by the National Abortion Federation at www.prochoice.org (retrieved April 2, 2003).

54. From "The Army of God Manual, Classic Third Edition," publicized at www.armyofgod.com/AOGsel6.html (retrieved April 3, 2003).

55. The woman, Crystal Davis, was quoted in Jeffrey Gettleman with David M. Halbfinger, "Suspect in '96 Olympic Bombing and 3 Other Attacks Is Caught," *New York Times*, June 1, 2003, 1.

56. According to the ELF web site, www.earthliberationfront.com.

57. From the statement of James F. Jarboe, Domestic Terrorism Section Chief, Counterterrorism Division, Federal Bureau of Investigation, on "The Threat of Eco-Terrorism," before the House Resources Committee, Subcommittee on Forest and Forest Health, February 12, 2002.

58. Washingtonpost.com: Live Online, www.washingtonpost.com (retrieved April 5, 2003).

59. www.earthliberationfront.com (retrieved April 5, 2003).

60. Abroad, extremists among the animal rights and environmental movements went further than their American counterparts. Thus, Volker van der Graaf, an activist on behalf of animal rights and environmental protection, assassinated the Dutch right-wing politician Pim Fortuyn in May 2002 during the national election campaign in Holland. During his trial, van der Graaf said that he had targeted Mr. Fortuyn because of the politician's dangerous ideas, especially with respect to animals, the environment, immigrants, Muslims, and asylum seekers.

61. Bruce Friedrich, a PETA official, was cited by Michael Spector, "The Extremist: The Woman behind the Most Successful Radical Group in America," *New Yorker*, April 14, 2003, 52.

62. Posted on the JDL's web site, www.jdl.org (retrieved September 27, 2004).

63. "Defense League Scored by Rabbi," *New York Times*, May 18, 1969, 81.

64. "About the Jewish Defense League," www.adl.org (retrieved September 26, 2004).

65. Anthony Leviero, "President Resting," *New York Times*, November 2, 1950, 1.

66. "Madness in Washington," *New York Times*, March 2, 1954, 24.

67. The excerpts are from "Text of Note Found near the Blast," *New York Times*, January 25, 1975, 10.

68. From FBI report, "Terrorism in the United States 1999," www.fbi.gov/publications/terror/terror99.pdf.

Religious Terrorism: Political Violence in the Name of God

As THE TITLE OF THIS CHAPTER SUGGESTS, RELIGIOUS TERRORISM, just like secular terrorism, has political ends. Secular terrorists are motivated by political ideologies (e.g., neo-Nazi groups by Hitler's racist white supremacist views; left-wing groups like the Red Army Faction and Red Brigades of the past by Marxist ideas) or widely accepted principles, such as the right to self-determination or to equality. Religious terrorists are motivated by their strong desire to live according to their religion's teachings and follow God's will, but they also have political grievances and goals. Thus, whether they are Christians, Jews, Muslims, Buddhists, Hindus, members of other religions, or devoted to self-declared religious sects (e.g., the Japanese Aum Shinrikyo), extremists commit violence for both religious and political ends. Mark Sedgwick has pointed out,

> Just as religious terrorism turns out to have important political elements, "secular" terrorism also has important religious elements. Many nationalists have spoken of their cause as "sacred," and it is not hard to conceive of a leftist speaking of the cause of the opposed masses." A Russian terrorist of the first wave [of terrorism] wrote of terrorism as "uniting the two sublimities of human nature, the martyr and the hero."[1]

But although secular terrorists may invoke religious rhetoric and imagery, they are solidly grounded in worldly justifications. Religious or pseudoreligious terrorists share the belief that their deeds are what God wants them to do, even what God commands them to do. According to Magnus Ranstorp, "Despite having vastly different origins, doctrines, institutions, and practices, these religious extremists are united in their justification for employing sacred violence either in efforts to defend, extend or revenge their own communities or for millenarian or messianic reasons."[2]

Religious Fanatics and Terrorism

Paul Hill (left), a devout Christian, killed Dr. John Bayard Britton, a Florida abortion provider; Mohammed Atta (middle), a devout Muslim, was the leader of the 9/11 terrorist team. that killed nearly 3,000 persons; Dr. Baruch Goldstein (right), a devout Jew, killed 29 worshippers in a Hebron mosque. All three claimed to act in the name of God.

The following three examples demonstrate how strongly religious terrorists believe that divine guidance gives them the strength to commit violence for what they consider to be just causes on earth and in heaven.

Christians and Sacred Terrorism

Case Study

On July 29, 1994, Paul Hill, an antiabortion activist, waited in front of an abortion clinic in Pensacola, Florida, for Dr. John Bayard Britton and his bodyguard James Herman Barrett, a retired Air Force Lieutenant Colonel, to arrive. As their car entered the parking lot, Hill first shot Barrett and, after reloading his shotgun, aimed at Britton. He killed both men. When he was arrested by police officers a few minutes later, he proclaimed loudly, "I know one thing, no innocent babies are going to be killed in this clinic today."[3] Well-known in radical antiabortion circles, Hill did not act impulsively, but planned his lethal attack carefully and, so he felt, under the guidance and as an instrument of God. From his prison cell, he later described his preparation and justification:

> I was not standing for my own ideas, but God's truths—the same truths that have stopped blood baths and similar atrocities throughout history. Who was I to stand in God's way? He now held the door open and promised great blessing for obedience. Was I not to step through it?
>
> When Monday arrived, I knew I had to decide. When I went from mentally debating whether to act, in general, to planning a particular act, I felt some relief. Romans 14:23b says ". . . and whatever is not from faith is sin." If I had not acted when I did, it would have been a direct and unconscionable sin of disobedience. One of the first things I told my wife, after the shooting was, "I didn't have any choice!" That cry came from the depths of my soul. I was certain, and still am, that God called me to obey His revealed will at that particular time.

(continued)

Christians and Sacred Terrorism (continued)

This conviction did not weaken during his time in prison. In Hill's own words,

The inner joy and peace that have flooded my soul since I have cast off the state's tyranny makes my 6 × 9 cell a triumphant and newly liberated kingdom. I shudder at the thought of ever returning to the bondage currently enforced by the state.

But Hill also hoped for worldly rewards, namely, that his deed would radicalize the pro-life movement. As he put it, "using the force necessary to defend the unborn gives credibility, urgency, and direction to the pro-life movement which it has lacked, and which it needs in order to prevail." He thought that his deed "would also help people to decide whether to join the battle on the side of those defending abortionists, or the side of those defending the unborn."[4] Before he was executed by injection in September 2003, Hill said with a smile on his face, "I expect a great reward in heaven. I am looking forward to the glory." But again, he also thought of immediate goals right here on earth, when he said, "I think it [killing the man he called 'the abortionist' and his bodyguard] was a good thing and instead of people being shocked at what I did, I think more people should act as I acted."[5] For Hill, a former minister in the Presbyterian Church in America and the Orthodox Presbyterian Church, his had been a "defensive action" on behalf of the unborn in that he prevented his victim from ever killing defenseless babies again.

His supporters shared his conviction. The day Hill was executed, one antiabortion extremist declared, "Paul Hill should be honored today. The abortionists should be executed and the judges that rule it's okay to kill children should be run out of Dodge."[6] On its web site, the extreme antiabortion "Army of God" continues to praise Paul Hill as an "American hero."

Muslims and Sacred Terrorism

In February 1998, Osama bin Laden and three like-minded men signed a *fatwa*, or religious edict, in the name of Al Qaeda's newly established "World Islamic Front" that called on all Muslims "in accordance with God's will" to "kill the Americans and their allies—civilians and military. . . ." The declaration detailed America's "crimes and sins" in the Middle East and left no doubt about the political goals of the holy war it calls for—remove Americans and their allies from the Middle East. In particular, bin Laden gives three justifications:

Firstly, for over seven years America has occupied the holiest places of the Islamic lands, the Arabian peninsula, plundering its wealth, dictating to its leaders, humiliating its people, terrorizing its neighbours and turning its bases there into a spearhead with which to fight the neighbouring Muslim peoples.

Secondly, despite great devastation inflicted upon the Iraqi people at the hands of the Judeo-Crusader alliance [during and after the first Gulf War], and despite the terrible number of deaths—over one million—despite all this, the Americans are trying to repeat these horrific massacres again. . . .

> *Thirdly, while these wars are being waged by the Americans for religious and economic purposes, they also serve the interests of the petty Jewish state, diverting attention from its occupation of Jerusalem and its murder of Muslims there.*

Just as Paul Hill considered it his Christian duty to obey God's will and kill abortion providers to protect their victims, bin Laden claimed that it is "in accordance with the words of God Almighty . . . to liberate the al-Aqsa Mosque [in Jerusalem] and the Holy Mosque [in Mecca] from their [the enemies'] grip, so that their armies leave all the territory of Islam. . . ." The declaration calls "with God's permission on everyone who believes in God and wants reward to comply with His will to kill the Americans . . . ."[7]

As Mohammed Atta, the leader of the 9/11 terrorist team, wrote in his handwritten instructions for the members of his team, "When the storming begins, strike like heroes who are determined not to return to this world. Glorify [Allah, i.e., cry 'Allah is Great'], because this cry will strike terror in the hearts of the infidels. . . ." Atta's instructions reminded his comrades repeatedly that they were acting on behalf of God and that their behavior during this mission must reflect its sacred nature.

> *You must not show any signs of nervousness or stress, and be joyful, happy, cheerful and calm, because you are about to carry out an action that Allah loves and that pleases him.*
>
> *And don't confuse or panic your brothers, but encourage them, reassure them and remind them. And how beautiful it is to read from the Koran, "Let them fight in Allah's name, those who would trade this temporal life for the afterlife." And also, the Sublime's saying, "Do not consider those who were killed for the sake of Allah dead."*

Finally, the 9/11 attackers were told that they must "not take revenge for yourself, but make your strikes and everything in the name of Allah."[8]

After 9/11, bin Laden praised the nineteen terrorists as "young men, for whom God has created a path . . ." and insisted that "jihad is without doubt mandatory for all Muslims. . . ."[9]

Case Study

Jews and Sacred Terrorism

In the early morning of February 25, 1994, Dr. Baruch Goldstein, a well-known resident of the Jewish settlement Kiryat Arba near the West Bank town of Hebron and an active member of the religious right-wing organization Kach, went to the shrine at the Tomb of the Patriarchs in Hebron/al Khali. Built over the site where Abraham, Sara, and other revered religious figures are buried, the shrine provided Jews and Muslims separate worship halls. This morning, Dr. Goldstein went right to the Muslim side, pulled an assault rifle from under his coat, and fired 111 shots, killing twenty-nine Muslim worshippers and injuring many more before he himself was beaten to death.

(continued)

Jews and Sacred Terrorism (continued)

Although Goldstein did not leave an explanatory note, the political realities in the mid-1990s and the teachings of his late spiritual mentor Rabbi Meir Kahane explained his immediate political and higher religious motives. Like others of the so-called messianic right in Israel, Dr. Goldstein was upset about political developments: the Oslo Peace Agreement negotiated by Israel's Prime Minister Yitzhak Rabin and PLO leader Yassir Arafat, the freeze on further Jewish settlements in the occupied territories, and the growing attacks by Palestinian extremists on Jewish settlements. As Ehud Sprinzak explained,

> Goldstein suffered a severe crisis in the months before the Hebron massacre. Not only was the future of Judea and Samaria put in great doubt, but the neighboring Palestinians became increasingly aggressive and violent. As the community's emergency physician and the doctor responsible for first aid to Jewish victims of terrorism, Goldstein was exposed to the consequences of these circumstances more, perhaps, than anybody else. Several victims of the intensifying Palestinian terrorism died in his hands. . . .[10]

These, then, were the immediate political grievances. But how did Goldstein's religious convictions figure into the Hebron massacre? For many years a disciple of Rabbi Meir Kahane, Baruch Goldstein ultimately became what Sprinzak called "[t]he new Kahane Jew"[11] who acted in accordance with the glorification of violence that the rabbi preached. Kahane and his followers "not only responded to violence but also produced it in new acts of death and destruction, a spiral of violence that continued long after the zealous rabbi's death."[12] In Kahane's "catastrophic messianism" the central point is that "the Messiah will come in a great conflict in which Jews triumph and praise God through their successes. . . . Anything that humiliated the Jews was not only an embarrassment but a retrograde motion in the world's progress toward salvation."[13]

For Kahane, both Arabs and secular Jews prevented the Israeli people's redemption that would come only after all Arabs were removed from the sacred land of Israel. According to Sprinzak, Goldstein believed in Kahane's tenet:

> There are numerous indications that following the 1990 assassination of the rabbi, whom Goldstein loved dearly, the consecutive disasters after the 1992 elections, especially the Oslo agreement, Goldstein started to slowly move into a desperate messianic defiance. He felt that only a catastrophic act of supreme Kiddush Hashem (sanctification of the name of God) could change, perhaps, the course of history and put it back on the messianic track [Kahane's prescription for redemption]. A responsible person who never was trigger happy, he had to carry out this exemplary mission.[14]

In other words, Goldstein unloaded his shotgun on worshipping Muslim Arabs in the conviction that this was the will of God.

While many Israelis condemned Baruch Goldstein for his lethal act of terrorism, he was an instant hero for members of the religious right. At his burial, one fellow settler said, "There's no question about it, he was a great man. There's no question about it."[15] Another settler added, "This was desperation for a man who was a moral man for every instant of his life."[16]

Defending the Faith in "Cosmic Wars"

The similarities among the three cases are striking in that terrorist violence was sanctioned by Christian, Muslim, and Jewish leaders of extreme movements and carried out by their followers in the conviction that they acted on behalf of God and in defense of their faith, their tradition, right, and interest. The men who committed the lethal acts of terrorism lived seemingly normal and moral lives before they resorted to violence against what they perceived as forces of evil. Such conversions can occur when persons slip into what Albert Bandura has described as "moral disengagement" that "is accomplished by cognitively restructuring the moral value of killing, so that the killing can be done free from self-censoring restraints."[17] And since religious terrorists believe they follow God's orders, they can displace responsibility for their deeds. According to Bandura, when it comes to displacement of responsibility, "[t]he higher the authorities, the more legitimacy, respect, and coercive power they command, and the more amenable are people to defer to them."[18] Once terrorists reach this psychological stage, they are convinced to fight "satanic" enemies in a "cosmic war."[19] According to Mark Juergensmeyer,

> The process of creating satanic enemies is part of the construction of an image of cosmic war. . . .
>
> When the opponent rejects one's moral or spiritual position; when the enemy appears to hold the power to completely annihilate one's community, one's culture, and oneself; when the opponent's victory would be unthinkable; and when there seems no way to defeat the enemy in human terms—all of these conditions increase the likelihood that one will envision one's opponent as a superhuman foe, a cosmic enemy. The process of satanization is aimed at reducing the power of one's opponents and discrediting them. By belittling and humiliating them—by making them subhuman—one is asserting one's own superior moral powers.[20]

Religious terrorists draw strength from their conviction that they are totally right, good, and moral and that their enemy is totally wrong, evil, and immoral. As Jessica Stern has pointed out, "[r]eligious terrorism attempts to destroy moral ambiguities." The idea of defeating the evil and Satan in an existential battle for God was central to Paul Hill's, Baruch Goldstein's, and Mohammed Atta's convictions. When he decided to kill Dr. Britton and his guard, Paul Hill considered the "abortionist's knife as [the] 'cutting edge of Satan's current attack' on the world."[21] When he decided to kill worshipping Muslim Arabs, Baruch Goldstein had come "to the conclusion that unless stopped by a most dramatic act that would shake the foundations of Earth and please God, the peace process would disconfirm the dream of redemption."[22] When Mohammed Atta and his team flew hijacked airplanes into the World Trade Center towers and the Pentagon, they considered themselves warriors in a sacred war against an alliance of Jews and Crusaders led by America that Osama bin Laden had called Satan.

Audrey Kurth Cronin lists the following five reasons that make religious terrorists more dangerous than right-wing, left-wing, and nationalist/separatist extremists:

- Religious terrorists' belief that they are involved in a "Manichaean struggle of good against evil. . . ." All nonbelievers are legitimate targets.
- Religious terrorists' desire "to please the perceived commands [to commit violence] of a deity."
- Religious terrorists' complete disregard for "secular values and laws."

- Religious terrorists' alienation from the existing social system. "They are not trying to correct the system . . ., they are trying to replace it."
- Religious terrorists' "dispersed popular support in civil society." For example, "groups such as al-Qaeda are able to find support from some Muslim non-governmental foundations throughout the world, making it a truly global network."[23]

Are some practitioners of sacred terrorism "evil" and others perhaps not? After interviewing many religious extremists and their supporters, Stern made a distinction. According to Stern, "Few of the terrorists described in these pages are single-mindedly thoughtful villains like those who masterminded the September 11 attacks. In some cases the ethical basis of their actions is complicated."[24] More specifically, she made the following distinction:

> Although none of the terrorism described in this book can be described as morally acceptable, at least in my view, the pro-life doctor killers probably come closest and are worth examining in detail for that reason. Unlike the September 11 hijackers, the doctor killers are discriminating: they target individuals who, in their view, are in the business of murder.[25]

But considering that Osama bin Laden, Al Qaeda, and like-minded individuals and groups believe also that Americans collectively are guilty of killing innocent Muslims, the difference between doctor killers and the 9/11 killers is in the number of victims, not in the moral distinction between justifiable and nonjustifiable homicide.

The Proliferation of Religious Violence

In 1980, during the Iran hostage crisis, the Department of State did not include religious organizations on its list of terrorist groups, but nearly two decades later, more than half of the listed international terrorist groups were of the religious variety.[26] In 2006, the "Terrorism Knowledge Base" of the National Memorial Institute for the Prevention of Terrorism (MIPT) listed 202 domestic and international religious terrorist groups.[27] Not surprisingly, most of these organizations were at the same time listed in the nationalist/separatist category. Thus, the MIPT data list Hamas and Hezbollah as both religious and nationalist groups. This dual classification of many such groups is the only possible system since such organizations have religious as well as political objectives.

Although the lines between religious and other types of terrorism—especially the nationalist/separatist variety—are blurred, the MIPT data reveal a significant increase in the number and severity of incidents carried out by religious groups, whether their motivations are purely religious or a mixture of political and religious objectives. In the thirteen years from 1980 through 1992, religious groups committed a total of 240 acts of international terrorism, killing 806 persons and injuring 1,192. During that same time period, communist/socialist and nationalist/separatist groups committed far more acts of terrorism, namely 1,045 and 1,039, respectively. In the thirteen years from 1993 through the end of 2005, the number of international terrorist incidents perpetrated by wholly or partially religious groups more than doubled, to 509; even more striking was the dramatic increase in fatalities (5,857) and injuries (22,885). While nationalist/separatist groups were responsible for more attacks than other types of groups, they committed far less terrorism than in the previous period. Terrorist incidents by communist/socialist groups declined even more sharply, to 331.[28] Since the MIPT "Knowledge Base" does not contain domestic terrorism statistics before 1998, these trend data are limited to international terrorist incidents for both time periods. If domestic incidents from countries all over the world were included, the number would be significantly higher. Nevertheless, the available data attest to a significant increase in terrorism by religious groups in the last dozen or so years.

For David Rapoport, the 9/11 attacks and similar violence by Al Qaeda and like-minded groups and cells are part of a wave of religious terrorism that began at the end of the 1970s and overlapped the "New Left Wave," which, apart from a few exceptions, disappeared after the end of the Cold War. Since the "Anarchist Wave" (beginning in the 1880s) and the "Anti-Colonial Wave" (beginning in the 1920s) preceded the "New Left Wave" (beginning in the late 1960s), he considers the "Religious Wave" as the fourth in the history of modern terrorism and Islam the most important religion in this latest period—but not the only one. Unlike Rapoport, who names three near simultaneous events (the "Iranian Islamic Revolution in 1979, the start of the Islamic *hijri* calendar, and the Soviet invasion of Afghanistan") as starting points of the "Fourth Wave," Mark Sedgwick considers 1967 as the crucial date:

> It was the shockingly sudden and complete defeat of the Arab armies by Israel in that year that began the shattering of the Arab nationalist dream incarnated by Egypt's President Nasser, a process completed by President Sadat's concessions at Camp David in 1979. . . .
>
> [I]t was after 1967 that the re-Islamization of Egyptian society started. The Arabs who went to fight for Islam in Afghanistan were in the middle of the wave, not at the start of it. The fourth wave, then, started not in Iran or Afghanistan, but in Palestine and Israel, in almost the same year that the third wave started in Europe and—to a lesser extent—in America.[29]

Like Rapoport, this writer considers the Iranian Islamic revolution and the Soviet invasion of Afghanistan (not the start of the fifteenth hijri century) as triggers of the "Fourth Wave," not the Arab–Israeli war of 1967. While the "re-Islamization of Egyptian society started"[30] after that war, the more immediate result was the establishment of secular Palestinian terrorist organizations that fit into the third or "New Left Wave" and actually cooperated with European Marxist terrorist groups.

Alienation, Humiliation, and Fear

Although Sedgwick argues that Al Qaeda's short-term or immediate goals are more political than religious and "owe more to European radicalism than to Islam," he also recognizes that the organization is "clearly marked by Islam, and not only in its ultimate [religiously defined] aims. Al Qaeda's potential constituency is the world's Muslims, and the means it uses to mobilize support in this constituency are derived from Islam."[31] The connection between shared Islamic concepts and images and terms on the one hand and the need to recruit members and sympathizers on the other is important in that it provides the movement with a large pool of potential supporters. Al Qaeda is not unique in this respect. As Juergensmeyer notes,

> The groups that have made a long-term impact, such as Hamas, the Khalistan movement [in India], Christian Identity, and the Jewish right wing, have used violence not

only to draw attention to themselves but also to articulate the concerns of those within their wider cultures.

Radical though they may be, they have represented widely held feelings of alien-ation and oppression, and for this reason their strident language and violent acts have been considered by their cohorts as perhaps intemperate but understandable.[32]

Those who have studied religious terrorists seem to agree that underneath their tough words and deeds, there is a great deal of alienation, humiliation, and even fear. Stern concluded that the grievances expressed by religious terrorists "often mask a deeper kind of angst and a deeper kind of fear. Fear of a godless universe, of chaos, of loose rules, and of loneliness. . . ."[33] It is not unusual that religious extremists are frustrated by the loss or pending loss of their privileged station in society. Thus, radi-cal elements in the Christian Identity movement do not hide that they hate African Americans and Jews, whom they blame for all the ills in American society and in par-ticular "for pornography, for the lack of morality, for the economic situation in America, for minority rights over white rights, and for kicking god out of schools."[34] Since many of the rank-and-file members of such groups have at best finished high school, work in low-wage jobs, or are unemployed, they blame nonwhite, non-Christian groups for their predicament. In other societies, for example in the Middle East, the frustration of university-educated males stems often from their inability to find high-level jobs that require the skills they have.

After her conversations with Kerry Noble, a leader in the Christian Cult, the Covenant, and the Arm of the Lord (CSA), a Christian Identity group, and many reli-gious extremists abroad, Stern concluded,

[T]he grievances Noble described were similar to those of religious extremists around the world. Al Qaeda's complaints about the new world order sound remarkably simi-lar to Kerry Noble's for example. Ayman Zawahiri, Osama bin Laden's second in command, accuses Western forces of employing international institutions such as the United Nations, multinational corporations, and international news agencies as weapons in their "new crusade" to dominate the Islamic world. They often reject feminism in favor of "family values," whether their families are in Oklahoma or Peshawar.[35]

Real or perceived humiliation, too, seems to drive males into violent groups. Thus, extremists like Al Qaeda's Ayman al-Zawahiri believe that "violence is a way to cure Muslim youth of the pernicious effects of centuries of humiliation at the hands of the West." Similarly, Christian Identity extremists join violent groups to regain their mas-culinity and forget that they were humiliated by gender and racial equality. Thus, Kerry Noble told Stern that "he felt strong for the first time in his life when he joined a violent, racist cult." He said he had been humiliated from elementary school on, when he was forced to play on the girls' side in physical education classes.[36] And vio-lent Jewish individuals and groups as well "see the peace process and giving up the occupied territories as humiliating to Jews."[37]

Whether Christian, Jewish, Muslim, Buddhist, Sikh, or devoted to idiosyncratic sects, religious extremists and fanatics resort to violence in opposition to the overbear-ing, permissive, change-oriented, postmodern world that spreads secular values and in the process threatens and even destroys their way of life. This explains why the imme-diate objectives of these groups and individuals are political. They choose the path of violence in efforts to regain control of their environment and remake the world around them according to their vision in order to achieve their ultimate religious ideal—eventually. In the process, though, they distance themselves from the mainstream tenets of their respective religions. Even when aware that they are out of step with the mainstream of their faiths, religious extremists in various parts of the world tend to insist that "their groups are in fact revivals of the original forms of their traditions."[38] Unfortunately, the targets of religious terrorism are often unable or unwilling to distinguish between nonviolent mainstream religions and their teachings on the one hand and the "new religions" of extremist leaders that justify terrorism in the name of God. As a result, a whole religion may be stereotyped by the image of its most extreme fringe groups.

Well before the 9/11 attacks, terrorism scholar Magnus Ranstorp recognized the causes and dangers of the "virtual explosion of religious terrorism in recent times" when he stated:

> The uncertainty and unpredictability in the present environment as the world searches for a new world order, amidst an increasingly complex global environment with ethnic and nationalist conflicts, provides many religious terrorist groups with the opportunity and ammunition to shape history according to their divine duty, cause, and mandate while it indicates to others that the end of the time itself is near.[39]

This assessment sums up the setting that is conducive to the proliferation of international religious terrorism and the domestic variety as well. Indeed, many seemingly domestic religious terrorists—for example, adherents of Christian Identity in the United States or Al Qaeda-like groups in Arab countries (e.g., Hezbollah)—are driven by grievances that transcend the domestic context. Ironically, in many instances, the same religious extremists who resent what they perceive as the negative effects of globalization, exploit vehicles of globalization, most of all global communication and transnational arms and drug trafficking, to finance their organizations and terrorist operations.

However, in spite of the long history of terrorism in all religious settings, among the adherents of the same and different religions, and in spite of the numerous similarities between these violent fanatics, the self-proclaimed warriors in the name of Islam pose at the present time the greatest threat because of the large number of individuals, cells, organizations, and even networks devoted to the so-called jihadi cause. The following section therefore deals exclusively with the theoretical underpinnings of the jihadi movement, its justification of violence, and the impact of jihadi ideology on contemporary terrorists' holy war against infidels in their own and other religions.

The Jihadi Movement and Political Violence

Shortly before the 2008 presidential election, during an appearance on NBC-TV's *Meet the Press* program, former Secretary of State Colin Powell criticized opponents of Senator Barack Obama who claimed that he was a Muslim. The retired general added, "What if he was? Is there something wrong with being a Muslim in this country? The answer is no, that's not America. Is there something wrong with some 7-year-old Muslim American kid believing that he or she could be president?"[40] This was a much-needed civics lesson on tolerance and on the fundamental value of equality in a nation of immigrants. As Mark Juergensmeyer noted, "Most Muslims regard Islam as a religion of peace, and Christians and Jews regard their own religion in the same way."[41]

Yet, it is indisputable that since the mid-1990s, and even more so since the attacks of September 11, 2001, the most serious terrorist threat has been closely tied to the most extreme strain of Muslim revivalism. After 9/11, there was a sudden surge of interest in Islam in the United States and elsewhere in the West. University courses on Islam were oversubscribed and books on the subject were written and bought in unprecedented numbers. But more Americans were not interested and remained clueless.

In 2006, Jeff Stein, the national security editor at *Congressional Quarterly*, concluded his series of interviews with Washington's counterterrorism officials in Congress, the FBI, and other agencies with the question, "Do you know the difference between a Sunni and a Shiite?" He was not looking for theological explanations, but rather some basic knowledge about the rivalries between the two groupings and their political strengths and differences in Iraq and other settings. As he reported that "most American officials I've interviewed don't have a clue. That includes not just intelligence and law enforcement officials, but also members of Congress who have important roles overseeing our spy agencies. How can they do their jobs without knowing the basics?"[42] One would assume that none of these clueless counterterrorism experts knew any details about the ideology of those they fought in the "war against terror." The following section explains the various constituent groups within the overall Muslim population and, in particular, the religiopolitical underpinnings of the ideas that fuel the violent mission of Al Qaeda Central's leaders as well as like-minded groups and individuals.

Muslims

Of the about 1.3 billion Muslims around the world, 85% are Sunnis and the rest Shias or Shi'ites. They all follow the teachings of the Prophet Muhammad and the Qu'ran. The two branches of Islam split after Muhammad's death, and to this day Sunnis believe that the most competent among his companions were rightly succeeding him, whereas Shias believe that Muhammad's descendants were his spiritual heirs, with his son-in-law Ali first in line. Vali Nasr has explained that the Sunni–Shia division "somewhat parallels the Protestant-Catholic difference in Western Christianity."[43] In the post–9/11 era, there is particularly in the West a notion that Islam is the problem, that Islam encourages violence. But John Esposito cautioned that, "[i]n discussing political Islam, it is important to distinguish between mainstream and extremist movements. The former participate within the political system, whereas the latter engage in terrorism in the name of Islam."[44] The vast majority of Muslims do not agree with their extremist and violent brethren, especially not when the religious fanatics harm women, children, and old people or attack fellow Muslims and harm Muslim interests.

Islamists

Within the Muslim population at large, Islamists, who strive for the establishment or strengthening of the Islamic state on the basis of Islamic law, constitute the next largest component on both the Sunni and Shia sides. Fueled by a strong religious revival since the 1960s and growing dissatisfaction with their authoritarian, pro-Western governments, religion, mosques, and mullahs became a rallying point when there was no space allowed for any other. The use of the mosque-mullah network was critical in the Iranian revolution, as have been private (nongovernmental) mosques and their imams in Egypt and many other countries.[45]

Most Islamists support peaceful change, but a growing minority believes that violence will advance their cause. The oldest and most influential Islamist movement is the transnational Muslim Brotherhood that was founded in Egypt in 1928 by Hassan al-Banna in opposition to the British-backed monarchy. In the mid-twentieth century, it spread throughout the Arab world and took root in countries such as Algeria, Libya, the Palestinian territories, Sudan, Syria, and Tunis. Officially, the Brotherhood has claimed to oppose violence but it makes an exception for Palestinians in their fight against Israelis. In reality, however, the Muslim Brotherhood in Egypt and affiliates elsewhere have resorted to terrorist means in various settings and situations. As the 9/11 Commission Report noted, "In some countries, its [the Brotherhood's] oppositional role is nonviolent; in others, especially Egypt, it has alternated between violent and nonviolent struggle with the regime."[46] In some instances, the most violent elements formed their own units within the Brotherhood; in other cases, they established separate and more extremist groups.

Salafis and Wahhabis

The Salafi movement within the larger Muslim population comprises the most puritanical form of Sunni Islam and promotes the return to the original teachings of the Prophet Muhammad and his companions. Some observers have compared this school of thought to the seventeenth-century Puritan movements in England and America. Salafis believe that the Qu'ran and the Prophet Muhammad's practices (Hadith), not the later interpretations of these sources by Islamic scholars, are the most authentic guidelines for the devout Muslim. Like other puritanical movements, Salafis believe that the end of Islam's golden age, when Muslim rule extended into Europe, was caused by their own "rulers and people who turned away from the true path of their religion, thereby leaving Islam vulnerable to encroaching foreign powers eager to steal their land, wealth, and even souls."[47] Afghanistan under the rule of the Taliban movement reflected best what the Salafi school of thought envisions as the societal ideal.

The most influential Salafis are Saudi clerics who preach an old version of Salafism called Wahhabism, an eighteenth-century movement named after its founder, Muhammad bin Abd al Wahhab. Since the modern kingdom of Saudi Arabia was established in 1932, Wahhabi clerics have enjoyed a great deal of influence on all aspects of their country's religious, political, social, and cultural realities. The symbiotic relationship between Saudi rulers and Wahhabi leaders spread religious puritanism and intolerance throughout the kingdom, and it also bought the ruling House of Saud protection from violent upheaval arising from Salafi opposition to westernized members of the royal family and to the influence of the West on the Saudi Arabian peninsula. This arrangement came with a price tag: The Saudi government and wealthy Saudis financed the spread of Wahhabi militancy throughout the Middle East as well as in other parts of the world, including Europe and the United States. In more recent times, moreover, Saudi Arabia has produced growing numbers of terrorists. Fifteen of the nineteen 9/11 terrorists were citizens of Saudi Arabia. And records of foreign nationals who entered Iraq between August 2006 and August 2007 to fight within the Islamic State of Iraq, an Al Qaeda–affiliated group, revealed that of the 595 entries that listed the nationality of these jihadis, 41% were of Saudi Arabian origin.[48]

Jihadis

Although most Salafis do not engage in violence and do not support the terrorist acts of fellow Salafis, today's most dangerous and by far most numerous terrorist groups and cells are part of the Salafi movement. Marc Sageman speaks of the "global Salafi jihad" as a revivalist movement "stretching from Morocco to the Philippines, eliminating present national boundaries." He characterizes Al Qaeda as the "vanguard" of the jihadi movement.[49] In another expert's view,

> Osama bin Laden and Al-Qaeda symbolize a global jihad, a network of extremist groups threatening Muslim countries and the West, whose roots have proved deeper and more pervasive than most had anticipated. This new global threat, which emerged from the jihad against the Soviet Union's occupation of Afghanistan, has exploded across the Muslim world from Central, South, and Southeast Asia to Europe and America.[50]

In terms of personnel, organization, and tactics, the origins of the global jihadi movement can indeed be traced back to the Arab *mujaheedins'* fight against Soviet invaders and against Afghan government troops in the 1980s, but the well-developed ideology of militant jihad that is at the core of the theoretical underpinnings, teachings, and actions of Al Qaeda and others in the contemporary jihadi movement has much deeper roots.

Jihadi Ideology

Utilizing a "citation analysis" of texts available in print and on jihadi web sites to identify the most influential theorists in the movement and differentiating between leading medieval and modern radical thinkers, two scholars found that in the first category the works by Ibn Taymiyya are most popular among contemporary jihadis, whereas Sayyid Qutb is most influential among modern thinkers in this respect.[51]

The texts authored by Taymiyya, a jurist living in the thirteenth and fourteenth centuries, offer a universal rationale for fighting foreign invaders—at his time a call to fight against the Mongols or Tartars and today a perfect justification of violent jihad against Westerners that are present and/or have interests in the Muslim world. Taymiyya held that fighting invaders was not only the right but the duty of every devoted Muslim. He wrote furthermore that Mogul rulers who had converted to Islam were no real Muslims and that they and any other Muslim group not fully observing Islamic law must be defeated—a license to fight a holy war against Muslim rulers and regimes that violate the tenets of puritan Islam.

As for modern jihadi theorists calling for jihad against non-Muslims and the overthrow of local apostate regimes, the dominant ideologue remains to this day the late Egyptian Sayyid Qutb, perhaps the last of the influential laypersons in the jihadi movement as compared to trained Islamic and jihadi theological experts that are dominant today. The turning point in Qutb's life was his two-year stay in the United States in the late 1940s, during which he began his metamorphosis from admirer of America and the West to jihadi revolutionary. Rejecting what he perceived as the moral decadence and materialism of Western societies, he joined the Muslim Brotherhood upon his return to Egypt, rose to be the organization's leading ideologue, and eventually clashed with the government. Allegedly involved in a plot to assassinate Egyptian president Gamal Abdel Nasser, Qutb was imprisoned and tortured but later allowed to write. In his most influential work, "Milestones," a manifesto of revolutionary religiopolitical Islam, Qutb

The Meaning of Jihad

When Osama bin Laden and four other leaders of jihadi groups in Egypt, Pakistan, and Bangladesh issued a *fatwa*, or religious edict, in February 1998, it was titled "The World Islamic Front for *Jihad* against the Jews and Crusaders." In the text, bin Laden explained that "[r]eligious scholars throughout Islamic history have agreed that *jihad* is an individual duty when an enemy attacks Muslim countries. . . . After faith, there is no greater duty than fighting an enemy who is corrupting religion and the world."[52] Bin Laden, other Al Qaeda leaders, and their followers, supporters, and sympathizers around the globe use the term *jihad* frequently to describe their terrorist mission and deeds. Not surprisingly, the term has negative connotations in the West.

The literal meaning of *jihad* is striving or struggling in the path of God and the Prophet Muhammad. And there is a distinction between the *greater jihad*, as personal spiritual and moral struggle, and the *lesser jihad*, as a violent struggle for the good of Islam. This distinction goes back to Muhammad, who reportedly said, "We return from the lesser jihad [warfare] to the greater jihad [the personal struggle to live a moral life]."[53] As for the more controversial of the two, Sageman explains,

> The lesser jihad is the violent struggle for Islam. Traditional Islamic jurispru-
> dence saw jihad as an obligation in a world divided into the land of Islam (dar
> al-Islam) and the land of conflict (dar ak-harb). The Muslim community, the
> umma, was required to engage in a jihad to expand dar al-Islam throughout the
> world so that all humankind could benefit from living within a just political
> social order. One school of interpretation diluted this belligerence by introducing
> the notion of land treaty (dar al-suhl), which had concluded a truce with dar-al-
> Islam and was not subject to jihad.[54]

When it comes to the belligerent or lesser jihad, there is another distinction between defensive and offensive jihad—the first against intruders in Muslim territory, such as the mujahideens' fight against Soviet invaders of Afghanistan or against American and other Western invaders of Iraq; the second to conquer non-Muslim land and convert infidels.

declared that both Marxism and the West's model of democracy and capitalism had failed and that the world was harmed most of all by the loss of moral values. It was the responsibility of true Muslims to bring the world back onto the right path; this, however, was only possibly after self-purification within the Muslim community. For Qutb, the world consisted of two camps: (1) Islam and (2) *jihiliyya*, the part characterized by barbarism, decadence, and unbelief—a state that existed in the world before the Prophet Muhammad delivered his divine message. According to Qutb, the choice is between those two camps—between the good and the evil, God and Satan. For him, far more people, Muslims included, are on the side of *jihiliyya* and therefore all Muslims have the duty to "take up arms in this fight. Any Muslim who rejects his ideas is just one more nonbeliever worthy of destruction."[55] Qutb wrote of the need "to initiate the movement of Islamic revival in some Muslim country" that would set "an example in order to fashion an example that will eventually lead Islam to its destiny of world domination."[56] For this to happen, he hoped for a vanguard that would translate his ideas into reality.

These ideas came to guide contemporary jihadi terrorists, especially the leading strata—Qutb's vanguard. Egyptian Ayman al-Zawahiri, who later rose to become Al-Qaeda's second in command, was on the frontline in Qutb's vanguard in that "the same year [1966] that Sayyid Qutb went to the gallows, al-Zawahiri helped form an underground cell devoted to overthrow the government and establish an Islamic state. He was fifteen years old."[57] Osama bin Laden, too, came to embrace the tenets of Qutb's extremist teachings, as did other leaders and followers in the global jihadi network. Indeed, Qutb's younger brother and keeper of his legacy was reportedly one of bin Laden's advisors.[58]

Excerpts from Communications by Osama bin Laden and Ayman al-Zawahiri

From bin Laden's post–9/11 message, Oct. 7, 2001

God has struck America at its Achilles heel and destroyed its greatest buildings, praise and blessings to Him. America has been filled with terror from north to south and from east to west, praise and blessings to God. What America is tasting today is but a fraction of what we have tasted for decades. . . . So when God Almighty granted success to one of the vanguard groups of Islam, He opened the way for them to destroy America utterly. I pray to God Almighty to lift them up to the highest Paradise.

From bin Laden's remarks during interview with Al-Jazeera, Oct. 21, 2001

I say that the battle isn't between the al-Qaeda organization and the global Crusaders. Rather, the battle is between Muslims—the people of Islam—and the global Crusaders. . . . These young men that have sacrificed themselves in New York and Washington, these are the ones that speak the truth about the conscience of our *umna*, they are its living conscience, which sees that it is imperative to take revenge against the evildoers and transgressors and criminals and terrorists, who terrorize the true believers. So, not all terrorism is restrained or ill-advised. There is terrorism that is ill-advised and there is terrorism that is a good act. . . . So, America and Israel practice ill-advised terrorism, and we practice good terrorism, because it deters those from killing our children in Palestine and other places.

From a taped bin Laden message, addressed to the American people, aired by Al-Jazeera, January 19, 2006

You have tried to prevent us from leading a dignified life, but you will not be able to prevent us from a dignified death. Failing to carry out jihad, which is called for in our religion, is a sin. The best death to us is under the shadows of swords. Don't let your strength and modern arms fool you. They win a few battles but lose the war. Patience and steadfastness are much better. We were patient in fighting the Soviet Union with simple weapons for 10 years and we bled their economy and now they are nothing. In that there is a lesson for you.

From an al-Zawahiri videotape and remarks addressed to President-elect Barack Obama, November 19, 2008

As for the crimes of America which await you [President-elect Obama], it appears that you continue to be captive to the same criminal American mentality towards the world and towards the Muslims. The Muslim Ummah received with extreme bitterness your hypocritical statements to and stances towards Israel, which confirmed to the Ummah that you have chosen a stance of hostility to Islam and Muslims. . . . you have climbed the rungs of the presidency to take over the leadership of the greatest criminal force in the history of mankind and the leadership of the most violent Crusade ever against the Muslims. And in you and in Colin Powell, [Condoleezza] Rice and your likes, the words of Malcolm X (may Allah have mercy on him) concerning "House Negroes" are confirmed.

You also must appreciate, as you take over the presidency of America during its Crusade against Islam and Muslims, that you are neither facing individuals nor organizations, but are facing a Jihadi awakening and renaissance which is shaking the pillars of the entire Islamic world; and this is the fact which you and your government and country refuse to recognize and pretend not to see.[59]

Although there are dozens of modern and premodern theorists who have contributed or added to one or the other aspect of jihadi ideology, Qutb has remained for the time being the most influential one. Important here is that all influential theorists are hardliners and are in favor of violence. According to Sageman, "Salafi ideology determines its [the jihadi movement's] mission, sets its goals, and guides its tactics."[60] Even the training of self-described holy warriors and martyrs in the service of jihad is guided by this extreme ideology. After studying the doctrines for terrorist training as articulated by leading theorists, Brynjar Lia concluded,

> When preparing recruits for waging a terrorist campaign or participating in a protracted guerilla war, the jihadi theorists unanimously agreed that ideological indoctrination and spiritual preparation should take precedence over physical and military training. In order to produce the kind of battle-hardened, martyrdom-seeking fighters that have filled the ranks of jihadi groups of the past, the jihadi theorists devote extraordinary attention to spiritual training.[61]

Not only recruits are the targets of the missionary fanaticism that permeates the jihadi movement. Wherever these extremists get a foothold, they force their convictions onto the population. Reporting from Iraq in the summer of 2008, Alissa J. Rubin wrote,

> Diyala residents and officials say [that] militants from Al Qaeda in Mesopotamia have worked to instill their radical Islamist vision in the population. Almost immediately

after moving in four years ago, they began holding religion classes for men and women. "Even in Baquba, my niece went to some; she was shaken," said Shamaa Abad al-Kader, the headmistress of a school for girls in Muqdadiya who also serves on Diyala's provincial council. "They gathered people in the villages; they brought women into Baquba and gave them lectures on how to behave," Ms. Kader said. "These Al Qaeda men were going into the schools, into the mosques and they forced people to listen to them. My niece said the man who came to her school had a long beard and a sword with him."[62]

In Afghanistan, jihadis of the resurging Taliban used violence to force fellow Afghans to live according to their extremist Salafi convictions, as they had during their fundamentalist movement's five-year reign. During that period, girls were not allowed to get an education, but this changed after the Taliban was toppled in the wake of the post–9/11 invasion by a U.S.-led coalition force. When the Taliban regained strength in former strongholds like Kandahar, teachers and female students became the particular targets of brutal and often lethal attacks. In one incident, Taliban militants doused a group of school girls and their teachers with acid, several of whom were hospitalized with burnt faces. When arrested, the men confessed that "a high-ranking member of the Taliban had paid the militants 100,000 Pakistani rupees ($1,275) for each of the girls they managed to burn."[63] The Kabul government called the attack "un-Islamic," but for Taliban jihadis this sort of terrorism was part of their holy fight to resurrect Afghan as model of pure Salafi society.

To sum up, terrorism in the name of God has been practiced by the adherents of all major religions and by pseudoreligious sects. Today, however, jihadis commit far more and far more lethal terrorist attacks and pose by far the greatest threat inside and outside the Muslim world.

Notes

1. Mark Sedgwick, "Al-Qaeda and the Nature of Religious Terrorism," *Terrorism and Political Violence* 16:4 (Winter 2004): 808.
2. Magnus Ranstorp, "Terrorism in the Name of Religion." Working paper available from Columbia International Affairs Online http://www.ciaonet.org.arugula.cc.columbia.edu:2048/wps/ram01/index.html.
3. "Anti-Abortion Killer Executed." CBS News, September 3, 2003, http://www.cbsnews.com/stories/2003/09/04/national/main571515.shtml.
4. Excerpts are from Paul Hill, "Defending the Defenseless," http://www.armyofgod.com/PHill_ShortShot.html.
5. "Anti-Abortion Killer Executed."
6. Ibid.
7. The text of bin Laden's 1998 *fatwa* is available on several Internet sites; the excerpts chosen were taken from Bruce Lawrence, ed., *Messages to the World: The Statements of Osama bin Laden* (London: Verso, 2005).
8. The so-called "The Last Night" letter was found in Mohammed Atta's luggage after the 9/11 attacks. See http://intelfiles.egoplex.com/911project/atta-last-night.pdf.
9. Lawrence, 107, 115.
10. Ehud Sprinzak, "Extremism and Violence in Israel: The Crisis of Messianic Politics." *Annals of the American Academy of Political and Social Science* 555 (January 1998): 123.
11. Ibid., 120.
12. Mark Juergensmeyer, *Terror in the Mind of God: The Global Rise of Religious Violence* (Berkeley: University of California Press, 2001), 57.
13. Ibid., 54.

14. Sprinzak, 123.
15. Quote is from a report by ABC News on *World News Sunday*, February 27, 1994.
16. Ibid.
17. Albert Bandura, "Mechanisms of Moral Disengagement," in Walter Reich, ed., *Origins of Terrorism: Psychologies, Ideologies, Theologies, States of Mind* (New York: Cambridge University Press, 1990), 164.
18. Ibid., 174, 175.
19. These terms are used by Juergensmeyer, chs. 8 and 9.
20. Ibid., 182–83.
21. Jessica Stern, *Terror in the Name of God: Why Religious Militants Kill* (New York: HarperCollins, 2003), 167.
22. Ibid.
23. Audrey Kurth Cronin, "Behind the Curve: Globalization and International Terrorism," *International Security* 27:3 (Winter 2002/3): 42.
24. Stern, xxv.
25. Ibid.
26. According to Juergensmeyer, 6.
27. http://www.tkb.org/Category.jsp?catID=10.
28. These statistics are drawn from the "MIPT Knowledge Base" of the National Memorial Institute for the Prevention of Terrorism, http://www.tkb.org/Home.jsp.
29. Sedgwick, 797.
30. Ibid.
31. Ibid., 805.
32. Juergensmeyer, 221.
33. Stern, xix.
34. This is what Terry Noble, a leader in a Christian Identity organization, told Mark Juergensmeyer. See Juergensmeyer, 193.
35. Ibid., xviii.
36. Stern, 286.
37. Stern, 285.
38. Juergensmeyer, 222.
39. Ranstorp, 8.
40. Colin Powell made this statement as guest of the NBC News program *Meet the Press* on October 19, 2008.
41. Mark Juergensmeyer, "Religion as a Cause of Terrorism," in Louise Richardson, ed., *The Roots of Terrorism* (New York: Routledge, 2006), 134.
42. Jeff Stein, "Can you tell a Sunni from a Shiite?" *New York Times*, October 17, 2006, available at: http:// www.nytimes.com/2006/10/17/opinion/17stein.html, (accessed December 6, 2008).
43. Vali Nasr, *The Shia Revival: How Conflicts within Islam Will Shape the Future* (New York: Norton, 2006), 34.
44. John L. Esposito, "Terrorism and the Rise of Political Islam," in Richardson, ed., *The Roots of Terrorism*, 146.
45. Ibid., 147.
46. *The 9/11 Commission Report* (New York: W.W. Norton, 2004), 466, footnote 11.
47. Ibid, 50.
48. "Al-Qa'ida's Foreign Fighters in Iraq." Harmony Project, Combating Terrorism Center at West Point, available at: http://ctc.usma.edu/harmony/pdf/CTCForeignFighter.19.Dec07.pdf.
49. Marc Sageman, *Understanding Terror Networks* (Philadelphia: University of Pennsylvania Press, 2004), 1.
50. Esposito, "Terrorism and the Rise of Political Islam," 145.
51. William McCants and Jarret Brachman, "Militant Ideology Atlas." Executive Report compiled and published by the "Combating Terrorism Center" at West Point.
52. Bruce Lawrence, ed., *Messages to the World: The Statements of Osama bin Laden* (London: Verso, 2005), 60–61.
53. This quote is from Esposito, 149.
54. Sageman, 2.

55. 9/11 Commission Report, 51.

56. Lawrence Wright, *The Looming Tower: Al Qaeda and the Road to 9/11* (New York: Knopf, 2006), 31.

57. Ibid, 37.

58. According to Youssef Aboul-Enein, "Sheik Abdel-Fatahl Al-Khalidi Revitalizes Sayid Qutb." West Point: The Combating Terrorism Center United States Military Academy.

59. Excerpts are from Lawrence, ed., *Messages to the World*; Fox News, http://www.foxnews.com/story/0,2933,454624,00.html, and Information Clearing House, http://www.informationclearinghouse.info/article11615.htm (accessed December 5, 2008).

60. Sageman, 1.

61. Brynjar Lia, "Doctrines for Jihadi Terrorist Training," *Terrorism and Political Violence* 20 (4) (October–December 2008): 537.

62. Alissa J. Rubin, "Despair Drives Suicide Attacks by Iraqi Women," *New York Times*, July 5, 2008. See http://www.nytimes.com/2008/07/05/world/middleeast/05diyala.html?sq=despair%20drives%20suicide%20attacks%20by%20Iraqi%20Women&st=cse&scp=1&pagewanted=print.

63. Abdul Waheed Waffa, "10 Arrested for Afghan Acid Attack," *New York Times*, November 25, 2008. Available at: http://www.nytimes.com/2008/11/26/world/asia/26afghan.html?scp=6&sq=taliban%20and%20school%20girls&st=cse (accessed November 25, 2008).

CHAPTER 6

The Making of Terrorists: Causes, Conditions, Influences

DURING A UNITED NATIONS CONFERENCE ON POVERTY IN MARCH 2002, President George W. Bush said that the United States was ready to challenge "the poverty and hopelessness and lack of education and failed governments that too often allow conditions that terrorists can seize and try to turn to their advantage."[1] A few months later, however, in an interview with Radio Free Europe/Radio Liberty, the president suggested otherwise when he stated that there was no direct link between poverty and terrorism. "Poverty is a tool for recruitment amongst these global terrorists," Bush said. "It's a way for them to recruit—perhaps. But poverty doesn't cause killers to exist, and it's an important distinction to make."[2] No doubt, the president had the kind of terrorism in mind that had led to the attacks on 9/11, but in expressing different assessments of the roots of terrorism, he reflected the different viewpoints in the long-running expert debate on this issue. There is no doubt that terrorism cannot be understood without exploring the real and perceived grievances of groups and individuals who resort to political violence. Grievances of this nature are of a domestic or international nature—or both. But although the same or similar conditions breed terrorists in some countries and not in others, scholars have put forth a multitude of explanations.

The idea that socioeconomic conditions, such as poverty, lack of education, and high unemployment, provide fertile ground for terrorism predates the rise of international terrorism in the last thirty-five years or so and, more importantly, the recent focus on the roots of terrorism in Arab and Muslim countries. Based on his research

Terrorism and Gender: Female Terrorists Are No Exceptions

Contrary to common wisdom, women have always played leading and supporting roles in many terrorist organizations. Ulrike Meinhof (left) was a co-founder of the German Baader-Meinhof terrorist group, also known as the Red Army Faction. Fusako Shigenobu (right) founded the Japanese Red Army and was involved in a number of international terrorist incidents in the 1970s. Pretty Leila Khaled (center), who participated in hijackings of the Popular Front for the Liberation of Palestine more than thirty years ago, was known as terrorism's glamour girl.

examining the lynching of black Americans in the nineteenth and twentieth centuries by whites and the economic conditions over a long period of time, Arthur Raper concluded that the number of lynching attacks peaked in times of economic downturns and subsided in years of economic improvement.[3] But using more advanced economic indicators, other researchers did not find a relationship between the ups and downs in lynching incidents and economic conditions.[4] For example, there was no surge in these attacks during the Great Depression of the 1930s.

At first sight, the argument that poverty breeds terrorism also carries little weight with respect to experiences in the West from the late 1960s through the 1980s, when some of the world's richest countries (e.g., Germany, Italy, France, Belgium, and the United States) produced a relatively large number of very active terrorist groups of the left-wing variety. The founders, leaders, and rank-and-file members of the most prominent terrorist organizations during that period, from the Italian Red Brigades to the German Red Army Faction and the French Direct Action, came typically from middle-class or upper-middle-class families and had studied at universities. The same was true for left-wing terrorists in the United States; many of them had finished college and earned professional degrees (medicine, law, teaching, social work, and so on). But, as Brent Smith and Kathryn Morgan found in their research, in the last decades of the twentieth century, right-wing terrorists in the United States had very different demographic characteristics than their left-wing counterparts: One-third of the right-wingers had not graduated from high school, only about 12% had a college degree, and a large number of them were "unemployed or impoverished self-employed workers."[5] In other words, the same society with the same macro socioeconomic conditions produced one type of terrorist that came from the well-to-do segment of society and another type from the lower socioeconomic strata.

Regardless of such findings, the idea that terrorism is the result of "poverty, desperation, and resentment" in less developed countries around the globe has survived as a plausible explanation in the search for the causes of group-based political violence.[6] However, statistical evidence tells another story. As Walter Laqueur has pointed out, "In the forty-nine countries currently designated by the United Nations as the least developed, hardly any terrorist activity occurs."[7] Other recent studies have contradicted the economic deprivation thesis with respect to terrorism and terrorists in the Middle East. Claude Berrebi examined a wealth of data on individual terrorists in the West Bank and Gaza, on the general population in those areas, and on the economic conditions over time. He concluded,

> Both higher standards of living and higher levels of education are positively associated with participation in Hamas or PIJ [Palestinian Islamic Jihad]. With regard to the societal economic condition, I could not find a sustainable link between terrorism and poverty and education, and I interpret this to mean that there is either no link or a very weak indirect link.[8]

Research by Alan B. Krueger and Jitka Maleckova came to similar conclusions with respect to the Lebanese Hezbollah; their evidence suggests "that having a higher living standard above the poverty line or a secondary school or higher education is *positively* associated with participation in Hezbollah."[9] The same research also found "that Israeli Jewish settlers who attacked Palestinians in the West Bank in the early 1980s were overwhelmingly from high-paying occupations."[10] Like Berrebi, Krueger and Maleckova found no evidence for a direct causal relationship between poverty and education on the one hand and participation in or support of terrorism on the other.

Focusing on militants in the Lebanese Hezbollah organization who had already undertaken or were willing to carry out suicide missions, one researcher found that most of these terrorists or would-be terrorists "are from poor families" and "geoculturally immobile."[11] But in the absence of in-depth comparisons between the living standard of the population at large and actual or would-be suicide bombers, the meaning of "poor" in this context is not quite clear. Perhaps Berrebi's research explains the different findings: With respect to the Palestinian groups he studied, Berrebi found that suicide bombers came from higher economic circumstances and had a higher education than the population at large but came "from lower socio-economic groups when compared to other, non-suicidal, terrorists."[12] Based on his empirical data analysis, James A. Piazza did not find evidence for what he calls the "rooted-in-poverty thesis" at all.[13]

These findings have profound implications for policy-makers in their fight to attack the roots of terrorism. If indeed economic and educational conditions do not cause terrorism, efforts to improve economic conditions, especially individual incomes, living conditions, health care, and educational opportunities, would not decrease the number of terrorists and their supporters or do away with terrorism altogether. But so far, policies continue to be guided in many instances by the assumption that aid to improve the economic circumstances of countries or regions is part of prudent counterterrorism strategy. Thus, in the spring of 2009, when the Taliban ally of Al Qaeda gained territorial control in Pakistan and intensified its violence in both Pakistan and Afghanistan, the Obama administration pushed for a massive U.S. aid package that in part aimed at financing school, hospital, and road projects in the Taliban stronghold Swat Valley and similarly contested regions in Pakistan.

It has been argued that changes in the content of education would be a more promising way to go. In her examination of textbooks, teachers' guides, and other official material used in schools on the West Bank and in Gaza, Daphne Burdman found that

> *Palestinian children are urged to violent actions against Israelis even when it is likely that they will be injured or die. They are encouraged to desire rather than fear the circumstances, because they will find a place in Paradise with Allah. . . . .*[14]

Like Burdman, Berrebi has suggested that efforts to reduce terrorism should focus on changes in the curriculum for children on the West Bank and in Gaza. Similar issues have arisen with respect to other countries and regions. For example, in the aftermath of 9/11, there were reports about and criticism of schools and textbooks in Saudi Arabia that encouraged intolerance and hate against non-Muslims. Similar indoctrination of the young was reportedly practiced in Islamic schools in North America and other parts of the world that received financial support from Saudi Arabia. Students of an Islamic school in northern Virginia told a reporter that some of their teachers "teach students that whatever is kuffar [non-Muslim], it is okay to hurt or steal from that person."[15]

But while propaganda of hate might well condition its receivers to support and even commit political violence, it is far from clear, however, whether removing hateful texts and indoctrination from schools would reduce terrorism significantly or eradicate it. After all, terrorism has flourished in all kinds of environments—in democratic and nondemocratic societies, in settings where young people were and were not indoctrinated into committing violence. Some scholars, among them Ted Gurr, consider liberal democracies less vulnerable to political violence than authoritarian systems because dissent and conflict can be brought into the legitimate political process. Indeed, Gurr's research indicates that repressive regimes have a higher incidence of political violence than liberal democratic settings.[16] But after analyzing global data on terrorist incidents from 1980 through 1987 with respect to the sites of terrorist strikes and the nationality of attackers and victims, William Eubank and Leonard Weinberg concluded that during the 1980s "terrorist violence was far more common in stable democracies than in autocratic settings" and that the perpetrators and the victims of terrorism were more likely to be the citizens of stable democracies than of less stable or partial democracies and of countries with limited authoritarianism or absolutism.[17]

How can one explain such contradictory findings? The most plausible explanations point to the fact that the two research projects covered different time periods and, more importantly, focused in the first case on domestic terrorism data and in the second case on international terrorism data. Both explanations seem reasonable. Citizens who live in countries with repressive regimes have more reasons to use violence against the ruling clique, but in the absence of civil liberties, it is likely that the authorities detect and crush opposition groups that have committed, or plan to commit, terrorism. If terrorist acts do occur in closed societies, the targeted governments have the means to prevent, curb, or spin the news coverage of such events. Democracies offer citizens opportunities to participate in the decision-making process, but when groups or individuals conclude that their grievances are not adequately addressed, they may be more inclined to resort to violence than their counterparts under authoritarian rule—if only because the free press will spread their "propaganda of the deed."

However, according to Piazza's research there are also variables that transcend the peculiarities of political systems and serve as important predictors of terrorism, namely, "population [size, historical development], ethno-religious diversity, increased state repression and, most significantly, the structure of party politics."[18]

All of this leads to the conclusion that terrorists emerge in poor and in rich countries, in democratic and in authoritarian states, in stable and in nonstable countries, and in societies whose textbooks teach or do not teach hate of other ideological, religious or ethnic groups.

In the absence of a universal model that identifies the conditions that breed group-based political violence and terrorists, experts in the field have looked beyond the environmental conditions for other explanations. If, under the same conditions, some people become terrorists while others do not, it is not far-fetched to suspect that an individual's traits and psychological makeup affect, or even determine, whether he or she selects or rejects the terrorist path. Terrorism scholars are not of one mind in this respect, but have proposed different approaches and explanations, among them the following: (1) Terrorists make rational choices, (2) terrorists are guided by personal traits, and (3) terrorists are the products of social interaction.

Terrorism as a Result of Rational Choice

Borrowing from the Prussian military theorist Carl von Clausewitz, who noted that war is the continuation of diplomacy, Gary Sick has suggested that terrorism "is the continuation of politics by other means."[19] While not discounting the possibility that persons with a predisposition to violence and fanatic beliefs are especially drawn to terrorism, Sick emphasizes that terrorism is the result of a deliberate choice made in particular political environments—at least in the early stage of a group's life span. "Their [group members'] choice of terrorism, as opposed to other possible forms of [political] behavior, is a function of the political environment," he writes. For Richard Shultz, too, terrorism "is calculated violence" that is "goal directed" and "employed in pursuit of political objectives."[20] In her exploration of terrorism as a logical choice, Martha Crenshaw concurs when she states that

> Terrorism is likely to be a reasonably informed choice among available alternatives, some tried unsuccessfully.[21]

Thus, the Weathermen group in the United States was formed when its founders concluded that the anti–Vietnam War, antiauthority protests staged by the Students for a Democratic Society did not further their ideological goals. Similarly, the Red Army Faction in Germany emerged as the radical offspring of the Socialist Student Association. The Army of God, and other extreme antiabortion groups that resorted to terrorist methods, emerged and grew when its founders and recruits determined that the mainstream pro-life movement's attempts to work within the legitimate political process to outlaw legalized abortions were in vain.

Based on many years of research, Ehud Sprinzak rejected the notion of terrorists as psychologically challenged types or crazies and concluded, "Terrorism is not the product of mentally deranged persons. Terrorism, and ideological terrorism in particular, is a political phenomenon par excellence and is therefore explicable in political terms."[22] On this count, Christopher Harmon agrees with Sprinzak and discards the notion of terrorist acts as mindless, stating,

> It is mostly on the surface that terrorism appears to be madness, or mindless. Behind the screaming and the blood there lies a controlling purpose, a motive, usually based in politics or something close to it, such as a drive for political or social change inspired by religion.
> The terrorist is not usually insane; he or she is more usually "crazy like a fox."[23]

Richard Rubenstein, too, considers terrorists as quite normal people who turn to violence under certain political circumstances, are "more like us than we ordinarily care to admit," and are "no more or less fanatical than the young men who charged into the Union cannonfire at Gettysburg or those who parachuted behind German lines into France."[24] Along the same lines, Lawrence Freedman concludes,

A psychological profile of a model terrorist cannot be drawn. The personalities are disparate. The context and circumstances within which terrorism, both political and ecclesiastical, has been carried out are diverse in chronology, geography, and motive.[25]

Recognizing that terrorists have "short-term organizational objectives and long-term political objectives," Louise Richardson characterized the more immediate or "secondary motives" as the "Three Rs" for "revenge, renown, and reaction."[26] No doubt, revenge for real or perceived injustice and humiliation, renown in the sense of getting publicity and glory, and reaction, and the wish for reaction and overreaction on the part of their targets, are common motives of all kinds of terrorist groups. In deciding to pursue the goals that Richardson calls the "Three Rs," terrorists presumably make some rational considerations.

The notion that terrorism is political in nature, goal oriented, and the result of rational or logical choices among several alternatives fits into the instrumental paradigm that recognizes terrorism as a means to specific political ends, such as removing foreign influence from a country or region, removal of a regime, or national independence.[27]

Terrorism as a Result of Personal Traits

Jerrold Post takes issue with the suggestion that terrorism is the result of rational choices made by the perpetrators of political violence. Instead, he argues that "political terrorists are driven to commit acts of violence as a consequence of psychological forces."[28] Based on his interviews with terrorists as well as memoirs and court records, Post suggests that "people with particular traits and tendencies are drawn disproportionately to terrorist careers."[29] A study of the background of 227 left-wing terrorists, most of them active in the Baader-Meinhof group or Red Army Faction, confirmed the idea that particular experiences and personality traits make some people more prone to become involved with terrorism than others. In the case of German left-wing terrorists, researchers found the following:

No less than 69 percent of the men and 52 percent of the women reportedly had clashes with parents, schools, or employers—33 percent with their parents, 18 percent with employers—or prior records of criminal or juvenile offenses, many of them repeated entries. Although there are no exact population averages or control groups with which to compare, the percentages are so large as to suggest in many cases a conflict-ridden youth aggravated by parental death, divorce, remarriage and other misfortunes of modern society.[30]

Konrad Kellen described this type of background using the example of Hans Joachim Klein, an eventual defector from the Red Army Faction. As a small boy and teenager, Klein was constantly mistreated and beaten by his father. According to Kellen,

When Klein was in his teens, a girlfriend gave him a small chain to wear around his neck; the father ripped the chain off and beat him once again. Suddenly, however, young Klein rebelled and slapped his father's face, expecting to be killed a moment later for his transgression. But the old man treated his son with courtesy and respect from that moment on! The lesson for the younger Klein was probably that force and the infliction of pain can do the trick. . . . Presumably Klein concluded, at some level, that if he could do this to his father, he could do it to the state as well.[31]

Despite the fact that many left-wing German terrorists had troubled backgrounds, Merkl has argued that "every German terrorist could just as well have turned away from terrorism, being a creature endowed with free will; and some did."[32] But what Jeffrey Ross has called individuals' "facilitating traits," such as alienation, depression, or antisocial behavior, may drive persons to join terrorist movements—especially when a particular group setting gives them for the first time in their lives the feeling that they belong, that they count.[33] Randy Borum takes a sensible in-between position by concluding that "[c]ertain life experiences tend to be commonly found among terrorists" and "[h]istories of childhood abuse and trauma appear to be widespread. . . . None of these contribute much to a causal explanation of terrorism, but may be seen as markers of vulnerability, as possible sources of motivation, or as mechanism for acquiring or hardening one's militant ideology."[34]

If one believes that terrorists are steered by their personal traits and a "special psycho-logic [that] is constructed to rationalize acts they are psychologically compelled to commit," as Post suggests, the instrumental paradigm falls on its face: Terrorism is not seen as the means to a particular political end, as a way to further one's political causes; rather, terrorism is the end itself, or, as Post puts it, "Individuals become terrorists in order to join terrorist groups and commit acts of terrorism."[35]

Terrorism as a Result of Social Interaction

In her studies of members of the Italian Red Brigades, Donatella della Porta found that social interaction and social ties, not personal traits, explain why individuals join terrorist groups. Della Porta's research revealed that "in as many as 88 percent of the cases in which the nature of the tie with the recruiter is known, she or he is no stranger; in 44 percent, she or he is a personal friend; and in 20 percent, she or he is a relative."[36] Similarly, a study of Lebanese Shiite terrorists established that they were "recruited by and from the concentric circles of familyship, friendship, or fellowship."[37] That is precisely what Marc Sageman found when he analyzed the personal background of 172 members of the global Salafi jihad movement, including Al Qaeda as its vanguard.[38] There was no evidence that these jihadis were brainwashed and enlisted by distinct recruiting efforts; rather, the key was, according to Sageman,

Social affiliation through friendship, kinship, and discipleship; progressive intensification of beliefs and faith leading to the acceptance of the global Salafi jihad ideology; and formal acceptance to the jihad through the encounter of a link to the jihad.[39]

And then there are terrorist organizations that provide social services in communities that otherwise would not have health care, schools, or security forces. The Lebanese Hezbollah and the Palestinian Hamas are good examples of groups that consist of a community service arm, a political branch, and a terrorist corps.

By coming to the aid of needy people in their communities, these organizations create large reservoirs for the recruitment of terrorists—especially in their religious schools. Potential recruits are often chosen at a very young age and well before they themselves have decided to become a terrorist. Instead, they are groomed for their future role. According to Loretta Napoleoni, "People are not only carefully selected, their background is analyzed minutely, and every single detail is taken into consideration. If a candidate is judged to be suitable, he is indoctrinated, fed a special diet of religion, spiritualism and violence."[40] In the last several years, Western Europe has become an especially fertile breeding ground of new jihadis—young members of the Muslim diaspora who are disillusioned and alienated from the societies they live in. Whether in London or Birmingham, Paris or Marseilles, Berlin or Cologne, and many other communities in the United Kingdom, France, Germany, and neighboring countries, some of these Muslim newcomers are likely to seek out and become part of social networks of fellow Muslims, where they join friends, relatives, or acquaintances. While pointing out that "the history of radical Islamism and the terrorist cells in Western Europe remains to be written," Walter Laqueur is nevertheless certain about one aspect:

The idea that over time a European Islam would develop that was more liberal and open seemed to have been premature at the very least. As a result a new generation grew up who were artificially assimilated and in large part deeply disaffected. Among these sections the preachers of jihad found their followers.[41]

But in his review of relevant research Malise Ruthven found evidence that neither alienation nor the embrace of religious and ideological extremism are the driving forces behind the establishment of terrorist jihadi cells. Instead, "[t]he people who form terror groups have to know and trust one another. In most Muslim societies it is kindship, rather than shared ideological values, that generates relations of trust."[42]

Gender and Terrorism

Following the terrorist drama in a packed Moscow theater in the fall of 2002, one commentator asked, "Who did not feel a deep unease at the sight of the female Chechen terrorists in the Moscow theater before it was stormed, with their eyes peering through the masks of their black burqas, with their Kalashnikovs, and their explosives strapped to their bodies?" Probably expressing the sentiments of many observers, the writer pointed out that terrorism is always disturbing, but that "there's an extra level of disquiet when the terrorists are female."[43] The shock value of terrorism is far greater when perpetrated by women because in such cases a common assumption is that if "women decide to violate all established norms about the sanctity of life, they do so only as a last resort."[44] As a result, when female terrorists, especially suicide terrorists, strike, they get far more media attention than their male counterparts. Moreover, media professionals are far more inclined to explore the motives, the causes of female terrorists than of their male counterparts.[45] This is, of course, precisely what terrorist groups want: mass-mediated debates about their causes and grievances.

Female terrorists are not a recent phenomenon. Although there were in the past and are today more male than female terrorists, both as leaders and as followers, taken together the number of women in these organizations was and is substantial.

According to Christopher Harmon, "More than 30% of international terrorists are women, and females are central to membership rosters and operational roles in nearly all insurgencies."[46] Other estimates range from 20% to 30% for many domestic and international terrorist groups. The membership of some terrorist organizations was and is all male, and a few have been known to have only female members, but most of the groups are composed of both men and women. Typically, far-left terrorist groups have emphasized the recruitment of females, and far-right groups have been much less interested in recruiting women willing to commit violence. As Harmon observed,

> If the presence of women helps to illuminate the recruitment patterns of successful leftist groups, a relative absence of women in the active hard core is a revealing indicator of different recruitment patterns among neo-Nazis and similar rightist militant groups. The latter generally do not seek out and promote women members. That approach, the product of culture and ideology, may be one of the more decisive weaknesses of these groups, which remain stuck on the political margins and are also overwhelmingly male.[47]

Regardless of the far-left/far-right divide in this respect, terrorists in all kinds of countries, regions, and continents and with all kinds of causes have for a long time recognized the advantage of incorporating females into their operations. Karla J. Cunningham has noted,

> Not only have women historically been active in politically violent organizations, the regional and ideological scope of this activity has been equally broad. Women have been operational (e.g., regular) in virtually every region and there are clear trends toward women becoming more fully incorporated into numerous terrorist organizations. Cases from Colombia, Italy, Sri Lanka, Pakistan, Turkey, Iran, Norway, and the United States suggest that women have not only functioned in support capacities, but have also been leaders in organizations, recruitment, and fund-raising, as well as tasked with carrying out the most deadly missions undertaken by terrorist organizations.[48]

Indeed, since the beginning of modern-day terrorism, females were actively involved in political violence—beginning with their roles in the anarchist bombings of nineteenth-century Europe. Women played particularly prominent roles in the post–World War II era—especially among far-left terrorist groups in the United States, Western Europe, Japan, and Latin and Central America. During the 1970s and 1980s, the names of many of these female terrorists became well known along with those of their male comrades. Females strove in other types of groups and in other parts of the world as well. To mention just a few examples of high-profile female terrorists, apart from those in the well-known Baader-Meinhof or Weather Underground types of organizations, Lolita Lebron was a participant in the 1950 terrorist attack in the U.S. House of Representatives by the Puerto Rican separatist group FALN (see Chapter 4); as a member of the Popular Front for the Liberation of Palestine, Leila Khaled participated in hijackings in 1969 and 1970; Kim Hyon Hui was one of the North Korean terrorists responsible for the 1987 bombing of a South Korean airliner that killed all 115 persons on board; and in 1991, a female member of the Tamil Tigers organization in Sri Lanka, known only by the name "Dhanu," assassinated Indian party leader Rajiv Gandhi during one of his election campaign appearances.

In a number of prominent terrorist organizations, women were represented in large numbers as rank-and-file members and also held leadership positions. Thus, the original Red Army Faction in Germany had fifty-one male and thirty-nine female members. Ulrike Meinhof and Horst Mahler formulated the group's ideological program. The successors of the original Baader-Meinhof group had more female than male leaders—ten women and six men. During the life span of the original Red Brigades in Italy, the organization's leadership included twelve men and seven women.[49] When arrested and imprisoned, female terrorists have proven more committed to the terrorist cause and their comrades than their male counterparts. However, while women were very much involved in the violent activities of such groups, it is also true that these organizations did not have a large number of members so that the actual number of women was quite small. According to Cindy Ness, there is no reason "to believe that these groups could have recruited females in substantial numbers given that they lacked broad-based support or the extensive infrastructure necessary to enlarge their operations."[50]

In the early 1980s, Martha Crenshaw noted,

There has been considerable speculation about the prominent position of women in terrorist groups (not prominent in comparison to the number of women in the population at large but in proportion to the number of women active in politics or in leadership roles). It will be interesting to find out if female participation in violence will have an effect on general social roles or on the stereotyping of women.[51]

To what extent the role of women in social, political, and professional settings is affected by female roles in terrorist groups, if at all, is difficult to assess. But stereotypical images and prejudices do enter into some of the arguments put forth in the discussion of the perennial question: Why do women become terrorists? A number of explanations have been advanced—all of them guided by deep-seated cultural gender stereotypes.

For the Sake of Love

Probably the most common view is that women become terrorists to follow their lovers, husbands, or perhaps brothers or male friends into the organization. Others believe that personal tragedies or disappointments drive women into close-knit terrorist groups that give them the sense of belonging and help them forget their troubles. This view "diminishes women's credibility and influence both within and outside organizations," as Karla Cunningham has suggested, and it is widely held by experts and the public. Robin Morgan has argued that women would have rather died than admit the fact that love motivated them to join terrorist groups.[52] In Morgan's view, Ulrike Meinhof, one of the founders and leaders of the RAF, Leila Khaled, the PFLP hijacker, or Shigenobu Fusako, the founder and leader of the Japanese Red Army—all females in terrorist organizations—were and are merely token terrorists and victims of male dominance, power, and coercion. Looking upon terrorism as inherently male, Morgan has described it as "the intersection of violence, eroticism, and what is considered 'masculinity.' "[53]

Recently, female members of white supremacy organizations, such as the Ku Klux Klan, have actually spread the word that most of them joined because of their husbands or boyfriends. According to one longtime female KKK member, a woman who used the pseudonym "Klaliff," "My introduction into the White Pride Movement (WP Movement) was in college where I fell in love with another college student, a man who had been an activist in the WP Movement." She revealed that many women got involved because they had a boyfriend in the Movement. "I cannot speak for all women in the WP Movement," Klaliff wrote, "but I see the men in the WP Movement as manly men with strong ideals and courage."[54] The writer furthermore noted that she married her husband because of "his [WP] beliefs."[55]

Typically, however, both male and female terrorists are inspired and enlisted by relatives, friends, and acquaintances—no gender differences with respect to recruits and recruiters! That is also true, when it comes to recruitment by coercion or, as practiced by the Tamil Tigers, by kidnapping children. The Liberation Tigers of Tamil Eelam kidnap both boys and girls when not enough volunteers join the organization. According to UNICEF, the United Nations Children's Fund, "5,666 children were abducted between the cease fire in 2002 [between the Sri Lankan government and the Tigers], when many child soldiers were released, and July [2006], although UNICEF believes only about a third of abductions are reported."[56] Parents shy away from alerting the authorities because they are singled out for revenge attacks. While the Tigers are responsible for most of such kidnappings, the breakaway Karuna faction that allied itself with the government abducts children as well. After a 16-year old girl was kidnapped as she walked by herself on a road, a nun in her church school blamed the mother for not protecting her daughter. "Now nobody knows were she is," the nun said.[57]

Addressing the characteristics of female suicide bombers in particular, Debra D. Zedalis found that the "selection of women for suicide operations and the methods used to persuade them generally are similar to those employed for men. The recruiters take advantage of the candidates' innocence, enthusiasm, personal distress, and thirst for revenge."[58] Like their male counterparts female terrorists are predominantly young and may have "experienced the loss of a close friend or family member."[59] Like male terrorists, women terrorists are single, married, widowed, or divorced; some have children, others are childless. In one thus far unique case, a pregnant member of the Kurdish Workers Party carried out a suicide mission killing several Turkish soldiers.

Demonstration of Gender Equality

In the 1970s, sociologists, psychologists, and political observers pointed to the feminist movement as the most likely explanation for the large number of females in left-wing terrorist groups.[60] Criminologist Freda Adler explained female terrorist activity in an interview with the *New York Times* as a "deviant expression of feminism."[61] According to the *Times*, Dr. Adler said that the publicity surrounding terrorism gives female terrorists "a platform to say, 'I am liberated from past stereotypes, I am accepted in the ultimate masculine roles.' "[62] Earlier, in her book *Sisters in Crime*, Adler wrote, "Despite their broad political pronouncements, what the new revolutionaries [such as female members of the Weather Underground] wanted was not simply urban social gains, but sexual equality."[63] Pointing in particular to the female terrorists of the Symbionese Liberation Army, she added,

> *That such women turned so drastically toward a new and highly volatile identity caused a good portion of the nation to ask incredulously, "How could women do this sort of thing?" Perhaps the question itself was the very point of the episode. The fires which consumed the ramshackle Los Angeles house where the small band staged its last shoot-out also burned away a large part of the prevailing American illusion about women.*[64]

In Europe, experts provided similar explanations for the large number of female members in terrorist organizations, such as the Red Brigades in Italy and the Red Army Faction in West Germany. According to one news account in 1977, "Italian and German sociologists and news commentators, all of them men, have suggested over the last few weeks that the significant female membership in radical and terrorist groups was an unwelcome consequence of the women's liberation movement."[65] Male sociologists and commentators in Europe were not the only ones to blame women's lib. A female German politician stated, "These women demonstratively negate everything that is part of the established feminine character."[66] A male professor in Munich wondered whether these female terrorists "see violence in society as [the] prerogative of males and ask, 'Why shouldn't we participate?'"[67] The former neighbor of the notorious female terrorist Susanne Albrecht complained, "She sang Communist songs all night and never cleaned the stairs."[68]

More recently, female terrorists in traditionally male-dominated societies have been hailed for furthering gender equality. Yassir Arafat, at the height of the second Intifada, told thousands of women during a speech in Ramallah, "Women and men are equal. You are my army of roses that will crush Israeli tanks."[69] Soon thereafter, in early 2002 and following the first female suicide bombing in Israel proper, Abdel Hamuda, the editor of an Egyptian weekly, declared that this was a monumental event in that it "shattered a glass ceiling" and "elevated the value of Arab women and, in one moment, and with enviable courage, put an end to the unending debate about equality between men and women."[70] But it is far from clear that a larger segment of these women became terrorists in a quest for gender equality.

Take the example of female Palestinian suicide terrorists. Living in a milieu in which gender inequality is deeply rooted in religious and cultural traditions, young women with personal disappointments and emotional problems are particularly vulnerable to being recruited and trained as "martyrs." Indeed, after talking to the families and friends of four female suicide bombers and interviewing several women who had been recruited but did not finish their mission, Barbara Victor wrote,

> I discovered the hard reality that it was never another woman who recruited the suicide bombers. Without exception, these women had been trained by a trusted member of the family—a brother, an uncle—or an esteemed religious leader, teacher, or family friend, all of whom were men. What I also discovered was that all four who died, plus the others who had tried and failed to die a martyr's death, had personal problems that made their lives untenable within their own culture and society.[71]

These women's social environment made them vulnerable to male manipulation and exploitation. In Victor's judgment, "there were, in fact, very different motives and rewards for the men who died a martyr's death than for the women."[72] It seems that whereas men justified the rationale for "martyrdom" in political terms, women were told by their male handlers that their own or a male family member's transgressions could only be redeemed by killing themselves to kill Israelis and enjoy happiness in paradise.

Can Real Women Become Terrorists?

This question points to the image of the female terrorist is that of the deviant woman—as masculine, not feminine. This view was widely held in the past, but it is still alive and well in the twenty-first century. In early 2002, an article in a leading U.S. news magazine linked terrorism to male hormones. The authors wrote, "Testosterone has always had a lot to do with terrorism, even among secular bombers and kidnappers like Italy's Red Brigade and Germany's Baader–Meinhof gang. As Andreas Baader himself once declared, 'F—cking and shooting are the same thing.'"[73] In this case, the reader was explicitly told that terrorism is a male domain. At the same time, the implicit message was that female terrorists are aberrations, the exceptions to the rule, not real females.

Given such stereotypes, Cindy Ness concluded that "the secular terrorist group and the religious terrorist group alike must historicize itself in such a way that its actions are not viewed as a rapture from 'decent' behavior but rather a transition whereby an old gender value is seen as being given new expression."[74] Thus, the Tamil Tigers, for example, do not retreat from their culture's esteem for chastity and motherhood and rejection of female warriors, but draw also from Hindu mythology to justify women freedom-fighters in extraordinary circumstances. According to Ness, "on all occasions other than when their military projects are coordinated, the sexes remain segregated with the LTTE. Females live in separate camps, run their own military organizations, and plan their own projects."[75] Similarly, religious groups like Hamas characterize female terrorists "as defenders of Islam, not by their stepping out of accepted social norms. . . ."[76] To put it differently, terrorist organizations find explanations to counter the idea that female members are not really women. As a sociologist with knowledge of the Tamil Tigers put it, "behind the appearance of every uniformed female fighter, is a tender, gentle and passionate young woman with all the qualities attributed to femininity."[77]

Tactical Advantages of Female Terrorists

Although, as noted above, female terrorists are not rare, the conventional wisdom is that females are far less likely than males to commit political violence. As a result, women have far better chances to carry out terrorist attacks without being intercepted than their male comrades. This has been long recognized by terrorists who oversee their groups' operations and are responsible for the success of attacks. Women are simply less likely to be suspects and therefore less likely to be denied access to potential targets and areas for attacks; they are less frequently selected for thorough security checks than males, and can fake pregnancies for the sake of hiding weapons and explosives. As former German terrorist Bommi Bauman, member of a successor cell of the Baader-Meinhof group observed,

> If a man in a high position, perhaps knowing that he may be a target for terrorists, is approached by a woman, he may think, she is a prostitute. Women can go straight to the target's doorstep; sometimes they do it in pairs, two women, saying they are lost. If two men approached him, he would be suspicious.[78]

What Bauman described was precisely the script for several of the kidnappings and assassinations conducted by West German terrorists in which women exploited the fact that they were not as suspicious as men—although it was well known that females were well represented in these groups. Terrorists elsewhere followed this blueprint as well. Before Dhanu, a female member of the Tamil Tigers, assassinated Rajiv Gandhi, she had "garlanded him, bowed at his feet, and then detonated a bomb that killed them both."[79] Playing the role of a female admirer of Gandhi, she didn't have any problem with getting close to him. It is telling that one of the members of a two-person backup team was a young woman as well. The Kurdistan Workers Party, too, decided to use female members for suicide attacks because of their tactical advantages. But women were also more inclined to become human bombs because they wanted to prove themselves useful in a struggle in which they often could not match the physical strength of their male comrades. More recently, the wave of terrorist attacks against Russian targets by female suicide bombers was partially explained as Chechen groups taking advantage of the fact that Chechen females were able "to move more freely than Chechen men, who are routinely harassed by Russia's police and security services."[80] In early 2004, after Hamas claimed responsibility for dispatching the first female suicide bomber to kill Israelis, the group's spiritual leader, Sheik Ahmed Yassin, cited "purely tactical reasons" when asked why his organization had decided on selecting a woman, saying, "It could be that a man would not be able to reach the target, and that's why they had to use a woman."[81]

The authorities in some societies came to understand over time that female terrorists were just as likely as their male comrades to commit deadly acts of terrorism. When West Germany was faced with a wave of terror by the Red Army Faction and its successor groups, the country's counterterrorism units were allegedly ordered by their superiors to "shoot the women first."[82] In responding to the increased attacks by Chechen females, Russian authorities expanded their security checks to women with scarves and other clothing typical of Muslim women. In the long run, therefore, it is possible, if not likely, that the gender advantage will fade once it is clear that attacks by female terrorists are not exceptions, but common occurrences. For this to happen, however, it is not enough for top officials to understand that the female paradox is a myth in the realm of terrorism; rather, the men and women who implement anti- and counterterrorist policies day in and day out must have this understanding as well—and act accordingly. But this seems easier said than done. The U.S. Department of Homeland Security, for example, developed an official profile of a typical terrorist that focused on males only. Jessica Stern criticized this as "an important weakness in our counterterrorism strategy" and warned,

> Profiling men exclusively, and also focusing so tightly on countries known to harbor terrorists, are significant loopholes that have not been closed despite the FBI's recognition that al Qaeda has begun recruiting women, and despite the discovery last spring that an MIT-trained female scientist may have been providing logistical support to al Qaeda.[83]

Even in societies that have experienced repeated attacks by women terrorists, there is still a tendency to view and treat females differently. Israel is a perfect example here. In January 2004, when a 22-year-old Palestinian woman, pretending to be crippled, told Israelis at a Gaza checkpoint that she had metal plates in her leg that would sound the alarm, they allowed her to wait for a woman to search her in a special area. Moments later, the woman blew herself up and killed four Israelis. Lamenting the cynical exploitation of his soldiers' consideration for the dignity of women, the officer in charge said,

> We're doing our best to be humanitarian, to consider the problems associated with searching women. She said she had a medical problem, that's why the soldiers let her in, to check her in private because she is a woman. That's very cruel, cynical use of the humanitarian considerations of our soldiers.[84]

The lesson here is this: While there are no profound gender differences with respect to terrorists' motives and actions, most societies continue to deem females less suspect and less dangerous than males. Indeed, indications are that more women will be recruited by terrorist groups in the future: After analyzing cross-national opinion surveys in fourteen Muslim countries, two scholars concluded that female respondents were more likely to support terrorism in defense of Islam.[85]

There is also evidence that female terrorists can be more committed to the terrorist cause and their comrades than their male counterparts. With respect to the Italian Red Brigades and similar groups, Luisella de Cataldo Neuberger and Tiziana Valenti found that a larger proportion of male members collaborated with law enforcement and distanced themselves from the activities and goals of their terrorist organizations, when imprisoned, than did their female counterparts. Although not enough data are available for the first generation of RAF, women seemed less inclined than men to cooperate with the authorities once they were behind bars.[86]

The Lack of a Universal Terrorist Profile

Since a universal terrorist profile does not exist, the idea that the roots of terrorism are best understood by considering a number of variables and that different factors explain different types terrorism makes sense.

But when everything is said and done, it seems impossible to understand the roots of particular kinds of terrorism without considering the real or perceived political, socioeconomic, or religious grievances that feed into the formation of terrorist ideologies and serve as justifications for terrorist acts. "However impoverished and reduced it may be," Michel Wieviorka wrote, "there is always an ideology underlying a terrorist action."[87] This may be more the case for the founding fathers and mothers of terrorist groups than for the rank-and-file members. But in order to function and flourish, the founders and their heirs must translate real or perceived grievances into an ideological framework or mission statement. According to Jessica Stern, "The most important aspect of organization is the mission. The mission is the story about Us versus Them. It distinguishes the pure from the impure and creates group identity. The organization's mission statement—the story about its raison d'etre—is the glue that holds even the most tenuous organizations together."[88]

The Stages Leading to Terrorism

Terrorism is rarely, if ever, the result of a sudden impulse. People do not become terrorists on the spur of the moment. Groups and individuals resort to political violence when they make the move into the last stage of a process. By distinguishing between social movements, antimovements, and terrorism, Wieviorka recognized different types of opposition groupings with different degrees of resistance to the existing power or powers and different courses of action coupled with their possible transitions from one type to another.[89] Similarly, Ehud Sprinzak identified three stages in liberal democracies—from strong opposition to intense opposition (with protests and even small-scale violence) to outright terrorist activity: (1) crisis of confidence, (2) conflict of legitimization, and (3) crisis of legitimacy.[90] Once a group enters into the last stage, its grievances turn increasingly into intense hate of the enemy, who is dehumanized. "The regime and its accomplices are now portrayed as 'things,' 'dogs,' 'pigs,' 'Nazis,' or 'terrorists.' The portrayal is not accidental and occasional but repeated and systematic."[91] This pattern of dehumanizing the enemy applies to all types of terrorist groups.

Because of his Vietnam policy, President Lyndon B. Johnson was called "baby killer" by the most extreme voices in the radical left of the 1960s; after the events at Waco, Texas, right-wing extremists called federal agents "baby killers" and Attorney General Janet Reno "butcher of Waco."

Members of the German Red Army Faction also moved gradually into the last motivational stage. According to Merkl, "Once an enemy had been declared and made into the absolute moral evil, the world became simple, and any means were justified for fighting this evil. Soon the 'struggle' itself became the goal, and this in turn could satisfy deep personal needs."[92] A member of the Italian Red Brigades explained the terrorist mindset and motivation when in search of a victim this way:

Then you have singled out your victim; he is physically there; he is the one to be blamed for everything. In that moment there is already the logic of the trial in which you have already decided that he is guilty; you only have to decide about his punishment. So you have a very "emphatic" sense of justice; you punish him not only for what he has done but also for all the rest. Then, you don't care anymore which responsibilities that person has; you give him them all . . . he is only a small part of the machine that is going to destroy all of us.[93]

Expressing his hatred of Israelis, one Arab terrorist said, "You Israelis are Nazis in your souls and in your conduct. . . . Given this kind of conduct, there is no choice but to strike at you without mercy in every possible way."[94] In defense of suicide missions, an Islamic terrorist said, "This is not suicide. Suicide is selfish, it is weak, it is mentally disturbed. This is *istishad* (martyrdom or self-sacrifice in the service of Allah)."[95]

First dehumanization, then the justification of killing as morally and religiously justified, are part of what Albert Bandura describes as a mechanism of moral disengagement on the part of groups that decide to commit terrorism:

One set of disengagement practices operates on the construal of the behavior itself. People do not ordinarily engage in reprehensible conduct until they have justified to themselves the morality of their actions. What is culpable can be made honorable through cognitive reconstrual. In this process, destructive conduct is made personally and socially acceptable by portraying it in the service of moral purposes. People then act on a moral imperative.[96]

In examining the causes of terrorism, Martha Crenshaw distinguishes between two major factors: (1) the preconditions that are at the heart of political, socioeconomic, or religious grievances felt by societal subgroups, and (2) the precipitants or specific events that trigger terrorist acts.[97] This twofold causation (see Table 6.1) can be traced with respect to most, if not all, groups or individuals who perpetrate terrorism. Although this chapter has discussed at some length the underlying political and personal circumstances as causes of terrorism, trigger events need further explanation. Typically, military or other violent government actions, often reactions to nonviolent or violent dissent, serve as catalysts for the formation of terrorist groups. Thus, brutal police actions against protesters during the Democratic Party's 1968 National Convention in Chicago triggered the formation of the Weathermen. One year earlier, the killing of a German student (Benno Ohnesorg) by the police during a demonstration in West Berlin against a visit of the Shah of Iran triggered massive student demonstrations as the prelude to the formation of the Red Army Faction. The defeat of the Arab states by Israel in the 1967 war became the precipitant for the formation of

TABLE 6.1

Causes of Terrorism/Formation of Terrorist Groups

Preconditions	Trigger Events
Grievances	Domestic, international, or both
	Internal, external, or both
Reactions:	**Reactions:**
Articulation of dissent and ideological differences	Most radical individuals split from larger opposition segment
Alienation from those in power	Core of leaders forms group for the purpose of more militant action: terrorfare
Nonviolent protests	Recruitment of members
Possibly some violence	Dehumanization of the enemy and moral disengagement
	Securing of resources (weapons, finances, hideouts, etc.)
	Result: Terrorist Acts

Source: Author.

Palestinian terrorist groups, just as the first Persian Gulf War in 1991 and the use of Saudi Arabian bases by the U.S. military influenced the emergence of bin Laden's Al Qaeda terrorist organization. Even the terrorist actions of lone wolves can be associated with trigger events. For example, the 1993 inferno at Waco, Texas, hardened the antigovernment feeling of American right-wing groups and was the trigger event for Timothy McVeigh, who was responsible for the Oklahoma City bombing on the second anniversary of the events at Waco.

The Roots of Terrorism: No Simple Answers

Recognizing a whole range of causes for the emergence of terrorism and the difficulty of identifying one or a few predominant ones, Jessica Stern wrote,

> *I have come to see terrorism as a kind of virus, which spreads as a result of risk factors at various levels: global, interstate, national, and personal. But identifying these factors precisely is difficult. The same variables (political, religious, social, or all of the above) that seem to cause one person to become a terrorist might cause another to become a saint.*[98]

Taken together, then, a variety of political, socioeconomic, and religious motives combined with personal conditions and trigger events provide clues for understanding the making of terrorists and the formation of terrorist groups, the motivations of individual recruits, and the decisions to commence violent campaigns. But in the absence of a predominant causal model, it is always difficult for target societies to fully comprehend the complex causes of a particular terrorist threat and more thorny yet to attack the roots of terrorism.

Notes

1. "Bush Ties Foreign Aid to Reform," CBSNews.com, March 22, 2002, www.cbsnews.com/stories/2002/03/21/politics/printable/504248.shtml (retrieved June 30, 2003).
2. Jeffrey Donovan, "U.S.: Analysts See Weak Link between Poverty and Terrorism," www.rferl.org/nca/features/2002/11/27112002205339.asp (retrieved June 29, 2003).
3. Arthur Raper, "The Tragedy of Lynching," Patterson Smith Reprint Series in Criminology, *Law Enforcement, and Social Problems*, Publication no. 25 (Montclair, NJ: Patterson Smith, 1969; originally published 1933).
4. C. Hovland and R. Sears, "Minor Studies of Aggression: Correlation of Lynchings with Economic Indices," *Journal of Psychology* 9 (1940): 301–10.
5. Brent L. Smith and Kathryn D. Morgan, "Terrorists Right and Left: Empirical Issues in Profiling American Terrorists," *Studies in Conflict and Terrorism* 17:1 (January–March 1994): 51.
6. See Allen Hammond, "Economic Distress Motivates Terrorists," in Laura K. Egendorf, ed., *Terrorism: Opposing Viewpoints* (San Diego, CA: Greenhaven Press, 2000), 77.
7. Walter Laqueur, *No End to War: Terrorism in the Twenty-first Century* (New York: Continuum, 2003), 15. The list of the world's least developed countries was based on several criteria: low per capita income, weak human resources, and low-level economic diversification.
8. Claude Berrebi, "Evidence about the Link between Education, Poverty, and Terrorism among Palestinians," unpublished paper, 2003, 1.
9. Alan B. Krueger and Jitka Maleckova, "Education, Poverty and Terrorism," unpublished paper, 2002, 1.
10. Ibid.
11. Ayla Schbley, "Defining Religious Terrorism: A Causal and Anthological Profile," *Studies in Conflict and Terrorism* 26:2 (March–April 2003): 119.
12. Berrebi, 1.
13. James A. Piazza, "Rooted in Poverty? Terrorism, Poor Economic Development, and Social Cleavages." *Terrorism and Political Violence* 18:1 (Spring 2006), 170.
14. Daphne Burdman, "Education, Indoctrination, and Incitement: Palestinian Children on Their Way to Martyrdom," *Terrorism and Political Violence* 15:1 (Spring 2003): 97.
15. Valerie Strauss and Emily Wax, "Where Two Worlds Collide; Muslim Schools Face Tension of Islamic, U.S. Views," *Washington Post*, February 25, 2002, A1.
16. Ted Gurr, "Political Protest and Rebellion in the 1960s: The United States in World Perspectives," in Hugh Graham and Ted Gurr, eds., *Violence in America* (Beverly Hills, CA: Sage, 1979), 59–73.
17. William Eubank and Leonard Weinberg, "Terrorism and Democracy: Perpetrators and Victims," *Terrorism and Political Violence* 13:1 (Spring 2001): 160, 161.
18. Piazza, 159.
19. Gary G. Sick, "The Political Underpinnings of Terrorism," in Charles W. Kegley, Jr., ed., *International Terrorism: Characteristics, Causes, Controls* (New York: St. Martin's, 1990), 51.
20. Richard Shultz, "Conceptualizing Political Terrorism," in Kegley, 45.
21. Martha Crenshaw, "The Logic of Terrorism," in Walter Reich, ed., *Origins of Terrorism: Psychologies, Ideologies, States of Minds* (New York: Cambridge University Press, 1990), 10, 11.
22. Ehud Sprinzak, "Extreme Left Terrorism in a Democracy," in Reich, 78.
23. Christopher C. Harmon, *Terrorism Today* (London: Frank Cass, 2000), 201.
24. Richard E. Rubenstein, *Alchemist of Revolution* (New York: Basic Books, 1987), 5.
25. Cited in Rubenstein, 5.
26. Louise Richardson, *What Terrorists Want: Understanding the Enemy, Containing the Threat* (New York: Random House, 2006), ch. 4.
27. For more on the instrumental approach, see Martha Crenshaw, "Theories of Terrorism: Instrumental and Organizational Approaches," in David C. Rapoport, ed., *Inside Terrorist Organizations* (London: Frank Cass, 2001), 13–31.
28. Jerrold M. Post, "Terrorist Psycho-Logic: Terrorist Behavior as a Product of Psychological Forces," in Reich, 23.
29. Ibid., 25.
30. The results of a study of German terrorists are cited and commented on by Peter H. Merkl, "West German Left-Wing Terrorism," in Martha Crenshaw, ed., *Terrorism in Context* (University Park: Pennsylvania State University Press, 1995), 203–4.

31. Konrad Kellen, "Ideology and Rebellion: Terrorism in West Germany," in Reich, 58.

32. Merkl, 204.

33. Jeffrey Ian Ross, "Beyond the Conceptualization of Terrorism: A Psychological-Structural Model of the Causes of This Activity," in Craig Summers and Eric Markusen, eds., *Collective Violence* (Lanham, MD: Rowman & Littlefield, 1999).

34. Randy Borum, *Psychology of Terrorism* (Tampa: University of South Florida, 2004).

35. Post, 25, 35.

36. Donatella della Porta, "Left-Wing Terrorism in Italy," in Crenshaw, *Terrorism in Context*, 140.

37. Schbley, 119.

38. The global Salafi movement aims to restore authentic Islam and to establish one united Islamist state reaching from Morocco to the Philippines.

39. Marc Sageman, *Understanding Terror Networks* (Philadelphia: University of Pennsylvania Press, 2004), 135.

40. Loretta Napoleoni, *Modern Jihad: Tracing the Dollars behind the Terror Networks* (London: Pluto Press, 2003), 132.

41. Laqueur, 67, 68.

42. Malise Ruthven, "The Rise of the Muslim Terrorists." The New York Review of Books, May 29, 2008, 33.

43. Kevin Meyers, "The Terrible Sight of a Female Terrorist," www.telegraph.co.uk/opinion/main.jhtml?xml=/opinion/2002/10/27/do2707.xml (retrieved July 20, 2003).

44. Alexis B. Delaney and Peter R. Neumann, "Another Failure of Imagination?: The Spectacular Rise of the Female Terrorist," *International Herald Tribune*, September 6, 2004.

45. Ibid.

46. Harmon, 212.

47. Ibid., 220.

48. Karla J. Cunningham, "Cross-Regional Trends in Female Terrorism," *Studies in Conflict and Terrorism* 26:3 (May–June 2003): 175.

49. These numbers are mentioned in Luisella de Cataldo Neuberger and Tiziana Valentini, *Women and Terrorism* (New York: St. Martin's Press, 1996), 8, 9.

50. Cindy D. Ness, "In the Name of the Cause: Women's Work in Secular and Religious Terrorism," *Studies in Conflict and Terrorism* 28:5 (2005) (September–October), 356.

51. Martha Crenshaw, "Introduction: Reflection on the Effects of Terrorism," in Martha Crenshaw, ed., *Terrorism, Legitimacy and Power: The Consequences of Political Violence* (Middletown, CT: Wesleyan University Press, 1983), 24.

52. Robin Morgan, *The Demon Lover: The Roots of Terrorism* (New York: Washington Square Press, 2001), 204.

53. Ibid., xvi.

54. Klaliff, "Women in the White Pride Movement," http://women.stormfront.org/writings/women.htm (retrieved October 20, 2003).

55. Ibid.

56. Nick Meo, "Tamil Tigers Eye Young Recruits." *Newsday*, October 25, 2006, A28.

57. Ibid.

58. Debra D. Zedalis, "Female Suicide Bombers," http://www.strategicstudiesinstitute.army.mil/pdffiles/PUB408.pdf, 8.

59. Ibid.

60. Donatella della Porta, "Left-Wing Terrorism in Italy," in Crenshaw, *Terrorism in Context*, 141.

61. Judy Klemesrud, "A Criminologist's View of Women Terrorists," *New York Times*, January 9, 1979, A24.

62. Ibid.

63. Freda Adler, *Sisters in Crime* (New York: Waveland Press, 1975), 20.

64. Ibid., 21, 22.

65. Paul Hofmann, "Women Active among Radicals in Western Europe," *New York Times*, August 14, 1977, 7.

66. Hanna-Renate Laurien, a conservative, was quoted by Kim Wilkinson, "The Hit Women," *Newsweek*, August 15, 1977, 30.

67. Michael Getler, "Women Play Growing Role in Slayings by West German Terrorist Groups," *Washington Post*, August 6, 1977.

68. Ibid.

69. Barbara Victor, *The Army of Roses: Inside the World of Palestinian Women Suicide Bombers* (New York: Rodale, 2003), 19.

70. James Bennett, "Arab Press Glorifies Bomber as Heroine," *New York Times*, February 11, 2002, 8.

71. Victor, 7.

72. Ibid.

73. Christopher Dickey and Gretel C. Kovach, "Married to Jihad," *Newsweek*, January 14, 2002, 48.

74. Ness, 361.

75. Ibid., 363.

76. Ness, 366, quotes Adele Balasingham, the wife of a close advisor to the Tamil Tiger leadership.

77. Ibid., 364.

78. Harmon, 219, 220.

79. Cunningham, 180.

80. Steven Lee Myers, "Female Suicide Bombers Unnerve Russians," *New York Times*, August 7, 2003, 1.

81. Hamas's first female suicide bomber was Reem al-Reyashi, a 22-year-old mother of two small children. Yassin was quoted in Greg Myre, "Gaza Mother, 22, Kills Four Israeli Soldiers," *New York Times*, January 15, 2004, A3.

82. *Shoot the Women First* was therefore chosen as the title of a book exploring the phenomenon of female terrorists. See Eileen MacDonald, *Shoot the Women First* (New York: Random House, 1992).

83. Jessica Stern, "When Bombers Are Women." *The Washington Post*, December 18, 2003, A35.

84. Brigadier-General Gadi Shamni, the Gaza divisional commander, was quoted in Chris McGreal, "Human-bomb Mother Kills Four Israelis at Gaza Checkpoint," *The Guardian*, January 15, 2004, 17.

85. C. Christine Fair and Bryan Shephard, "Who Supports Terrorism? Evidence from Fourteen Muslim Countries," *Studies in Conflict and Terrorism* 29 (2006): 51–74.

86. Cataldo Neuberger and Valentini, especially ch. 1.

87. Michael Wieviorka, *The Making of Terrorism* (Chicago: University of Chicago Press, 1993), 10.

88. Jessica Stern, *Terror in the Name of God: Why Religious Militants Kill* (New York: HarperCollins, 2003), 142.

89. Wieviorka, ch. 1.

90. Sprinzak, 64–85.

91. Ibid., 82.

92. Merkl, 206.

93. Della Porta, 150.

94. Quoted by Jerrold M. Post, Ehud Sprinzak, and Laurita M. Denny, "The Terrorists in Their Own Words: Interviews with 35 Incarcerated Middle Eastern Terrorists," *Terrorism and Political Violence* 15:1 (Spring 2003): 178.

95. Ibid., 179.

96. Albert Bandura, "Mechanisms of Moral Disengagement," in Reich, *Origins of Terrorism*, 163.

97. Crenshaw, "The Causes of Terrorism," 114.

98. Stern, 283.

CHAPTER 7

From State Sponsors to Involuntary Hosts

ALTHOUGH TERRORIST ORGANIZATIONS ARE NONSTATE ACTORS, some of them are generously sponsored or partially supported by the governments of nation-states. Decision-makers in target countries emphasize the complicity of governments because it is easier to threaten and punish state sponsors than it is terrorist organizations. Just as governments in the Eastern Bloc and Soviet client states elsewhere sponsored anti-Western terrorism during the Cold War (see Chapter 3), state support has remained an important factor in bolstering terrorists and their deeds.

According to three laws (section 6(j) of the Export Administration Act, section 40 of the Arms Export Control Act, and section 620A of the Foreign Assistance Act), U.S. secretaries of state are required to designate states as sponsors of terrorism if they determine that they have "repeatedly provided support for acts of international terrorism."[1] This designation triggers the following sanctions against state sponsors of terrorism:

I. A ban on arms-related exports and sales.
II. Controls over exports of dual-use items, requiring 30-day Congressional notification for goods or services that could significantly enhance the terrorist-list country's military capability or ability to support terrorism.
III. Prohibitions on economic assistance.
IV. Imposition of miscellaneous financial and other restrictions, including:

Requiring the United States to oppose loans by the World Bank and other international financial institutions;

Exception from the jurisdictional immunity in U.S. courts of state sponsor countries, and all former state sponsor countries (with the exception of Iraq), with respect to claims for money damages for personal injury or death caused by certain acts of terrorism, torture, or extrajudicial killing, or the provision of material support or resources for such acts;

Denying companies and individuals tax credits for income earned in terrorist-list countries;

Denial of duty-free treatment of goods exported to the United States;

Authority to prohibit any U.S. citizen from engaging in a financial transaction with a terrorist-list government without a Treasury Department license; and

Prohibition of Defense Department contracts above $100,000 with companies in which a state sponsor government owns or controls a significant interest.[2]

The State Department's list of state sponsors of terrorism shrunk in the last few years from seven to merely four: Iraq was taken off the list after the U.S.-led invasion and the demise of Saddam Hussein; Libya was scratched in 2006 after Muammar Qaddafi agreed to abandon the country's WMD programs and renounced terrorism; North Korea's elimination from the list in 2008 was Washington's reward to Pyongyang for agreeing to nuclear inspection requirements. However, about three months into the Obama presidency, North Korea re-started the Yongbyon plant that can make arms-grade plutonium and ordered U.N. inspectors to leave the country. According to the U.S. Department of State's "Country Report on Terrorism 2008," the following states remained on the list: Cuba (since 1982), Iran (since 1984), Sudan (1993), and Syria 1979).

Cuba to this day and North Korea up to the fall of 2008 remained on the list and thus subject to sanctions although there was no evidence that these countries provided support to terrorist groups as they had during the Cold War era. Indeed, the State Department's report for 2003 admitted this explicitly with respect to North Korea when it stated, "The Democratic People's Republic of Korea (DPRK) is not

A Product of State Sponsorship: The Lebanese Hezbollah

After hijacking a TWA airliner in April 1985, members of the Lebanese Hezbollah held dozens of passengers hostage in hideouts around Beirut and, at one point, invited the international media to a news conference to publicize their demands. The Iranian government had its hand in the establishment and long-term support of this group, which was founded in 1982.

known to have sponsored any terrorist acts since the bombing of a Korean Airlines flight in 1987."[3] Why, then, was the DPRK still listed as a sponsor of terrorism at the time? According to the report, "Pyongyang has not taken substantial steps to cooperate in efforts to combat international terrorism." This sounded as if the State Department, after 9/11, expanded its definition of terrorism sponsors to include states whose governments were not involved in the fight against terrorism. Strangely, North Korea was not removed from the list because of an official renouncement of terrorism but rather in the wake of Pyongyang's on-and-off-again agreement to nuclear inspections. Indeed, months before the State Department withdrew North Korea's designation, the department's 2007 country report noted that North Korea still harbored four members of the Japanese Red Army that had hijacked an airliner in 1970.[4]

At the end of the twentieth and the beginning of the twenty-first centuries, Cuba, too, was no longer an active sponsor of terrorism except for providing safe haven to some members of terrorist groups. In listing the remaining state sponsors of terrorism, the State Department explained with respect to Cuba,

Although Cuba no longer actively supports armed struggle in Latin America and other parts of the world, the Cuban government continued to provide safe haven to several terrorists. Members of ETA, the FARC, and the ELN remained in Cuba during 2008, some having arrived in Cuba in connection with peace negotiations with the governments of Spain and Colombia. Cuban authorities continued to publicly defend the FARC.[5]

But there was also a hint of a possible change in Cuba's approach to terrorism in the last year of the Bush administration. As the State Department report noted, "on July 6, 2008, former Cuban President Fidel Castro called on the FARC to release the hostages they were holding without preconditions. He has also condemned the FARC's mistreatment of captives and of their abduction of civilian politicians who had no role in the armed conflict."[6] For years, other direct and indirect sponsors of terrorism were missing from the State Department's list for various political reasons. For example, in spite of Pakistan's long-standing support for groups that committed terrorist acts in Kashmir, the Pakistani government's cooperation in the U.S.-led campaign against international terrorism kept the country off the list of sponsors. But the State Department's most glaring omission from the list of terrorism supporters was Saudi Arabia, whose rulers had a long tradition of allowing the channeling of huge amounts of money to terrorist groups and to organizations known to be breeding grounds and recruitment centers for terrorists.

States that sponsor international terrorism over longer periods of time share several characteristics: repressive governments, ambitious political and/or religious goals that transcend their own borders, and a tendency to blame an outside enemy (or enemies) for their own domestic or regional problems. Governments and terrorists cooperate when both sides determine that they benefit from such a relationship (see Table 7.1). Typically, state sponsors provide support in the form of training camps, safe havens, financial resources, logistical expertise, weapons, and so on. In return, terrorist groups carry out terror strikes against targets that sponsor states cannot attack without risking retaliation. For more than two decades, Iran has systematically and generously provided organizations abroad with literally all kinds of support that terrorists need. The Iranian model is by far the most comprehensive one, as the following case study demonstrates.

TABLE 7.1

Needs of Terrorists and Motives of State Sponsors

What Terrorists Need	Why States Sponsor Terrorism	State Sponsors Listed by the U.S. Government in 2008
Bases of operation	Shared goals and grievances	Iran
Training facilities	Same enemy(ies)	
Financial support	Want terrorists to carry out violent acts	Sudan
Weapons	Ability to deny involvement in terrorism	Syria
Intelligence/logistic support	Avoidance of counterterrorist strikes	Cuba
Opportunities for recruitment	Divert domestic radicals' frustrations to outside target(s)	
Safe havens		

Source: Author.

Case Study

Iran: The Premier Model of State-Sponsored Terrorism

Since the early 1980s, Iran has been the most striking example of active state sponsorship of terrorism. The Islamic Revolutionary Council, an eleven-member clerical group, was established in 1981 to supervise and coordinate support for Islamic revolutionary groups in Islamic countries. The council's assemblies were established to lend support to such movements in Lebanon, in Bahrain, in Iraq, on the Arabian Peninsula, and elsewhere. The Corps of the Islamic Revolutionary Guards was chosen to advise and train Islamic revolutionary movements. Over the years, Iran has supported terrorists abroad in a variety of ways, among them the following:

PROPAGANDA: Soon after the establishment of the Islamic Republic, Iran began to broadcast to Muslim states in the Persian Gulf region to praise the Iranian revolution and encourage the overthrow of "un-Islamic" rulers said to be under the influence of the West, especially the United States. Propaganda campaigns spread to other regions.

TRAINING CAMPS: During the 1980s, the Revolutionary Guards established several facilities in various parts of Iran (e.g., Qom and Mashad) to train radical Shi'ites from abroad. They were instrumental in the establishment of the Hezbollah in Lebanon and training facilities in the Bekaa Valley.

FINANCIAL SUPPORT: Beginning in September 1981, when the Islamic Revolutionary Council was established under the Ayatollah Khomeini with the declared goal of exporting the Iranian revolution, the government made available funds for the purpose of supporting non-Iranian revolutionary forces. Experts estimated that the Lebanese Hezbollah alone received tens of millions of dollars annually from Tehran to pay its members, especially members trained as terrorists, and to branch out into education, health care, and welfare—all important services to sustain and expand popular support.

SUPPLY OF WEAPONS: Iran has provided arms to Islamic revolutionaries—at times by channeling them through other countries. Hezbollah, for example, is said to have gotten arms via Syria. Weapons were shipped elsewhere as well. In early 2001, for example, Israeli Special Forces intercepted a ship in the Red Sea with fifty tons of weapons aboard before it reached its destination, the Gaza Strip. The shipment originated in Iran.

DIPLOMATIC SUPPORT: Iran used diplomatic channels in support of Hezbollah—for example, when the organization had differences with the Syrian government.

SAFE HAVENS: Terrorists on the run found a safe haven in Iran. In some instances, these individuals hijacked planes and forced pilots to land in Iran, where they were welcomed and protected.

SPONSORED GROUPS: Of the Iranian population, 89% are Shi'ite Muslims, 10% are Sunni Muslims, and 1% are listed as "other." Most support has gone to Shi'ite groups, such as Hezbollah, but Iran has also supported Sunni Muslim organizations, such as Hamas and the Palestinian Jihad, and secular Palestinian terrorist organizations, such as the Popular Front for the Liberation of Palestine–General Command. Common to all groups is their violent opposition to the state of Israel.

Following 9/11, the U.S. government accused Iran of harboring members of Al Qaeda—even after the Iranian government turned over several members of that group to their countries of origin. While some observers expressed doubts about the alleged friendly ties between the Shi'ites in Iran and the Sunnis of Al Qaeda, others speculated that some segments of the Iranian security forces provided safe havens to Al Qaeda terrorists after the American-led invasion of Afghanistan in response to 9/11 forced many of them to leave Afghanistan.

But whether ties between Iran and Al Qaeda ever existed or not, "Iran has been one of the world's most active sponsors of terrorism," as Daniel Byman has noted. "Tehran has armed, trained, inspired, organized, and otherwise supported dozens of violent groups over the years. Iran has not only backed groups in its Persian Gulf neighborhood, but also terrorists in Lebanon, Israel, Bosnia,

(continued)

Iran: The Premier Model of State-Sponsored Terrorism *(continued)*

the Philippines, and elsewhere."[7] However, it was the 34-day war between Hezbollah and Israel in the summer of 2006 that put the limelight once again on Iran's role as terrorism's sponsor-in-chief and on Hezbollah as Tehran's proxy in the conflict with Israel. According to one account,

> The Iranians may not have been physically present on the frontlines in Lebanon, but they were active there nonetheless. A number of Revolutionary Guard members were killed in the Israeli incursion into the town of Baalbek (close to the Syrian border) on August 1, and Israeli intelligence claims that Iranians helped Hezbollah fire the land-to-sea missile that almost destroyed an Israeli warship in mid-July. Most of Hezbollah's arms—including modern antitank weapons and the thousands of rockets that rained down on Israel—came from Iran (as well as Syria). Iranian advisers had spent years helping Hezbollah train and build fortified positions throughout southern Lebanon.[8]

Similarly, the full magnitude and scope of arms smuggled from Iran into the Gaza Strip became clear during the violent Israeli–Hamas clash in late 2008/early 2009, when large numbers of rockets from the Gaza Strip reached far further South into Israel than previous missiles and mortars launched by Hamas.

Former and Current State Sponsors

Iraq

Before the fall of Saddam Hussein, the Iraqi government sponsored terrorism for many years, providing arms, logistical support, training camps, and safe havens mostly to secular Palestinian groups that fought Israelis and citizens of countries known as supporters of Israel. In 2002, Abu Nidal, one of the most notorious Palestinian terrorist leaders, died in Baghdad under mysterious circumstances. Abu Abbas, a leader of the Palestine Liberation Front, was caught by the U.S. military in his Iraqi hideout after the fall of Baghdad in 2003. He reportedly died during his detention in Iraq. Before the first Persian Gulf War commenced in early 1991, Abbas had warned that his organization would unleash a wave of anti-Western terrorism if the U.S.-led coalition were to attack Iraq. But the threatened terror campaign never materialized.

Before his regime fell in 2003, Saddam Hussein paid each family of Palestinian suicide bombers $10,000 (later on, $25,000), to reward them for the "martyrdom" of their loved ones. Iraq also supported Iranian dissident groups, among them the terrorist organization Mujahedin-e-Khalq. But there was no credible evidence, nor was it likely, that Iraq's government supported Al Qaeda. Bin Laden despised Saddam Hussein because Iraq's president was a secular ruler and thus, in the Al Qaeda leader's eyes, an enemy of the type of fundamentalist Islamic regime and society that bin Laden has promoted as the only acceptable model for Muslim countries. For secular rulers like Saddam Hussein, bin Laden's call for the establishment of Islamic republics in the region and his pan-Islamic dreams of one Muslim nation stood in the way of joining Al Qaeda in a united front against the American enemy. For bin Laden and his associates, the removal of Saddam Hussein was nearly as high on their priority list as the ouster of Saudi Arabia's rulers. Nevertheless, before and after the invasion of Iraq in early 2003, the Bush administration insisted that Iraq had ties to Al Qaeda and perhaps to the 9/11 terrorists. According to the U.S. Department of State, Al Qaeda terrorists in northern Iraq "concocted suspect chemicals" and "tried to smuggle them into Russia, Western Europe, and the United States to terrorist operations."[9] These activities, the report concluded, would be inconceivable "without the knowledge and acquiescence of Saddam's regime."[10] In reality, the Ansar-al-Islam group that allegedly linked Iraq and Al Qaeda operated in northern Iraq in an area that was not under the control of Saddam Hussein's government. Although it mentioned reports of contacts between Iraqi officials and bin Laden and other Al Qaeda members, the National Commission on Terrorism Attacks upon the United States did not find evidence for either a "collaborative relationship" between Iraq and Al Qaeda in general or for Iraq's cooperation in the 9/11 attacks.[11]

In May 2003, after the fall of Saddam Hussein's regime, President George W. Bush lifted all sanctions against Iraq because the country was no longer a state sponsor of terrorism. A year later, however, the U.S. State Department gave the following explanation of why Iraq remained on Washington's list of terrorist states:

> Iraq became a central front in the global war on terrorism as [the U.S.-led] Coalition and Iraqi authorities faced numerous attacks by a disparate mix of former regime elements, criminals, and some foreign fighters—including Islamic extremists linked to Ansar al-Islam, al-Qaida, and Abu Mus'ab al-Zarqawi.[12]

As an unintended consequence of Iraq's occupation by the U.S.-led Coalition, the country had become a hotbed of terrorism and a major boost to the recruitment efforts of Al Qaeda and similar Islamic groups.

Libya

During the 1970s and particularly the 1980s, Libya was one of the most notorious sponsors of terrorism, providing Palestinian terrorists and European groups associated with Palestinian organizations with training facilities and logistical and financial support. Moreover, Libyan citizens—believed to be government agents—committed terrorist acts, among them the bombing of Pan Am Flight 103 in December 1988, although Libya's ruler, Muammar Qaddafi, denied his own or his government's involvement. During those years, Libya supported not only secular Palestinian and left-wing Western European groups but also revolutionary movements in Southeast Asia. In 2000, Qaddafi sent a Libyan official who was acquainted with the Abu Sayyaf terrorist group to the southern Philippines, where the Muslim separatists held several European hostages. Qaddafi's emissary convinced the Abu Sayyaf leaders to release several European hostages in exchange for a $1 million ransom payment per hostage. The Libyans called their ransom "development aid" and achieved quite a coup: On the one hand, they dished out money for terrorist operations, and on the other, they played the role of humanitarians who freed German, French, and Finnish hostages from unbearable captivity in the jungle.[13]

After 9/11, Muammar Qaddafi gave repeated assurances that Libya was ready to join the war against terrorism—especially against Islamic extremists, Osama bin Laden, and members of the Al Qaeda–led terrorism network. And in December 2003, President Bush and British Prime Minister Tony Blair revealed that the Libyan president had agreed to abandon the country's weapons of mass destruction programs. But in 2004, while American oil companies hoped for the removal of U.S. sanctions and a return to Libya's oil fields, Saudi Arabian authorities arrested four men who were allegedly involved in a Qaddafi-inspired plot to assassinate Crown Prince Abdullah. Still, in the summer of 2006 the State Department took Libya off its terrorism sponsor list and in 2008, Washington and Tripoli formally restored diplomatic ties with Libya that had been cut twenty-eight years earlier.

Sudan

After the 1986 U.S. bombing raids on Libyan targets in retaliation for anti-American terrorism, Qaddafi was no longer eager to harbor terrorists and provide them with training facilities. The next stop for some of the militants was the Sudan. Once an Islamic government was established following a coup in 1989, Sudan provided a host of mostly Islamist terrorist groups with training camps and other resources. According to one source, these camps were utilized by terrorists from Libya and Egypt as well as by members of Hezbollah, Hamas, several Filipino groups, and militant Islamicists from Algeria and Tunisia.[14] What all of these groups had in common was their aim of overthrowing the governments in their respective countries and establishing Islamist states. In 1991, stripped of his Saudi citizenship, Osama bin Laden and his associates moved to the Sudan, where they were welcomed by the Sudanese authorities with open arms.

In 1994, the Sudanese government extradited the Venezuelan Carlos Ramirez Santos, better known as "Carlos the Jackal" and one of the most notorious left-wing terrorists, to France. This move was designed to change Sudan's international image as a terrorist haven. It proved an unsuccessful maneuver. One year later, the United Nations imposed sanctions against the Sudan. In 1996, under pressure from Washington, the Sudanese government offered to allow Saudi Arabian or U.S. authorities to take Osama bin Laden into their custody. Lacking enough evidence to prosecute him as a terrorist, the Clinton administration refused the offer and so did Saudi Arabia. Instead, bin Laden and his group moved to Afghanistan.

Although the United Nations lifted its sanctions after the Sudanese authorities arrested several dozen terrorists following the events of 9/11, the United States refused to take the country off its list of state sponsors. In its report for 2008, the State Department praised the Sudanese government for remaining "a cooperative partner in global counterterrorism efforts" and for continuing "to pursue terrorist operations directly involving threats to U.S. interests and personnel in Sudan."[15] But there remained concern because "Al-Qa'ida (AQ)-inspired terrorist elements, and elements of both Palestine Islamic Jihad (PIJ), and HAMAS remained in Sudan."[16]

Syria

Traditionally, the government of Syria limited its support of terrorism to secular and religious groups poised to fight for Arab, and especially Palestinian, interests and against Israel. To begin with, Syria had a direct grievance against Israel, namely, Israel's occupation of the Golan province since the Six-Day War in 1967. Over the years, Syria allowed terrorists to reside inside its borders. The Islamic Resistance Movement, Hamas; the Popular Front for the Liberation of Palestine; the Popular Front for the Liberation of Palestine–General Command; and Islamic Jihad were the most visible groups operating in Syria's capital, Damascus. The Syrian authorities also had close ties to the Lebanese Hezbollah, and they allowed Iran's Revolutionary Guards and terrorists from various parts of the world to use training camps in Lebanon's Beqaa Valley. One expert concluded in the late 1990s,

> Damascus Airport, for example, is known to be a popular trans-shipment point for Iranian arms and equipment destined for Hezbollah camps and operatives through-out the Middle East. Additionally, Syria also contributes through the vital provision of safe houses and offices from which innumerable organizations have been able to recruit potential trainees.[17]

The support for Palestinian or pro-Palestinian terrorists continued in the early twenty-first century. There was, however, no hard evidence that Syria sponsored Al Qaeda or Al Qaeda related groups. Indeed, after 9/11, the U.S. State Department noted that the Syrian government "cooperated significantly with the United States and other foreign governments against al-Qaida, the Taliban, and other terrorist organizations and individuals. It has also discouraged any signs of public support for al-Qaida, including in the media and at mosques."[18] It seems that Syria's relationship with and support for terrorist groups have always been dictated by the government's domestic and foreign policy interests and are, according to Byman, "nuanced and complex, reflecting Damascus's desire to both exploit terrorist groups and limit them."[19] In its annual assessment of terrorism state sponsors for 2008, the State Department expressed particular concern about the close ties between Damascus and Tehran. The report noted that "[t]hroughout the year, Syria continued to strengthen ties with fellow state sponsor of terrorism, Iran" and that "President Asad repaid a 2007 visit to Damascus by Iranian President Ahmadinejad with a visit of his own to Tehran in early August, his third visit since 2005."[20]

The Case of Saudi Arabia

Martha Crenshaw wrote, shortly after the attacks of 9/11, that for thirty years most acts of international terrorism against the United States were committed "because of United States support for unpopular local governments or regional enemies."[21]

Add to this the fact that oppressive regimes in the region were not unhappy when their most militant critics directed their fury and terror against others, namely, the United States and Israel. Indeed, for the sake of protecting their own back, these regimes channeled the hatred of these groups to outside targets. To that end, some of the regimes also provided financial support to terrorists or allowed individuals and organizations within their countries to do so as long as the militants did not strike inside their borders.

While other countries in the region, especially those on the oil-rich Arabian Peninsula, supported and/or tolerated terrorism that targeted Israel, Saudi Arabia's role in financing a global network of terrorist breeding grounds was unique. According to a staff report for the National Commission on Terrorism Attacks upon the United States,

> Saudi Arabia has long been considered the primary source of al Qaeda funding, but we found no evidence that the Saudi government as an institution or senior officials within the Saudi government funded al Qaeda. Still, al Qaeda found fertile fundraising ground in the Kingdom, where extreme religious views are common and charitable giving is essential to the culture and, until recently, subject to very limited oversight.[22]

But whether the Saudi government, some of the princes of the House of Saud, or their wives transferred funds directly to Al Qaeda or related cells and individuals was of less concern than the well-known practice of Saudi Arabia's rulers of indirectly facilitating preachers of hate and terror abroad. Loretta Napoleoni describes an extensive "mosque network," sponsored by Saudi Arabian funds, as "the ideological partner of the terror financial network; it complements it and is as complex and comprehensive a web as its monetary counterpart."[23]

This global mosque network is the result of a symbiotic relationship between the guardians of Wahhabism, the most fundamentalist version of Islam, and the ruling House of Saud. In return for the religious leadership's support of Saudi Arabia's rulers, the government has traditionally supported the strict implementation of Wahhabi teaching and Wahhabism's missionary zeal. Because Muslims are required to make charitable donations (known as *zakat*), a great deal of money flows into the coffers of charitable organizations in the oil-rich countries around the Persian Gulf. For many years, most of the generous giving by wealthy Saudis went to "government-linked charities with the dual mission of doing good works and propagating the country's strict Wahabbi Islam."[24] In order to divert growing opposition to their own regime, the Saudi rulers encouraged the Wahhabi colonization drive "as a release valve for the most extreme religious strains inside Saudi Arabia."[25] This was especially the case after the end of the first Persian Gulf War. According to Dan Murphy,

> In the 1990s, many of the kingdom's most militant and committed preachers and young men were sent overseas to work and preach. They were given tacit approval for militant activities abroad so long as the same methods were not brought to bear against the monarchy, which men like Osama bin Laden consider to be corrupt and illegitimate.[26]

By establishing mosques, financed by Saudi charities, Wahhabi mullahs found first of all fertile ground in those parts of the world where Muslims had not enjoyed religious freedom for a long time, namely, in several of the newly independent former Soviet republics. Mosques and religious schools were also established in Africa, South and Southeast Asia, and elsewhere in the developing world. While aggressive in those regions, the approach was more discreet in the West. But the result was all the same, as Napoleoni observed:

> In the West, the Mosque Network's main operations have been recruiting and fundraising. So successful have they been in performing these tasks that several mosques have now become hotbeds of potential terror fighters, who have been fed an explosive mixture of religion and political ideology.[27]

Contrary to the Saudi rulers' intention to export the domestic discontent, Osama bin Laden and his followers did not lose sight of their number-one target. Beginning in 2003 and intensifying in 2004, Al Qaeda cells mounted a deadly terrorist offensive inside Saudi Arabia. Starting in May 2003 with the truck bombing of a Riyadh housing compound for Westerners that killed thirty-five persons and injured more than two hundred, there was a multitude of bold attacks on foreigners, including one on the U.S. consulate in Jedda in late 2004, as well as kidnappings and executions. The immediate victims of these acts of terrorism were mostly Americans and other foreigners, but the House of Saud was a target as well. Bin Laden and his followers wanted to drive foreigners, including those working in the oil industry and U.S. military personnel, out of the country and thereby weaken Saudi Arabia's economy and defense. The offensive was at least partially successful in that some foreign companies reduced their presence in Saudi Arabia.

When Governments Reconsider Their Support for Terrorism

State support for terrorism and specific terrorist groups does not necessarily last forever. On the contrary, in the past governments have frequently reconsidered their ties to terror groups and ceased or altered their support. Thus, after allowing Palestinian terrorists to reside and train in Libya for years, Colonel Qaddafi asked these groups to leave his country because he feared further retaliatory strikes by Israel and the United States. And when the Libyan ruler claimed that he had turned his back on terrorism and was in support of the post–9/11 war on terrorism, he campaigned for an end to U.S. sanctions and the return of U.S. oil companies in order to revitalize Libya's economy. Obviously, Qaddafi recognized that the economic costs of supporting terrorism were far higher than the ideological benefits. But Libya's retreat from sponsoring terrorism seems the exception not the rule. As Byman concluded,

> State sponsorship of terrorism is a complex problem that cannot easily be solved. Despite diplomatic protests, economic sanctions, and even military pressure Iran, Pakistan, and Syria have supported numerous terrorist groups for decades. The Taliban persisted in its support for al-Qa'ida until US-backed forces toppled it from power. Many other states also backed terrorist groups, at times even risking war to do so.[28]

Failed and Failing States and "Brown Areas"

The typical state sponsor of terrorism displays a strong central government firmly in control of its territory, but weak states present problems with respect to terrorism as well. In the absence of a strong central government, terrorists have free reign in the territory of these countries, or parts thereof. Colombia is a good example in that the central government manages to exert its authority over some parts of the country but not in others. As a result, a number of domestic terrorist and paramilitary groups control chunks of the country and, at times, fight each other for what they perceive as valuable pieces of real estate—especially those where farmers grow coca plants, the prime ingredient in cocaine.[29] Yemen is an example of a failed state in which effective governmental authority is no longer exercised. Failed states, like failing states, are breeding grounds for terrorists. Yemenis were among the many Al Qaeda adherents who were trained in bin Laden's camps in Afghanistan. And an Al Qaeda cell in Yemen carried out the lethal attack on the USS *Cole* in 2000 while the American warship made a refueling stop in the port of Aden.

And then there are states with functioning central governments that nevertheless contain geographical areas in which the government cannot or does not try to exert its authority and control. The territory of the Philippines, for example, contains what has been defined as "brown areas"—geographical enclaves "where there is minimal or zero presence of the state both functionally and territorially."[30] As a result, the Abu Sayyaf group, an Al Qaeda affiliate, has operated and prevailed in the southern Philippines in spite of repeated efforts by government troops to destroy the terror organization once and for all.

From the American perspective, one of the most explosive "brown areas" is the so-called tri-border-area (TBA), where Argentina, Brazil, and Paraguay meet. According to Benedetta Berti,

> The Triple Frontera is one of the most important commercial centers of South America, with approximately 20 thousand people transiting on a daily basis from the neighboring states to the free-trade area of Ciudad del Este in Paraguay. The intense volume of people and goods entering the TBA, together with its porous borders, are two important factors that originally attracted criminal and armed groups to this area. Additionally, the relative ease with which money is locally laundered and transferred to and from regions overseas constitutes a very powerful incentive to maintain a base of operations in the TBA.[31]

No wonder that terrorist organizations with very different agendas and ideologies have found a haven to exchange operational expertise and financial resources. Hezbollah in particular has for decades a strong presence here and taken "advantage of the extensive network of immigrants of Lebanese origin residing in the area."[32] Al Qaeda leaders obviously recognized the opportunities offered by the triple frontier region because a map of the area was found in an Al Qaeda safe house in Afghanistan. While there is no conclusive evidence that Al Qaeda Central was ever active in the TBA, jihadis have reportedly established training facilities in this brown area and are using the region as a launching pad to recruit all over Latin America:

> A recent Argentine intelligence report mentions Uruguaiana, a Brazilian town on the border with Argentina, and Cascavel in Paraguay, as places where Muslim merchants with suspicious connections have surfaced.[33]

According to terrorism expert Walter Purdy, this "region is one of the world's emerging threat areas that terrorists could use to stage attacks."[34]

Involuntary Host Countries

When governments invite or allow terrorists to operate, train, or hide within their borders, their countries are what one may call "voluntary hosts" of terrorist organizations and/or individual members. But there are far more nation-states that have become involuntary hosts of either domestic or international terrorists than there are state sponsors or voluntary hosts. As discussed above, because failing or failed states are unable to defeat terrorists, they often become involuntary hosts of terrorist groups. But liberal democracies are just as vulnerable to becoming involuntary host countries and hideouts for terrorists as are failing and failed states—albeit for very different reasons.

Democratic countries and their peoples provide an environment conducive to breeding their own terrorism and attract terrorists from abroad because of their commitment to freedom and civil liberties. Political and religious tolerance, open borders, freedom of movement, increased diversity of the populace because of immigration, and political asylum opportunities are among the reasons why terrorists seek out democratic states. Terrorists know that it is much easier to operate in free societies than under repressive regimes—unless they are allied with those regimes. If there was any question about the abundance of terrorist cells in democratic states that do not share the characteristics of failing and failed states, the post–9/11 years removed such doubts. After all, investigations uncovered that

Al Qaeda operatives and like-minded cells existed and operated in the United States, Canada, the United Kingdom, France, Germany, Italy, Spain, Belgium, and the Netherlands, as well as in other democracies in Europe and elsewhere.

All told, then, state sponsors of terrorism are only part of the story about the connections between nation-states and terrorists. Failing and failed states frequently become natural breeding grounds for terrorists without government support. But well-functioning democratic states, too, are increasingly cast in the role of involuntary hosts of terrorists, especially Islamic fanatics who are either aliens or first-generation immigrants.

Notes

1. U.S. Department of State, "Country Reports on Terrorism," April 2008, available at http://www.state.gov/s/ct/rls/crt/2007/103711.htm, (accessed January 13, 2009).
2. Ibid.
3. U.S. Department of State, "Overview of State-Sponsored Terrorism," in "Patterns of Global Terrorism 2003," April 29, 2004, 1, www.state.gov/s/ct/rls/pgtrpt/2003/31644pf.htm.
4. U.S. Department of State, "Country Reports on Terrorism," April 2008.
5. U.S. Department of State, "Country Reports on Terrorism 2008," released April 30, 2009, chapter 3. The report is available at http://www.state.gov/s/ct/rls/crt/2008/index.htm.
6. Ibid.
7. Daniel Byman, *Deadly Connections: States that Sponsor Terrorism* (New York: Cambridge University Press, 2005), 79.
8. Ze'ev Schiff, "Israel's War With Iran." *Foreign Affairs* (November/December 2006), http://www.foreignaffairs.org/20061101faessay85603/ze-ev-schiff/israel-s-war-with-iran.html.
9. U.S. Department of State, "Overview of State-Sponsored Terrorism," in "Patterns of Global Terrorism 2002," released April 30, 2003, 4.
10. Ibid.
11. National Commission on Terrorist Attacks upon the United States, "Overview of the Enemy," Staff Statement no. 15, June 16, 2004.
12. U.S. Department of State, 2004, 5.
13. For more on this episode, see Brigitte L. Nacos, *Mass-Mediated Terrorism: The Central Role of the Media in Terrorism and Counterterrorism* (Lanham, MD: Rowman & Littlefield, 2002), ch. 3.
14. Thomas Hunter, "Bomb School: International Terrorist Training Camps," *Jane's Intelligence Report,* March 1, 1997.
15. U.S. Department of State, "Country Reports on Terrorism 2008."
16. Ibid.
17. Hunter.
18. U.S. Department of State, 2004.
19. Byman, 117.
20. U.S. Department of State, "Country Reports on Terrorism 2008."
21. Martha Crenshaw, "Why America? The Globalization of Civil War," *Current History* (December 2001): 425.
22. National Commission on Terrorist Attacks.
23. Loretta Napoleoni, *Modern Jihad* (London: Pluto Press, 2003), 128.
24. Dan Murphy, "Saudi Crackdown on Charities Seen as Incomplete," *Christian Science Monitor,* June 9, 2004, www.csmonitor.com/2004/0609/p07p02-wome.html.
25. Ibid.
26. Ibid.
27. Napoleoni, 131.
28. Byman, 273.
29. In June 2004, for example, members of the left-wing FARC killed thirty-four coca farmers in northeastern Colombia who reportedly worked for a right-wing paramilitary group, in an effort

to regain control over an area they had lost to the paramilitaries. See Juan Forero, "Attack by Columbia Rebels Threatens Fragile Talks," *New York Times*, June 17, 2004, A3.

30. Ibid., 140.
31. Benedetta Berti, "Reassessing the Transnational Terrorism-Criminal Link in South America's Tri-Border-Area." Terrorism Monitor 6:18, September 22, 2008. Available at http://www.jamestown.org/single/?no_cache=1&tx_ttnews[swords]=8fd5893941d69d0be3f378576261ae3e&tx_ttnews[exact_search]=Reassessing%20the%20Transnational%20Terrorism-Criminal%20Link&tx_ttnews[categories_1]=11&tx_ttnews[tt_news]=5172&tx_ttnews[backPid]=7&cHash=92fa20c09b, accessed May 13, 2009.
32. Ibid.
33. A. Brownfeld, "Terrorists in the Triple Frontier," *Jane's Terrorism and Security Monitor*, February 12, 2003.
34. Ibid.

CHAPTER 8

Common Thread: Goals, Targets, Tactics

Aᴸᴛʜᴏᴜɢʜ ꜱᴏᴍᴇ ᴘᴇʀꜱᴏɴꜱ ᴀʀᴇ ᴘꜱʏᴄʜᴏʟᴏɢɪᴄᴀʟʟʏ ᴍᴏʀᴇ ᴘʀᴏɴᴇ to become terrorists than others, it would be a mistake to dismiss terrorists and their deeds as crazy or capricious. Instead, as Bruce Hoffman has noted, a terrorist group's course of action—the selection of targets and tactics—is shaped by a variety of factors, among them the organization's ideology.[1] Indeed, there is little doubt that the ideology of a group, whether well or ill defined, determines the goals, the targets or victims, and, to some degree, the tactics or methods of terror as well.

As for the goals, terrorists tend to have two sets of political objectives, namely, short-term and long-term goals; and typically, they have both sets in mind when they plan and execute an act of violence. In the case of Lebanese and Palestinian groups that were responsible for a series of hijackings and kidnappings in the 1970s and 1980s, the short-term objective most of the time was to win the release of imprisoned comrades. One shorter-term goal of Hezbollah was to force the pullback of American and French troops from Lebanon. Once the American and French forces had been withdrawn following a horrific terror strike against their bases near Beirut in 1983, the group explained its ultimate long-term goal in an "Open Letter to Downtrodden in Lebanon and the World":

> As for Israel, we consider it the American spearhead in our Islamic world. It is the usurping enemy that must be fought until the usurped right is returned to its owners. . . .
>
> This Islamic resistance must continue, grow, and escalate, with God's help, and must receive from all Muslims in all parts of the world utter support, aid, backing, and participation so that we may be able to uproot this cancerous germ and obliterate it from existence.[2]

When the Weather Underground, the Symbionese Liberation Army, or the Baader-Meinhof Red Army Faction pulled off bank robberies, their short-term goals were clear: They wanted money to support their lives in the underground. But they rationalized their crimes and their booty as means to further their ultimate or long-term goals—revolutionary systemic changes. In the case of the Red Army Faction, this meant nothing short of an international revolution. As one of the RAF's members described it,

> *Even if the masses in the European metropolis don't put themselves on the side of the revolution—the working class among us is privileged and takes part in the exploitation of the Third World—the only possibility for those who build the Vanguard here, who take part in the struggle here, is to destroy the infra-structure of imperialism, destroy the apparatus.*[3]

Do Terrorists Achieve Their Goals?

On the one hand, if one considers the philosophy and objectives of the Baader-Meinhof group and associated cells, it is crystal clear that they failed to achieve, or even further, their ultimate or strategic goals. On the other hand, they were quite successful in realizing their short-term or tactical objectives, such as the release of fellow terrorists. In this respect, the West German radical left was representative of other left-wing terrorists of this period in that these movements often did succeed in their short-term agendas. The same is true of other types of terrorists (right-wing, nationalist,

Arafat: From Terrorist Outcast to Legitimate Leader

Once denied a visa by the U.S. Department of State to visit the United Nations' headquarters in New York because he was considered a dangerous international terrorist, Yassir Arafat was later accepted as a legitimate Palestinian leader. This picture shows Arafat (second from left) at a 1995 summit in the Oval Office with President Bill Clinton, Vice President Al Gore, Egyptian President Hosni Mubarak, Israeli Prime Minister Yitzhak Rabin, and Jordan's King Hussein.

single-issue, and so on) as well. Given this mixed bag of successes and failures, it has been argued that "the scorecard of struggle between nation-states and terrorists is not so clear."[4] While acknowledging terrorists' tactical successes, Robert A. Feary concluded in regard to their ultimate objectives that the result "is hardly a source of encouragement for terrorists."[5]

To be sure, the battlefield of terrorism is littered with utter failure in terms of long-term or ultimate strategic goals. But there were David-beats-Goliath results as well. One of the terrorist success stories was written by the Irgun Zvai Leumi, a Jewish militant group that operated in what was then the British mandate in Palestine and committed terrorist acts against British targets. The most deadly and most notorious of these attacks targeted the British headquarters at the David Hotel in Jerusalem in 1946, resulting in the deaths of ninety-one persons. The terrorist campaign led to the withdrawal of the British from Palestine and the establishment of the state of Israel soon thereafter. According to David Fromkin,

> Of course, Britain might have withdrawn anyway, at some other time or for some other reason. But that is really beside the point, for the Irgun wanted independence then and there, in order to open up the country for refugees from Hitler's Europe. They got what they wanted when they wanted it by doing it their own way.[6]

Similarly, the terrorist tactics of the National Liberation Front (FLN) forced France to withdraw from its North African colony of Algeria and open the way to Algeria's national independence.

So, does terrorism work? Sometimes it does, in that one "can find, well before Yassir Arafat's reception at the United Nations in 1974, historical illustrations of terrorism's efficacy."[7] However, citing the cases of Israel and Algeria, Fromkin has argued, "Terrorism wins only if you respond to it in the way that the terrorists want you to."[8] Philip Jenkins concluded the case of the Algerian FLN demonstrated that terrorism and terrorists can realize their long-term goals. According to Jenkins,

> Several other movements have made the transition from loathed terrorists to respected politicians. At some stages of its history, the African National Congress used terrorist actions, but in 1994, the ANC became the governing party of South Africa, the most powerful state in black Africa. In Northern Ireland, the Irish Republican Army has often employed savage violence against civilians and noncombatants, of a sort that can only be described as terrorism. By the late 1990s, leading IRA supporter Gerry Adams was a prominent figure in Northern Irish politics and a member of the British Parliament. In Israel, too, the condemned Jewish terrorists of the 1940s had by the 1980s risen to the status of respected political leaders.[9]

All in all, then, the terrorist rate of success is pretty high when it comes to short-term goals but quite low when it comes to long-term objectives. Yet, the fact that some terrorist movements did accomplish their ultimate goals in the past continues to encourage contemporary terrorists' belief that they, too, may become exceptions to the rule.

The Selection of Targets

Once an ideological rationale has been embraced and the ultimate or long-term goal or goals have been established, the range of acceptable targets "is determined by a number of factors, and the terrorists' ideology is central to this process, not only because it provides the initial dynamic for the terrorists' actions, but because it sets out the moral framework within which they operate."[10] Ideology is more important than other factors because the doctrine "defines how the members of a group see the world around them."[11] More importantly, the terrorist doctrine identifies the pool of enemies from which the victims will be selected. The West German Red Army Faction (RAF), for example, considered the United States and NATO (including West Germany, a member state) as the core of the hated imperialist system. Thus, American citizens and NATO representatives and facilities were logical and legitimate targets. While the Italian Red Brigades (RB) shared the RAF's hate of the global imperialist evil, in reality the movement's ultimate goal was the removal of the Italian regime. The result was, as C. J. M. Drake has pointed out, that the German left-wing terrorists' priority targets were the U.S. military and high-level German officials in politics and the corporate world. The RAF picked as victims individuals whom the group perceived as symbols of gross injustices and wrongdoing. Italian terrorists, on the other hand, attacked mostly low- and middle-level targets—with a few exceptions, such as the kidnapping and killing of former Prime Minister Aldo Moro in 1978. Nearly all of the RB's targeted persons were Italians.[12]

The examples of the RAF and RB demonstrate that even when groups share the same ideological framework and the same enemies, they can differ in the selection of their victims. For the Italian terrorists, all police officers were legitimate and explicitly selected targets; for the West German terrorists, low-level police officers were never intentional targets—even though several were killed by accident during terrorist operations. Inside the West German terrorist movement, a marked change occurred after the founders of the RAF—Ulrike Meinhof, Horst Mahler, and Andreas Baader—had been arrested. On several occasions, their "heirs" targeted "innocent" people with no symbolic meaning. This was the case in several hijackings of airplanes. Reportedly, the RAF founders rejected these strikes against innocents as the "willful dilution of the moral thrust of the first RAF by later recruits"; and one of them, Klaus Juenschke, complained about "this degenerate crew that has the nerve . . . to boast of this cowardly murder and to present it as a new quality in the anti-imperialist struggle . . . in Western Europe."[13] By and large, however, even the new generation of German terrorists adhered to the careful selection of military, political, or corporate targets.

For many years, anti-American terrorism affected civilians who seemed to be randomly selected because they happened to be at the wrong place at the wrong time. However, often the victims were "not selected purely at random."[14] Instead, terrorists targeted U.S. citizens, persons carrying Israeli passports, members of a particular religious group (namely, Jews), or simply those who visited a particular country. The Lebanese terrorists who hijacked a TWA airliner in 1985, for example, collected all passports and asked one of the flight attendants to sort out Israelis and passengers with Jewish-sounding names. After a terrorist assault on Lod Airport in Israel in 1972, during which a number of foreign tourists were killed, one of the terrorists explained that "there are no innocent tourists in Israel."[15] The rationale was that if you are not for us, you are against us, or, as some terrorists have put it, "If you are not part of the solution, you are part of the problem."[16] Similarly, following the first World Trade Center bombing in 1993, the perpetrators of the first major international terrorist act on American soil stated,

> The American people are responsible for the actions of their government and they must question all of the crimes that their government is committing against other people. Or they—Americans—will be the targets of our operations that could diminish them.[17]

Osama bin Laden explained his jihad against all Americans in similar terms. He explicitly cited the will of God as the ultimate endorsement when he wrote, "All these crimes and sins committed by the Americans are a clear declaration of war on God, his messenger, and Muslims."[18]

In the conflict between Israelis and Palestinians, members of Palestinian terrorist groups, too, have rationalized the indiscriminate targeting of Israelis on the basis of what they consider the justice of their cause. This mindset is reflected in the remarks of Palestinian militants:

> *The organization did not impose any limits with regards to damage or scope or nature of the armed attacks. The aim was to kill as many Jews as possible and there was no moral distinction between potential victims, whether soldiers, women or children.*
>
> *When it came to moral considerations, we believed in the justice of our cause. . . . I don't recall ever being troubled by moral questions.*[19]

The mastermind and perpetrator of the Oklahoma City bombing in 1995, Timothy McVeigh, also justified the indiscriminate killing of innocents for his cause. After he had disclosed his plan to bomb the Alfred P. Murrah Federal Building to his friend Michael Fortier, he was asked about the fate of all the people in the building. McVeigh answered, "Think about the people as if they were storm troopers in *Star Wars*. They may be individually innocent, but they are guilty because they work for the Evil Empire."[20]

In sum, then, the overall ideological framework and the associated assignment of blame for their grievances will guide some terrorists to select a limited number of target types and others to pinpoint huge groups of people, even a whole nation or several nations, as legitimate targets.

Terrorist Methods: From Primitive Bombs to WMD

Describing the mindset of terrorists as they justify their violent means to achieve political ends, J. Bowyer Bell observed that for terrorists,

> *the recourse to violence, often the last option, is a legitimate means to shape the future. The present is intolerable and violence the only way. As one Palestinian fedayi said, "We would throw roses if it would work." Since it does not, they throw bombs.*[21]

The metaphor of the rose-throwing terrorist is, of course, in sharp contrast to the real-life damage that terrorists have caused for many years and to the fact that terrorists have used all kinds of violent methods—from stabbing or strangling their victims to dispersing nerve gas. The most obvious reason for changes in terrorist tactics over time was simply the availability of ever more convenient and potent means to attack and harm the targets of terrorism. Throughout the centuries, terrorists embraced each new technology for their purposes, from the revolver to sticks of dynamite, fertilizer bombs, rockets, and sarin gas. Advances in transportation technology, too, have affected the choice of terrorist methods as the derailment of trains, the hijacking of airplanes and ships, the suicide bombing of crowded buses, or the explosion of car or truck bombs have attested to—not to mention the attacks of 9/11, when terrorists turned airliners into devastating missiles.

The selection of one or more targets and of the method of attack go hand in hand. Both decisions are affected by the following factors:

- The degree of access to targets
- The level of protection provided for targets
- The general state of counterterrorist measures in the targeted society
- The risks involved for the attacker(s)
- The probability of carrying out a successful mission

For terrorists, nothing is more important than executing an act of terror successfully. As George Habash put it, "The main point is to select targets where success is 100% assured."[22] There are additional factors that figure into the selection of the particular terrorist method to be used in a given operation:

- The terrorists' level of training and skills
- The availability of financial resources, mobility, and hideouts
- The available weaponry
- The decision to either limit a strike to the immediate victim(s) and spare innocent bystanders or attack indiscriminately regardless of the number of innocent bystanders

Modern terrorists have a broad range of choices when deciding on a particular mode of attack. A quarter of a century ago, terrorism experts Robert Kupperman and Darrell Trent warned that terrorists were not only using "pistols, submachine guns, and bombs" but that they also had attempted to use "heat-seeking, surface-to-air rockets (SA-7s) and Soviet-made antitank weapons (RPG-7s) and that German terrorists had threatened to disperse mustard gas and nerve agents."[23] The more sophisticated among terrorist groups often write and distribute their own instruction manuals that describe the range of weapons recommended for terrorist strikes. Thus, the Provisional Irish Republican Army issued a pamphlet describing various tactics, "including preparation and use of a variety of explosives, special culvert bombs for burial beneath roadways, and deployment of snipers. The text also mentioned submachine guns, pistols, grenades, rifles, automatic rifles, mortars, and rocket launchers." According to one expert, "All these [weapons] have been deployed in past strikes by the IRA, and all remain in regular service today. In that respect the IRA is very typical for contemporary terrorism."[24] This IRA list of suitable terrorist weapons shows that contemporary terrorist groups have access to a larger variety of weapons.

Most Common Methods of Terrorist Attacks

Bombings

Suicide bombings

Assassinations

Armed attacks

Missile attacks

Hijackings

Kidnappings

Mass disruption/mass destruction

Bombing sites is by far the most often used terrorist method with the distinct type of suicide bombing not far behind. In the past several years, heavily armed terrorists and insurgents resorted increasingly to armed attacks on persons. The November 2008 attacks in Mumbai, India, was a shocking case of terrorists staging armed attacks on civilians in hotels and other facilities. But such attacks are most common when terrorists or guerrillas control some territory, or have support in the population, and/or operate in a region that is not controlled by policy and security forces. Large and well-armed and well-equipped groups come to mind here, such as the FARC in Colombia, the Taliban in Afghanistan and Pakistan, and various terrorist and insurgent groups in Iraq. Not surprisingly, then, the number of armed attacks skyrocketed in the last several years, with the vast number of incidents occurring in Iraq, Afghanistan, and Pakistan. For 2007, for example, the U.S. Counterterrorism Center's statistics of worldwide terrorism incidents reveal that right after "conventional" bombing and suicide bombing combined (16,932 incidents), armed attack (11,411 incidents) was the second most often used terrorist method. Like conventional bombers, armed attackers strike at the time and place of their choice, tend to surprise their victims, and have the advantage even if their targets are armed themselves. In the past, armed attacks ranked low in the hierarchy of terrorist methods.

Terrorist actions result in either conclusive incidents or incidents of duration. Bombings, assassinations, and suicide missions are conclusive incidents because the actual acts occur in fractions of seconds—armed attacks can last longer—whereas hijackings and kidnappings are incidents of duration because these terrorist events last for longer periods of time—hours, days, weeks, months, or even years. Although in a different league in terms of the likely damage, terrorism aimed at causing mass disruption and mass destruction also fits the category of conclusive incident as far as carrying out these tactics is concerned. The following sections summarize the characteristics of various terrorist methods or tactics.

BOMBINGS For a long time, terrorists have preferred bombings to all other methods of attack because no other weapons are as readily available as incendiary or explosive devices. Just as important, this is an "easily learned technique that can be undertaken with minimal risk to the perpetrator" in that the "bomber operates with time and distance on his side."[25] Putting timers on devices allows perpetrators to detonate the explosives at the time of their choosing. Bombs come in many forms and "the possible operations for their use are almost infinite."[26] In most instances, terrorists' bombs are of the "do-it-yourself" variety because, as experts know, crude but potent bombs "can be fabricated from seemingly innocuous materials found in the open market."[27] Detailed instructions on the ingredients of bombs and how to mix or assemble them are readily and legally available in bookstores, in libraries, and on the Internet.

The web site of the Animal Liberation Front (ALF), for example, has posted the "ALF Primer," which describes in detail how to build simple incendiary devices to commit arson, how to best place them in targeted facilities, and how to avoid being caught by the police. In the "Getting Started" section of the primer, the ALF details a "simple way to create an incendiary device" and a "different version of the same device" to be used by arsonists.[28] A variety of potent homemade explosives are described in easily available books, such as *The Anarchist Cookbook* or *Home Workshop*

Explosives. In June 2003, one customer reviewer of *The Anarchist Cookbook* wrote the following on the Amazon.com web site:

> *Almost all (with the exception of a few) of the things in here are accurate in the sense that they show you BASICALLY how to do something, but also in the sense that the way it tells you how to do it is so dangerous that it will most likely fail. . . . If you really want to know how to make homemade exploseives [sic] try "Home Workshop Explosives" by Uncle Fester, now that book is a real deal. This books [sic] techniques are tooken [sic] from military handbooks that date back to about 30 years ago!*[29]

In October 2001, a Brazilian reader of Uncle Fester's *Home Workshop Explosives* wrote in a customer review on the Amazon.com site, "WOW! I just received the 2nd Revised Edition and Uncle Fester made a miracle: changed the best into something better. . . . If you want the very best book on explosives manufacture [sic], this is the only one to have."[30]

But one doesn't even have to buy a book; instructions for putting together bombs were easy to come by in the past and still are today. Following the pipe bomb explosion in the Centennial Olympic Park in Atlanta in July 1996, the CNN.com web site carried a story that detailed in its text and an accompanying illustration how such a device is put together. Readers learned the following:

> *A pipe bomb is a fairly simple device—literally a length of a pipe capped at both ends and filled with an explosive. Often they are packed with nails and screws to heighten damage. . . . The pipes can be filled with low-order gunpowder or higher-order plastique. It can be rigged to go off instantly or with a timer.*[31]

Seven years after the initial posting, the same story was still available on CNN's web site. However, while the CNN story seemed to provide basic information about the nature of pipe bombs unwittingly, other web sites carried explicit instructions on building explosives such as Molotov cocktails and bombs consisting of fertilizer and fuel.[32] The terrorist conspirators whose truck bomb nearly toppled one of the World Trade Center towers in 1993 did not encounter any problems when they bought the chemicals needed for putting together a powerful bomb. Simon Reeve describes how Ramzi Yousef, the mastermind of the first World Trade Center bombing, and his associates proceeded:

> *Yousef, also using the name "Kamal Ibraham," one of his 11 aliases he used during his six months in the US, began ordering chemicals from a local firm called City Chemical, including 1,000 lbs (454 kg) of urea, 105 gallons of nitric acid, and 60 gallons of sulphuric acid. Yousef told City Chemical's salesman he knew exactly what he wanted: the nitrogen content of the urea crystals had to be 46.65 per cent and the sulphuric acid had to be 93 per cent pure.*[33]

Timothy McVeigh and his accomplice, Terry Nichols, also purchased with ease the ingredients for the powerful truck bomb that completely destroyed the large Alfred P. Murrah Federal Building in Oklahoma City. According to Lou Michel and Dan Herbeck,

> *On September 30 and October 18 [1994], Terry Nichols purchased a combined total of four thousand pounds of ammonium nitrate using the alias Mike Havens. McVeigh purchased smaller amounts. Whenever the opportunity presented itself, he pulled into the local feed and seed store of a small town and loaded up his car with fifty-pound*

bags of ammonium nitrate. He thought nothing of tossing ten bags into the backseat of the Road Warrior; he would have filled the trunk, too, if he weren't concerned about the unequal distribution in weight.

Between McVeigh and Nichols, they made about eight purchases before they had the amount of ammonium nitrate they needed.[34]

Terrorists have also used plastic explosives with devastating results. The bombing of Pan Am Flight 103 in late 1988 was accomplished by the explosion of a small sheet of Semtex, a plastic explosive that was available at the time from the Czech Republic and Libya. The Irish Republican Army "used it independently and liberally for bombs, such as those carried in a briefcase, or as a detonator for larger fertilizer bombs, just as non-Irish groups often do."[35]

Dynamite was the first explosive used by terrorists. The anarchists of the nineteenth century hailed Alfred Nobel's invention as the "tool for the destruction of society" in prose and even in poems.[36] Dynamite is still used by modern terrorists. Typically, terrorists steal sticks of dynamite from military stockpiles, construction sites, or mines. More than 100 years ago, anarchist John Most tried to assemble an incendiary letter bomb, a device that modern-day terrorists have built and deployed as well—albeit in more sophisticated forms. The "Unabomber," Theodore Kaczynski, for example, killed and injured all of his victims by mailing them letter bombs.

ASSASSINATIONS   If they use bombs to assassinate their enemy, terrorists have a better chance of avoiding arrest than when using handguns. Depending on the circumstances, even the assassin who shoots his or her victim from close range may be able to flee the scene. In early 2002, for example, two assassins killed an Italian government consultant, Marco Biagi, in Bologna by firing several shots as their victim entered his home. Both shooters sped away on a scooter. The Greek terrorists who in 2000 assassinated Stephen Saunders, a British military attaché, in Athens shot him with a .45-mm pistol and got away. But by and large, shooting a target from close range is riskier than other tactics. Take the case of Yigal Amir, the young Israeli who killed Prime Minister Yitzhak Rabin in order to stop the Middle East peace process. Amir used a Beretta pistol to shoot Rabin and was immediately subdued and arrested by security forces.

SUICIDE ATTACKS   When nineteen members of the Al Qaeda organization flew hijacked airliners into buildings in New York and Washington, D.C., on September 11, 2001, they introduced the United States to a terrorist tactic that until then had been widely used and feared in other parts of the world: suicide attacks. Immediately, the type of attack was compared to the practice of kamikaze during World War II, when some 4,600 Japanese nationals committed suicide by crashing their planes into enemy targets. But unlike the kamikaze flights that were undertaken as part of a country's war effort, the more recent suicide attacks were carried out by groups or individuals. As Adam Dolnik recalled before the 2003 defeat of Saddam Hussein's regime in Iraq,

The modern practice of suicide bombings has its roots in Lebanon. The first major suicide attack by a non-state group occurred in December 1981, when 27 people died and more than 100 were wounded in the bombing of the Iraqi Embassy in Beirut. This attack was claimed by Al Dawa (The Call), the Iranian-backed Shia group that seeks to topple Saddam Hussein's regime in Iraq.[37]

For most Americans, however, the history of the modern suicide practice dates back to 1983, when a member of the Lebanese Hezbollah drove a truck laden with explosives into the American Embassy in Beirut, killing himself and more than 60 other persons. Six months later, another member of the same organization ignited a truck bomb as he drove into the U.S. Marine barracks near Beirut airport, killing 241 Americans. Another lethal suicide attack against the French military stationed in Lebanon was carried out nearly simultaneously and resulted in the death of 58 French paratroopers. Indeed, more than 500 individuals died within a one-year period, from November 1982 to November 1983, as the result of five major suicide attacks in Lebanon. Lawrence Eagleburger, then undersecretary of state for political affairs in the Reagan administration, said at the time that it was nearly impossible to defend oneself if a driver is willing to kill himself.[38] American and French troops were withdrawn from Lebanon, and the Israeli Defense Forces retreated into the southern part of the country. The success of the suicide missions was undeniable.

From the perspective of terrorists, suicide terrorism has a number of advantages compared to other terrorist methods. According to Bruce Hoffman, "Suicide bombings are inexpensive and effective. They are less complicated and compromising than other kinds of terrorist operations. They guarantee media coverage. The suicide terrorist is the ultimate smart bomb."[39] The efficacy of the suicide tactic is best understood by terrorists themselves. After interviewing 250 of the most militant Palestinians in the 1990s, Nasra Hassan wrote,

> A Palestinian security official pointed out that, apart from a willing young man, all that is needed is such items as nails, gunpowder, a battery, a light switch, and a short cable, mercury (readily obtainable from thermometers), acetone, and the cost of tailoring a belt wide enough to hold six or eight pockets of explosives. The most expensive item is transportation to a distant Israeli town. The total cost of a typical [suicide] operation is about a hundred dollars.[40]

Furthermore, the planners of suicide missions do not have to make escape plans or fear the arrest of their operatives and the revelation of organizational secrets. More importantly, organizations that embrace suicide attacks as their tactic of choice appreciate that this terrorist method is more likely to succeed than most other means. According to Nasra Hassan,

> Military commanders of Hamas and Islamic Jihad remarked that the human bomb was one [of] the surest ways of hitting a target. A senior Hamas leader said, "The main thing is to guarantee that a large number of the enemy will be affected. With an explosive belt or bag, the bomber has control over vision, location, and timing."[41]

Suicide attacks are especially horrifying to target societies—for a number of reasons. First of all, as one expert concluded, this tactic is "reliably deadly" and "on average kills four times as many people as other terrorist acts."[42] Secondly, suicide attacks have lasting effects on the psyche of the target society because no one knows when, where, and how the next suicide attack will occur.

Because of their operational and psychological effectiveness, modern-day suicide attacks spread from Lebanon to an increasing number of other venues, among them Sri Lanka, Turkey, Chechnya, Argentina, and, of course, Israel. As Adam Dolnik has pointed out, religiously motivated terrorists are not the only ones who have embraced this tactic in the last three decades. To be sure, many of the suicide operations conducted by groups in the Middle East were and are carried out by devout Muslims. But secular groups have adopted the same tactic. In Lebanon, only about half of all suicide attacks recorded since the early 1980s were carried out by members of Hezbollah and Amal, both Shi'ite groups; several secular organizations were responsible for the rest. Similarly, although Hamas and the Palestinian Islamic Jihad, both religious Muslim groups, embraced suicide attacks as their most effective weapon against Israelis, the more secular Al-Aksa Martyrs Brigade followed suit beginning in late 2001.[43]

But it was the Lebanese Hezbollah that created the mythos of the explosives-laden martyr in the Arab world and beyond—mostly because of the TV images that were broadcast after such attacks. The result was what Christoph Reuter calls an extremely successful "martyr-marketing."[44] This marketing assures that there is never a shortage of individuals willing to die for a cause that they learn to perceive as far more important than their own lives. Nasra Hassan has described the postincident glorification efforts after suicide attacks by Palestinian militants:

> The [suicide] operation doesn't end with the explosion and the many deaths. Hamas and Islamic Jihad distribute copies of the martyr's audiocassette or video to the media and to local organizations as a record of their success and encouragement to young men. His [the suicide bomber's] act becomes the subject of sermons in mosques, and provides material for leaflets, posters, videos, demonstrations, and extensive coverage in the media. Graffiti on walls in the martyr's neighborhood praise his heroism. Aspiring martyrs perform mock reenactments of the operation, using models of exploding cars and busses.[45]

Religious terrorists undertake suicide missions in the belief that they will be rewarded with a privileged existence in paradise; secular suicide terrorists do not expect rewards from God. But the latter are also indoctrinated by sectlike groups that insist on absolute subordination to whatever their "higher cause" may be. This explains the suicide terrorism of the Liberation Tigers of Tamil Eelam (LTTE), commonly known as the Tamil Tigers, and the Kurdistan Workers Party (PKK). Although suicide bombings by Middle Eastern groups received far more publicity in the last twenty or so years, Sri Lanka (formerly Ceylon) experienced more such acts than any other country—an estimated 200 since the end of the 1980s. In their fight against the Sinhala-dominated central government, the LTTE's suicide corps, the Black Tigers, have almost always targeted government officials and symbols of power as well as the country's infrastructure. In January 1996, for example, a group of suicide bombers attacked Sri Lanka's Central Bank, killing 86 persons and injuring more than 1,300. And in July 2001, an even larger contingent of suicide bombers attacked the International Airport in Columbo, destroying or damaging thirteen military and civilian planes. Reuter has described the indoctrination of designated LTTE suicide bombers as brainwashing.[46] Recruits learn that it is a disgrace to be caught alive by the enemy. For that reason, all members of the organization carry capsules of potassium cyanide, which they are required to bite into "when injured or when on the verge of capture."[47] The left-wing PKK conducted 15 suicide missions in southern Turkey during the late 1990s, targeting in all instances government representatives, members of the military, and military installations. The vast majority of the victims were policemen and soldiers, but a few civilians were killed and injured unwittingly. Like the Black Tigers in Sri Lanka, the PKK suicide bombers did not kill themselves in the name of God and a fast track to eternal life in heaven, but rather to strengthen the group's political cause.

Following the first suicide bombings by militant Muslim groups in Lebanon, Shi'ite clerics were faced with the question of whether their religion condemned or allowed these acts. Sayyid Muhammad Husayn Fadlallah, for example, declared first that based on his knowledge of Islamic law, he had reservations about using suicides for political ends. But, as Martin Kramer has pointed out, "Fadlallah eventually gave them [suicide attacks] the fullest possible endorsement short of an explicit *fatwa*."[48] This did not, however, resolve the issue for the Muslim clergy in Lebanon or elsewhere. To this day, some religious leaders, whether Shi'ites or Sunnis, sanction martyr missions against civilians if undertaken within a strategy of self-defense, while others speak out against this tactic.

Dolnik found that since the early 1980s, eighteen terrorist organizations striking in fifteen countries carried out more than 300 suicide missions. None of these attacks killed and injured as many individuals or caused as much damage as the multiple kamikaze flights into symbolic buildings in New York and Washington, D.C., on September 11, 2001—not to mention the additional damage to the U.S. psyche. From the perspective of their masterminds, the suicide operations of 9/11 were successful; Osama bin Laden and his lieutenants expressed this much in their post–9/11 communications. As long as terrorists consider suicide attacks as the most effective of their tactics, they will continue to rely on human bombs and human missiles.

Robert A. Pape has rejected religious fanaticism as a plausible explanation for this phenomenon, arguing instead that "suicide terrorism follows a strategic logic, one specifically designed to coerce modern liberal democracies to make significant territorial concessions."[49] In other words, it is not whether a group is religious or secular, but it is its nationalist aspirations that determine the tactical choice of suicide attacks. This conclusion fails to explain why some groups that fight for self-determination and statehood do practice suicide terrorism and why others with the same aspirations do not. Why have Palestinians embraced this method, but not the ETA and IRA? It seems that fanatical devotion to a religion and/or a charismatic leader of godlike stature is still the best explanation. In the case of the LTTE, its founder and leader, Vellupillai Prabhakaran, exercises godlike absolute control over the cadre, and the organization "resembles in its core more a sect."[50] In this respect, the LTTE and the PKK were like twins, according to Reuter, in that before his capture, Abdullah Ocalan's status in the PKK was the same as that of Prabhakaran in the LTTE: Ocalan was God or at least a saint, and the "PKK became a de facto sect."[51] Michael Radu, too, has characterized the Tamil Tigers and the Kurdish Workers Party as operating "more like religious sects under the absolute control of a charismatic leader."[52] After studying several nationalist groups, Aaron Horwitz identified a cultural tradition of glorifying suicide for the collective good as the one most powerful determinant: Where the tradition exists and is exploited by leaders, suicide terrorism has proven an attractive option; where no such tradition exists, suicide attacks have not been embraced as a terrorist tactic.[53]

Given the high publicity value of suicide terrorism, it is hardly surprising that the most lethal of such missions are sometimes claimed by two or more organizations that operate in the same environment. This underlines an observation by Mia Bloom, namely that "[u]nder conditions of group competition, there are incentives for further groups to jump on the 'suicide bandwagon' and ramp up the violence in order to distinguish themselves from the other organizations."[54] Whether such "outbidding" occurs depends also on the reaction of those in whose name terrorist groups and their members claim to act. According to Bloom, "If the domestic environment supports the use of suicide terror and an insurgent group does not use the tactic, they tend to lose market share and popularity."[55] In such a situation, a group may also try to regain support by launching suicide missions. Finally, competition between groups may also influence the selection of suicide terrorists that promise special attention of friends and foes—females rather than males, younger rather than older volunteers. In November 2006, for example, Hamas scored big in terms of news coverage and an outpouring of massive Palestinian support after the organization claimed sole responsibility for a suicide bombing carried out by the oldest suicide bomber by far on record: a 64-year old mother of nine and grandmother of thirty-six.

HIJACKINGS Operations that aim at taking and holding hostages as bargaining chips demand careful and sophisticated preparations. Beginning in the late 1960s, the hijacking of a commercial airliner was for a while the preferred terrorist tactic. Generally, these operations were carried out by at least two, but often more than two, terrorists who took control by threatening crew members and passengers with hand grenades and/or handguns. Whenever hijackers forced the pilots to land their planes in a country whose government was either sympathetic to them or too weak for a rescue attempt, they were able to negotiate for their immediate demands—typically, the release of fellow terrorists from prison or the payment of ransom. When a hijacked plane touched down in an environment that was not hospitable to the terrorists aboard, the hijackers would threaten to harm hostages unless they were assured free passage out of the country. Whatever the particular circumstances, only sophisticated groups can pull off a skyjacking with the prospect of success because this tactic "demands patience on the part of the operatives and an ability to handle a 'duration operation.'"[56]

The risks that hijackers take in these operations depend in large part on the counterterrorist measures at the airports of departure and aboard the chosen planes. Good airport security can detect terrorists' weapons before they can be brought aboard a plane; armed sky marshals aboard an airliner can overpower terrorists and prevent them from taking control; and, finally, well-trained counterterrorist commandos can storm a hijacked plane on the ground. Indeed, once all of these counterterrorist means were in place in an increasing number of countries, the number of hijackings began to decrease in the 1980s.

KIDNAPPINGS To kidnap one or more persons requires even more operational know-how and favorable conditions in order to succeed. To take hostages in a friendly environment or one in which the authorities are unable to provide for law and order is, of course, far less risky than finding hideouts in a hostile environment. The terrorists who held American hostages in Lebanon during most of the 1980s did not have to fear discovery and arrest because they were able to hide and operate in areas that they controlled or that were surrounded by sympathizers. In the past, hostage situations have often worked in favor of the captors in that the targeted governments or private corporations gave in to the demands in order to free the hostages. Terrorist groups in Colombia and elsewhere in Latin America, for example, have kidnapped foreigners on numerous occasions and released their hostages when their employers in North America or Europe paid the ransom demanded.

Whatever the circumstances, a kidnapping coup "requires intricate planning, split-second timing, a large support apparatus to sustain the group holding the victim, and the ability to remain secure while still communicating demands or negotiating with third parties."[57] Past hostage situations often ended with the eventual release of the captives, but there were other endings as well. In the 1980s, for example, Lebanese terrorists murdered two of their hostages, William Buckley and William Higgins. But whereas terrorist kidnappers in the past used this tactic to pressure governments into giving in to their demands, the more recent kidnappings by Al Qaeda and affiliate cells had a different motive all along. They did not want to bargain, but preferred to kill their hostages in the most barbaric ways possible in order to send warnings to their target audiences by publicizing videotapes of their victims' gruesome ordeals and executions. This tactic was evident in early 2002, when kidnapped *Wall Street Journal* reporter Daniel Pearl was brutally murdered by terrorists in Pakistan. A year later, a young American contractor, Nicholas Berg, was beheaded by terrorists in Iraq, and an American engineer, Paul Johnson, Jr., suffered the same fate in Saudi Arabia.

MISSILE ATTACKS ON FIXED AND MOVING TARGETS   In November 2002, a surface-to-air missile was fired at an Israeli jetliner that was carrying a large group of tourists from the Kenyan resort of Mombasa back to Israel. Luckily, the rocket missed its target. There was no doubt that terrorists had launched the projectile at a time when a car bomb killed fourteen persons in the lobby of an Israeli-owned hotel in the same resort. This was not the first time terrorists had used this tactic. In September 2000, for example, a rocket was fired from a handheld launcher at a distance of only a few hundred yards onto Great Britain's Intelligence Headquarters in the heart of London. Officials suspected that renegades of the Irish Republican Army were responsible for the incident. Although the pictures taken after the audacious attack showed only minimal damage to the well-known MI6 building—once featured in a James Bond film (*The World Is Not Enough*)—these images heightened the fear of an escalation of terrorist violence in London and elsewhere in England. For years, the IRA used mortars and homemade launchers to attack military and civilian targets. According to Christopher Harmon,

> One of the most creative and ingenious use[s] of mortars was popularized by the IRA and by Japanese terrorists of the "Middle Core Faction" during the 1970s and 1980s. The groups place mortars in the back of an altered vehicle, creating a truly "mobile launcher" for urban terrorism. The method was used in 1991 in a bold attack on 10 Downing Street [the prime minister's residence]. It proved to be a psychological victory that could have had an even greater impact had one of the shells not struck a tree in the Prime Minister's garden rather than the residence itself.[58]

If they have the financial resources, today's terrorists do not have to rely on homemade mortars but can acquire sophisticated handheld missile launchers to hurl lethal rockets against fixed and moving targets. The facilitators of such sinister transactions are either some renegade countries or the striving black market that reaches into literally all continents.

Launching projectiles against enemy targets, even if done from some distance, comes with some risks. Unless terrorists operate in a friendly environment, operate within failed or failing states, or have secured getaway routes, there is always the risk of being caught.

Weapons Training in Al Qaeda's Afghan Camps

Ahmed Ressam, an Algerian national, testified for the prosecution during the trial against his fellow terrorist Moktar Haouari. In the following text, which is excerpted from his testimony, he describes his weapons training in Al Qaeda's Khalden and Deronta camps in Afghanistan ("Q" stands for question, "A" for answer):

Q. During those five or six months at that camp did you receive training?

A. Yes, I received training.

Q. What type of training did you receive first?

A. I received training in light weapons, handguns, and small machine gun and a large one, RPG.

Q. Explain what an RPG is.

A. It is a small rocket launcher that is used in fighting in the mountains and in cities against tanks.

Q. What type of training did you receive next?

A. I received training in explosives.

Q. What type of explosives did you have?

A. How to make a charge, the types of explosives, TNT, C4.

Q. What is C4?

A. It's a plastic explosive, and there is another one that was called black plastic.

Q. Were you taught applications for the use of these explosives in that training?

A. One involved the types of explosives and then one is called sabotage.

Q. What did the sabotage part of the training consist of?

A. How to blow up the infrastructure of a country.

Q. Can you tell us what your next training was?

A. I also got training in urban warfare.

Q. Describe in a few sentences what that training was.

A. We learned how to carry out operations in cities, how to block roads, how to assault buildings, and the strategies used in these operations.

Q. Did you receive training in tactics as well?

A. Yes.

Q. What types of things are you talking about were you taught in tactics.

A. How to assassinate someone in operation.

Q. You were trained to use cyanide by placing the cyanide near the air intake of a building, correct?

A. They gave us examples, but we did not try them out actually.

(continued)

Weapons Training in Al Qaeda's
Afghan Camps (continued)

Q. Other experiments that you conducted at the Deronta camp included experiments with other poisons, correct?

A. Yes.

Q. One of the things you learned at the Deronta camp was how to mix poisons with other substances, put them together and smear them on doorknobs; do you remember that?

A. Yes, I did say that.

Q. Any person who would touch the doorknob would soon have poison running through their bloodstream, correct?

A. Yes, that's true; the poison will infiltrate his body.

Q. And kill him or her, correct?

A. Yes.[59]

MASS DISRUPTION AND MASS DESTRUCTION Without hurling bombs and missiles or assassinating individuals, without toppling skyscrapers, taking hostages, or releasing poison gas, terrorists can inflict great damage on literally any society they target. In early 1995, for example, "high-tech" terrorists cut the cables of Germany's public communication agency at three key underground crossroads in Frankfurt and disrupted all computer, telephone, and fax service in parts of the city—including the international airport, hospitals, and office buildings. Fortunately, the communications blackout did not cause planes to crash or patients to die. But the group that claimed responsibility, *Keine Verbindung* (No Connection), demonstrated the vulnerability of the communication system.

Terrorists who aim at seriously disrupting a country's or region's infrastructure could aim at hitting electric power grids and gas pipelines. A blackout of the New York stock exchanges, the leading Wall Street firms, and the backup systems that were established in the wake of 9/11 would affect and perhaps paralyze the domestic and global financial markets. The accidental breakdown of the electric power supply structure in part of the American Midwest and Northeast as well as in neighboring Canada on August 14, 2003, affected an estimated 50 million people, giving them a bitter taste of what would happen in the wake of massive terrorist attacks on power grids and other vital parts of the infrastructure. Such incidents do not simply disrupt the lives of people in the immediately affected areas but cause ripple effects that are felt throughout the country and abroad and that inflict high costs on individuals, the business community, and markets.

Even the mere threat of causing major disruption can have chaotic consequences, as happened in 1995, when a bomb threat was made against the air traffic control center responsible for directing traffic at two New York airports (John F. Kennedy and LaGuardia) and at Newark Airport in New Jersey. Although the bomb threat proved to be a hoax, landings and takeoffs at these three major airports were interrupted for hours; this, in turn, affected air traffic in the rest of the country as well. In the past, terrorist groups have repeatedly tried to damage electric power grids and pipelines in various parts of the world but have not caused a great deal of damage and disruption. But the potential of more sophisticated and more determined terrorists succeeding in such endeavors is high.

Security experts are especially worried about the prospect of devastating cyberterrorism. There is reason for concern because in 2002, the FBI made a shocking discovery as its agents investigated a mysterious pattern of surveillance of Silicon Valley computer systems:

> Working with experts at the Lawrence Livermore National Laboratories, the FBI traced trails of a broader reconnaissance. A forensic summary of the investigation, prepared for the Defense Department, said the bureau found "multiple casings of sites" nationwide. Routed through telecommunications switches in Saudi Arabia, Indonesia and Pakistan, the visitors studied emergency telephone systems, electrical generation and transmission, water storage and distribution, nuclear power plants and gas facilities.
>
> Some of the probes suggested planning for conventional attack, U.S. officials say. But others homed in on a class of digital devices that allow remote control of services such as fire dispatch and of equipment such as pipelines. More information about those devices—and how to program them—turned up on al Qaeda computers seized this year, according to law enforcement and national security officials.[60]

One of the nightmares that haunts security experts is a scenario in which terrorists launch a major physical attack in conjunction with a cyberstrike that prevents swift action by emergency response professionals. Imagine 9/11–like events and simultaneous cyberattacks that knock out the 911 emergency systems and/or the electric power grid in the affected cities and regions. There are other dangers as well. For example, computers could be used to "remotely access cereal processing plants, change the levels of iron supplement, and sicken or kill the children of a nation as they eat their breakfast."[61] Or, terrorists could remotely alter the pressure in a gas line and cause a valve to fail so that "a block of a sleepy suburb detonates and burns."[62] No wonder that even before Al Qaeda became the most dangerous terrorist organization, experts warned,

> The danger today stems from induced disasters of vastly different magnitude. The vulnerability of society's life-supporting physical networks literally invites focus on sabotage and the low-intensity warfare of terrorist attacks. If successful, such assaults could exceed the self-healing limits of society.[63]

Seen this way, the step from terrorism of mass disruption to terrorism of mass destruction can be rather small or nonexistent. Pointing to new weapons of mass destruction (WMD), Robert Bunker wrote,

> While no such weapons have been utilized by terrorists to date, one troubling trend has developed recently involving laser strikes on commercial aviation and airborne law enforcement assets primarily in the Los Angeles metropolitan region since 1996. These include still unexplained incidents against Ontario, Pomona, and San Diego police helicopters. Lasers make ideal terrorist weapons and, in fact, possess a number of advantages over surface-to-air missiles (SAMs) in the areas of availability, functioning, and operational deployment. To further complicate matters, lasers, like computers, are drastically falling in price and their performance levels are greatly increasing.[64]

Weapons of mass destruction pose the ultimate threat. The abbreviation WMD, as noted above, stands for "weapons of mass destruction." But experts speak increasingly of CBRN (for chemical, biological, radiological, and nuclear) weapons, because WMD can also stand for "weapons of mass disruption." Following the dismantling of the Eastern Bloc and the Soviet Union, stockpiles of nuclear weapons became accessible, and scientists and technicians who developed nuclear arms and chemical and biological agents in Russia and elsewhere in the East were for hire. Whether through official channels, the Russian Mafia, or some unpaid scientists, some of these dangerous weapons and some of the human expertise found their way into countries with known ties to terrorist groups. The idea that terrorists might resort to weapons of mass destruction is a nightmare that was in the past merely the stuff of fiction. In his novel *The Turner Diaries*, right-wing leader William Pierce described how biological, chemical, and nuclear weapons were used for the neo-Nazi conquest of North America and Europe. Now the threat of catastrophic terrorism is real. The most publicized case involved the Aum Shinrikyo cult in Japan and its repeated release of sarin nerve gas in 1995. But the Sri Lankan Tamil Tigers were the first terrorist group to resort to a chemical weapon when it launched a poison gas attack against a Sri Lankan military facility in 1990—half a decade before the sarin nerve gas attack in Japan shocked the world.[65]

In the United States, evidence has surfaced that "white supremacist, Christian Identity and elements of the militia movement have been experimenting with chemical and biological agents. However, these have been almost entirely low-grade incidents . . . [that] can hardly be described as the use of 'weapons of mass destruction.' "[66] The same can be said of an incident in 1984, when the Rajneesh cult poisoned salad bars in ten restaurants located in the Oregon community they lived in. The plan was to make enough citizens sick so that they were unable to vote against the sect's candidate in an upcoming local election. Yet the anthrax incident on the heels of the 9/11 attacks drove home the point that there is a clear and present danger of terrorists using biological or chemical agents as weapons of mass destruction. This was indeed the judgment of a pair of experts in the field, who made the following assessment:

> Both chemical and biological agents can be obtained from government laboratories through the terrorist-organised crime nexus. By developing links with rogue scientists, terrorist groups can also purchase the equipment required to produce these agents in the open market. Although some biological agents are relatively difficult to produce, the process of production is within the reach of contemporary terrorist groups with access to university-qualified members, collaborators, supporters and sympathisers.[67]

So far, terrorist groups have not gotten hold of nuclear arms. But Aum Shinrikyo and Al Qaeda tried to buy highly enriched plutonium from sources in Russia and other republics of the former Soviet Union in order to build their own nuclear weapons. It does not necessarily take the financial resources of a bin Laden to acquire potent weapons. Just as the U.S. Army is known to have lost track of large quantities of explosives stored in military facilities such as Fort Bragg, it is not impossible that groups or individuals could steal nuclear, biological, or chemical materials by breaking into some laboratory. And there is always the chance that a government that does not dare to fight openly against real or imagined enemies will supply terrorists with weapons of mass destruction—even of the nuclear kind.

Nearly ten years ago, a group of experts warned of a post–Cold War "nuclear anarchy" unless the United States and the international community prevented the worst-case scenario from unfolding. In case of inaction, they warned, "Terrorist groups would be able to shop at the Russian nuclear bazaar. Consider Hamas with nuclear weapons; the Red Brigade with nuclear weapons, the Chechens with nuclear weapons."[68] But Russia's stored nukes and their vulnerability to theft and sale to the highest bidders are not the only danger in this respect. In addition to Russia, seven other countries have nuclear weapons (China, France, India, Israel, Pakistan, the United States, and the United Kingdom); and by 2004, experts believed that North Korea had the material to build several nuclear weapons and that Iran was working toward the same goal. Whether provided by state sponsors or acquired on the nuclear black market, nukes in the hands of terrorists have become the ultimate terror threat. According to Rohan Gunaratna and Peter Chalk,

> With terrorist propensity to conduct mass casualty attacks, it is a question of time that Al-Qaeda or another terrorist group will acquire, develop and use a CBRN weapon in the foreseeable future. Unless a state sponsor provides a nuclear weapon to a terrorist group, it is highly unlikely that a terrorist group will be able to gain access to a nuclear weapon. However, it is likely that a terrorist group will acquire, develop or use a chemical, biological, or a radiological weapon.[69]

Today, no society can be confident that terrorists will continue to rely on "conventional" weapons and shy away from weapons of mass disturbance and mass destruction. In spite of this threat, Allison Graham, a leading expert on weapons and national security, suggests that the ultimate terrorist catastrophe is preventable by an urgent, aggressive, multifaceted effort of "denying terrorists access to nuclear weapons and weapons-grade material."[70]

Most Likely CBRN Weapons in the Hands of Terrorists

States, terrorist groups, and individual terrorists could develop or acquire a multitude of chemical, biological, radiological, and nuclear materials in order to commit lethal and catastrophic political violence. Some groups inside and outside the United States have developed or acquired biological or chemical agents and tried to deploy them. Other terrorist organizations made similar efforts without succeeding. Some incidents receive far greater publicity than others. In 1995, after the Japanese Aum Shinrikyo cult attacked the Tokyo subway system with sarin, the incident was widely reported around the world. But evidence that extremists in the United States had managed to buy dangerous biological agents received little media attention. Jessica Stern found that in 1995 alone, there were three known cases that involved "survivalists" and "white supremacists" acquiring biological agents. According to Stern,

> In March [1995] two members of the Minnesota Patriots Council were arrested for producing ricin with which to assassinate a deputy U.S. marshal who had served papers on one of them for tax violations.
>
> In May, just six weeks after the Aum Shinrikyo incident, Larry Wayne Harris, a former member of neo-Nazi organizations, bought three vials of Yersinia pestis, the bacterium that causes bubonic plague, which killed nearly a quarter of Europe's population in the mid-fourteenth century.

In December a survivalist was arrested for trying to carry 130 grams of ricin across the border into Canada.[71]

Some of the most feared CBRN weapons that terrorists might use are the following:

CHEMICAL

Mustard gas is a chemical agent in gas or liquid form that in some states smells like mustard, but it has nothing to do with the mustard people eat with frankfurters and other foods. Mustard gas attacks the skin and causes severe blisters. When inhaled, it damages lungs, other organs, and even the cells' DNA, which can result in cancer and birth defects. Although not as lethal as some other chemical agents, when used as a weapon, mustard gas is likely to inflict permanent injuries and suffering. There is no known case in which terrorists produced or acquired mustard gas.

Sarin, whether in the gas or liquid form, is among the most lethal of chemical weapons. It is far more deadly than cyanide and is able to kill victims within minutes. Whether inhaled or absorbed through the skin, this chemical material attacks the nervous system, muscles, and organs. The Japanese Aum Shinrikyo cult produced sarin in the 1990s in its own laboratories and used it as a terrorist weapon in its 1995 attack on the Tokyo subway system.

VX, a chemical agent, is considered the most lethal nerve gas known. When absorbed through the skin, VX attacks the nervous system and tends to kill victims within a very short time. It is believed that amateurs cannot produce this deadly material, but the scientists of the Aum Shinrikyo cult did produce traces of VX and used it in several assassination attempts, in which one victim was killed.

BIOLOGICAL

Anthrax is a type of bacteria that is well known in the United States as a biological weapon because a few weeks after the 9/11 attacks, a still-unknown person mailed letters with anthrax spores to a number of people in the media and in politics. Anthrax can enter the body through even the tiniest cut in the skin, through inhalation, and by ingestion with food. When anthrax spores are inhaled and enter the lungs, without treatment most victims die. The skin and stomach forms of anthrax are thought to be less lethal.

Smallpox is a virus that is easily spread from person to person and, in the past, it often killed millions of people during a single year. Declared eradicated more than thirty years ago, only the United States and Russia are known to have the smallpox virus stored—the United States in the Centers for Disease Control and Russia in a repository that once fed the Soviet Union's biological weapons program. It seems unlikely that terrorists would use this virus because it is highly contagious. But there are concerns that a financially strong terrorist organization with scientists in its ranks could perhaps acquire smallpox through unemployed experts in the field who once worked in the Soviet Union's bioweapons program.

Botulinum toxin is the most poisonous biological agent known. According to one account, in its most concentrated form "one pound of it, if properly dispersed, could in theory kill a billion people."[72] The bacteria that produce the botulinum toxin are sometimes found in soil. When exposed to a potent form of botulinum toxin, victims suffer muscle paralysis and die within a short time.

It was reported that scientists in the Aum Shinrikyo cult "had tried to make germ weapons from anthrax and botulinum" and that they "had staged as many as a dozen unsuccessful germ attacks in Japan from 1990 to 1995."[73]

Ricin is a protein toxin that can be inhaled, ingested, or injected. Contained in castor beans, it can be extracted so that it is "two hundred times more potent than cyanide."[74] Since no antidote is known, victims will die. In early 2003, British police found a small quantity of ricin in a building in the outskirts of London and arrested seven Muslim extremists in connection with it.

RADIOLOGICAL

Dirty bombs are conventional explosive devices that also contain radioactive material. When a dirty bomb is set off, the dynamite (or whatever explosives are used) will spray the radioactive material and contaminate the targeted site. Depending on the radiation potency, weather conditions, and speed of emergency responders, the number of victims killed would vary. If, for example, a dirty bomb were to explode in New York's Times Square, this site and its environment would be uninhabitable for a long time. If terrorist groups were to get hold of radioactive material, it would be easy for them to construct a dirty bomb. There were reports that Al Qaeda had in fact built such a radiological weapon in Afghanistan before 9/11.

NUCLEAR BOMBS Documents found in Al Qaeda's former safe houses in Afghanistan revealed that bin Laden and his group were interested in learning as much as possible about nuclear weapons. Indeed, since the 1990s, bin Laden has tried to acquire nuclear capabilities but there is no evidence that these efforts were successful. The Aum Shinrikyo cult, too, was interested in building nuclear weapons. Before he left office in early 2005, U.S. Attorney General John Ashcroft warned,

If you were to have nuclear proliferation find its way into the hands of terrorists, the entire world might be very seriously disrupted by a few individuals who thought to impose their will, their arcane philosophy, on the rest of mankind.[75]

Still, the nuclear nightmare scenario seems less likely than the threat of terrorists deploying chemical, biological, and even radiological weapons. Some experts reject the "alarmist scenarios" of catastrophic biological or chemical terrorism that are reinforced by certain government officials, sensational news reports, and Hollywood movies. But even the antialarmist school does not completely rule out such attacks. According to Jonathan B. Tucker and Amy Sands, "The historical record suggests that only a tiny minority of terrorists will be motivated to carry out an indiscriminate chemical or biological attack, and that few if any of this subset will possess the necessary technology and expertise to actually accomplish this." While pointing out that incidents of "state-sponsored" terrorism of this sort have been very rare, Tucker and Sands recognize also that "ad hoc or 'transnational' terrorist organizations, such as the group that bombed the World Trade Center, have inspired growing concern because they may be loosely affiliated with a state sponsor and hence less constrained [than governments]."[76]

At the end of 2008, the U.S. Commission on the Prevention of Weapons of Mass Destruction, Proliferation, and Terrorism concluded,

The number of states that are armed with nuclear weapons or seeking to develop them is increasing. Terrorist organizations are intent on acquiring nuclear weapons or

the material and expertise needed to build them. Trafficking in nuclear materials and technology is a serious, relentless, and multidimensional problem.

Yet nuclear terrorism is still a preventable catastrophe. The world must move with new urgency to halt the proliferation of nuclear weapons nations—and the United States must increase its global leadership efforts to stop the proliferation of nuclear weapons and safeguard nuclear material before it falls into the hands of terrorists.[77]

Notes

1. Both of these points are articulated by Bruce Hoffman, *Inside Terrorism* (New York: Columbia University Press, 1998), 157.
2. "Open Letter to Downtrodden in Lebanon and the World," in Walter Laqueur and Yonah Alexander, eds., *The Terrorism Reader* (New York: NAL Penguin, 1987), 318.
3. The West German terrorist Michael Bauman is quoted in David C. Rapoport, "The International World as Some Terrorists Have Seen It: A Look at a Century of Memoirs," in David C. Rapoport, ed., *Inside Terrorist Organizations* (London: Frank Cass, 2001), 44.
4. Robert Kupperman and Darrel Trent, *Terrorism: Threat, Reality, Response* (Stanford, CA: Hoover Institution, 1979), 7.
5. Robert A. Feary, "Introduction to International Terrorism," in Marius H. Livingston, ed., *International Terrorism in the Contemporary World* (Westport, CT: Greenwood Press, 1978), 31, 32.
6. David Fromkin, "Strategy of Terrorism," in Charles W. Kegley, Jr., ed., *International Terrorism: Characteristics, Causes, Control* (New York: St. Martin's, 1990), 57.
7. Kupperman and Trent, 17.
8. Fromkin, 61.
9. Philip Jenkins, *Images of Terror: What We Can and Can't Know about Terrorism* (New York: Aldine de Gruyter, 2003), 81.
10. C. J. M. Drake, "The Role of Ideology in Terrorists' Target Selection," *Terrorism and Political Violence* 10:2 (Summer 1998): 53.
11. Ibid., 56.
12. For an excellent account of the relationship between ideology and target selection and the differences between the RAF and RB, see Drake, 53–85.
13. Peter H. Merkl, "West German Left-Wing Terrorism," in Martha Crenshaw, ed., *Terrorism in Context* (University Park: Pennsylvania State University Press, 1996), 192.
14. Donna M. Schlagheck, *International Terrorism* (Lexington, MA: Lexington Books, 1988), 2.
15. Brian Michael Jenkins, "Der internationale Terrorismus," *Aus Politik und Zeitgeschehen* B5/87: 25.
16. This slogan was popular among the radical Left in the United States and was attributed to Huey Newton of the Black Panther Party. See Jenkins, 25.
17. From a letter published in the *New York Times* on March 28, 1993, 35.
18. "Jihad against Jews and Crusaders, 23 February 1998," www.washingtonpost.com/wp-dyn? article&node=&contentId=A4993-2001Sep2.
19. Jerrold M. Post, Ehud Sprinzak, and Laurita M. Denny, "The Terrorists in Their Own Words: Interviews with 35 Incarcerated Middle Eastern Terrorists," *Terrorism and Political Violence* 15:1 (Spring 2003): 181, 183.
20. Lou Michel and Dan Herbeck, *American Terrorist: Timothy McVeigh and the Oklahoma City Bombing* (New York: Regan Books, 2001), 166.
21. J. Bowyer Bell, "Terror: An Overview," in Livingston, 38.
22. George Habash is quoted in Bowman H. Miller and Charles A. Russell, "The Evolution of Revolutionary Warfare: From Mao to Marighella to Meinhof," in Kupperman and Trent, 191.
23. Kupperman and Trent, 5.
24. Christopher C. Harmon, *Terrorism Today* (London: Frank Cass, 2000), 111.
25. Miller and Russell, 193.
26. Ibid.
27. Kupperman and Trent, 52.
28. www.animalliberationfront.com (retrieved July 21, 2003).

29. Amazon.com web site, www.amazon.com (retrieved July 21, 2003).
30. Ibid.
31. "Pipe Bombs: Low-Tech, Lethal Tools of Terror," www.cnn.com/US/9607/27/pipe.bomb.explain/.
32. One such site, Raisethefist.com, described how to build all kinds of bombs from crude pipe bombs to very potent explosives based on ammonium nitrate fertilizer mixed with gasoline. After the operator of the anarchist site and writer of the guide to explosives was arrested in early 2002, it was no longer accessible. A successor site did not carry the guide.
33. Simon Reeve, *The New Jackals: Ramzi Yousef, Osama bin Laden and the Future of Terrorism* (Boston: Northeastern University Press, 1999), 146.
34. Michel and Herbeck, 164, 165.
35. Walter Laqueur, *A History of Terrorism* (New Brunswick, NJ: Transaction Publishers, 2002), 59.
36. Harmon, 113.
37. Adam Dolnik, "Die and Let Die: Exploring Links between Suicide Terrorism and Terrorist Use of Chemical, Biological, Radiological, and Nuclear Weapons," *Studies in Conflict and Terrorism* 26:1 (January–February 2003): 25.
38. Eagleburger is quoted in Christoph Reuter, *Mein Leben ist eine Waffe* (Munich: Bertelsmann, 2002), 95.
39. Bruce Hoffman, "The Logic of Suicide Terrorism," *Atlantic Monthly*, June 2003, 40.
40. Nasra Hassan, "An Arsenal of Believers," *New Yorker*, November 19, 2001, 39.
41. Ibid.
42. Hoffman, 42.
43. See Dolnik, 22–27.
44. Reuter, 128.
45. Hassan, 41.
46. Reuter, 349.
47. Dolnik, 24.
48. Martin Kramer, "The Moral Logic of Hizballah," in Walter Reich, ed., *Origins of Terrorism* (New York: Cambridge University Press, 1990), 144.
49. Robert A. Pape, "The Strategic Logic of Suicide Terrorism," *American Political Science Review* 97:3 (August 2003): 343.
50. Reuter, 344–45.
51. Ibid., 356, 358.
52. Michael Radu, "Radical Islam and Suicide Bombers," article distributed by the Foreign Policy Research Institute, October 21, 2003.
53. Aaron Baruch Horwitz, "Charisma, Repression, and Culture: The Making of a Suicide Terrorist," unpublished senior thesis, Department of Political Science, Columbia University.
54. Mia Bloom, *Dying to Kill: The Allure of Suicide Killing* (New York: Columbia University Press, 2005), 94.
55. Ibid., 95.
56. Miller and Russell, 195.
57. Ibid.
58. Harmon, 113.
59. Excerpts from the original court transcription were posted on the web site of the Public Broadcasting System, www.pbs.org/wgbh/pages/frontline/shows/trial/inside/testimony.html (retrieved June 24, 2003).
60. Barton Gellman, "The Cyber-Terror Threat," *Washington Post, weekly edition,* July 1–14, 2002, 6.
61. Robert J. Bunker, "Weapons of Mass Disruption and Terrorism," *Terrorism and Political Violence* 12:1 (Spring 2000): 40.
62. Ibid.
63. Robert Kupperman and Jeff Kamen, *Final Warning: Averting Disaster in the New Age of Terrorism* (New York: Doubleday, 1989), 109.
64. Bunker, 35.
65. The Tamil Tigers' poison gas attack is mentioned by Bruce Hoffman, "A Nasty Business," *Atlantic Monthly,* January 2002 (retrieved from the ProQuest database on August 10, 2003).
66. David Claridge, "Exploding the Myth of Superterrorism," *Terrorism and Political Violence* 11:4 (Winter 1999): 136.

67. Rohan Gunaratna and Peter Chalk, "Terrorist Training and Weaponry," in *Counter Terrorism*, 2nd ed., October 2002, Janes, www.janes.com (retrieved June 20, 2003).

68. Graham T. Allison et al., *Avoiding Nuclear Anarchy* (Cambridge, MA: MIT Press, 1996), 73.

69. Gunaratna and Chalk.

70. Graham Allison, "How to Stop Nuclear Terror," *Foreign Affairs* (January–February 2004), www.foreignaffairs.org (retrieved October 4, 2004).

71. Jessica Stern, *The Ultimate Terrorist* (Cambridge, MA: Harvard University Press, 1999), 7–8.

72. Judith Miller, Stephen Engelberg, and William Broad, *Germs: Biological Weapons and America's Secret War* (New York: Simon & Schuster, 2001), 39.

73. Ibid., 154.

74. Ibid., 215.

75. According to an Associated Press report. See "Ashcroft: Nuke Threat the Largest Danger," www.yahoo.com/news?tmpl=story&u=/ap/20050128/ (accessed January 28, 2005).

76. Jonathan B. Tucker and Amy Sands, "An Unlikely Threat," *Bulletin of the Atomic Scientists* 55:4 (July/August 1999): 46–52.

77. Commission on the Prevention of Weapons of Mass Destruction, Proliferation and Terrorism, *World At Risk.* (New York: Vintage Books, 2008), xix, xx.

CHAPTER 9

Organizational Structures and the Financing of Terror

Traditionally, most terrorist movements have organized along the lines of the predominant hierarchical model of other organizations, whether they were of the legitimate kind, such as governments or corporations, or the illegitimate variety, such as crime syndicates. One leader or a group of leaders occupy the top of the organizational pyramid, while lieutenants and rank-and-file members populate the lower levels. The chain of command here is comparable to that in the military in that decisions are made at the top and communicated to and carried out by those below. The Provisional Irish Republican Army (IRA), for example, has been described as a "hierarchically-organized authoritarian structure ensuring both operational and non-operational efficiency."[1] Similarly, the Lebanese Hezbollah has been known to be governed "on the national and local level by the supreme political-religious leadership, composed of a small and select group of Lebanese *ulama* [community of learned men expressing the true content of Islam]."[2] The oldest among the Palestinian militant groups are perfect examples of hierarchical organizations built around forceful leaders— from Yassir Arafat's PLO and Al Fatah to the Abu Nidal Organization, George Habash's Popular Front for the Liberation of Palestine, and Abu Abbas's Palestine Liberation Front. The absolute commitment to the causes of their group displayed by the Black Tigers, the LTTE's suicide brigade in Sri Lanka, and of all Tamil Tigers has been related to the strict hierarchical indoctrination and command system under the control of LTTE's charismatic founder Vellupillai Prabhakaran. Similarly, under the leadership of Abdullah Ocelan, who was arrested in 1999 and put behind bars in Turkey, the Marxist Kurdistan Workers Party was commanded from the top.

More recently, however, terrorist movements have increasingly abandoned the hierarchical structure and adopted the "leaderless resistance" principle once practiced by the Communist party. In a 1992 pamphlet, Louis Beam, a notorious American right-wing extremist, explained the advantages of dropping the hierarchical organization model as a means of preventing government agents from infiltrating and destroying the movement. Instead, the idea is to have all groups and individuals operate independently from one another and from a central command. According to Beam,

> *At first glance, such a type of organization seems unrealistic, primarily because there appears [to be] no organization. The natural question thus arises as to how are the "Phantom cells" and individuals to cooperate with each other when there is no inter-communication or central direction? The answer to this question is that participants in a program of Leaderless Resistance through Phantom cells or individual action must know exactly what they are doing, and how to do it. It becomes the responsibility of the individual to acquire the necessary skills and information as to what is to be done. This is by no means as impractical as it appears, because it is certainly true that in any movement, all persons involved have the same general outlook, are acquainted with the same philosophy, and generally react to a given situation in similar ways.[3]*

When he wrote the article, Beam had firsthand experience with the vulnerability of hierarchical organizations. He had been the Grand Dragon of the Texas Knights of the Ku Klux Klan and presided as the leader from the top of its organizational pyramid. For a long time, law enforcement agencies were very successful in penetrating the Klan organizations. Disillusioned with this sort of scrutiny, Beam joined the white supremacy group Aryan Nations in order to promote and practice the leaderless cell concept. While acknowledging that independent cells or lone wolves needed to keep up with the "organs of information distribution such as newspapers, leaflets, computers, etc.," Beam failed to

Spain's 9/11: Catastrophic Train Bombings

Members of several autonomous European terrorist cells, all subscribing to Osama bin Laden's declaration of war against the United States and the West, were responsible for the deadly train bombings in Spain on March 11, 2004. This picture shows rescue workers searching one of the train wrecks in Madrid.

mention that it fell to leaders to provide such motivational and informational resources. But by emphasizing the responsibility of the individual in the leaderless resistance model, Beam recognized fully well that one person or a very small group is able to function as a "patriotic" resistance cell against "state tyranny."[4] The Oklahoma City bomber Timothy McVeigh was a perfect example of the functioning of an independent cell. There is no reason to believe that McVeigh received direct instructions, assistance, or financial resources from higher-ups in right-wing organizations. But he kept informed about the radical antigovernment sentiments in these circles and read fiction and nonfiction that detailed how to vanquish federal agents. Mir Aimal Kansi, a Pakistani who attacked and killed employees at the entrance to the CIA headquarters near Washington, D.C., in 1993 acted as a lone wolf or leaderless cell in a larger cause—the holy war declared by Islamic extremists against the United States.

Secular right-wing and left-wing organizations, single-issue groups, and religiously motivated movements embraced the concept of "leaderless cells" before and after Louis Beam discovered and promoted it. For example, when the founders of the Baader-Meinhof group and the Red Army Faction were in prison, their followers outside established "Revolutionary Cells" that continued to fight for the cause. Modern-day anarchists in the United States and elsewhere, particularly the Antifa (for antifascist) movement in Western Europe, rely on this organizational principle, as do the militia movements, the Animal Liberation Front, the Earth Liberation Front, and a host of other single-issue movements in the United States and Europe.

For many extremists, terrorism becomes "a career as much as a passion."[5] They become full-time or professional terrorists in contrast to others who are part-time or amateur terrorists. The members of the Marxist terror groups of the 1970s and 1980s became professional terrorists, if only because they had to operate underground; many committed adherents of the far-right antigovernment movements fall into the amateur category. As long as leaders (who tend to be full-timers) articulate the ideology of a particular movement, groups with predominantly professional members and those with overwhelmingly amateur adherents both prefer increasingly the leaderless resistance model.

Jihadis too, have bought into this principle. Thus, the so-called *Encyclopedia of Jihad*, at times available online, "provides instructions for creating 'clandestine activity cells,' with units for intelligence, supply, planning and preparation, and implementation."[6] Pointing out that this trend poses particular problems for law enforcement in the West, Jessica Stern has noted,

> In one article on the "culture of jihad" available on-line, a Saudi Islamist urges bin Laden sympathizers to take action without waiting for instructions. "I do not need to meet the Sheikh [Osama bin Laden] and ask his permission to carry out some operation," he writes, "the same as I do not need permission to pray, or to think about killing the Jews and the Crusaders that gather on our lands."[7]

But leaders remain crucial in one respect: Without leaders taking up a cause, formulating a philosophy, and convincing others to embrace what they preach, there will be neither hierarchical movements nor independently operating cells. Even when forceful individuals take the initiative, terrorist cells or larger organizations emerge only when actual or potential domestic and/or international factions are sympathetic to a particular cause. Only a few in such constituencies may favor a violent course of action and pursue it actively, but sympathizers are crucial in terms of hideouts, financial support, and reaction to counterterrorist measures.

The Internet that facilitates all kinds of social networks is also instrumental in connecting networks of dispersed cells devoted to political violence In the process, new types of networks of groups, cells, or individuals, whether criminal or terrorist in nature, confront governments in a new type of conflict—what experts call "netwar."[8] The term *netwar* has a double meaning, indicating in the first place a cell-based organizational mode or network and, secondly, such networks' strong reliance on the Internet and other means of modern communication technology in order to communicate, coordinate, and indoctrinate. Or, to put it differently, the terrorists (or criminals) "depend on using network forms of organization, doctrine, strategy, and technology."[9] Recognizing that relatively new terrorist groups differ in their organizational philosophy and practice from older terrorist organizations, Michele Zanini observed,

> *The rise of networked arrangements in terrorist organizations is part of a wider move away from formally organized state-sponsored groups to privately financed looser networks of individuals and subgroups that may have strategic guidance but enjoy tactical independence. Related to these shifts is the fact that terrorist groups are taking advantage of information technology to coordinate activities of dispersed members. Such technology may be deployed by terrorists not only to wage information warfare, but also to support their own networked organizations.*[10]

Whether understood mostly as leaderless resistance cells that otherwise operate along traditional lines or as a trend toward the netwar principle that utilizes information technology, the basic idea of moving away from the strictly hierarchical organization was embraced by all kinds of domestic and transnational terrorist groups beginning in the 1980s. Two types of organizations in particular adopted the cell-based network mode early and wholeheartedly—the far right in the United States and Europe and extremist Islamic groups around the world. According to Michael Whine, "These types of organizations, comprised of geographically far-flung, radical, nonstate components make them ideal users of networks and proponents of Netwar."[11] Well before the attacks of September 11, 2001, Zanini described a transnational Arab terrorism network that was different from traditional organizations of this kind in that it consisted of a variety of relatively autonomous groups. According to Zanini,

> *The most notorious element of the network is Osama bin Laden, who uses his wealth and organizational skills to support and direct a multinational alliance of Islamic extremists. At the heart of this alliance is his own inner core group, known as Al-Qaeda ("The Base"), which sometimes conducts missions on its own, but more often in conjunction with other groups or elements in the alliance.*

What eventually became the most extensive terrorist network ever began as Al Qaeda's own move toward the cell model. Beginning in the mid-1990s, bin Laden sent trusted followers into many countries and regions to establish a global network of cells. In 1994, the first and perhaps most important of these cells was established in the United Kingdom.

The whole extent of the European cells became clear in the months and years after 9/11. During the trial of Al Qaeda operatives who had plotted to blow up a U.S. military base in Belgium, one of the prosecutors told the court that defendants had "established a 'spider's web' of Islamic radicals plotting attacks and recruiting fighters in Europe for al-Qaida and the now-deposed Taliban in Afghanistan."[12]

But the Al Qaeda network alone was not sufficient for bin Laden's grand design. In 1998, he convened a meeting in Afghanistan that was attended by the leaders of autonomous Islamic groups, among them the physician Ayman al-Zawahiri, the head of Egypt's Islamic Jihad, who soon thereafter became bin Laden's right-hand man. Also present were the leaders of Egypt's Gama'a al Islamiya, representatives of radical Pakistani groups, and the head of Bangladesh's Islamic Jihad. As a result of this meeting, the Al Qaeda leader established what he called the International Islamic Front for Jihad against the Jews and Crusaders (IIF), a quickly growing international alliance of existing groups in exclusively or partially Muslim countries. Although up to then strictly reserved for Sunni Muslims, Al Qaeda also reached out to and cooperated with Shi'ite groups, in particular the Lebanese Hezbollah, or Party of God, one of the best-organized—albeit hierarchical—organizations. Hezbollah is known as a Lebanese organization with interests in neighboring countries, but the group has supporters, if not cells, in North and South America, Africa, and Europe as well. Last but not least, as a result of his growing fame as an anti-American and anti-Western mastermind of terror, bin Laden inspired the establishment of numerous new cells in many parts of the world.

Taken together, the Al Qaeda cells and the International Islamic Front's network of associated but independent organizations, many of which contain a multitude of nodes, formed an expansive terrorist network with a presence on most continents and in dozens and dozens of countries. The organizations that bin Laden put together corresponded in many respects to the archetypal netwar design as described by theorists:

> Ideally, there is no single, central leadership, command, or headquarters—no precise heart or head that can be targeted. The network as a whole (but not necessarily each node) has little to no hierarchy; there may be multiple leaders. Decision making and operations are decentralized, allowing for local initiative and autonomy.
>
> The capacity of this design for effective performance over time may depend on the existence of shared principles, interests, and goals—perhaps an overreaching ideology—which spans all nodes and to which the members subscribe in a deep way.[13]

To be sure, as the head and heart of Al Qaeda and the IIF network, bin Laden was something like a chairman of the board, with al-Zawahiri as the chief executive officer at his side. Trusted associates headed the following committees with responsibilities in specific areas:

- The Political Committee, or *Shura*: responsible for issuing religious edicts or fatwa that justify and even order actions in the name of Islamic law—among them, terror against infidels
- The Military Committee: responsible for planning specific attacks and in charge of managing Al Qaeda's training camps
- The Finance Committee: responsible for the fund-raising, budgeting, and financing of Al Qaeda's living and operational expenses
- The Foreign Purchase Committee: responsible for the acquisition of technical equipment (e.g., computers), weapons, and explosives
- The Security Committee: responsible for intelligence, counterintelligence, and the protection of Al Qaeda leaders and facilities[14]

This elaborate organizational setup was first utilized during bin Laden's stay in the Sudan and later on in Afghanistan, where the Al Qaeda leader and his associates felt safe. An estimated 20,000 or so members of dozens of autonomous and affiliated

Cell System in Al Qaeda and the International Islamic Front

After he was convicted for his role in a conspiracy to bomb Los Angeles International Airport in December 1999, Algerian citizen Ahmed Ressam, who hoped for a reduced sentence, testified for the prosecution during the trial of a fellow terrorist and revealed details of Al Qaeda's organizational preferences ("Q" stands for question, "A" for answer):

Q. What camp were you assigned to in Afghanistan?

A. He sent me to Khalden Camp.

Q. Can you describe how the camp was organized?

A. It had people from all nationalities who were getting training there.

Q. Can you name some of the countries that were represented at the camp?

A. Yes, Jordanians, Algerians, from Yemen, from Saudi Arabia, from Sweden, from Germany also, French also, Turks also, and Chechnyans also.

Q. Which group were you part of?

A. I belonged to the Algerian group.

Q. Was security also taught at the camp?

A. Yes.

Q. Can you tell us generally what was taught about security?

A. One is to preserve your secrets. And when you work in a group, each person knows only what he is supposed to do, no more, to preserve your secrets. Avoid the places that are suspicious or will bring suspicion upon you, such as mosques.

Q. You said you were part of the Algerian group in the camp, correct?

A. Yes.

Q. Approximately how many people were in the Algerian group?

A. 30 or more, I don't remember precisely.

Q. Who were the leaders of the Algerian group?

A. The big person in charge was Montaz. He had others working with him, Abu Doha and Abu Jaffar.

Q. Tell us how the people in the Algerian camp were organized.

A. They were a large group divided into cells. Each cell had a certain area, for example, Europe. Each cell had its emir that was in control. They stayed in touch in Pakistan with Abu Jaffar and Abu Doha who was in Europe.

Q. Approximately how many people were in your cell?

A. I remember five.

Q. Were there discussions in your cell about conducting a terrorist operation?

A. Yes.

Q. Can you describe to the jury what that discussion was?

A. We were all to meet in Canada and we were all to carry out operations of bank robberies and then get the money to carry out an operation in America.[15]

groups and cells were trained by Al Qaeda operatives in camps in Afghanistan, the Philippines, Indonesia, Australia, Malaysia, and elsewhere. At the same time, Al Qaeda provided associated cells with financial resources, weapons, and logistics.[16]

After 9/11, when Al Qaeda's main hub in Afghanistan was lost, the network's secondary hubs (headquarters/camps of autonomous organizations) and nodes or cells became crucial to continuing the fight for the cause and to planning and carrying out terrorist activities. By 2003, terrorism expert Rohan Gunaratna explained,

> With the removal of its main Afghan base in October 2001, Al-Qaeda's leadership is now looking to associated groups to advance their territorial aims, as well as support Al-Qaeda's universal jihad. To this end, its organizers, trainers, financiers and human couriers have dispersed and are moving around the world to provide support to these groups.[17]

Although in hiding, bin Laden continued "to inspire many of the operatives he trained and dispersed, as well as smaller Islamic extremist groups and individual fighters who share his ideology."[18] But bin Laden was no longer involved in important decisions as he had been before when he personally "approved all al Qaeda operations, often selecting the targets and operatives."[19]

In the post–9/11 era, the following autonomous organizations were among the increasing number of groups that were part of the Al Qaeda/IIF network of terror:

Abu Sayyaf Group, a small separatist group fighting for the establishment of an independent Muslim state in the southern Philippines. The group engaged in kidnappings for ransom, assassinations, and bombings and expanded its operations into Malaysia.

'Asbat al Ansar (League of Followers), a Lebanese Sunni group that committed terrorism against domestic and international targets (among them, Americans).

Al-Gama'a al-Islamiyya (Islamic Group, or IG), Egypt's largest militant organization, which conducted many terrorist attacks inside Egypt. Senior members of the group signed Osama bin Laden's 1998 fatwa that declared war against the United States.

Al-Jihad, also called Egyptian Islamic Jihad, an extremist group founded in the 1970s, merged with Al Qaeda/International Islamic Front in 2001 but retained the ability to conduct independent operations.

Harakat ul-Mujahidin (Movement of the Warriors, HUM), a radical Pakistani group that committed terrorist acts in Kashmir. Fazlur Rehman Khalil, the longtime leader of HUM, was among the cosponsors of Osama bin Laden's 1998 declaration of war against the United States.

Jemaah Islamiya (JI), an extensive terrorism network in Southeast Asia with hubs and cells in Indonesia, Malaysia, southern Thailand, and the southern Philippines. The group cultivated strong ties to Al Qaeda. Many of JI's followers received training in bin Laden's training camps in Afghanistan as well as financial and logistical assistance. Jemaah Islamiya was responsible for the 2002 bombings of a Bali nightclub and the 2003 truck bombing of the Marriott Hotel in Indonesia's capital, Jakarta.

Lashkar-e-Tayyiba (Army of the Righteous, LET), a radical Sunni group in Pakistan with ties to Al Qaeda. Abu Zubaydah, a close bin Laden associate, was arrested in early 2002 in an LET safe house in Faisalabad, Pakistan.

There were indications that the network included several less well-known groups, as well, among them the Moro Islamic Liberation Front in the Philippines, the Al-Ansar Mujahadin in Chechnya, the Libyan Islamic Fighters Group, and the Tunisian Combatant Group. Moreover, through its above-mentioned cooperation with the Lebanese Hezbollah, Al Qaeda was able to make overtures to longtime Hezbollah allies among Palestinian extremists—in particular, Hamas and the Palestinian Islamic Jihad.

Al Qaeda's network structure proved crucial after the central leadership had fled Afghanistan and remained in hiding for many years. In some ways, Al Qaeda Central's expansion, especially after 9/11, resembles the organizational model of those multinational corporations that grow through mergers and acquisitions in different parts of the world and leave most, if not all decision-making to the various national or regional affiliates. In the case of Al Qaeda, its "peripheral elements are minimally dependent on its core leadership . . ."[20] But just as the headquarters of multinational corporations push for increased brand recognition and demand for their product, Al Qaeda uses virtual propaganda for the marketing of its brand of ideology. According to an early 2009 assessment,

> Physical sanctuary in Pakistan has provided immense value to al-Qa'ida's efforts to regain control over the movement, and it has allowed the core group to better enable its affiliated organizations. The organization has expanded through selective mergers and affiliations in Somalia, Yemen, South Africa, West Africa, the Levant and Algeria. The al-Qa'ida affiliates that developed in these regions present a lesser, yet persistent threat strengthening the brand, further perpetuating the movement. Affiliate organizations offer greater opportunities for al-Qa'ida as well as increased risk due to loss of control of its message, brand and target selection. Despite the risks, al-Qa'ida has continued to expand.[21]

To be sure, just as corporate mergers are not without risks, the addition of cells and hubs to a virtual network may prove problematic if the individual parts move away from the objectives of the core. All the more important is the constant effort of the central leadership to keep all parts connected via effective messaging strategies. It seems that more than seven years in hiding, Al Qaeda Central managed to expand and hold its global network together.

When Terrorist Groups Decline or End

Once the American-led coalition invaded Afghanistan and began its hunt for Osama bin Laden and other Al Qaeda leaders, many observers wondered whether the arrest or death of bin Laden would also mean the end of Al Qaeda and even the IIF. While bin Laden has remained on the run and in hiding, an estimated two-thirds of the Al Qaeda network's leaders were either arrested or killed in the post–9/11 years.[22] Yet, the loss of these associates and bin Laden's forced inactivity did not diminish the network's energy, but offered regional and local operatives opportunities to step into leadership roles. Indeed, of the network's first fourteen attacks since 9/11, nine were independently planned, financed, and carried out by local cells.[23] Therefore, many observers believed that even the capture or the arrest of bin Laden would not close down the terror network he created. On the contrary, bin Laden as a martyr could in fact result in more recruits and a strengthening of Al Qaeda and the IIF.

The case of Al Qaeda is not the first in which the removal or fugitive status of leaders led to greater decentralization. After the founders of Germany's Red Army Faction were arrested, they were not replaced by another set of similarly influential leaders. Instead, under the pressure of intensified police actions, the RAF operated along the line of the cell model. When Hamas's spiritual leader, Sheik Ahmed Yassin, was assassinated by Israel in early 2004, Dr. Abd-al-Azis al-Rantisi immediately succeeded Yassin. But the subsequent assassination of al-Rantisi raised questions about the organization's future structure. Observers wondered in particular whether Hamas would abandon the highly visible central leadership and organize its military wing in leaderless cells that would be less easily discovered and targeted by Israeli security forces.

The death or arrest of a strong group leader can also result in internal fights for his or her succession and weaken or even break up a group. This happened after William Pierce, the founder and leader of the right-wing National Alliance organization, died, and after Matthew Hale, the leader of the white supremacy World Church of the Creator group, was arrested. In both cases, the man at the top had operated like an absolute ruler who did not allow strong associates with meaningful positions at his side. As a result, there were no designated successors with enough influence to carry on.

Besides the organizational disintegration that is typically caused by a leadership vacuum or by disagreements between different group factions, Martha Crenshaw has mentioned two other reasons for the decline of terrorist groups, namely, the physical defeat of a group by the targeted government and a group's decision to abandon political violence.[24] Typically, the defeat of terrorist organizations comes in the form of massive police and/or military campaigns that result in the death or arrest of many members. This was the fate of Italy's Red Brigades, Uruguay's Tupamaros, and many other leftist organizations. When followed up with amnesties for both prisoners and terrorists in hiding, governments seem especially effective in rooting out political violence. Thus, when Tupamaros founder Raul Sendic Antonaccio was pardoned, he asked his comrades to abandon terrorism in exchange for peaceful political participation. The adoption of so-called repentance laws in Italy convinced a number of Red Brigades' members to throw in the towel.

Thus, one reason for a group giving up on the terrorist tactic is its de facto defeat by the targeted government. Of course, the most obvious reason for ending terrorism is the realization of a terrorist organization's objectives. An example here is the terrorism committed by Irgun Zvai Leumi in the British mandate in Palestine that led to the desired withdrawal of the British and the establishment of the state of Israel. Audrey Kurth Cronin lists the following seven "explanations for, or critical elements in, the decline and ending of terrorist groups in the modern era: (1) capture or killing of the leader, (2) failure to transition to the next generation, (3) achievement of the group's aims, (4) transition to a legitimate political process, (5) undermining of popular support, (6) repression, and (7) transition from terrorism to other forms of violence"[25] She also points out that more than one of these dynamics may bring about the weakening or demise of a group.

Financing Terrorism

After 9/11, U.S. President George W. Bush and his secretary of state, Colin Powell, stated that money is the oxygen or lifeblood of terrorism and that the administration was therefore intensifying efforts to dry up terrorist organizations' financial resources.

To follow the money trail is a solid counterterrorist tactic in that the flow of money can help to identify donors, middlepersons, and even recipient cells and their members, but there is no evidence that lack of money puts terrorist groups out of business. Surely, in order to support themselves, operate training facilities, acquire weapons, and travel, professional terrorists need substantial (and amateur terrorists need some) financial resources. And there are known cases in which terrorists had to scale down their plans because they lacked the necessary funds. Nimrod Raphaeli cites the first World Trade Center bombing in 1993 as one such incident in that "due to the lack of funds, the terrorists were unable to build as large a bomb as they had intended."[26] But by and large, terrorists have been very resourceful in financing their violence.

For a long time, Western observers assumed that Osama bin Laden's inherited fortune allowed him to support the terrorist operations in Afghanistan and around the world. But the National Commission on Terrorism Attacks upon the United States found that bin Laden's personal wealth was far more modest than was widely assumed. According to the commission,

> Bin Laden never received a $300 million inheritance. From about 1970 until approximately 1994, he received about $1 million per year—a significant sum, but hardly a $300 million fortune that could be used to finance a global jihad.[27]

The truth is probably somewhere in between the "huge fortune" and hard-pressed-for-money versions. If there was ever any shortage of money, Peter Bergen points out that "lack of money was no impediment to al Qaeda's almost simultaneous bombings of the American embassies in Kenya and Tanzania on 7 August 1998."[28] When governments deprive terrorists of their financial resources, they hope to prevent further acts of terror. But terror organizations have proven resourceful in finding new sources to finance their operations. After the U.S. government announced that it would aggressively go after terrorist funds, bin Laden declared such measures ineffective. "By the grace of Allah," he said, "Al-Qaeda has more than three different alternative financial networks."[29]

Martin S. Navias has identified three sources of funding that are unique to terrorist organizations and difficult to cut off.[30] But there is at least one additional (and not at all unique) way to finance terrorism. These are the four most common funding sources:

- **State sponsors provide financial support.** Such support can be indirect in that the sponsor government provides living quarters, training camps, weapons, and so on free of charge, and direct in that the terrorist group receives cash payments or can draw from legally established and funded bank accounts. There are many examples of this kind of support, for example, Iran's sponsorship of Hezbollah, Libya's past sponsorship of secular Palestinian groups, Saudi Arabia's monetary support of charitable front organizations for terrorists, or Saddam Hussein's generous payments to the families of Palestinian suicide bombers. Apart from confiscating funds in banks within their borders and putting pressure on state supporters, governments that are the targets of sponsored terrorist groups have difficulties in stopping this sort of support.
- **Private organizations/individuals provide donations.** The stronger the sentiments in favor of a terrorist group's motives and goals, the greater is the likelihood of organizations collecting a large number of small donations for, and wealthy individuals donating significant sums to, terrorist groups. As Navias points out, "Significantly, such funds may be generated in terrorist host states or in states that are the target of the terrorist group's activities or are at least hostile

to them."[31] This financing scheme is particularly crafty when the recipients of donations are involved not only in terrorism but in social services and legitimate political activities as well. The Palestinian Hamas, for example, provides educational opportunities, health care, and other social services while its military branch commits acts of terrorism. The Lebanese Hezbollah has carried out terrorist acts while participating in the legitimate political process.

- **Terrorists use their own legitimate businesses to fund violent acts.** This is by far the least likely way to finance terrorism, and the most obvious example is Al Qaeda. The organization was originally funded by Osama bin Laden's inheritance and by the profits of the commercial enterprises he established in the Sudan.[32] Of course, many hate groups that overtly or covertly encourage political violence rake in profits by selling books, T-shirts, posters, CDs, and other items—most often via their online stores.

- **Terrorists get involved in criminal activities to finance their operations.** The first three funding sources are significant, but many, if not most, terrorists groups are also involved in criminal activities in order to finance their operations. Typically, past and contemporary terrorists have committed bank robberies, pulled off kidnappings to extort ransom money, and engaged in profitable drug trafficking. Smuggling drugs has been a particularly popular source of funding for terrorist groups in the Middle East, in South Asia, Southeast Asia, and in Latin America. Focusing particularly on terrorism financing in Southeast Asia, Aurel Croissant and Daniel Barlow concluded,

Stripping away ideological goals, most terrorist organizations in the region have a strong tradition utilizing the same techniques as organized crime. Southeast Asia has long been a center for laundering and generating illegitimate funds from criminal activities such as illicit drug production and the small arms trade; decade old insurgent groups, ethnic armies, and organized crime have long used the region to acquire and channel funds to accomplish their purposes.[33]

When part of a loosely linked terrorist network, groups may transfer money to affiliates via front firms or charities. In the case of Al Qaeda and local affiliates, for example, "Funds flow into and out of Southeast Asia to support both Al Qaeda and local organizations. Once transnational terrorist organizations have generated funds from local activities or received funds from foreign sponsors, the money is distributed to allied front organizations or individuals . . ."[34]

South America's Tri-Border Area where the borders of Argentina, Brazil, and Paraguay converge is also notorious as a source of terrorism financing. A significant part of the money that is raised by terrorist groups here or transferred to them by their supporters stems from criminal activities, such as drug trafficking and counterfeiting of goods. Affiliates and supporters of Hamas, Hezbollah, and Al Qaeda along with Latin American groups raise a great deal of money here through criminal activities. Tracing these funds is difficult because "money transfers in this area is done through informal value transfer systems, such as the hawala system" or, in other words, outside conventional banks.[35]

To get their hands on money, terrorists use different illegal methods in different parts of the world. In the West, for example, they are likely to commit credit card fraud, sell forged passports, violate intellectual property rights, and smuggle persons illegally into countries.[36] But although essential for the operation of terror organizations and their violent activities, the lack of financial resources is unlikely to reduce terrorism significantly—if at all.

Terrorists have proven crafty in finding organizational arrangements and financial resources that they deem most effective in their campaign of violence and least likely to be disrupted by authorities hostile to their design.

Narco-Terrorism or Narco-Funded Terrorism?

As mentioned above, terrorist organizations in different parts of the world fund their activities by trafficking in narcotics. According to Laqueur, the Colombian FARC, for example, far from being an exception, "had an annual income of some $500 million in the late 1990s."[37] There is no doubt that the hefty sums that many terrorist organizations take in via drug trafficking represent the largest—and in some cases, the only—income. But it is far more precise to speak of "narco-funded terrorism" than to use the more common term "narco-terrorism," which blurs the differences between groups involved in political violence and those engaged in crime. For this very reason, Abraham H. Miller and Nicholas A. Dmask rejected the "narco-terrorism" characterization as a "myth" exploited since the 1980s by policy-makers interested in emphasizing the connection between drug traffickers and terrorists. While not denying that cooperative ties between terrorist organizations and drug cartels exist, Miller and Dmask also mention the turf battles and often deadly clashes between the two sets of groups. They use the Latin American example to pinpoint the fundamental differences between the goals of terrorist organizations and those of drug cartels:

> Left-wing insurgents seek to create economic structures where the government controls economic enterprises. Drug traffickers desire governments where intervention in the economy is at a minimum, where ideology is of minimal concern, and where bribery is easily accepted.
>
> What brings traffickers and insurgents together are not common goals but a common enemy—the government.
>
> The narco-terrorism idea is, consequently, based on simplistic stereotypes which emphasize the few similarities between terrorists and traffickers and ignore the many differences.[38]

A case in point is Colombia where the FARC and the smaller M19 (Movement 19 April) struggled for years with financial difficulties that weakened their recruitment and operational abilities. This changed in the early 1980s, when the left-wing revolutionary terrorists and the drug cartel found common ground: In exchange for protecting the members of the cartel from the military, the FARC was allowed to levy "a 10 per cent protection tax on all coca growers in areas under its control . . ."[39] Both sides profited greatly from the deal because their alliance led to a vast expansion of the narco-business. Nevertheless, the fundamental difference between the drug mafia and its terrorist partners remained in that for the former the lucrative criminal activity was the ultimate objective, whereas for the FARC and M19 involvement in and financial riches from the drug business was a means to their political ends, namely to further and one day realize their ideological agendas.

Notes

1. John Horgan and Max Taylor, "The Provisional Irish Republican Army: Command and Functional Structure," Terrorism and Political Violence 9:3 (Autumn 1997): 3.
2. Magnus Ranstorp, "Hizbollah's Command Leadership: Its Structure, Decision Making and Relationship with Iranian Clergy and Institutions," Terrorism and Political Violence 6:3 (Autumn 1994): 304.

3. Louis Beam, "Leaderless Resistance," *Seditionist* 12 (February 1992). The pamphlet is available on several web sites.

4. Ibid.

5. Jessica Stern, "The Protean Enemy," *Foreign Affairs* (July–August 2003): 28.

6. Ibid., 34.

7. Ibid., 34, 35.

8. See, for example, John Arquilla and David Ronfeldt, "The Advent of Netwar: Analytical Background," *Studies in Conflict and Terrorism* 22:3 (July–September 1999): 193–206.

9. Ibid., 193.

10. Michele Zanini, "Middle Eastern Terrorism and Netwar," *Studies in Conflict and Terrorism* 22:3 (July–September 1999): 247.

11. Michael Whine, "Cyberspace—A New Medium for Communication, Command, and Control by Extremists," *Studies in Conflict and Terrorism* 22:3 (July–September 1999): 232.

12. Constant Brand, "Suspect Convicted in Belgian Terror Trial," Associated Press, September 30, 2003 (retrieved from Yahoo!News on October 1, 2003).

13. Arquilla and Ronfeldt, 197.

14. This organizational structure was described in National Commission on Terrorism Attacks upon the United States, "Overview of the Enemy," Staff Statement no. 15, 2–3.

15. Excerpts from the original court transcription were posted on the web site of the Public Broadcasting System, www.pbs.org/wgbh/pages/frontline/shows/trial/inside/testimony.html (retrieved June 24, 2003).

16. For more on this, see Rohan Gunaratna, "Al-Qaeda's Operational Ties with Allied Groups," *Janes Intelligence Review*, February 1, 2003.

17. Ibid.

18. "Overview of the Enemy," 12.

19. Ibid., 11.

20. The Combating Terrorism Center, "Al-Qa'ida's Five Aspects of Power." *CTC Sentinel* 2:1 (January 2009), 4.

21. Ibid.

22. According to Marc Sagerman, who compiled a biographical database of the Al Qaeda network's operatives. See Terence Henry, "Al-Qaeda's Resurgence," *Atlantic Monthly*, June 2004, 54.

23. Ibid. Henry

24. Martha Crenshaw, "How Terrorism Declines," *Terrorism and Political Violence* 3:1 (Spring 1991): 70.

25. Audrey Kurth Cronin, "How al-Qaida Ends," *International Security* 31:1 (Summer 2006), 17–18.

26. Nimrod Raphaeli, "Financing of Terrorism: Sources, Methods, and Channels," *Terrorism and Political Violence* 15:4 (Winter 2003): 60.

27. "Overview of the Enemy," 4.

28. Peter Bergen, "The Bin Laden Trial: What Did We Learn?" *Studies in Conflict and Terrorism* 24:6 (November–December 2001): 430.

29. Bin Laden is cited by Raphaeli, 61.

30. Martin S. Navias, "Finance Warfare as a Response to International Terrorism," in Lawrence Freedman, ed., *Superterrorism: Policy Responses* (Malden, MA: Blackwell Publishing, 2002), 68, 69.

31. Navias, 68.

32. Reeves, ch. 9.

33. Aurel Croissant and Daniel Barlow, "Following the Money Trail: Terrorist Financing and Government Responses in Souteast Asia." *Studies in Conflict & Terrorism* 30: (February 2007): 135.

34. Ibid.

35. Benedetta Berti, "Reassessing the Transnational Terrorism-Criminal Link in South America's Tri-Border Area." *Terrorism Monitor* 6:18 (September 22, 2008). For more on the Tri-Border Area's important source for terrorist financing, see Matthew Levitt, Hamas: *Politics, Charity, and Terrorism in the Service of Jihad* (New Haven Yale University Press, 2006), 71–72.

36. Raphaeli, 61.

37. Walter Laqueur, *No End to War* (New York: Continuum, 2003), 225.

38. Abraham H. Miller and Nicholas A. Damask, "The Dual Myths of 'Narco-Terrorism': How Myths Drive Policy," *Terrorism and Political Violence* 8:1 (Spring 1996): 124.

39. Loretta Napoleoni, *Modern Jihad: Tracing Dollars behind the Terror Networks* (London: Pluto Press, 2003), 40.

PART 2

Counterterrorism

CHAPTER 10

Terrorism and America's Post–9/11 National Security Strategy

On SEPTEMBER 11, 2001, AT 8:30 P.M. EDT, A GRAVE PRESIDENT George W. Bush addressed a shocked nation from the Oval Office. At first, he called that day's devastating attacks on American soil by transnational terrorists "acts of mass murder." But toward the end of his short speech, he declared, "America and our friends and allies join with all those who want peace and security in the world, and we stand together to win the war against terrorism."[1] Contrary to the reference to crime at the outset, the war analogy was not meant as a rhetorical exclamation mark. Not law enforcement, but the use of military force became the centerpiece of Washington's post–9/11 response to transnational terrorism and threats that the administration linked to this kind of political violence. Robert Dalby observed that after 9/11 there was "the immediate assumption that the struggle against terror was a matter best prosecuted as a matter of warfare rather than by diplomacy and police action."[2]

Although the most deadly strikes in the history of modern terrorism, the destruction of the World Trade Center and the partial demolition of the Pentagon, symbols of America's economic might and military superiority, were not the first anti-American operations masterminded by Osama bin Laden and carried out by Al Qaeda or like-minded groups or cells. But the first World Trade Center bombing of 1993, the truck bombings of U.S. embassies in Kenya and Tanzania in 1998, the strike against the USS *Cole* in 2000, and violence against Americans in Saudi Arabia and elsewhere did not register as manifestations of a major national security threat. Instead, as Ian Lesser concluded in 1999 and thus before 9/11, "[m]ost contemporary analyses of terrorism focus on terrorist political violence as a stand-alone phenomenon, without reference to its geopolitical and strategic context."[3] This was hardly surprising because the realist conceptualization of geopolitics with its focus on the nation-state and the assumption that every state tries to maximize its national interest was the guidepost of American security and foreign policy. In this understanding, threats in the international context emanate from states—especially, from powerful states. Threats from nonstate actors do not fit the realist paradigm. As a result, international relations scholars ignored terrorism as well. Martha Crenshaw observed,

> [Before 9/11] the security studies and international relations fields were not especially hospitable to scholars interested in terrorism precisely because it was not considered an important problem for the discipline or for the development of grand strategy. As an intellectual approach, it did not lend itself to abstract theory or modeling. The study of terrorism was too policy-oriented to be of serious academic significance.[4]

When experts warned of terrorism as a serious threat to America's national security and suggested that it needed to be integrated into the national security strategy, they almost always thought of nightmare scenarios: weapons of mass destruction in the hands of terrorists. Identifying the preoccupation with body counts as the root of a limited perception of the transnational terrorist threat, Paul Pillar concluded,

> The underlying paradigm—that terrorism is to be measured in the numbers of dead Americans, and that counterterrorism is thus largely a matter of preparing for attacks (particularly CBRN attacks) that could cause many such deaths—is shared by people with widely different appraisals of the terrorist threat and of the priority and resources that should be devoted to countering it.[5]

While the bipartisan United States Commission on National Security/21st Century highlighted the danger of weapons of mass destruction in the hands of terrorists, it also pressed for a national security strategy and policies that included

President Bush outlines post–9/11 national security strategy at West Point

On June 1, 2002, President George W. Bush outlined the key elements of the post-9/11 national security strategy during his speech at the graduation ceremony of U.S. Military Academy cadets at West Point. By declaring that threats were to be dealt with before they become imminent, he paved the way for the invasion of Iraq and the removal of Saddam Hussein.

threats from nonstate actors. In its "Phase I Report on the Emerging Global Security Environment for the First Quarter of the 21st Century" that was released in September 1999, the commission made the following, utterly alarming and—as 9/11 would show—prophetic assessment:

> While conventional conflicts will still be possible, the most serious threat to our security may consist of unannounced attacks on American cities by sub-national groups using genetically engineered pathogens. Another may be a well-planned cyber-attack on the air traffic control system on the East Coast of the United States, as some 200 commercial aircraft are trying to land safely in a morning's rain and fog.[6]

The commission concluded that "[t]aken together, the evidence suggests that threats to American security will be more diffuse, harder to anticipate, and more difficult to neutralize than ever before. Deterrence will not work as it once did; in many cases it may not work at all."[7] Although the co-chairs of the panel, former Senators Gary Hart, a Democrat, and Warren Rudman, a Republican, as well former U.S. Representative Newt Gingrich, a commission member, testified before several congressional committees, their alarming predictions received "scant attention" as the *Financial Times* noted—belatedly— one day after 9/11.[8] Because almost all news organizations ignored the report completely, the public was not informed about the commission's dire conclusions.

The National Commission on Terrorism did not fare better when it released its report three months before the kamikaze attacks on the World Trade Center and the Pentagon. In their executive summary, the commissioners warned of dangerous groups operating inside the United States and abroad and that their objectives were more deadly than those of previously active terrorists."[9] The *Omaha World-Herald* editorialized that the commission "envisioned a level of evil more pervasive than common sense and experience suggest actually exists."[10] As a result, the public at large remained in the dark, as did probably many in the foreign policy establishment.

All of this changed on September 11, 2001. Since then, as one observer noted, "American concern for national security has been almost totally focused on, some might argue transfixed by, the problem of international terrorism and its likely reoccurrence on American soil."[11] And Crenshaw stated, "The attacks of September 11 propelled terrorism from obscurity to prominence in the wider field of international relations and foreign and security policy. It now took center stage in the grand strategy debate. Scholars who had previously ignored terrorism now acknowledged it was a major national security concern; in fact, some saw the threat of terrorism as an occasion for a complete reorientation of post–cold war foreign policy.[12]

President Bush and his closest advisers did not wait for the foreign policy establishment and international relations scholars to fit what was widely perceived as a novel type of catastrophic terrorism into a post–9/11 national security strategy and the nation's foreign policy priorities. Instead, the president's remarks on September 11, 2001, and his subsequent speeches signaled the end of piecemeal, case-by-case responses to terrorist incidents and the beginning of a newly emerging national security strategy built around the so-called war against terrorism, or what the administration eventually came to call "global war on terrorism" and still later "the long war." This war was to be fought against terrorist organizations, groups, cells, and individuals but also—and indeed most of all—against state sponsors of terrorism. The goal was not simply to defeat the perpetrators of terrorism and their state supporters but at the same time to replace authoritarian and repressive regimes by democratic ones and thereby rid the world of terrorism or at least reduce this threat.

Seven days after 9/11, the U.S. Congress authorized President Bush "to use all necessary and appropriate force against those nations, organizations, or persons he determines planned, authorized, committed, or aided the terrorist attacks that occurred on September 11, 2001, or harbored such organizations or persons, in order to prevent any future acts of international terrorism against the United States by such nations, organizations or persons."[13] Two days later, in his live televised address to a joint session of Congress and the American people, the president equated conventional warfare and the terrorist attack on the World Trade Center and Pentagon when he said,

> *On September the 11th, enemies of freedom committed an act of war against our country. Americans have known wars—but for the past 136 years, they have been wars on foreign soil, except for one Sunday in 1941. Americans have known the casualties of war—but not at the center of a great city on a peaceful morning. Americans have known surprise attacks—but never before on thousands of civilians. All of this was brought upon us in a single day—and night fell on a different world, a world where freedom itself is under attack.*[14]

It is noteworthy that both the congressional war authorization and the presidential address mentioned not only terrorist organizations and individuals but also "nations" as targets for military action in the nation's new war against terrorism. "Every nation, in every region, now has a decision to make. Either you are with us, or you are with the terrorists," the president said. "From this day forward, any nation that continues to harbor or support terrorism will be regarded by the United States as a hostile regime."[15] Although the 9/11 attacks were masterminded by Al Qaeda's leadership and carried out by 19 of its followers, decision-makers clung to the statecentric assessments and response options of the past that were better suited for fighting against nation-states rather than nonstate actors like Al Qaeda and the terrorist organization's affiliates.

Neo-conservative ideologues inside and outside the Bush administration recognized immediately that the war against terrorism offered an ideal pretext to further their agenda, which listed the toppling of Iraqi President Saddam Hussein as a priority. In the earliest months of the Bush presidency, the neo-cons had gained considerable influence in the White House and the Department of Defense. (For a short explanation of neo-conservative ideology, see the box on page 173). As deputy secretary of defense, Paul Wolfowitz in particular had pushed relentlessly for the removal of Iraq's president and the Baathist regime. According to Bob Woodward's account,

> *Wolfowitz had edgy, hawkish views. The reasons for getting rid of Saddam were: It was necessary and it would be relatively easy. Wolfowitz believed it was possible to send in the military to overrun and seize Iraq's southern oil fields—1,000 wells, which had about two-thirds of Iraq's oil production—and establish a foothold. . . . From the enclave, support would be given to the anti-Saddam opposition, which would rally the rest of the country and overthrow the dictator.*[16]

Wolfowitz advocated an immediate attack against Iraq. He "argued that if there were even a 10 percent chance that Saddam Hussein had been behind the 9/11 attacks, maximum priority should be placed on eliminating that threat. He also argued that the odds in fact were far greater than one in ten."[17] Wolfowitz and his boss, Secretary of Defense Donald Rumsfeld, failed to convince the president and other national security advisers to go to war against Iraq or simultaneously against Al Qaeda and the Taliban in Afghanistan and Saddam Hussein in Iraq, but at the direction of the president the

Neo-cons and Foreign Policy

Led intellectually by figures such as Paul Wolfowitz and Richard Perle and politically by Vice President Dick Cheney and Defense Secretary Donald Rumsfeld [and Wolfowitz], this group had its original roots in government in the staff of the late Washington Senator Henry M. "Scoop" Jackson and the administration of Ronald Reagan (calling themselves Jackson Democrats, then Reagan Democrats). They offer a very different view of the role of American military power in the world than previous administrations have held.

The neo-cons see the current power balance that is overwhelmingly in favor of the United States as a distinct opportunity that should be maintained for as long as possible. Their argument is that the United States can use its power to force change in countries around the world to foster political democracy and freedom that cannot be achieved by diplomatic, political, or economic efforts alone. Some of the neo-cons refer to the situation they favor as one of "benign hegemony," an evangelical worldview that places the United States at the core of global peace and democracy through the imposition or threat of employing U.S. force when that vision is resisted. Regime change in Iraq was the prototype of the employment of this strategy, which is stated most forcefully in the so-called Bush doctrine incorporated into the 2002 National Security Strategy of the United States of America.

The above excerpt is from Donald M. Snow, *National Security for a New Era* (New York: Pearson Longman, 2007).

Pentagon continued to plan for the invasion of Iraq. Just a few days after 9/11, "Bush told [Secretary of State] Rice that the first target of the war on terrorism was going to be Afghanistan. 'We won't do Iraq now,' the president said, 'we're putting Iraq off. But eventually we'll have to return to that question.'"[18]

The neo-cons were instrumental in shaping the Bush doctrine and its codification in the 2002 National Security Strategy of the United States of America, but their core ideas had been developed and expressed since the end of the Cold War.[19] In an assessment of the post–9/11 national security strategy, Simon Dalby wrote,

> *Little of this geopolitical thinking is very new, although some innovations were obviously needed in a hurry in September 2001 given the novelty of Osama Bin Laden's tactics. The key themes of American supremacy, the willingness to maintain overwhelming military supremacy over potential rivals and the proffered option of preventive war to stop potential threats from even emerging, were all sketched out in the first Bush presidency at the end of the cold war in the period following the war with Iraq in 1991 when Dick Cheney was Defense Secretary and Colin Powell and Paul Wolfowitz were at the heart of Washington's defense bureaucracy. The related key assumption that America has the right to assert its power to reshape the rest of the world to its liking also carries over from the early 1990s.*[20]

Unhappy with American defense policy during the Clinton years, leading neo-conservatives pushed their ideas about America's role in the post–Cold War's new world order in speeches, articles, studies, and books. Their home was the The Project for a

New American Century, a Washington think tank. In September 2000, one year before the events of 9/11, the organization published a lengthy report ("Rebuilding America's Defenses: Strategy, Forces, and Resources for a New Century"[21]) that called for a new national security strategy. "At present the United States faces no global rival," the report stated. "America's grand strategy should aim to preserve and extend this advantageous position as far into the future as possible."[22] The neo-cons wanted most of all a massive buildup of America's military to maintain and strengthen U.S. dominance around the globe. Like most security and foreign policy experts inside and outside of government, the neo-cons were preoccupied with nation-states and ignored nonstate terrorist groups and networks. Their security and foreign policy blueprint did not deal with terrorism at all and mentioned terrorists only once in the context of American dominance of the international state system:

> America's global leadership, and its role as the guarantor of the current great-power peace, relies upon the safety of the American homeland; the preservation of a favorable balance of power in Europe, the Middle East and surrounding energy producing region, and East Asia; and the general stability of the international system of nation-states relative to terrorists [emphasis added], organized crime, and other "non-state actors."[23]

The neo-cons' American exceptionalism trumped the tenets of realists and liberal internationalists so that the "neoconservative vision of American foreign policy provided the theoretical and policy content of the Bush doctrine which in turn underpinned the justification to invade Iraq in 2003 and depose the leadership of Saddam Hussein."[24] One expert noted that "9-11 gave the neo-cons the pretext on which to make their strategy of military primacy the operational code for the American state."[25] While a U.S.-led military coalition drove Al Qaeda and the Taliban out of Afghanistan and into Pakistan, administration officials were already planning the Iraq invasion and preparing the nation for the next front in the war against terrorism. The news media not only reported but in fact embraced the administration's arguments in favor of both military moves. Based on his content analysis of editorials and op-ed articles in elite newspapers, one scholar concluded that the Bush administration gained support for both the Afghanistan and Iraq wars "by linking security and moral indignation."[26] Presumably, the American public's strong support for both wars was influenced by media opinion-makers who bought into the administration's post–9/11 foreign policy and its "heavy dose of moralist opinion that condemned evil enemies and touted American virtues."[27]

Terrorism and America's Post–9/11 National Security Strategy

George W. Bush's State of the Union address on January 29, 2002, his graduation speech at West Point four months later, additional statements by the president and other high administration officials, and the 2002 "National Security Strategy of the United States" contained the basic elements of America's new national security strategy, or what has been called the Bush doctrine. As far as national security strategy and foreign policy were concerned, nothing changed in the following years. The principles enunciated in the 2002 document were also the most important components of "The 2006 National Security Strategy of the United States of America."[28]

To this end, each section began with a short "summary of National Security Strategy 2002" and was followed by updates under headers like "Successes and Challenges since 2002" and "The Way Ahead." After studying the 2006 document, one foreign policy expert concluded that "one would be hard pressed to find much evidence that the president has backed away from what has become known as the Bush doctrine."[29] The following section summarizes the three most important components of the Bush doctrine that relate to terrorism and counterterrorism according to the national security strategy.

I. Making the World Safer and Better

As the world's sole remaining superpower, the United States is determined to maintain and strengthen its global supremacy. According to the preamble of the 2002 "National Security Strategy" that the president signed, "The great struggles of the twentieth century between liberty and totalitarianism ended with the decisive victory for the forces of freedom—and the single sustainable model for national success: freedom, democracy, and free enterprise."[30] The United States will use its military, political, and economic might in the service of international peace and the spread of freedom, democracy, and economic progress. 9/11 is seen as wake-up call and opportunity to reshape the world in the American image. For this reason, the overriding premise and rationale of the Bush doctrine were articulated in distinctly upbeat passages, as the following excerpt attests:

> [T]he United States will use this moment of opportunity to extend the benefits of freedom across the globe. We will actively work to bring the hope of democracy, development, free markets, and free trade to every corner of the world. The events of September 11, 2001, taught us that weak states like Afghanistan can pose as great a danger to our national interests as strong states. Poverty does not make poor people into terrorists and murderers. Yet poverty, weak institutions, and corruption can make weak states vulnerable to terrorist networks and drug cartels within their borders.[31]

As one leading scholar put it, this view "is linked to the belief, common among powerful states, that its values are universal and their spread will benefit the entire world. Just as Wilson sought to 'teach [the countries of Latin America] to elect good men,' so Bush will bring free markets and free elections to countries without them."[32]

The Bush administration stated explicitly that "the aim of this strategy is to help make the world not just safer but better."[33] It was left to others to speculate how the president's faith as a born-again Christian figured into his post–9/11 foreign policy mission. One international relations expert wrote that "[t]here is reason to believe that just as his [George W. Bush's] coming to Christ gave meaning to his previously aimless and dissolute personal life, so the war on terrorism has become, not only the defining characteristic of his foreign policy, but also his sacred mission."[34]

II. Preemption Before Threats Become Imminent

The United States and other democracies are seriously threatened by terrorist organizations and rogue states that sponsor political violence and could supply terrorists with weapons of mass destruction. Acknowledging the dangers of asymmetrical warfare, the president said at West Point, "Enemies in the past needed great armies and great industrial capabilities to endanger the American people and our nation. The attacks of September the 11th required a few hundred thousand dollars in the hands of a few dozen evil and deluded men."[35] When the president spoke of WMD in this context, he mentioned states before terrorist groups: "When the spread of chemical and biological and nuclear weapons, along with ballistic missile technology—when that occurs, even weak states and small groups could attain a catastrophic power to strike great nations," he said. "Our enemies have declared this very intention, and have been caught seeking these terrible weapons."[36]

In the new geopolitical setting, deterrence along the line of the Cold War's mutual assured destruction (MAD) assumptions is thought to be obsolete and must be replaced by military preemption, if needed. In the President Bush's words:

For much of the last century, America's defense relied on the Cold War doctrines of deterrence and containment. In some cases, those strategies still apply. But new threats also require new thinking. Deterrence—the promise of massive retaliation against nations—means nothing against shadowy terrorist networks with no nation or citizens to defend. Containment is not possible when unbalanced dictators with weapons of mass destruction can deliver those weapons on missiles or secretly provide them to terrorist allies. We cannot defend America and our friends by hoping for the best. We cannot put our faith in the word of tyrants, who solemnly sign non-proliferation treaties, and then systemically break them. If we wait for threats to fully materialize, we will have waited too long. Our security will require all Americans to be forward-looking and resolute, to be ready for preemptive action when necessary to defend our liberty and to defend our lives.[37]

In the Bush doctrine, then, threats are to be dealt with before they become imminent. The 2006 "National Security Strategy" cited the Iraq Survey Group's finding that Saddam Hussein "continued to see the utility of WMD" and could have reactivated his WMD program but also noted that the group "found that pre-war intelligence estimates of WMD stockpiles were wrong."[38] Noting that "our intelligence must improve," the document left no doubt that the invasion of Iraq and the removal of Saddam Hussein was justified according to the preemption provision of the Bush doctrine.

III. Unilateral Use of Force

The United States will act unilaterally in the face of imminent threats when there may not be time or support for getting a consensus for preemptive action. As the 2002 "National Security Strategy" put it, "While the United States will constantly strive to enlist the support of the international community, we will not hesitate to act alone, if necessary, to exercise our right of self-defense. . . ."[39] This position was hardly surprising, because a "commitment to the maintenance of a unipolar international system and to the doctrine of preemption is unilateralist to the core."[40] In the months and years after 9/11, when Americans feared additional terror strikes, the notion of going it alone against terrorists and their state sponsors, if needed, was an easy sell for the administration.

However, unilateralism was not only part of the grand strategy that the neoconservatives pushed in the 1990s but also George W. Bush's preference before he became president. Once in the White House and before 9/11, "Bush displayed little willingness to cater to world public opinion or to heed the cries of outrage from European countries as the United States interpreted its interest and the interests of the world in its own way. Thus, the Bush administration walked away from the Kyoto treaty, the International Criminal Court, and the protocol implementing the ban on biological weapons. . . ."[41] The third pillar of the Bush doctrine projected the neo-conservatives' long-held contempt for international organizations, laws, treaties, and initiatives.

In sum, then, the 9/11 attacks, the threat of further strikes, and the war against terrorism were seized by the Bush administration as an opportunity to enshrine the principle of unilateralism along with the right to preemptive action and the use of U.S. superiority to reshape the world according to American values as the core components of America's national security strategy.

End of the Post–9/11 National Security Strategy?

More than three years after the Iraq invasion, it was reported that "[a]nalysts across the political spectrum say the Bush Doctrine—preventive war, choking the roots of terrorism by planting democracy, and brandishing power to force others into line— has failed."[42] After the Republican Party's dismal showing in the 2006 mid-term elections, the neo-conservative architects of the Bush doctrine and the Iraq war were one-by-one removed from their influential positions in the administration or lost in influence. In spite of the unchanged rhetoric on the part of the president and his team, the course of American foreign policy had already begun to veer from the doctrine's tenets. One clear sign was the Bush administration's willingness to engage in multilateral talks with North Korea, a country that the president had mentioned in early 2002 as one of the rogue states in the "axis of evil" along with Iraq and Iran.

Why, then, bother with an extensive review of a doctrine after the Bush administration moved away from important tenets of this strategy in the president's second term and after a new president took office?

Concluding that "[i]n its trial run, the Bush Doctrine has been found wanting," Andrew Bacevich suggested that there was an urgent need for Congress "to abrogate that doctrine" and thereby reduce "the likelihood that we will see more Iraqs in the future."[43] Philip Gordon, too, warned that major events and developments, such as another catastrophic terror attack in the United States, could result in foreign policy responses along the lines of the Bush doctrine.[44]

The problem was that nobody had come up with a comprehensive, alternative national security strategy as the basis of foreign policy guidelines for the post–9/11 world with its many serious problems—among them transnational terrorism. The 2008 presidential campaign demonstrated that anxieties about a possible revival of the Bush doctrine and the return of neo-conservatives to high-level policy-making positions were not far-fetched. During the campaign, Senator John McCain, whose foreign policy ideas were shaped by William Kristol, Robert Kagan, Randy Scheunemann, and other leading neo-conservative thinkers he consulted with regularly, continued to strongly defend the invasion of Iraq as justified. He took as tough a stand against Iran and North Korea as extreme neo-cons like John Bolton and Vice-President Richard Cheney even at a time, when the Bush administration had switched to diplomatic approaches.[45] For Democratic Senator Barack Obama, one of the early critics of the Iraq invasion, the unjustified Iraq war was fought at the expense of strong efforts in

Afghanistan to defeat the true villains of 9/11: bin Laden, other Al Qaeda leaders, and their Taliban allies. While agreeing that nuclear arms in the hands of Iranian rulers were unacceptable, Obama emphasized direct diplomacy and multilateral pressures and sanctions to discourage the nuclear ambitions of Iran and to diminish the likelihood of WMD in the hands of terrorists. Contrary to his Republican opponent, Obama favored U.S. strikes against known Al Qaeda hideouts in Pakistan's border region at a time when President Bush had already given a green light for such military measures. Once Barack Obama became the 44th U.S. president, expectations were that he and his national security advisers would sack the Bush doctrine and develop a very different grand strategy to guide U.S. foreign and defense policies.

As Michael Leiter, director of the National Counterterrorism Center, said during a speech in early April 2009,

> Counterterrorism is part of larger U.S. policy. Counterterrorism rarely, if ever, should be the lead in that policy. The challenges we face – the terrorism challenges we face are different in different regions of the world and are interconnected to broader U.S. policy interests. Counterterrorism should be, in most cases, the tail, and we should not wag the broader policy dog. I think it is important for me to say that because I want to make clear that the counterterrorism community understands its role. We should be influencing a lot of policy, we should be informing a lot of policy, but ultimately there are broader issues here. Whether or not it's in Pakistan and Afghanistan or Somalia, counterterrorism is not the only interest the U.S. government has.[46]

This chapter has dealt with the predominant factors of America's post–9/11 national security strategy, namely, the emphasis on the use of military power in the war against terrorism, but there were other, nonmilitary components as well, as was reflected in the 2008 "National Defense Strategy" signed by Robert Gates, who continued as secretary of defense in the Obama administration. Acknowledging the need for a long campaign against terrorist movements, the inclusion of military and nonmilitary approaches, and most of all the importance of enlisting the cooperation of foreign governments and actors, the 2008 "National Defense Strategy" stated,

> The use of force plays a role, yet military efforts to capture or kill terrorists are likely to be subordinate to measures to promote local participation in government and economic programs to spur development, as well as efforts to understand and address the grievances that often lie at the heart of insurgencies.
>
> Working with and through local actors whenever possible to confront common security challenges is the best and most sustainable approach to combat violent extremism. Often our partners are better positioned to handle a given problem because they understand the local geography, social structures, and culture better than we do or ever could. In collaboration with interagency and international partners we will assist vulnerable states and local populations as they seek to ameliorate the conditions that foster extremism and dismantle the structures that support and allow extremist groups to grow.[47]

Cooperating with governments, international organizations, and non-governmental organizations in countries or regions faced with "violent extremism" on their soil will neither guarantee the defeat nor retreat of transnational terrorists and insurgents by military and/or nonviolent means. Pressured by Washington, Pakistan's counterterrorist effort in the second half of 2008 was a case in point. Reporting from Pakistan's Bajaur region, a passageway to Afghanistan, Jane Perlez and Pir Zubair Shah wrote that after three months of heavy fighting and the most intense effort of the Pakistani Army to defeat the Taliban and al-Qaeda, the military controlled merely a small part of the tribal area. The reporters cautioned, therefore, "President-elect Barack Obama has pledged to make the conflicts in Afghanistan and Pakistan a top priority. The Bajaur campaign serves as a cautionary tale of the formidable challenge that even a full-scale military effort faces in flushing the Taliban and Al Qaeda from rugged northern Pakistan."[48] As Pakistan's military fought violent elements in the tribal region and U.S. Special Forces directed missiles against Taliban and Al Qaeda hideouts, foreign aid workers were also the targets of assassinations.[49] The situation was similar in neighboring Afghanistan, where NATO troops, often joined by Afghan soldiers, fought the Taliban and other insurgents but also built schools, roads, and bridges in and around remote villages. But when villagers needed to choose between cooperating with Taliban fighters who were planning another attack or warning U.S. soldiers who improved conditions in their communities, they tended to side with the former—if only out of fear. As in Pakistan, foreign aid workers in Afghanistan were killed and kidnapped by violent extremists.[50]

Whether governments are dealing with specific terrorist incidents or the ever-present threats by groups and movements, they need to assess what kind of short-term tactics and long-term strategies are most promising. The following chapter evaluates the utility of hard and soft power against terrorism and reviews the exercise of military and nonmilitary responses to terrorism before and after 9/11.

Notes

1. http://www.whitehouse.gov/news/releases/2001/09/20010911-16.html.
2. Simon Dalby, "Geopolitics, Grand Strategy and the Bush Doctrine," IDSS discussion paper, October 2005, 12.
3. Ian O. Lesser, "Countering the New Terrorism: Implications for Strategy," in Ian O. Lesser et al., eds., *Countering the New Terrorism* (Santa Monica, CA: Rand, 1999), 140.
4. Martha Crenshaw, "Terrorism, Strategies, and Grand Strategies," in Audrey Kurth Cronin and James M,. Ludes, eds., *Attacking Terrorism: Elements of a Grand Strategy* (Washington: Georgetown University Press, 2004), 77. Crenshaw's analysis distinguishes between strategy that "typically refers to military operations" and "is concerned with the relationship between means and ends . . .'"; grand strategy, which "represents a more inclusive conception that explains how a state's full range of resources can be adapted to achieve national security"; and "foreign policy defines the goals of strategy and 'grand' or high strategy" and "is a statement of purpose." (pp. 75, 76)
5. Paul R. Pillar, *Terrorism and U.S. Foreign Policy* (Washington, D.C.: Brookings, 2001), 5.
6. http://govinfo.library.unt.edu/nssg/Reports/NWC.pdf (accessed Oct. 1, 2008).
7. Ibid.
8. Edward Alden, "Report Warned of Attack on American soil," *Financial Times*, September 12, 2001, 5.
9. Report of the National Commission on Terrorism,"Countering the Changing Threat of Terrorism," Pursuant to Public Law 277, 105th Congress, 49.
10. "Secure, Yes, But Also Free," *Omaha World-Herald*, June 12, 2000, 6.
11. Donald M. Snow, *National Security for a New Era* (New York: Pearson Longman, 2007), 1.
12. Crenshaw, 82.
13. Authorization for Use of Military Force, September 18, 2001, Public Law 107-40 SJ Res. 23, 107th Congress. http://news.findlaw.com/wp/docs/terrorism/sjres23.es.html (accessed September 30, 2008).
14. http://www.whitehouse.gov/news/releases/2001/09/print/20010920-8.html (accessed September 29, 2008).
15. Ibid.
16. Bob Woodward, *Plan of Attack* (New York: Simon & Schuster, 2004), 22.
17. Louise Richardson, *What Terrorists Want: Understanding the Enemy, Containing the Threat* (New York: Random House, 2006), 189.

18. Ibid., 26.

19. "The National Security Strategy of the United States of America" of September 2002 is available at: http://www.whitehouse.gov/nsc/nss.pdf (accessed October 10, 2008).

20. Simon Dalby, "Geopolitics, Grand Strategy and the Bush Doctrine," IDSS Working Paper Series, Paper No. 90, October 2005, 3.

21. The Project for a New American Century, "Rebuilding America's Defenses: Strategy, Forces, and Resources" (Washington, September 1999), available at: http://www.newamericancentury.org/RebuildingAmericasDefenses.pdf (accessed October 10, 2008).

22. Ibid., 8.

23. Ibid., 17.

24. Brian C. Schmidt and Michael C. Williams, "The Bush Doctrine and the Iraq War: Neoconservatives vs. Realists." Paper presented at the Annual Conference of the British International Studies Association, Cambridge, UK, December 17–19, 2007, 5.

25. Dalby, 15.

26. Andrew Rojecki, "Rhetorical Alchemy: American Exceptionalism and the War on Terror." Political Communication 25:1 (January–March 2008), 81.

27. Ibid.

28. "The National Security Strategy of the United States of America," March 2006, http://www.whitehouse.gov/nsc/nss/2006/ (accessed October 10, 2008).

29. Philip H. Gordon, "The End of the Bush Revolution," Foreign Affairs (July/August 2006), http://www.foreignaffairs.org/20060701faessay85406/philip-h-gordon/the-end-of-the-bush-revolution.html?mode=print (accessed October 11, 2008).

30. "The National Security Strategy of the United States of America," September 2002, http://www.whitehouse.gov/nsc/nss.pdf (accessed October 1, 2008).

31. Ibid.

32. Robert Jervis, "Understanding the Bush Doctrine," Political Science Quarterly 118:3 (2003): 366.

33. Ibid., 1.

34. Ibid., 379.

35. http://www.whitehouse.gov/news/releases/2002/06/20020601-3.html (accessed September 1, 2008).

36. Ibid.

37. Ibid.

38. "2006 National Security Strategy," 23.

39. Ibid., 6.

40. Schmidt and Williams, 9.

41. Jervis, 374.

42. Carolyn Lochhead, "Iraq War has Bush Doctrine in Tatters," San Francisco Chronicle, August 27, 2006. Available at http://www.sfgate.com/cgi-bin/article.cgi?file=/c/a/2006/08/27/MNGL2KQ8H01.DTL (accessed October 1, 2008).

43. Andrew J. Bacevich, "Rescinding the Bush Doctrine," The Boston Globe, March 1, 2007. Available at: http://www.boston.com/news/globe/editorial_opinion/oped/articles/2007/03/01/rescinding_the_bush_doctrine/ (accessed October 11, 2008).

44. Gordon.

45. For a discussion of Senator McCain's foreign policy views, see David D. Kirkpatrick, "Response to 9/11 Offers Outline of McCain Doctrine," New York Times, August 17, 2008. Available at: http://www.nytimes.com/2008/08/17/us/politics/17mccain.html?scp=1&sq=outline%200f%20McCain%20doctrine&st=cse (accessed October 12, 2008).

46. From a speech delivered at The Aspen Institute in Washington, D.C., April 9, 2009. Transcript is available at http://www.nctc.gov/press_room/speeches/2009-04-09_aspen-inst-speech.pdf, accessed May 12, 2009.

47. National Security Strategy, June 2008, 9. Available at http://www.defenselink.mil/news/2008%20National%20Defense%20Strategy.pdf.

48. Jane Perlez and Pir Zubair Shah, "Pakistanis Mired in Brutal Battle to Oust Taliban," New York Times, November 11, 2008. Available at http://www.nytimes.com/2008/11/11/world/asia/11pstan.html?_r=1&hp=&oref=slogin&pagewanted=print.

49. In early November 2008, for example, U.S. aid worker Stephen D. Vance was shot to death by gunman as he arrived at his office in Peshawar. For the story, see http://www.nytimes.com/2008/11/13/world/asia/13pstan.html?scp=1&sq=aid%20worker%20killed%20&st=cse.
50. In October 2008, for example, Gayle Williams, a 34-year old member of the British Christian organization Serve Afghanistan was killed in Kabul by two gunmen on motorcycles. For the article, see http://www.nytimes.com/2008/10/21/world/asia/21afghanistan.html?scp=2&sq=aid%20worker%20killed%20&st=cse. Moreover, there were many instances in which foreign aid workers were kidnapped and killed or freed in exchange for the release of Taliban prisoners or the payment of ransom.

The Utility of Hard and Soft Power in Counterterrorism

OCTOBER 7, 2001: IN RESPONSE TO THE 9/11 STRIKES, MILITARY operations against targets in Afghanistan are launched by American and British forces. The objective is the destruction of Al Qaeda facilities, the apprehension of Osama bin Laden and his lieutenants, and the removal of the Taliban regime that has offered bin Laden and his organization safe haven inside Afghanistan. Soon after the initial assault on Taliban and Al Qaeda strongholds, the coalition ends the Taliban's rule, tears down Al Qaeda's camps, and forces Al Qaeda leaders and rank-and-file members to flee into Pakistan.

For years, the Afghanistan war was widely hailed as a success story in the fight against terrorism, although the Taliban and Al Qaeda were not mortally wounded. As the United States shifted its interest and military assets from Afghanistan to Iraq, Taliban and Al Qaeda leaders and fighters were able to regroup in their hiding places across the border in Pakistan and to launch violent attacks against coalition forces and their Afghan collaborators in Afghanistan.

October 31, 2008: Two missiles hit a house and a car in a village in North Waziristan, Pakistan, killing twenty people—among them Al Qaeda operative Abu Kasha and several other foreign members of the organization. Two hours later, two additional missiles hit targets in another village in South Waziristan, killing seven people, including several foreign militants.

Since similar attacks were frequently carried out by the U.S. military against Al Qaeda and Taliban targets in the tribal border region between Afghanistan and Pakistan, it was assumed that the missiles were once again fired by remotely piloted American aircraft. According to one account, these strikes raised the number of such missile attacks within the last three months to seventeen.

March 1, 2008: A predawn air strike by the Colombian military against a jungle camp of the Revolutionary Armed Forces of Colombia (FARC) just inside neighboring Ecuador kills Paul Reyes, one of the most influential leaders and the most prominent spokesperson of the FARC. Sixteen other members, among them Reyes's female partner, are also killed in the air raids.

While the well-executed military strike was a hard blow against the FARC, one of the most durable and most dangerous terrorist organizations, it also triggered a regional crisis. The governments of Ecuador, Venezuela, Nicaragua, and Chile condemned the attack within the borders of a sovereign state, and there was the possibility of an armed conflict. But within a week, the presidents of Colombia, Ecuador, and Venezuela met in Santa Domingo and settled the dispute.

Just as military force and the threat of force have their place in international politics, they are options and should remain options in counterterrorism. The preceding summaries of military actions against the Taliban and/or Al Qaeda in Afghanistan and Pakistan and against FARC operatives inside Ecuador's borders were examples of effective military actions against terrorist organizations. Yet, successful attacks against camps, missiles fired from unmanned drones, commando raids to free hostages, and the invasion of a nation-state tend to accomplish limited objectives (i.e., destruction of training camps, decimation or displacement of a group's or regime's leadership; freeing of hostages); they are less likely to destroy terrorist organizations for good, dry up state support for terrorism, or change public sentiments among those in whose name terrorists claim to act. In addition to a range of military responses, there are nonmilitary options that should be part of sound counterterrorist policies. To put it differently, both hard and soft power need to be considered as means to counter terrorism.

U.S. Special Forces: On the Hunt for Osama bin Laden

More than three years after 9/11, U.S. Special Forces, often in concert with the Afghan National Army and the Pakistani military, were still searching for Osama bin Laden, other Al Qaeda leaders, and leading members of the Taliban. This picture shows one of the U.S. soldiers of Task Force 31 in late March 2004 on the way to conduct joint village searches with members of the Afghan National Army in southeast Afghanistan.

Before Barack Obama took the oath of office in January 2008, Joseph Nye criticized the Bush doctrine (discussed in the previous chapter) as "based on a flawed analysis of power in today's world." Looking ahead to a different foreign policy approach by the incoming administration, Nye wrote, "Obama's election itself has done a great deal to restore American soft power, but he will need to follow up with policies that combine hard and soft power into a smart strategy of the sort that won the Cold War."[1] Nye recommended a mix of hard and soft power as basis for America's grand strategy in the post–Cold War era well before 9/11, but his power concept was and remains particularly useful in the context of the global terrorist threat and the need for effective counterterrorism strategy and policy.

Defining Power—Hard and Soft

The German sociologist Max Weber defined politics as "striving for a share of power or for influence in the distribution of power, whether between states or between groups of people contained within a single state." For Weber, "Anyone engaged in politics is striving for power, either power as a means to attain other goals (which may be ideal or selfish), or power 'for its own sake,' which is to say, in order to enjoy the feeling of prestige created by power."[2] Military power and economic muscle are, as Joseph Nye has put it, "examples of hard command power that can be used to induce others to change their positions. Hard power can rest on inducements (carrots) or threats (sticks)."[3] Whereas hard power is unequivocal, soft power is subtle. For Nye, soft power "co-opts people rather than coerces them. Soft power rests on the ability to set the political agenda in a way that shapes the preferences of others."[4]

In the fall of 2007, Secretary of Defense Robert Gates called on the U.S. government to invest more in the resurrection of America's soft power capacity, arguing that military force alone cannot defend America's interests around the world. Gates criticized as "shortsighted" the post–Cold War "gutting of America's ability to engage, assist, and communicate with other parts of the world—the 'soft power,' which had been so important throughout the Cold War. The State Department froze the hiring of new Foreign Service officers for a period of time. The United States Agency for International Development saw deep staff cuts—its permanent staff dropping from a high of 15,000 during Vietnam to about 3,000 in the 1990s. And the U.S. Information Agency was abolished as an independent entity, split into pieces, and many of its capabilities folded into a small corner of the State Department."[5]

Lost in the process was America's soft power expertise, especially with respect to public diplomacy. During the Cold War era information about the United States, its values, and its citizens' ways of life was beamed into the communist world and there were cultural and educational East–West exchanges as central soft power approaches.

Today's global information and communication networks, especially the Internet, offer new opportunities for new soft power approaches, including public diplomacy, especially in efforts to counter the propaganda of terrorist movements.

During her testimony as secretary of state designee before the Senate Foreign Relations Committee's confirmation hearing, Hillary Clinton spoke of the need for "soft power" and explained "smart power":

> The president-elect and I believe that foreign policy must be based on a marriage of principles and pragmatism, not rigid ideology. On facts and evidence, not emotion or prejudice. Our security, our vitality, and our ability to lead in today's world oblige us to recognize the overwhelming fact of our interdependence.
>
> We must use what has been called "smart power," the full range of tools at our disposal—diplomatic, economic, military, political, legal, and cultural—picking the right tool, or combination of tools, for each situation. With smart power, diplomacy will be the vanguard of foreign policy.[6]

In the post–Cold War world, asymmetric warfare that involved belligerents of vastly different military strength, not symmetric warfare between two sides of similar capacities, was most prevalent. This is unlikely to change in the foreseeable future. According to the National Intelligence Council's projections, "Terrorism is unlikely to disappear by 2025. . . ."[7] Instead, irregular forces—call them terrorists or guerrillas or insurgents—will continue to challenge the United States and/or other powerful nation states directly or indirectly. The experiences in Afghanistan and Iraq have shown that overwhelming power will not succeed in the context of asymmetric warfare—at least not without exercising soft power as well. As one expert put it, such conflicts "require the application of all elements of national power. Success will be less a matter of imposing one's will and more a function of shaping behavior—of friends, adversaries, and most importantly, the people in between."[8] Others expressed the same ideas more bluntly. With the conflict in its eighth year, Andrew Bacevich suggested that the "war in Afghanistan (like the Iraq War) won't be won militarily. It can be settled—if imperfectly—only through politics."[9]

What, then, are the hard and the soft power options in counterterrorism?

Military Hard Power

John Lewis Gaddis observed, shortly after the collapse of the World Trade Center and the partial destruction of the Pentagon, "No one, apart from the few people who plotted and carried out these events, could have anticipated that they were going to happen. But from the moment they did happen, everyone acknowledged that everything had changed."[10] Immediately after the kamikaze strikes on the territory of the world's most powerful (and, indeed, only) superpower, 9/11 was compared to the attack on Pearl Harbor. But by pointing to the similarity of the two sneak attacks, most commentators failed to mention the most obvious difference: In the case of Pearl Harbor, a government ordered the aggression and targeted members of the military; but in the case of New York and Washington, members of an international terrorist network planned and carried out the attacks on defenseless civilians. By equating the two events, it seemed logical to invoke the war metaphor. What political leaders and the media dubbed immediately as "Attack on America," an act of war, called for a likewise rhetorical response—the "war against terrorism" or the "war on terror" that President George W. Bush promptly declared. Noting that in the context of terrorism, the noun *war* is more likely to be followed by *on* rather than *against*, Geoffrey Nunberg explained,

> The "war on" pattern dates from the turn of the century, when people adapted epidemiological metaphors like "the war on typhus" to describe campaigns against social

evils like alcohol, crime and poverty—endemic conditions that could be mitigated but not eradicated. Society may declare a war on drugs or drunken driving, but no one expects total victory.

"The war on terror," too, suggests a campaign aimed not at human adversaries but at a pervasive social plague.[11]

That was the way John Kerry understood the meaning of the "war on terrorism." During the 2004 presidential campaign, he said that "the only realistic goal was to contain the problem, to reduce it to the status of nuisance rather than a central, encompassing fixation; he drew an analogy with containing prostitution and gambling."[12] Similarly, Paul Pillar suggested that a "central lesson of counterterrorism is that terrorism cannot be 'defeated'—only reduced, attenuated, and to some degree controlled."[13] President Bush, however, never retreated from what he considered the meaning and the objective of the "war on terrorism" or "war on terror" all along, namely, that this war "will not end until every terrorist group of global reach has been found, stopped, and defeated."[14]

Military Retaliation/Reprisal

To fight a real war in the context of terrorism and counterterrorism, the enemy must be in control of a nation-state or parts thereof. The Afghanistan war was such a case. The Taliban rulers who controlled most of the country had allowed bin Laden to establish the Al Qaeda headquarters and training camps in Afghanistan. This was a clear-cut case of a symbiotic relationship between the quasi-rulers of a nation-state and a terrorist organization that had plotted an unprecedented terror attack against the United States. When the Taliban leadership refused U.S. demands to expel or hand over bin Laden and his associates in the aftermath of 9/11, there was significant international support for removing Al Qaeda and its sponsors by waging war because "much of the world was prepared to accept our expanded definition of national self-defense—the standard required by Article 51 of the UN Charter."[15] The Afghanistan war was fought after an attack against the United States and was rationalized as both retaliation and prevention. For Paul Pillar, the "option of military force arises when there is a clear offense of a major, recent attack for which a state has been proven responsible. Day-to-day support for terrorist groups and terrorist-related activity lacks such clarity."[16] This strict requirement was not quite met in the case against the Taliban in that Taliban leaders or followers had neither planned not carried out the 9/11 attacks. Still, the Taliban leadership had very close ties to Osama bin Laden and Al Qaeda and may well have been aware of the 9/11 plot.

Retaliation or reprisal refers to punitive action taken after the fact, or, as Neil Livingstone put it, "Reprisals involve the extraction of punishment on those who have committed an illegal act for which there is no other form of peaceful redress."[17] When it comes to terrorism, the targets of military retaliation can be the terrorists themselves if they can be pinpointed in a particular location or a nation-state if its government can be identified as the perpetrators' sponsor. Theoretically, there is a distinction between reprisal and preemption, but in reality the boundaries are often blurred. Thus, the U.S. air strikes against Tripoli and Benghazi, Libya, in 1986 were in swift retaliation for Libya's involvement in the bombing of a West Berlin nightclub that was frequented by American GIs. But the military measures were also preemptive in that they were thought to discourage Libyan President Muammar Qaddafi from sponsoring further acts of terror. The Afghanistan war against Al Qaeda and the Taliban was both retaliatory and preemptive.

For reprisals to be legal and as such recognized under international law, they "cannot be capricious and open-ended and must conform to certain carefully defined conditions and limitations."[18] To begin with, efforts to find peaceful redress must have failed. Secondly, the retaliatory measures must be proportional to the initial act of aggression and must not harm innocents. Finally, many experts believe that there is only a limited time period after a terrorist strike for military reprisal to be "effectively linked to a precipitating terrorist incident. Under normal circumstances, such a window for military action is probably no more than seventy-two hours."[19] This last condition explains why the Israelis tend to retaliate very quickly to terrorist attacks. But limiting the time frame for legitimate retaliation reduces the chances of coming to a peaceful solution, which, admittedly, is very remote in most cases of terrorism. Pillar warns of "revenge for the sake of revenge," but he recognizes that "striking back may help to sustain the national morale" and suggests, "This has probably been the principal consideration in most of Israel's retaliatory strikes against terrorist foes."[20] Reprisals must be overt, not covert, "if they are to have a cathartic effect on the victimized nation or serve as a deterrent to future attacks."[21]

Although precision-guided bombs and missiles have increased the accuracy of surgical air strikes and reduced the risk of harming innocents, this option is not foolproof. Civilians continue to be killed and injured in these sorts of strikes. When these casualties (known as "collateral casualties" or "collateral damage") occur, the retaliating government will be condemned abroad and sometimes at home as well. After Hezbollah members crossed into Israel to capture Israeli soldiers in the summer of 2006, Israel responded with massive military attacks on terrorist strongholds in Lebanon. While Israel justified the war against Hezbollah as reprisal for the kidnapping of IDF members and as a means to prevent further terrorist rocket attacks from South Lebanon against Israeli civilians, critics condemned Israel for not first trying to redress the border incident peacefully and for harming large numbers of Lebanese civilians. The problem is, of course, that fighting terrorists is very different from fighting a country's army, in that terrorists tend to operate from and hide in civilian neighborhoods. But if the objectives of retaliatory and/or preventative actions are not fully achieved—as was the case for Israel in the 2006 conflict with Hezbollah—the effects can be detrimental to national morale and unity, while not necessarily a deterrent to future terrorist strikes.

After seemingly won by U.S.-led coalition forces, the Afghanistan war became a prolonged case of asymmetrical warfare between Al Qaeda terrorists and Taliban insurgents on one hand and U.S. military units as part of NATO forces on the other. However, one proponent of what he calls "offensive action and offensive military capabilities" has argued that "even unsuccessful offensive actions, which force terrorist units or terrorist cells to stay perpetually on the move to avoid destruction, will help reduce their capability" and that the "threat of offensive action is critical to exhausting the terrorists, whether they are with units in the field in Afghanistan or hiding out in cities and empty quarters across the world."[22]

But targeting terrorists that fight within military units, not exactly typical for terrorist organizations, is very different from using offensive military force against terrorists or insurgents who hide among civilians in cities, towns, or villages. One of many tragic examples of high-risk offensive actions against terrorists or insurgents during the "war on terrorism" was an August 2008 ground operation in the Afghan village of Azizabad by U.S. Special Operation Forces backed by air strikes. When the dust settled, more than 90 civilians—most of them women and children—were dead along with three dozen or so insurgents.[23] The damage to America's reputation in the Afghan village, in all of Afghanistan, and in the international community was once again far greater than the benefit of eliminating a few terrorists or insurgents. Military actions, especially when they involve the death of innocent bystanders, tend to rally supporters and recruit new ones. Thus, the surgical strike against the leading Al Qaeda operative al-Masri and his companions in Pakistan was followed by a surge in violence in Afghanistan and Pakistan by the Taliban and Al Qaeda terrorists.

While it was difficult enough to hunt terrorists in the mountainous terrain of hostile tribal areas along the Afghan–Pakistani border, there was an even greater problem with the nation-building task and the impossible dream of turning Afghanistan into a stable democracy. As president-elect, Barack Obama and Defense Secretary Gates agreed on sending thousands of additional troops to Afghanistan, the question was whether the Obama administration would change the Afghanistan mission to the original goal of taking out Al Qaeda Central.

Military Preemption

As part of his post–9/11 foreign policy, President Bush proclaimed the United States' right to wage preemptive wars against rogue states that threaten the national security of the United States and cannot be deterred. *Preemption* means "striking in advance of hostile action to prevent its occurrence and to avoid suffering injury."[24] Crucial here is the availability of reliable intelligence about a strike or strikes planned against a nation-state. If such evidence exists, preemptive military actions can be justified. But the bar of proof is high to justify all-out preemptive action. Discussing this in the context of terrorism, Neil C. Livingstone wrote long before 9/11,

> In fact, a nation carrying out a preemptive attack may appear to the rest of the world as an aggressor rather than a potential victim, and in order to win acceptance of its action, the nation engaged in the preemptive attack will have to make a strong and persuasive public case to justify its action. This, however, can be exceedingly difficult and in some instances impossible.[25]

Indeed, as Robert Jervis has pointed out, "[t]he very nature of preventive war means that the evidence is ambiguous and the supporting arguments are subject to rebuttal. If Britain and France had gone to war with Germany before 1939, large segments of the public would have believed that the war was not necessary."[26] For this reason, governments have by and large been reluctant to fight preemptive wars.

For the United States, this attitude toward preemption changed in terms of Iraq. By invading and occupying Iraq, the United States lost in many parts of the world the moral high ground that had motivated a large number of countries to join the military coalition against Al Qaeda and the Taliban in Afghanistan. With few exceptions, the international community did not buy Washington's premier reasons for going to war against Iraq: the presence of weapons of mass destruction in Iraq and the threat of Saddam Hussein providing terrorists—namely, Al Qaeda—with these weapons. If this was the reason for invading Iraq, North Korea, Iran, and Pakistan posed at the time greater and more immediate threats. But, as explained in the previous chapter in some detail, for President Bush the decisive factor in favor of preemptive war was not whether a threat was imminent. As the president explained during a TV interview,

> I believe it is essential—that when we see a threat, we deal with those threats before [emphasis added] they become imminent. It's too late if they become imminent.

It's too late in this new kind of war, and so that's why I made the decision I made [to go to war against Iraq].[27]

If the United States claims the right to wage war "against . . . emerging threats before they are fully formed," as the president did, this would justify preemptive strikes against many nation-states. Moreover, other countries could insist on the same right. Whatever the rationale for and against preemptive war may be, military might can defeat the armies of terrorism-sponsoring states and topple their regimes, but it cannot defeat globally dispersed terrorism networks.

The Iraq War was a case in which an invasion in the name of preventing catastrophic terrorism paved the way for groups and cells loyal to Al Qaeda or like-minded groups to flock into the country and unleash a wave of terrorism . The conflict did not start out as part of the "war on terrorism" but was fought and won against Iraq's Army. It was only after Iraq was defeated and Saddam Hussein toppled that the conflict changed into asymmetrical warfare between U.S. forces and their allies on one side and foreign terrorists and home-grown insurgents on the other. During Saddam Hussein's rule, Iraq itself was not a breeding ground of Jihadi terrorists and did not allow foreign extremists from all over the Arab and Muslim world to enter the country and unleash lethal violence against civilians. Ironically, the years following Iraq's initial defeat witnessed Iraqi and foreign militants carrying out waves of terrorist attacks—not only against members of the occupation forces but most of all against the civilian population in many parts of the country. If Iraq became indeed the most important front in the so-called Global War on Terror, as the Bush administration claimed, it was the direct result of the resentment and anger in the Arab and Muslim world triggered and nourished by the invasion and occupation of Iraq. In 2007, for example, more than 6,000, or 43%, of the more than 14,000 terrorist incidents worldwide occurred in Iraq; more than 13,000, or 60%, of the more than 22,000 persons killed by terrorists around the globe died in terrorist attacks in that country.[28]

The reported decline in terrorist attacks in 2008 came after a surge in U.S. troop deployment in the summer of 2007 and, perhaps more important, on the heels of the so-called Anbar Awakening, in which large numbers of Sunnis turned against foreign extremists of Al Qaeda Iraq, choosing instead to cooperate with the U.S. military, and of Shia cleric Moqtada al-Sadr's decision to rein in his Mahdi Army and focus on gaining power in the political process.[29]

Summing up, then, wars against state sponsors of terrorism can be waged and won but even the mightiest military forces are unlikely to defeat transnational terrorist organizations or networks. As Secretary Gates wrote just before President Obama's inauguration, "Direct military force will continue to play a role in the long-term effort against terrorists and other extremists. But over the long-term, the United States cannot kill or capture its way to victory."[30]

When it comes to transnational terrorism and in particular global terrorist networks, good old police work may be more promising than military action. Opting for a terrorism-as-crime understanding rather than the terrorism-as-war paradigm, one student of terrorism suggests,

Terrorism is a phenomenon that is global in its range, constant in its presence, and inevitably involves the commission of crime. Any national or international mechanism to counter it must be predicated on that understanding. Liberal democracies have well-developed legislation, systems, and structures to deal with crime; consequently, the criminal justice system should be at the heart of their counterterrorism efforts.[31]

A recent study of all terrorist groups that were active around the world from 1968 through 2006 found that 7% ended because of military force, 40% because of policing, and 10% because they realized their typically very limited objectives. According to the same research, 43% of all these organizations terminated their violence because of political solutions or settlements.[32] In other words, traditional criminal justice approaches and efforts to bring terrorist groups into the political process were far more successful in ending terrorism than military actions. Yet, as mentioned earlier, there are cases in which military force is an option and, at times, the best option.

Commando Raids

Short of going to war against state sponsors or conducting air strikes against terrorist sponsor states and terrorist groups, commando attacks on terrorist homes and training grounds, the use of commandos to hunt down terrorists, and the utilization of surrogates to attack terrorists are options chosen by various target countries. Using commandos increases the accuracy of attacks and minimizes the risk of harming innocents. But sending special forces teams into a hostile environment entails also the risk of members being captured, injured, and killed. Using surrogates, on the one hand, eliminates the risk of a country's own personnel being harmed and allows officials to deny responsibility if an attack fails or results in collateral damage. On the other hand, however, the sponsoring government may lose control over proxies. This was rumored in 1985 when a car bomb exploded in Beirut and killed innocent Lebanese bystanders. Allegedly, the CIA had hired indigenous operatives for the attack but lost control over their operation. More recently, during the post–9/11 invasion of Afghanistan, members of U.S. Special Forces paid Afghan tribesmen to assist in the hunt for bin Laden, Al Qaeda members, and Taliban leaders. But the Afghans were reportedly also taking bribes from the other sides and warned them of impending actions by the U.S.-led coalition.

There is also the option of using commandos for systematic retribution campaigns against perpetrators of particular terrorist acts. Generally, the governments and citizens of democratic countries are not in favor of eliminating terrorists by assassination. Yet, in certain predicaments, some experts recommend fighting ruthless terrorists with equally ruthless campaigns that "must be highly selective, fought in secret, targeting only those responsible and never acknowledging guilt."[33]

The model for retribution campaigns remains Israel's response to an attack on the country's athletes at the 1972 Olympic Games in Munich. Prodded by then Prime Minister Golda Meir, the best and brightest of Israel's military and intelligence elite formed a commando unit with the code name *Mivtzan Elohim*, meaning "Wrath of God." Members were charged with hunting down every member of Black September, the group responsible for the Munich operation. For years, Wrath of God commandos tracked down leaders and followers of Black September in the Middle East and in Europe, killing them one by one until the job was done in 1979. Along the way, mistakes were made—for example, when an Arab in Scandinavia was falsely identified as the Palestinian leader of the Munich attack and killed. But, as one observer wrote approvingly, "Despite some spectacular foul-ups . . . Mossad [Israel's intelligence agency] has racked up a deadly record of hits on Palestinian terrorists without ever bragging about it. The terrorists know who did it, and that's enough for the Israelis."[34] Others recommended that the United States should establish a counterterrorist commando along the lines of the Wrath of God model as one more aggressive option in its counterterrorism posture.

Assassinations

"Wrath of God" was an assassination campaign. Governments typically do not speak about, or deny, their involvement in the assassination of terrorists. But in some situations, officials admit to such targeted killings as preventative and retaliatory actions, if only to satisfy a fearful populace's demand for more protection. Thus, in the fall of 2000, Israeli officials acknowledged publicly that their military was targeting and killing individual Palestinians accused of actual attacks on Israeli citizens or of planning such deeds. While Palestinians spoke of "state terrorism" and "assassinations," a highly placed government official in Israel explained these acts as countermeasures and said that the "most effective and just way to deal with terror is the elimination or incarceration of the people who lead these organizations."[35] After Israeli forces targeted an alleged mastermind of a Palestinian terror attack but killed several civilians in the process, Israeli Foreign Minister Shimon Perez reacted angrily when an interviewer used the term *assassination* to characterize the action. "Suicide bombers cannot be threatened by death," he argued. "The only way to stop them is to intercept those who sent them."[36] And Prime Minister Ariel Sharon made clear that "actions to prevent the killing of Jews" would continue.[37] Indeed, Israel intensified its campaign to kill the leaders of terrorist groups. But whether taking out Hamas leader Sheik Yassin, his successor, and a host of others in the higher circles of Palestinian terror groups reduced violence against Israel in the long run was far from sure. Even more than terrorist foot soldiers, their leaders become martyrs in death and attract new recruits.

After 9/11, there was a debate in the mass media in the United States on the best outcome of the ongoing hunt for Osama bin Laden. To arrest or to "neutralize" (i.e., assassinate) the Al Qaeda leader was the question. There was fear of a wave of terror attacks inside the United States if bin Laden was arrested and tried by the American judiciary. There was also concern that the United States could lose influence over the procedures if bin Laden was caught and brought before an international tribunal. As for neutralizing the Al Qaeda boss, assassinations were outlawed by the United States following the disclosure that the Central Intelligence Agency was involved in assassination plots against foreign leaders during the 1960s and 1970s. To be sure, bin Laden was not a head of state or leader in a nation-state. Nevertheless, after 9/11, the issue was whether the president and Congress should lift the ban on assassination when known terrorists were the targets. Michael Ignatieff proposed three conditions for targeted assassination in the fight against terrorism: "Only as a last resort, only when capture is impossible without undue risk to American lives and only where death and damage to innocent civilians can be avoided."[38]

President Bush did not repeal the executive order banning assassinations, nor did Congress introduce legislation to allow targeted assassinations of terrorists. But after 9/11, President Bush issued a finding that authorized the CIA to kill or capture terrorist leaders.[39] Indeed, in the fall of 2002, a pilotless Predator plane operated by the CIA fired a Hellfire antitank missile at a car in Yemen and killed a key Al Qaeda leader and five others. This operation was, no doubt, a targeted assassination coup. Similar Predator attacks targeted Al Qaeda and Taliban leaders in Afghanistan, albeit without success. Still, after 9/11 the assassination of terrorists was part of the American arsenal in the fight against terrorism.

Hostage Rescue Missions

In the late 1960s and early 1970s, when hostage-taking was the most popular terrorist tactic, military and police experts began to discuss suitable rescue methods. But, as Pillar has recalled, it was the "unsuccessful German attempt to rescue the Israeli athletes kidnapped at the Olympic Games in Munich in 1972 [that actually] led major European governments to develop highly skilled commando units with this mission."[40] Germany, for example, established a counterterrorist commando called Grenzschutzgruppe 9 (GSG-9) within its border patrol, and the United Kingdom designated the special commandos of the Special Air Service (SAS) as a counterterrorist force. Israeli commandos were the first to stage a spectacular rescue mission in 1976 after terrorists hijacked an Air France airliner en route from Tel Aviv to Paris and forced the pilot to land in Entebbe, Uganda. Although the Ugandan authorities supported the hijackers, who threatened to kill their Israeli hostages, an Israeli C-130 plane with eighty-six highly trained commandos aboard landed at the airport. Within a few minutes, the paratroopers struck down the terrorists and rescued ninety-five passengers. Although two passengers were killed in the crossfire and the leader of the rescue commando, Jonathan Netanyahu, died in the exchange, the raid on Entebbe became "a worldwide sensation—a clearcut victory against terrorism."[41]

Delta Force, perceived as counterterrorist commandos, was already in the planning stage when officially established as a counterterrorism unit in November 1977 during the Carter presidency. In the previous months, commandos of Germany's GSG-9 had stormed a hijacked Lufthansa plane at the airport of Mogadishu, Somalia, rescuing all eighty-six passengers. Delta Force, under the command of Colonel Charles Beckwith, became a formidable counterterrorist asset—especially after becoming part of the so-called Special Operation Forces (SOF) that combined special units from each of the military services after the failure of the rescue mission during the Iran hostage crisis, which had been partially blamed on poor coordination between the various military services. (However, unlike Mogadishu, where the government of Somalia had welcomed the rescue raid by German commandos, the American rescue force flew into an extremely hostile environment in Iran. To be sure, Israeli commandos faced hostility at Entebbe as well—and succeeded—but without taking away from the brilliant execution of their coup, they had the benefit of surprise on their side because this was the first rescue of its kind.)

In recent times, foreigners have been typically taken hostage one at a time or in small groups and held in hideouts in Iraq, Pakistan, Afghanistan, Saudi Arabia, and elsewhere by transnational terrorists, which has made rescue attempts highly unlikely or impossible.

Although domestic rescue operations tend to be less problematic, they are not unlike efforts to free hostages held abroad when the captors' control territory within a state. Colombia is an instructive example. For years, the Revolutionary Armed Forces of Colombia (FARC) kidnapped and held hundreds of hostages, many of them for long periods of time and in spite of many attempts by Colombian security forces to free them. But the combined efforts of military intelligence and commandos eventually pulled off one of the most stunning, nonviolent hostage rescue coups on July 2, 2008, when they freed fifteen hostages from a FARC jungle camp—among them former Colombian presidential candidate Ingrid Betancourt and three Americans. After they had infiltrated the terrorist/guerrilla organization for months, the rescuers posed as FARC fighters and convinced guards that they had come with an order to gather the hostages from three different locations and march them to a centrally located place from where they would fly to a meeting with an international delegation. Camouflaged rescuers, real FARC fighters, and the hostages marched ninety through the jungle. When a helicopter landed, Colombian security forces disguised as FARC operatives got off, handcuffed the hostages, and ordered them aboard along with two of the FARC guards. As the latter were overpowered soon after lift-off, the hostages learned that they were finally free. Betancourt had spent more than six years, and the three American defense contractors more than five years, in captivity.

In sum, then, hostage rescue missions are far more likely to succeed when they are attempted in "permissive environments" rather than in "nonpermissive environments." A number of hostage rescue missions conducted by different counterterrorism commandos in various countries and in different parts of the world has affirmed this rule of thumb.

Non-Military Hard Power: Economic Sanctions

Like military actions, economic sanctions are imposed by governments in order to affect the behavior of the targets of such measures. Trade and foreign aid sanctions are meant to change the behavior of governments, whereas financial sanctions can be imposed against both states and non-state actors. Trade sanctions prohibit the exporting and importing of goods to and from target countries; foreign aid sanctions stop financial and other assistance, such as loans, to targeted governments; financial sanctions concentrate typically on the freezing of financial assets of foreign governments or organizations so that they cannot be moved from the frozen bank accounts. All of these economic sanctions have been imposed as counterterrorist measures by the U.S. government.

Indeed, when the U.S. Department of State identifies states as sponsors of terrorism, this designation triggers automatically a multitude of U.S.-imposed sanctions that include the prohibition of certain exports and access to a variety of foreign assistance programs. In addition, specific sanctions tend to be legislated against sponsor states. But sanctions require careful consideration. While sanctions inflict costs on the targeted states and in some cases on organizations, they also result in losses to the businesses and workers of exporting sectors in the country that imposes sanctions. Moreover, unless other countries decide in favor of sanctions, unilaterally imposed measures of this kind tend to be less harmful than intended. In the past, even the United States' allies in Europe were not at all eager or willing to join the Unites States in a multilateral sanction regime. This was true with respect to Iran, Syria, and Cuba.

Whatever the reason for sanctions, the "scholarly literature on economic statecraft is generally skeptical, portraying the use of economic sanctions and other strategies as ineffective or even counterproductive."[42] Robert Pape, for example, concluded that based on the evidence "economic sanctions are not likely to achieve foreign policy objectives."[43] However, Pillar points to Libya as probably the "best case of sanctions helping to shape a state sponsor's behavior on terrorism-related matters."[44] In the Libyan case, as a study by Stephen D. Collins revealed, unilateral economic sanctions by the United States (and the bombing of Libyan cities) did not discourage the Qaddafi government from sponsoring terrorism, but UN-backed multilateral economic sanctions did reduce Libyan-supported terrorist attacks markedly.[45] The multilateral sanctions imposed by the UN Security Council were particularly intended to press Libya to surrender the suspects in the terrorist attack on Pan Am Flight 103.

Thus, "[t]he evidence clearly demonstrates that following the application of multilateral sanctions Libyan support for terrorism declined precipitously. . ."[46] Similarly, when Muammar Qaddafi signaled in late 2003 his willingness to dismantle weapons of mass destruction, this decision was unquestionably influenced by his desire to end all sanctions in order to improve his country's economy.

Drying Up Financial Resources

Money has been identified as the most important fuel of terrorism. Most recently, President George W. Bush and U.S. Secretary of State Colin Powell called money the oxygen and lifeblood of terrorism as they ordered measures to dry up the financial resources of Al Qaeda and other terrorist groups in the wake of 9/11. To be sure, terrorists need money to support themselves, their training facilities, their weaponry, and the planning and execution of their terrorist actions. But Pillar has correctly pointed out that efforts to defeat terrorism by imposing financial controls encounter two major problems in that (1) terrorism in terms of killing innocents is cheap, and (2) "the money that does flow in the terrorist world is extremely difficult to track."[47] Tracking terrorists' financial resources is severely hampered by several factors, among them their habit of using false names and their preference for using unorthodox financial transactions—among them money laundering—and getting involved in criminal activities, such as drug trafficking. Moreover, actual terrorist attacks are rather cheap. Although prepared for many months in advance and involving dozens of people besides the actual suicide bombers, the whole 9/11 plot did not cost more than $400,000. The Madrid train bombings that required two years of preparations were staged for an estimated $10,000. And even the most devastating explosive belts for single suicide bombers can be assembled for around $100. Following the money trail may be more successful in identifying the members of terrorist cells and thereby increasing law enforcement officials' chances of hunting down and arresting terrorists, and less successful at putting terror organizations once and for all out of business.

Soft Power and Counterterrorism

Besides hard power, namely military and economic measures, there are also less drastic options available in response to specific terrorist incidents and terrorism threats in general. In assessing the utility of soft power, one needs to distinguish between state sponsors and terrorist groups or networks.

Deterrence

Like many other leading international relations scholars and policy-makers, Robert Jervis believes that contemporary terrorist threats "cannot be contained by deterrence" because "[t]errorists are fanatics, and there is nothing that they value that we can hold at risk; rogues like Iraq [under Saddam Hussein] are risk-acceptant and accident prone. The heightened sense of vulnerability increases the dissatisfaction with deterrence."[48] Richard Betts concludes that deterrence has a "limited efficacy" for countering today's major terrorist threats.[49] But Robert F. Trager and Dessislava P. Zagorcheva argue that "the claim that deterrence is ineffective against terrorists is wrong." According to these two political scientists,

> Even seemingly fanatical terrorists, intensely motivated by religious beliefs, are not irrational in a sense that makes them impossible to deter.

> [S]ome essential elements of terrorist support systems are likely to be less moti-
> vated and therefore vulnerable to traditional forms of deterrence, particularly at early
> decision nodes in the lengthy process of preparation required for major attacks.
>
> Even the most highly motivated terrorists, however, can be deterred from certain
> courses of action by holding at risk their political goals, rather than life and liberty.

For Trager and Zagorcheva "the ability to hold political ends [of terrorist groups] at risk . . . stands by far the best chance of fracturing the global terrorist network, one of the most important objectives of counterterrorism policy."[50]

Diplomacy

The prospect for deterrence is different with respect to state sponsors of terrorism. But without diplomatic contacts, without talking to the sponsors of terrorism and terrorist groups it is impossible to figure out whether there are prospects for deterrence or not.

For nearly four decades, the United States has insisted that it will not negotiate with terrorists and will not give in to terrorists' demands. This policy was put in place during the Nixon administration and officially embraced by all administrations thereafter. Yet, diplomacy represents a useful instrument in efforts to solve specific terrorist situations, to convince other governments to join counterterrorist measures, and to suspend their support of terrorists. Diplomatic efforts tend to be especially urgent during hostage situations, when the well-being and even the lives of victims are at stake. During the Iran hostage crisis, there were many attempts to find diplomatic solutions to the deadlock—even though the United States and Iran had broken off their diplomatic ties. In this case, members of the Swiss embassy in Tehran and officials of the United Nations were among the third parties that negotiated on behalf of the United States, and, eventually, Algerian officials were instrumental in brokering the agreement that led to the end of the crisis. Diplomacy had a chance because Iranian authorities had great influence over the hostage-holders. During the TWA hijacking crisis in 1985, there was also a great deal of media diplomacy that involved Washington officials and Lebanese individuals explaining their positions and responding to each other's suggestions and demands on television. More importantly, contacts between Washington officials and the Israeli government and the role of the Red Cross were crucial in negotiating the release of Arab prisoners by Israel and the freeing of the hostages by their Hezbollah captors.

Going the diplomatic route does not guarantee satisfactory solutions. Although the United States and the Taliban did not have diplomatic relations, the military actions against both Al Qaeda and Taliban facilities in Afghanistan were preceded by indirect diplomatic exchanges facilitated by third parties, especially Pakistan. But failed efforts in some instances should not discourage diplomatic initiatives in other cases. In the words of the National Commission on Terrorism,

> Diplomacy is an important instrument, both in gaining the assistance of other
> nations in particular cases and convincing the international community to condemn
> and outlaw egregious terrorist practices . . . .
>
> The United States should strengthen its efforts to discourage the broad range of
> assistance that states provide to international terrorists. A key focus of this initiative
> must be to reduce terrorists' freedom of movement by encouraging countries to stop
> admitting and tolerating the presence of terrorists within their borders.[51]

Finally, diplomacy is "linked with all the [other] elements of counterterrorism," as Paul Pillar observed, whether one thinks of military measures, international cooperation in the areas of intelligence and law enforcement, efforts to dry up terrorists' financial resources, or economic sanctions.[52]

Severing diplomatic relations with terrorist sponsors, an option repeatedly chosen by the United States, demonstrates a targeted country's determination to punish state sponsors of terrorism. But this option eliminates direct diplomacy as a counterterrorist instrument aiming at the exploration of incentives that could weaken a government's willingness to support terrorism.

Of course, even without formal diplomatic ties, direct government to government contacts are not out of the question and can be one factor in paving the way for policy changes on the part of a state sponsor of terrorism. Again, Libya is the most obvious case in point. In 2003 the country was taken off the U.S. State Department's list of state sponsors of terrorism after American–Libyan contacts resulted in Moammar Qadhafi's decision to discontinue his WMD program and any involvement in terrorism; he furthermore agreed to compensate the families of victims that perished in Libyan sponsored terrorist incidents. By the end of 2008, 28 years after diplomatic ties were broken off between Washington and Tripoli, the two countries were ready to restore full diplomatic relations. As mentioned before, Qadhafi's desire to end his country's economic and political isolation influenced his decision greatly, but diplomacy was instrumental in sealing the ultimate outcome.

Take the case of North Korea: Not military might but joint diplomatic efforts by the United States, China, Japan, Russia and South Korea brought North Korea, another longtime member on the State Department's list of terrorism sponsors, to the negotiating table. As a result, Pyongyang took the first, small steps to dismantle its Yongbyon nuclear reactor and promised a long-delayed declaration of its nuclear program and verification regime. In turn, the United States pledged to lift economic sanctions, remove North Korea from its list of terrorist sponsors, and open the door for international aid once the verifiable denuclearization process was in place. To be sure, this was not a happy end to this story, but rather another opening in a difficult and protracted on-going negotiation process. By early 2009, North Korea evicted international nuclear inspectors and began reprocessing spent fuel rods to extract plutonium for the production of nuclear arms. And, again, there were international efforts to resume negotiations.

Whether the U.S. president should directly negotiate with Iranian leaders or not was a major bone of contention during the 2008 presidential campaign, with Barack Obama agreeing to talk to America's adversaries, including Iran, without prior conditions and John McCain rejecting direct and highest-level diplomacy. At the same time, the Bush administration sent contradictory signals. In May 2008, President Bush said in a speech before the Knesset and immediately after mentioning Iran's President Mahmoud Ahmadinejad,

> Some seem to believe that we should negotiate with the terrorists and radicals, as if some ingenious argument will persuade them they have been wrong all along. We have heard this foolish delusion before. As Nazi tanks crossed into Poland in 1939, an American senator declared: "Lord, if I could only have talked to Hitler, all this might have been avoided." We have an obligation to call this what it is—the false comfort of appeasement, which has been repeatedly discredited by history.[53]

Two months after the president categorically rejected a dialogue with Iranian leaders and attacked those who recommended direct talks, the U.S. State Department's third-ranking official, William J. Burns, traveled to Geneva to participate in talks, along with representatives of the European Union, with Iran's nuclear negotiator Saeed Jalili. Although the Geneva meeting ended without any tangible results, there were reports that the U.S. administration and the Iranian government were considering the opening of interest sections in each other's capitals. Comments in Washington and Tehran on the possibility of informal diplomatic representations were in substance and tone a marked departure from President Amadinejad's and President Bush's usually combative rhetoric and Vice-President Cheney's long practice of saber rattling. Given President Obama's position on direct diplomacy with Iran, Cuba, and other adversaries, considerations by both sides of some kind of official representation in each other's capitals seemed like a good prelude to going the diplomatic route in order to change the policies of a terrorist sponsor state.

Talking to Terrorist Groups

Whether to talk to and negotiate with terrorist groups depends first of all on the particular circumstances. Hostage situations are the most likely cases when governments are willing to deal directly or indirectly with terrorists in order to save the lives of fellow citizens. In the Iran hostage crisis, in the arms-for-hostages deals between Washington and Tehran for the sake of Americans held hostage by Hezbollah in Lebanon, and in many other less prominent cases, governments and corporations have negotiated and struck deals with terrorists, without admitting it, to free hostages. This practice continues to this day.

Giving in to the demands of terrorists in order to free hostages is problematic because such bargains might encourage further hostage takings by the same groups or by other organizations.

It is far more difficult, if not impossible, to negotiate the abandonment of terrorism and bringing groups into the domestic and/or international political process. Northern Ireland serves as an excellent example. After decades of bloody violence and a long, protracted peace process, Northern Ireland finally turned the corner in early 2007, when Sinn Fein, the political wing of the Irish Republican Army, and the Democratic Union Party, representing the Protestant majority, formed a government in which Ian Paisley, the long-time Protestant opponent of any meaningful political role for the Catholic minority, became the first minister (or prime minister) and Martin McGuinness, a former IRA commander, the deputy first minister. As the case of Northern Ireland demonstrates, negotiated peace agreements rarely hold after the first try; instead, it is far more likely that the road to peace is paved with broken accords and renewed outbreaks of violence. Cease-fire agreements between the Sri Lankan government and the Tamil Tigers, between Spain's government and the Basque ETA, and between the Israeli government and Hamas have been repeatedly negotiated and broken. Yet, given the poor track record of military actions in ending terrorism, the negotiation route may well be the most promising option in certain cases.

One needs to recognize that the goals and ideologies of organizations determine whether there are opportunities for common ground and compromises. Separatist groups may be inclined to settle for a significant degree of political, economic, and social autonomy short of full independence, if only because they risk otherwise the support of their constituencies. Organizations with uncompromising objectives, on the other hand, will not move from their ultimate goals. While it was possible to negotiate with Marxist militants, such as the Baader-Meinhof terrorists in Germany, about the release of their hostages in return for freeing some of their imprisoned comrades, it did not make sense to talk about the group's categorical stand on its final objective: the destruction of capitalism and democracy in the Federal Republic of Germany and elsewhere in the West. Religious terrorists, too, tend to have absolute demands and goals that defy compromise. A comparison between the secular Palestinian al-Fatah, a terrorist organization before—at least officially—it abandoned terrorism, and the religious Palestinian Hamas is instructive. While al-Fatah has been open to settling for a compromise two-state solution with Israel, Hamas has not retreated from its ultimate objective—the removal of Israel from the map of the Middle East.

While recognizing the difficulties and risks involved in opening a dialogue with terrorists—especially after 9/11—Daniel Byman has examined the potential benefits of such talks by reviewing past contacts between governments and terrorist groups, such as the PIRA, ETA, and the PLO. He also assesses possible talks between the United States and Hezbollah and/or Hamas—without mentioning the pros and cons of talking to Al Qaeda's leaders.[54] Aware that suggestions to actually talk to Al Qaeda might be considered "tantamount to treason," Louise Richardson nevertheless writes,

> *If anything, we appear to know less about the nature of our adversaries in the war on terrorism than we did when we began. We take as a given that their demands are so extreme as to be nonnegotiable, but it would be worth finding out if that is, in fact, the case.*
>
> *Ayman al-Zawahiri has clearly emerged as the chief spokesman and strategist of the al-Qaeda leadership, and while it is far from clear that he has the authority to carry his followers with him, the opportunity to engage him is one that should not be missed, no matter how much opprobrium we hold for him.*[55]

Interestingly, al-Zawahiri, in a videotape released in December 2006, said that the United States would ultimately have to talk to "the real forces in the Islamic world"—presumably meaning the Al Qaeda leadership.[56] In other words, Al Qaeda's second-in-command signaled the desire for U.S.–Al Qaeda negotiations.

On this issue, this writer sides with those who reject talks with Osama bin Laden or his lieutenants because of the organization's nonnegotiable goals. Negotiations would elevate Al Qaeda and the global like-minded terrorist network to legitimate political actors without any incentive to abandon violence. As one expert put it,

> There is no sign that al Qaeda has changed its thinking on the utility of violence. And it is hard to conceive of a viable process of primary negotiations in which al Qaeda could be included. Al Qaeda has global aspirations and no firm territorial base, and there is no clearly defined territory in which its aims could be satisfied through constitutional means. Under these conditions, opening negotiations would be a counterproductive move: it would provide al Qaeda with political legitimacy . . . .[57]

A more promising course of actions, one that Richardson recommends as well, would concentrate on weakening support and sympathies among those Arabs and Muslims in whose name Al Qaeda and like-minded groups claim to commit their violent deeds. Terrorists need the good will of those they claim to represent in order to draw moral support and new recruits. Thus, there is a need for a public diplomacy initiative that utilizes the information and communication means of the twenty-first century.

Public Diplomacy

When it comes to the Arab and Muslim world, public opinion polls in Pakistan, Saudi Arabia, Indonesia, and several other countries have revealed that the strong support for Osama bin Laden and his causes has a soft underbelly and could be softened more so with the right public diplomacy approaches. Kenneth Ballen, president of the Terror Free Tomorrow organization that has conducted extensive surveys in Muslim countries, found significant resentment toward the United States but at the same time potential for a dramatic turnaround in favor of America without drastic policy adjustments.[58]

Take the example of Pakistan. Eighty percent of respondents in a June 2008 survey said that Al Qaeda's top goal was standing up to America; 57% agreed with that objective. The same survey revealed that only one-third of Pakistanis had a favorable opinion of bin Laden and Al Qaeda. When asked what would improve their opinion of the United States, the vast majority considered educational scholarships and U.S. visas, free trade between the two countries, American disaster relief, medical aid, and resources to build schools and train teachers as measures to better Pakistanis' esteem of America. The most surprising result was that a larger percentage of bin Laden supporters than of nonsupporters reacted positively to U.S. measures deemed likely to improve Pakistanis' attitudes toward America and Americans. Or take Indonesia, where public opinion became much more favorable toward the United States and much less positive toward bin Laden after American-led relief efforts following the deadly tsunami of 2005. With these and similar results in other Muslim countries in mind, Ken Ballen wrote,

> What our surveys uncovered is that the U.S. would witness dramatic improvements in the view of the United States among the overwhelming majority of Muslims, including those who express support for al Qaeda and Bin Laden, if we demonstrate respect and caring for people in their daily lives through practical, relatively achievable steps such as increasing direct humanitarian assistance (medical, education, food), visas and better trade terms.[59]

For this to work, Washington decision-makers, not just those in the Department of State, must consider how to explain and justify U.S. policies—actions and nonactions—and how to gauge the effects of those policies on foreign publics. In short, there is a need for effective public diplomacy.

Unlike traditional, government-to-government diplomacy, public diplomacy is conducted by one government and aimed at foreign publics. So far, the record of American post–9/11 public diplomacy in the Arab and Muslim world has been a fiasco and thus a far cry from the success story during the Cold War. The three pillars of American public diplomacy of the Cold War era—the spread of information via foreign language broadcasts into the communist world, cultural exchanges, and educational exchanges—need to be adapted to the global realities of the twenty-first century.[60] In the age of information, when a multitude of global television and radio networks and the Internet provide instant news, information, and communication, the successful broadcast strategies of the past will no longer work. There are more vehicles and opportunities to reach and engage larger audiences overseas than ever before—but only with innovative programs conceived, produced, and presented by professionals who speak the languages and know the cultures of the target audiences and, of course, the public relations goals of the United States.

Although well financed, the U.S. government's Arab-language television network al-Hurra and radio station al-Sawa, for example, have neither displayed the excellence of their Cold War predecessors, such as "Voice of America" or "Radio Free Europe," nor found promising new approaches for a completely different media and communication environment. As for the Internet, Secretary of Defense Robert Gates was right on target when he said the following:

> [P]public relations was invented in the United States, yet we are miserable at communicating to the rest of the world what we are about as a society and a culture, about freedom and democracy, about our policies and our goals. It is just plain embarrassing that al-Qaeda is better at communicating its message on the internet than America. As one foreign diplomat asked a couple of years ago, "How has one man in a cave managed to out-communicate the world's greatest communication society?" Speed, agility, and cultural relevance are not terms that come readily to mind when discussing U.S. strategic communications.[61]

While a modernized public diplomacy model must focus on the Internet's ample opportunities for virtual cultural and educational exchanges, it should never do so at the expense of direct cultural and educational exchanges since surveys reveal that many Arabs and Muslims are in favor of such interactions.

Finally, public diplomacy should also target moderate Muslim clerics and opinion-makers, such as media personnel, particularly news analysts, editorial writers, and columnists, and encourage and even press them to speak out against terrorism that is carried out in the name of Islam. In the wake of the 2004 terrorist attack by Chechen separatists on a Russian school in Beslan, a number of Muslim clerics condemned the attacks—but such condemnations were often not categorical but permitted explicitly or implicitly such lethal strikes against Israelis and other infidels who had not, like Russia, supported the Palestinian cause. Others Muslim leaders have pointed out that most of the deadly and gruesome terrorism attacks at the dawn of the twenty-first century have been perpetrated by Muslims. At the height of the violent uproar over the Danish cartoons that depicted the Prophet Muhammad, some Arab opinion-makers questioned the Muslim world's mass protests against drawings and its collective silence about jihadis who beheaded their western hostages and posted the videotapes of these executions on the Internet. Since these moderates are the best hope for promoting movements toward nonviolence and the ultimate failure of violence in their own communities, countries, and regions, they should be the particular targets of mass-media and personal communication efforts.

Conciliation and Peace

One viable option—the effort on the part of democratic governments to offer conciliation, compromise, and peace to individuals or organizations instead of fighting and repressing them—is frequently omitted from responses to terrorism. As Peter C. Sederberg has pointed out,

> We tend to underestimate the possibility that the democratic principles themselves may suggest effective response. Negotiations, compromise, and conciliation rest at the heart of democratic processes, but commentators usually dismiss them as irrelevant or even dangerously ineffective.[62]

A chance for conciliation and compromise may exist if individual terrorists recognize the hopelessness of their struggle and if organizations are not dead-set on totally destroying the state they fight. Italy's "repentance" law of 1980, for example, was an effort to lure individual terrorists away from the Red Brigades, win their collaboration, and thereby weaken and defeat the terror organization. To be sure, the time was right, in that the growing brutality of the Red Brigades' terror strikes horrified an increasing number of its members, some of whom no longer believed that their armed struggle could succeed. But while some terrorists took the opportunity, many others did not. Identifying "group dynamics" as keeping terrorists in the fold, Donatella della Porta found that

> [m]any of the militants who were in the process of quitting terrorism were in fact compelled to react to the "betrayal" of some of their fellow comrades by confirming their loyalty to the organization. Solidarity toward comrades also influenced the process of quitting underground organizations. Interviews expressed such sentiments as "You do not give up on the basis of an individual decision."[63]

In June 2004, after a series of deadly terror attacks in Saudi Arabia, King Fahd called on militant followers of Al Qaeda to turn themselves in to the law enforcement authorities within a one-month period in which "the door of forgiveness" would be open. This limited amnesty was offered with the warning that unless militants surrendered, they would face the full might of state wrath. Shortly after the amnesty was announced, two of Saudi Arabia's most wanted terrorists surrendered. But a Saudi group linked to Osama bin Laden predicted in an online news release that the initiative would end in "utter failure . . . to stop the jihad."[64] There was no threat in this particular case, but would-be defectors might not have left their groups for fear of being punished. The limited amnesty was not successful at all.

Just like conciliation efforts directed at individuals, peace initiatives aimed at bringing governments and organizations together and finding nonviolent compromises have had mixed results in the past. In South Africa, a long process of peace involving the minority government and the African National Congress (ANC) was successful in that it led to the establishment of a democratic government in 1994. After the "getting-to-know-each-other" phase, the parties set a negotiation agenda and agreed on visible compromises: The government released ANC prisoners, and the ANC terminated its armed struggle. This was followed by actual negotiations, the implementation of the negotiated agreement, and, finally, a process of "truth and conciliation."[65] The willingness of all parties to participate in negotiations to resolve the century-old conflict in Northern Ireland in the 1990s peacefully moved them toward a lasting, nonviolent, political solution. In the Middle East, a negotiated solution of the Israeli–Palestinian conflict seemed repeatedly on track in the last decades, but opponents of compromise on both sides derailed the peace process at crucial junctures. Although negotiations between the Spanish government and the Basque separatist group ETA resulted in a cease-fire agreement in the 1990s, in the long run the terrorists rejected a compromise solution and resumed their campaign of terror.

It seems that conflicts between states and domestic groups that commit terrorism are more susceptible to conciliation and compromise than are clashes between a nation-state on the one hand and foreign terror groups or an international terrorism network on the other. Secular groups may be more willing than religious organizations to partake in negotiations. Individual followers of Osama bin Laden may be lured away from their terrorist activities by amnesty offers, but it is unlikely that the leaders of the global Al Qaeda terror network and their principal foe—the United

States—would travel the road of reconciliation and compromise. And yet, conciliation should never be discounted as one of many options for responding to terrorism. Indeed, governments can use a stick and carrot at the same time or, as Sederberg suggested, "combine conciliatory and repressive elements."[66]

Notes

1. Joseph Nye, "Obama's Foreign Policy Must Combine Hard and Soft Power," *The Huffington Post*, December 3, 2008, available at http://www.huffingtonpost.com/joseph-nye/obamas-foreign-policies-m_b_147108.html?view=print (accessed December 11, 2008).
2. The quotes are from Max Weber's lecture "The Profession and Vocation of Politics," available at http://www.as.ysu.edu/~polisci/syllabi/weber.htm (accessed December 11, 2008).
3. Joseph S. Nye, Jr., *The Paradox of American Power* (New York: Oxford University Press, 2002), 8.
4. Ibid., 9.
5. Defense Secretary Robert Gates made these remarks in his Landon Lecture at Kansas State University, November 26, 2007. The text of the lecture is available at http://www.defenselink.mil/speeches/speech.aspx?speechid=1199 (accessed December 1, 2008).
6. Secretary of State Hillary Clinton made these remarks during her testimony as Secretary of State designee before the U.S. Senate Foreign Relations Committee's confirmation hearing on January 13, 2009. For transcript, see http://www.npr.org/templates/story/story.php?storyId=99290981 (accessed January 14, 2009).
7. National Intelligence Council, "Global Trends 2025: A Transformed World," available at http://www.dni.gov/nic/NIC_2025_project.html.
8. Defense Secretary Robert Gates made these remarks in his Landon Lecture at Kansas State University, November 26, 2007.
9. Andrew J. Bacevich, "Think Again: What's Our Definition of Victory?" *Newsweek*, December 8, 2008, 38.
10. John Lewis Gaddis, "And Now This: Lessons from the Old Era for the New One," in Strobe Talbot and Nayan Chanda, eds., *The Age of Terror* (New York: Basic Books, 2001), 3.
11. Geoffrey Nunberg, "How Much Wallop Can a Simple Word Pack?" *New York Times*, July 11, 2002, sec. 4, 7.
12. Donald M. Snow, National Security for a New Era (New York: Pearson Longman, 2007), 299.
13. Paul Pillar, *Terrorism and U.S. Foreign Policy* (Washington, DC: Brookings Institution Press, 2001), 218.
14. President Bush's Address to the Joint Session of Congress, September 20, 2001.
15. Ibid., 15.
16. Pillar, 168.
17. Neil C. Livingstone, "Proactive Responses to Terrorism: Reprisals, Preemption, and Retribution," in Charles W. Kegley, Jr., ed., *International Terrorism* (New York: St. Martin's, 1990), 220.
18. Ibid.
19. Ibid.
20. Pillar, 101.
21. Livingstone, 222.
22. Barry R. Posen. "The Struggle against Terrorism: Grand Strategy, Strategy, and Tactics," *International Security* 26:3 (Winter 2001–2002): 47.
23. Carlotta Gall, "Evidence Points to Civilian Toll in Afghan Raid," *New York Times*, September 9, 2008, available at http://www.nytimes.com/2008/09/08/world/asia/08afghan.html?_r=1&hp=&oref=slogin&pagewanted=print, (accessed September 9, 2008).
24. Ibid.
25. Neil C. Livingstone, "Proactive Responses to Terrorism: Reprisals, Preemption, and Retribution," in Charles W. Kegley, Jr., ed., *International Terrorism* (New York: St. Martin's, 1990), 223.
26. Robert Jervis, "Understanding the Bush Doctrine," in Demetrios James Caraley, ed., *American Hegemony: Preventive War, Iraq, and Imposing Democracy* (New York: Academy of Political Science, 2004), 9.

27. From a transcript of NBC News, *Meet the Press*, February 8, 2004 (retrieved from the LexisNexis electronic archive).

28. According to the National Counterterrorism Center's "2007 Report on Terrorism" released on April 30, 2008, available at http://www.terrorisminfo.mipt.org/pdf/NCTC-2007-Report-on-Terrorism.pdf (accessed September 1, 2008).

29. As the *Washington Post* reported before the release of Bob Woodward's most recent book, *The War Within: A Secret White House 2006–2008*, the surge "was not the primary factor behind the steep drop in violence" in Iraq. Woodward mentions intelligence and military officials' "new covert techniques" that helped to locate and target leading terrorists and insurgents besides the "Anwar Awakening" and the restraint of the Mahdi Army. The article is available at http://www.washingtonpost.com/wp-dyn/content/article/2008/09/04/AR2008090403160.html. In his response, National Security Adviser Stephen Hadley insisted that the troop surge of 2007 was the decisive factor that made the other improvements possible. For the Hadley statement, see http://www.whitehouse.gov/news/releases/2008/09/20080905-5.html.

30. Robert M. Gates, "A Balanced Strategy: Reprogramming the Pentagon for a New Age," *Foreign Affairs* (January/February 2009): 29.

31. Lindsay Clutterbuck, "Law Enforcement," in Audrey Kurth Cronin and James M. Ludes, eds., *Attacking Terrorism: Elements of a Grand Strategy* (Washington: Georgetown University Press, 2004), 141.

32. Seth G. Jones and Martin C. Libicki, *How Terrorist Groups End: Lesson for Countering al Qa'ida* (Santa Monica, CA: Rand Corporation, 2008), chapter 2.

33. Holger Jensen, "The United States Should Retaliate against Terrorist Groups," in Laura K. Egendorf, ed., *Terrorism: Opposing Viewpoints* (San Diego, CA: Greenhaven Press, 2000), 164.

34. Ibid.

35. Deborah Sontag, "Israel Acknowledges Hunting Down Arab Militants," *New York Times*, December 22, 2000, A12.

36. Perez was quoted in Clyde Haberman, "In the Mid-East This Year, Even Words Shoot to Kill," *New York Times*, August 5, 2001, sec. 4, 3.

37. Ibid.

38. Michael Ignatieff, "Lesser Evils," *New York Times Sunday Magazine*, May 2, 2004. Available at http://www.nytimes.com/2004/05/02/magazine/lesser-evils.html?scp=1&sq=michael%20ignatieff,%20lesser%20evils&st=cse (accessed May 20, 2009).

39. For more on the CIA authority, see James Risen and David Johnson, "Threats and Responses: Hunt for Al Qaeda; Bush Has Widened Authority of CIA to Kill Terrorists," *New York Times*, December 15, 2002, 1.

40. Pillar, 98.

41. David C. Martin and John Walcott, *Best Laid Plans: The Inside Story of America's War against Terrorism* (New York: Harper & Row, 1988), 35.

42. Stephen D. Collins, "Dissuading State Support of Terrorism: Strikes or Sanctions?" *Studies in Conflict & Terrorism* 27:1 (January/February 2004): 3.

43. Robert Pape, "Why Economic Sanctions Do Not Work," *International Security* 22 (Fall 1997): 110.

44. Pillar, 167.

45. Collins.

46. Ibid., 15.

47. Pillar, 94, 95.

48. Jervis, 7.

49. Richard Betts, "The Soft Underbelly of American Primacy," in Demetrious James Careley, ed., *September 11, Terrorist Attacks, and U.S. Foreign Policy* (New York: Academy of Political Science, 2002), 46.

50. Robert F. Trager and Dessislava P. Zagorcheva, "Deterring Terrorism: It Can Be Done," *International Security* 30:3 (Winter 2005/2006): 88–89.

51. Countering the Changing Threat of International Terrorism: Report of the National Commission on Terrorism, Pursuant to Public Law 277, 105th Congress, 17, 18.

52. Pillar, 73.

53. The transcript of President George W. Bush's speech on May 15, 2008 is available at http://www.whitehouse.gov/news/releases/2008/05/20080515-1.html.

54. Daniel Byman, "The Decision to Begin Talks with Terrorists: Lessons for Policymakers," *Studies in Conflict and Terrorism* 29 (2006): 403–14.

55. Louise Richardson, *What Terrorists Want: Understanding the Terrorist Threat* (New York: Random House, 2006), 212.

56. For summary of the video release of December 23, 2006, see http://memri.org/bin/articles.cgi?Page=subjects&Area=iwmp&ID=SP140506 (accessed December 29, 2008).

57. Peter R. Neumann, "Negotiating with Terrorists," *Foreign Affairs* 86:1 (January/February 2007), 136.

58. For survey summaries and news accounts about them, see Terror Free Tomorrow's web site http://www.terrorfreetomorrow.org/

59. Ken Ballen, "Even al Qaeda Supporters Can Be Won Over," *Los Angeles Times*, June 14, 2008, available at http://www.terrorfreetomorrow.org/upimagestft/LATWashMonth.pdf

60. For public diplomacy in the information age, see Geoffrey Cohen and Amelia Arsenault, "Moving from Monologue to Dialogue to Collaboration: The Three Layers of Public Diplomacy," in Geoffrey Cohen and Nicholas J. Cull, eds., *Public Diplomacy in a Changing World.* (Philadelphia: THE ANNALS 616 (March 2008)), 46–52.

61. The remarks were made during the Landon Lecture at Kansas State University, November 26, 2007. The transcript of the speech is available at http://www.defenselink.mil/speeches/speech.aspx?speechid=1199 (accessed September 1, 2008).

62. Peter C. Sederberg, "Conciliation as Counter-Terrorist Strategy," *Journal of Peace Research* 32:3 (1995): 298.

63. Donatella della Porta, "Left-Wing Terrorism in Italy," in Martha Crenshaw, ed., *Terrorism in Context* (University Park: Pennsylvania State University, 1995), 153.

64. Reuters, "Qaeda Says Saudi Militant Amnesty Will Fail," *Yahoo! News*, June 30, 2004, www.yahoo.com (retrieved July 6, 2004).

65. For more, see "Reconciliation and Community: The Future of Peace in Northern Ireland," Conference Report, Project on Justice in Times of Transition, June 6–8, 1995, Belfast, Northern Ireland.

66. Sederberg, 299.

CHAPTER 12

Balancing Security, Liberty, and Human Rights

A GOVERNMENT'S FIRST DUTY IS TO PROTECT THE LIVES AND the property of its citizens. Therefore, political leaders tend to take extraordinary measures during times of crisis in the name of providing security. But after devastating terrorist strikes, democratic governments must resist the temptation to go too far—otherwise, they play into the hands of the very same terrorists they set out to defeat. Terrorists want to change the behavior of the societies they attack. When they strike democracies, they want to scare their targets into weakening or abandoning their most esteemed values: their respect for civil liberties and for human rights. This was precisely what bin Laden wanted to accomplish with the attacks of 9/11, and he believed in fact that he succeeded. In an interview with Al Jazeera, bin Laden said,

> The values of this Western civilization under the leadership of America have been destroyed. Those awesome symbolic towers that speak of liberty, human rights, and humanity have been destroyed. They have gone up in smoke.
>
> The proof came, when the U.S. government pressured the media not to run our statements that are not longer than a few minutes. They felt that the truth started to reach the American people, the truth that we are not terrorists as they understand it but because we are being attacked in Palestine, Iraq, Lebanon, Sudan, Somalia, Kashmir, the Philippines, and everywhere else.[1]

While he overstated by far what was happening in the United States and elsewhere in the West, bin Laden left no doubt that he was delighted about his enemies' reactions. Earlier terrorists anticipated also that governments would overreact and, as a result, frustrate and infuriate their own citizens. Well before 9/11, Paul Wilkinson warned against "overreaction" and repressive measures that "could destroy democracy far more rapidly and effectively than any campaign by a terrorist group." But he also cautioned against "underreaction" in the face of terrorist threats.[2] In other words, governments must strive for a balance between providing security on the one hand and respecting civil liberties and human rights on the other, between effective anti- and counterterrorist measures on one side and highly esteemed societal values on the other.

What is the distinction between anti- and counterterrorism? In the 1980s, Marc A. Celmer wrote that "antiterrorist actions are designed as defensive measures to prevent the occurrence of terrorism as opposed to counterterrorist measures, which are offensive in nature and are designed to respond to a terrorist act."[3] While antiterrorism is still understood as defensive in nature, the common meaning of counterterrorism transcends offensive measures. When threatened by terrorism, governments adopt and implement a whole range of policies and measures in order to prevent further terrorist strikes. Hunting down terrorists, punishing supporters of terrorist activities, launching retaliatory strikes, tightening security measures, and strengthening preparedness programs are all parts of an overall counterterrorism strategy. Typically, a host of governmental institutions and actors as well as the private sector get involved in counterterrorist measures. Counterterrorism, then, encompasses strategies and tactics adopted in response to terrorism. According to one encyclopedia entry,

> Counter-terrorism is not specific to any one field or organization, it involves entities from all levels of society. For instance, businesses have security plans and sometimes share commercial data with government. Local police, fire fighters, and emergency personnel (often called "first responders") have plans for dealing with terrorist attacks. Armies conduct combat operations against terrorists, often using special forces.[4]

Antiterrorist policies and actions, then, are part of the overall counterterrorist approaches that a country adopts in response to terrorism and the threat thereof.

Years before the U.S. government adopted its first comprehensive anti- and counterterrorism laws, European democracies, such as Germany, Greece, and the

Money, Time, Patience: The Price of Heightened Security Measures

Because the 9/11 terrorists passed the existing security checks on their way to hijacking four commercial airliners, the United States invested heavily in measures to improve airport security. While experts do not agree whether these efforts have resulted in greater security, travelers need extra time and patience when they and their carry-on luggage are checked thoroughly by security personnel.

United Kingdom, enacted many measures in response to frequent terrorist strikes within their borders. Between 1970 and 1989, the Federal Republic of Germany adopted ten amendments to its criminal code that provided the judiciary and police with more justifications for investigating and arresting suspects. After 9/11, "Rasterfahndung," a combination of profiling and data mining that had been used in the Federal Republic's struggle against the Red Army Faction and its successor groups, was revived. Describing the earlier practice, Peter Katzenstein wrote,

> A newly developed "computer matching" (Rasterfahndung), tailored to the fight against terrorism, scans large data sets to identify overlapping clusters of what are regarded as suspicious traits, in the hope of targeting police work more efficiently and effectively. For example, in the 1970s the police got access to the files of the West German utility companies and identified those customers who paid their bills in cash or through third parties. This group of potential suspects was narrowed down further through checks with data on residence registration, which is compulsory in West Germany, automobile registration, receipt of social security or child care payments as well as other data sources. What remained was a list of names of potential terrorist suspects: those who did not receive pensions or child allowances, who were not registered, had no automobiles and who paid their utility bills in cash or through third parties. Traditional police investigation, including surveillance and house searches, was concentrated on this list of potential suspects.[5]

The post–9/11 Rasterfahndung concentrated on Muslims and Arabs in their twenties and thirties and data assembled by travel agencies, telecommunication companies, universities, and other public and private institutions. In early 2006, Germany's Constitutional Court (Bundesverfassungsgericht) ruled in the case of a Moroccan plaintiff that Rasterfahndung is legal only in the face of a "real threat" to the security of the country or the life of a citizen.

Within months after 9/11, Germany enacted two comprehensive antiterror laws with many far-reaching provisions that, for example, expanded jurisdiction of law enforcement agencies beyond German borders, allowed authorities to ban religious groups if they promoted violence, and expanded the power of border patrol agents to screen and search persons and their belongings. In 2006, following the botched plot to bomb two German trains by Lebanese students, Chancellor Angela Merkel and her government pushed for expanded closed-circuit camera systems in train stations and other public places. A camera at the Cologne main terminal had provided the grainy images of two young men boarding a train and led to the quick arrest of one of the would-be bombers.

Beginning with the Northern Ireland Act of 1973 that toughened emergency provisions to deal with terrorism in Northern Ireland, the United Kingdom enacted several antiterrorism laws. Like Germany, the United Kingdom enacted several more comprehensive laws in reaction to 9/11 and the multiple suicide attacks on London's transit system in July 2005: the Crime and Security Act of 2001, the Prevention of Terrorism Act of 2005, and the Terrorism Act of 2006. Even before the events of 2001, when British authorities were mostly concerned about terrorism in the context of the conflict in Northern Ireland, British intelligence and law enforcement agencies were authorized by the Regulation of Investigatory Powers Act of 2000 and the 2001 Crime and Security Act "to evaluate communications data for patterns suggestive of terrorist activities."[6] Moreover, to monitor communications data, a law enforcement or intelligence agency need only to complete a written application, which is considered by a designated individual within the body or agency.[7] As John Yoo testified before a U.S. Senate Committee,

> The British have greater power [than American law enforcement] to detain a terrorist without criminal charge. Section 23 of the Terrorism Act of 2006 sets forth a procedure under which a suspect may be detained for up to 28 days before he must be charged with a crime or released. After 48 hours, judicial approval is required, and is required a second time if the authorities wish to detain the suspect beyond 7 days. The judge does not need to find probable cause, but must be satisfied that "there are reasonable grounds for believing that the further detention of the person to whom the application relates is necessary to obtain relevant evidence whether by questioning him or otherwise or to preserve relevant evidence," and "the investigation in connection with which the person is detained is being conducted diligently and expeditiously." The suspect has access to counsel and may make written or oral communications before the judge; however, the suspect and his counsel may also be excluded from portions of the hearing. The British government has already invoked this power to detain the individuals arrested in conjunction with the August, 2006 plot to blow up airliners departing Britain. This allowed the plot to be halted, but also allows more evidence to be gathered prior to formally charging the suspects with crimes.[8]

Coming on the heels of successful and failed suicide bombings in London, the Antiterrorism Act of 2006 made it a crime to glorify or encourage political violence. But just like earlier German and Greek laws that prohibited the glorification of terrorism in news reports or the publication of communications by terrorists during a terrorist incident, this particular provision was too broad to be effective.

Beginning in the 1980s, the United States, too, responded with legislative and executive initiatives to each major anti-American act of terrorism. But until 1996, when the Congress and President Bill Clinton reacted to the Oklahoma City bombing, antiterrorism laws did not intrude markedly on the civil liberties of individuals. During the 1980s, when Americans abroad as well as diplomatic and private American facilities in foreign countries were frequently the targets of terrorism, presidents and both houses of Congress were eager to demonstrate that they were doing something. Typically, presidents established commissions and asked them for recommendations and congressional committees held hearings. Administration officials and members of Congress, regardless of whether they were Democrats or Republicans, were eager to claim that they had initiated or sponsored legislation to tighten security in the air, on water, and on foreign soil. During this period, the Omnibus Diplomatic Security Act of 1986 became the most comprehensive package of new or revised security laws. For example, this act directed the State Department to establish a Diplomatic Security Service, intensify the protection of U.S. embassies and other governmental facilities abroad, and expand a facility construction program to harden diplomatic missions overseas. The act (Public Law 99–399) also established a reward program for the capture of terrorists, a program to provide for greater security at U.S. military bases abroad, measures for seaport and shipboard security, initiatives to combat nuclear terrorism, and a framework for the compensation of terrorism victims.

Strongly affected by the first World Trade Center bombing in 1993 and introduced in Congress two months before the Oklahoma City bombing, the Antiterrorism and Effective Death Penalty Act of 1996 (Public Law 104–132) was in some respects a softened version of what President Clinton had asked for. For example, a provision that would have given police more authority in the surveillance of suspected terrorists was scratched. Still, opponents rejected the measure as containing "some of the worst assaults on civil liberties in decades."[9] The law made it a crime for individuals or groups, whether citizens or noncitizens, to provide money or material support to groups designated by the secretary of state as foreign terrorist organizations; another section provided for the establishment of a special court to handle the deportation of aliens suspected of terrorist activities while protecting classified information. The Antiterrorism Act required for the first time that plastic explosives must contain chemical "taggents" that allow law enforcement to track their source. Acknowledging the pleas of victims of terrorism and their families, this law allowed U.S. citizens to bring civil actions against the governments of countries that the secretary of state had designated as state sponsors of terrorism.

None of the previously adopted laws, executive orders, and other government initiatives came close to the burst of post–9/11 measures taken by the White House, the Congress, the Department of Justice, and other parts of the U.S. government. According to Laura Donohue, in the eight weeks following the events of 9/11, "the President issued dozens of Proclamations and Executive Orders and the Executive Branch engaged in a widespread antiterrorist campaign. Congress introduced 323 bills and resolutions and adopted 21 laws and resolutions relating to the attacks and the war against terrorism."[10] Within days of the terror attacks on New York and Washington, D.C., the Bush administration presented Congress with proposals to expand police and prosecutorial powers to enhance the fight against terrorism. Some six weeks later, both houses of Congress voted in overwhelming majorities for the Uniting and Strengthening America by Providing Appropriate Tools Required to Intercept and Obstruct Terrorism Act, which is better known by its catchy name: the USA PATRIOT Act of 2001 (Public Law 107–56). Few lawmakers, if any, were familiar with the details of the hastily written provisions of the bill when they cast their votes. In the absence of news reports that described and scrutinized the most important provisions of either the legislative proposals or the final version of the bill that the president signed into law, the public remained clueless as to the content of the new law.

The USA PATRIOT Act vastly increased the authority of government agents to track and gather information by conducting "sneak and peek searches" in homes, offices, or other private places without informing the targets of such searches in advance. The government's wiretap authority was expanded, as was information sharing among various federal agencies. By simply certifying a need for the material sought in an investigation of international terrorism, government agents got the authority to subpoena any individual's records at places such as libraries, bookstores, telephone companies, Internet providers, and universities. The act directed the U.S. attorney general (AG) to hold foreigners who were suspected terrorists for up to seven days before charging them with a crime or beginning deportation procedures. As Laura Donohue put it, "The USA PATRIOT Act not just allowed but required the detention of anyone the AG had reasonable grounds to believe was connected to terrorism or was a threat to national security. The statute did not specify a time period. Detention without trial could continue until the suspect was either deported or determined no longer a threat."[11] Furthermore, the law stipulated the establishment of a system to fingerprint and photograph foreigners at their entrance point into the United States, a controversial measure that was in place by the beginning of 2004.

Supporters of the act emphasized that many of its most controversial provisions would expire in 2005 unless renewed by congressional and presidential actions. But this did not pacify conservative and liberal critics, who—as they became aware of the details in the USA PATRIOT Act—rejected a number of provisions as assaults on constitutionally guaranteed civil liberties. Pointing to the vastly different reactions to the massive antiterrorism law, Charles Doyle of the Congressional Research Service wrote, "Although it is not without safeguards, critics contend some of its provisions go too far. Although it grants many of the enhancements sought by the Department of Justice, others are concerned that it does not go far enough."[12]

David Cole and James Dempsey concluded that "the PATRIOT Act radically transformed the landscape of government power, and did so in ways that virtually guaranteed repetition of some of law enforcement's worst abuses of the past."[13] Such fears were justified. The inspector general of the U.S. Department of Justice found dozens of cases in which the civil liberties and civil rights of detained terrorism suspects were violated in the enforcement of the PATRIOT Act. One of the cases described in the inspector general's report concerned "allegations that during a physical examination a Bureau of Prisons physician told the inmate, 'If I was in charge, I would execute every one of you, because of the crimes you all did.'"[14] The same physician was accused of treating other inmates "in a cruel and unprofessional manner."[15] After a Bureau of Prisons investigation substantiated the allegations, the physician was reprimanded—not fired. Far more troubling than this mistreatment of individuals was the inspector general's conclusion that many of the foreign detainees "languished in unduly harsh conditions for months, and that the department had made little effort to distinguish legitimate terrorist suspects from others picked up in roundups of illegal immigrants."[16] Most of these detainees in detention centers in the United States were held for immigration violations—in many cases for many months without an opportunity to have their cases reviewed by an independent judiciary authority.

In April 2005, the U.S. Senate and House of Representatives held the first in a series of oversight hearings in a prolonged debate on whether to renew the sixteen provisions of the USA PATRIOT Act set to expire at the end of the year. There was wide agreement that most parts of the comprehensive law were uncontroversial tools for law enforcement agencies in their efforts to prevent terrorism. But loud voices on the left and right of the political spectrum demanded the removal or modification of those parts of the USA PATRIOT Act that went too far in allowing the FBI and other agencies to curb political dissent and spy on Americans. Particularly controversial were those sections allowing the government to get access to medical, library, and other personal records and to search a person's home—in both cases without notifying individuals of such actions.

While the original USA PATRIOT Act of 2001 was passed by huge majorities in both houses of Congress (98–1 in the Senate and 356–56 in the House), there was somewhat more opposition four years later, when the Senate voted 89–11 and the House 280–138 for the USA PATRIOT Improvement and Reauthorization Act of 2005 and the USA PATRIOT Additional Reauthorization Amendments Act of 2006. Still, overwhelming majorities of both parties cast their votes in favor of these bills—perhaps because they strengthened congressional and judicial oversight in several areas, especially with respect to wiretapping, access to personal records, and "sneak and peek" search warrants. But when President Bush signed both acts into laws (P.L. 109–177 and P.L. 109–178) in March 2006, his signing statement made clear that he reserved the right to ignore such oversight provisions.

President's Statement on H.R. 3199, the "USA PATRIOT Improvement and Reauthorization Act of 2005"

Today, I have signed into law H.R. 3199, the "USA PATRIOT Improvement and Reauthorization Act of 2005," and then S. 2271, the "USA PATRIOT Act Additional Reauthorizing Amendments Act of 2006." The bills will help us continue to fight terrorism effectively and to combat the use of the illegal drug methamphetamine that is ruining too many lives.

The executive branch shall construe the provisions of H.R. 3199 that call for furnishing information to entities outside the executive branch, such as sections 106A and 119, in a manner consistent with the President's constitutional authority to supervise the unitary executive branch and to withhold information the disclosure of which could impair foreign relations, national security, the deliberative processes of the Executive, or the performance of the Executive's constitutional duties.

The executive branch shall construe section 756(e)(2) of H.R. 3199, which calls for an executive branch official to submit to the Congress recommendations for legislative action, in a manner consistent with the President's constitutional authority to supervise the unitary executive branch and to recommend for the consideration of the Congress such measures as he judges necessary and expedient.

George W. Bush

The White House,

March 9, 2006.

Several months before the second version of the USA PATRIOT Act became the law of the land, President Bush confirmed news reports that the National Security Agency (NSA) was eavesdropping without warrants on international telephone and e-mail communications of American citizens and noncitizens in this country who were suspected of being in contact with terrorists. This NSA practice violated the Foreign Intelligence Surveillance Act of 1978 (FISA) that excluded U.S. citizens and resident aliens from electronic surveillance and requires authorization by a special Foreign Intelligence Surveillance Court for the electronic surveillance of suspected foreign intelligence agents inside the United States. Shortly after 9/11, President Bush authorized the NSA to wiretap U.S. citizens and foreign nationals without warrants issued by the FISA court. When the warrantless wiretap practice was revealed, some of President Bush's harshest critics suggested that he had broken the law and should be impeached. But, as Eric Lichtblau reported, nothing really changed in the year following the eavesdropping revelations: "For all the sound and fury in the last year, the National Security Agency's wiretapping program continues uninterrupted with no definitive action by either Congress or the courts on what, if anything, to do about it. . . ."[17]

President Bush, however, pushed for and won the legalization of greater spying powers in the last year of his second term. On July 2008, he signed the FISA Amendment Act (FAA) of 2008 into law after enough Democrats (including then

Senator Barack Obama) and Republicans in both congressional chambers voted in favor of significantly "updating" the original FISA law. In the first place, the new FISA version expanded (1) the administration's power for up to seven days to undertake emergency wiretapping of foreigners without court warrants in "exigent" national security circumstances and (2) the emergency wiretapping of citizens to seven days without court warrants as long as the attorney general certifies the wiretap target's connection to terrorism. Moreover, the new law provided legal immunity to telecommunication companies that carried out illegal wiretaps for the Bush administration in the post–9/11 years.

Whereas the supporters of the FAA emphasized the need for greater security during the war on terrorism, the opponents wanted to uphold fundamental and constitutionally guaranteed liberties. Thus, during the signing ceremony at the White House President Bush said,

> Today I'm pleased to sign landmark legislation that is vital to the security of our people. The bill will allow our intelligence professionals to quickly and effectively monitor the communications of terrorists abroad while respecting the liberties of Americans here at home. The bill I sign today will help us meet our most solemn responsibility: to stop new attacks and to protect our people.[18]

But Senator Chris Dodd, one of the most outspoken opponents of the bill, declared,

> With one stroke of his pen, the President has ensured that the truth behind his unprecedented domestic spying regime will never see the light of day. But the fight must go on. I will continue to stand up for the rule of law and the civil liberties of all Americans at every opportunity, and will strongly support efforts to challenge the constitutionality of this decision in the courts. I can only hope that the courts will be able to correct the mistake the Congress and President have made.[19]

Less than 24 hours after the FISA Amendment Act of 2008 was signed into law, the American Civil Liberties Union (ACLU) filed a lawsuit on behalf of a number of plaintiffs who challenged the constitutionality of the new law. In particular the ACLU's brief complained,

> The [new] law not only essentially legalized the secret warrantless spying program the president approved in late 2001, it gave the government expanded spying powers, including the power to conduct dragnet surveillance of Americans' international communications without ever telling a court who it intends to spy on, what phone lines and email addresses it intends to monitor, where its surveillance targets are located, why it's conducting the surveillance or whether it suspects any party to the communication of wrongdoing.[20]

It was once again left to the courts to decide whether the constitution was on the side of proponents or opponents of the FAA provisions. Just as the Bush administration, the Obama administration tried to fend off legal actions against warrantless wiretaps by invoking the "state secrets" doctrine. But the U.S. Court of Appeals for the Ninth Circuit in California rejected the government's appeal to dismiss a suit by the al-Haramain Islamic Foundation that alleged that the organization had been the target of illegal wiretaps by the National Security Agency. The three judge panel did not embrace the Justice Department's argument that the proceedings would reveal state secrets but gave green light to the plaintiffs' legal proceedings. In the second case, the Obama administration repeated the "state secrets" claim of the Bush administration in a suit filed by

AT&T customers against the telecommunication company for cooperating with the National Security Agency's wiretap program. This was one of about 40 suits against telecoms filed around the country after President Bush acknowledged in 2005 that he had allowed the NSA to monitor communications between U.S. residents and suspected terrorists abroad without warrants. In short, then, in the first weeks and months of the Obama administration there were more similarities than differences in the positions taken on these wiretapping cases.

The Rights of "Enemy Combatants"

Controversies arose also over the legal rights of so-called enemy combatants, who were held in Guantanamo Bay, the U.S. military base in Cuba, and over the torture and abusive treatment of foreign nationals held in American-controlled detention facilities in Afghanistan, Iraq, Guantanamo, and elsewhere. By characterizing hundreds of foreigners and a few American citizens as enemy combatants—not prisoners of war or criminals—President Bush and his administration denied these men the protections afforded prisoners of war under the Geneva Convention and the civil liberties that the U.S. Constitution extends to accused criminals. To be sure, post–9/11 terrorism did not fit the familiar threats associated with war and crime. But, as Ronald Dworkin pointed out,

> The fact that terrorism presents new challenges and dangers does not mean that the basic moral principles and human rights that the criminal law and the laws of war try to protect have been repealed or become moot. We must instead ask what different scheme—what third model—is appropriate to respect those principles while still effectively defending ourselves.[21]

The more than 600 foreign nationals held for years in Guantanamo Bay were either captured in Afghanistan as Al Qaeda or Taliban fighters or turned over to American authorities by foreign governments. Yet, according to international agreements, it was not up to the American side to unilaterally decide their legal status by declaring them "enemy combatants" or "unlawful combatants." Instead, as Anthony Lewis explained, "The Third Geneva Convention, which the United States has signed and ratified, says that when there is doubt about a prisoner's status, the question is to be determined by a 'competent tribunal.' That means an independent one. The Bush Administration has refused to comply with the Geneva Convention."[22]

For other observers, the issue was not as clear-cut. Assuming that the terrorist threat against the United States was, is, and will remain terribly serious, Michael Ignatieff outlined a "necessity of lesser evils" position in the fight against terrorism and suggested that

> [t]o defeat evil, we may have to traffic in evils: indefinite detention of suspects, coercive interrogations, targeted assassinations, even pre-emptive war. These are evils because each strays from national and international law and because they kill people or deprive them of freedom without due process. They can be justified only if they prevent the greater evil.[23]

But the outcome of this approach requires, too, that the formal and informal democratic institutions discharge their responsibilities and control the "lesser evils." As Ignatieff put it,

> Only if our institutions work properly—if Congress reviews legislation in detail and tosses out measures that jeopardize liberty at no gain to security, if the courts keep

executive power under constitutional control and if the press refuses to allow itself to become "embedded" with the government—can the moral and constitutional hazards of lesser evils be managed.[24]

During major crises, especially when national security is at stake, U.S. presidents tend to claim extraordinary powers. Past presidents were rarely checked by other actors and institutions inside and outside of government when they suspended fundamental civil liberties. For nearly three years, that seemed the case after 9/11. While perhaps expected from Congress, where the president's party controlled both houses, that still left the judiciary. However, as Lewis remarked,

The Supreme Court has usually been reluctant to intervene. When the Japanese relocation program [that removed 120,000 Americans of Japanese descent from their homes and confined them to camps on President Franklin D. Roosevelt's order] reached the Court, a majority declined to look past the military judgment that Japanese-Americans might be disloyal, though events had proved them false.[25]

However, with respect to the post–9/11 enemy combatants, the U.S. Supreme Court did rein in the president and the executive branch in several cases. First, a 6–3 majority ruled that foreign detainees in Guantanamo Bay had the right to apply for a writ of habeas corpus, the ancient right of prisoners to challenge the lawfulness of their detention.[26] Second, the Court decided that a U.S. citizen—although declared an enemy combatant by the executive branch—was entitled to his or her constitutional right of due process and that even the president did not have the power to deprive U.S. citizens of their Fifth Amendment rights to "life, liberty, or property, without due process of law." In a rare occurrence, the probably most liberal justice (John Paul Stevens) and the perhaps most conservative member of the Supreme Court (Antonin Scalia) were in the 7–1 Court majority in the case of Yaser Esam Hamdi, a U.S. citizen who was captured during hostilities in Afghanistan. In the prevailing opinion, Justice Sandra Day O'Connor wrote,

Striking the proper constitutional balance here is of great importance to the nation during this period of on-going combat. But it is equally vital that our calculus not give short shrift to the values that this country holds dear or to the privilege that is American citizenship. It is during our most challenging and uncertain moments that our nation's commitment to due process is most severely tested; and we must preserve our commitment at home to the principles for which we fight abroad.[27]

Taken together, these decisions made clear that, as Justice O'Connor put it, "a state of war is not a blank check for the president."[28] Rather than allow Hamdi's lawyers to challenge his detention in court, the U.S. Departments of Justice and Defense decided in a complete turnaround that the suspected terrorist Hamdi was not a threat at all. After he renounced his U.S. citizenship as a condition of his release, Hamdi was flown to Saudi Arabia and became a free man.[29]

As the administration pondered how to translate the Supreme Court's decisions into practice with respect to the Guantanamo prisoners, any satisfactory solution would still leave in limbo an unknown number of foreign nationals who were held, as human rights organizations charged, in secret U.S. detention facilities abroad. According to Human Rights First (formerly the Lawyers Committee on Human Rights), nearly three years after 9/11, the U.S. government was "holding prisoners in a secret system of off-shore prisons beyond the reach of adequate supervision, accountability, or law."[30] These detainees were being held for extended periods of time without access to legal counsel, without a right to have their imprisonment reviewed by an independent authority, and without visits by the International Red Cross, Human Rights Watch, or other organizations. This policy was and is indefensible. Even though he endorsed "lesser evils" against the terrorist threat, Ignatieff also insisted that "no detainee of the United States should be permanently deprived of access to counsel and judicial process, whether it be civilian federal court or military tribunal. Torture will thrive wherever detainees are held in secret. Conduct disgracing the United States is inevitable if suspects are detained beyond the reach of the law."[31]

The issue of how to try "enemy combatants" seemed finally decided in June 2006, when the U.S. Supreme Court ruled in *Hamdan v. Rumsfeld* that military commissions set up by the Bush administration violated the Geneva Conventions and the Uniform Code of Military Justice. Thus, the 5–3 decision in favor of Salim Ahmed Hamdan, who had worked in Afghanistan as Osama bin Laden's driver and bodyguard, held that "enemy combatants" are protected by the Geneva Conventions and, additionally, that the congressional Authorization for Use of Military Force Against Terrorists (AUMF) of September 2001 did not grant President Bush the authority to create new tribunals without congressional mandate.[32] Within a few months, the Congress adopted and President Bush signed into law the Military Commissions Act of 2006 (PL 1009–366) which contained provisions that reestablished the very military tribunals that the Supreme Court ruled unconstitutional in *Hamdan v. Rumsfeld* and denies aliens detained by the United States government and determined to be enemy combatants the right of habeas corpus. Fareed Zakaria concluded,

> The Military Commissions Act of 2006 eliminates habeas corpus for anyone defined
> as an "unlawful enemy combatant" as well as all aliens, including permanent
> residents—green-card holders—of the United States. . . . In effect, federal courts
> appear to have been stripped of their historic role in assessing the legality of deten-
> tions if the executive branch claims that these arrests are part of the war on terror.[33]

On December 14, 2006, Judge James Robertson of the United States District Court for the District of Columbia ruled that the Military Commissions Act did not allow Hamdan to contest his detention before a federal court. A year earlier, the same judge had granted Salim Ahmed Hamdan's habeas petition and thereby stopped his war crime trial at Guantanamo. But according to Judge Robertson, the Military Commissions Act "was unambiguous in denying Guantanamo detainees the use of a habeas corpus statute."[34]

Hamdan challenged the constitutionality of the congressional statute, but in October 2007 the U.S. Supreme Court refused to review his case. Charged with conspiracy and providing material support for terrorism, Hamdan's military commission trial took place in summer 2008 at Guantanamo. The six-member commission acquitted him of the more serious charge (conspiracy) and found him guilty of the lesser charge (providing material support). The prosecution asked for 30-year to life imprisonment but the commission opted for a 66-month prison term—61 months of which had been served already. In November 2008, Hamdan was sent to Yemen, where he was to serve the last month of his sentence.

At the time of Hamdan's release, about 250 "unlawful enemy combatants" remained in the Guantamo facility—about 100 of them citizens of Yemen. It was left to the Obama administration to decide what to do with those detainees and the

Guantanamo prison. During the campaign Obama said that Guantanamo was a sad chapter in American history and promised "we're going to close Guantanamo. And we're going to restore habeas corpus. . . . We're going to lead by example—by not just word but by deed. That's our vision for the future."[35] Indeed, Obama promised that as president he would close the Guantanamo detention facility within a year. During the transition period, he and his advisers worked on a solution that seemed to favor the release of some seemingly innocent detainees, the prosecution of others in criminal courts inside the United States, and the trial of those involving national security issues in a newly created court. Two days after his inauguration President Obama issued an Executive Order for the prompt closing of the Guantanamo Bay detention facility after an immediate review of all detainees' records.[36] But although he had criticized the military tribunals for Guantanomo inmates during his campaign, Obama reversed his stance when he revived military commissions four months into his presidency as "appropriate for trying enemies who violate the laws of war, provided that they are properly structured and administered."[37]

This change of mind came on the heels of another position that aligned the Obama administration early on with similar stances of the Bush administration. For example, during the Bush administration the Department of Justice argued for the dismissal of a suit by five men who had been victims of the CIA's so-called "extraordinary rendition" (the handing over of terrorist suspects to foreign governments that are known for human rights violations, such as torture) against the Boeing Company for flying the plaintiffs to their foreign destinations. Like the Bush administration, the Obama Justice Department invoked the "preservation of state secrets" defense. However, a three-judge panel of the Ninth Court of Appeal ruled in favor of the plaintiffs and dismissed the government complaint.[38]

Torture: Leaders and Followers

> . . . at Abu Ghraib prison, outside of Baghdad, an Iraqi prisoner . . . , Manadel al-Jamadi, died during an interrogation. His head had been covered with a plastic bag, and he was shackled in a crucifixion-like pose that inhibited his ability to breathe; according to forensic pathologists who have examined the case, he asphyxiated.[39]

In the fall of 2007, during his confirmation hearing before the U.S. Senate's Judiciary Committee, Attorney-General designate Michael Musakey claimed to be clueless as to the nature of waterboarding. He said that he did not know whether this interrogation technique constituted torture. In a letter to the committee, he seemed to side with the administration's position that CIA interrogations of terrorists or suspected terrorists are exempt from antitorture laws that the military and others must follow.[40] He was confirmed as the highest U.S. official to enforce the laws of the land. Once in office, Mukasey did not change his position. Instead, during an appearance before the Senate Judiciary Committee, he said that he would not rule out the use of torture in the future.[41]

Waterboarding has been used as a method of torture for hundreds of years. In more recent times, it has been practiced by state and non-state human rights violators. According to one account, "in some versions of the technique, prisoners are strapped to a board, their faces covered with cloth or cellophane, and water is poured over their mouths to stimulate drowning; in others, they are dunked head-first into water."[42] In the past, U.S. authorities considered this particularly gruesome interrogation method to be torture and punishable as a war crime. Thus, following WWII, "U.S. military commissions successfully prosecuted as war criminals several Japanese soldiers who subjected American prisoners to waterboarding. A U.S. army officer was court-marshaled in 1968 for helping to waterboard a prisoner in Vietnam."[43]

But that changed after 9/11. Waterboarding and other torture techniques were no longer off-limits in the "war on terror." A few reports about "aggressive interrogation" methods of so-called "enemy combatants" in U.S.-run prisons abroad had been published earlier, but most Americans learned about such gross human rights violations in the spring of 2004, when CBS News on 60 Minutes and Seymour Hersh in The New Yorker revealed the torturous treatment of detainees at Abu Ghraib. Administration officials blamed the isolated incidents on rogue soldiers, but eventually evidence showed that "harsh" interrogation practices—indeed, torture—were backed by opinions written and approved by legal experts in the White House and the Departments of Justice and Defense in express violation of the United Nations Convention against Torture, the U.S. Constitution, and the Uniform Code of Military Justice.[44]

Referring to what administration critics called "Torture Memos," Donald P. Gregg, national security advisor from 1982 to 1988 to then Vice President George H.W. Bush, wrote in 2004:

> Recent reports indicate that Bush administration lawyers, in their struggles to deal with terrorism, wrote memos in 2003 pushing aside longstanding prohibitions on the use of torture by Americans. These memos cleared the way for the horrors that have been revealed in Iraq, Afghanistan and Guantánamo and make a mockery of administration assertions that a few misguided enlisted personnel perpetrated the vile abuse of prisoners.
>
> I can think of nothing that can more devastatingly undercut America's standing in the world or, more important, our view of ourselves, than these decisions. Sanctioned abuse is deeply corrosive—just ask the French, who are still seeking to eradicate the stain on their honor that resulted from the deliberate use of torture in Algeria.[45]

But in spite of evidence to the contrary, the administration denied that detainees were being or had been tortured. After the U.S. Congress adopted and the president signed a bill with antitorture provisions in October 2006, President George W. Bush insisted in his signing statement that the new law "will allow the Central Intelligence Agency to continue its program for questioning key terrorist leaders and operatives. . . ."[46] He claimed that it was the president's prerogative to decide what methods CIA interrogators were allowed to use. But in the same breath, he continued to tell Americans and the rest of the world, "The United States does not torture. It's against our laws and it's against our values. I have not authorized it."[47] Similarly, right after Vice President Richard Cheney stated in a radio interview the "dunk in water" (meaning waterboarding) in the interrogation of detainees was a "no-brainer," he added, "We don't torture. That's not what we're involved in."[48]

The White House clung to the "we-do-not-torture" line even after CIA director Michael V. Hayden admitted in early 2008 that waterboarding had been used during the interrogations of three leading Al Qaeda figures: Abu Zabaydah, Abd al-Rahim al-Nashiri, and Khalid Sheik Mohammed.[49] In reaction, a White House spokesperson said that President Bush would "authorize waterboarding future terrorism suspects if certain criteria are met."[50] And Vice President Cheney "vigorously defended the use of harsh interrogation techniques on a few suspected terrorists, saying that the methods made up "a tougher program, for tougher customers."[51] Neither the president nor vice president considered waterboarding or "harsh interrogation techniques" to be torture. Not surprisingly, on March 8, 2008, President Bush announced during his regular Saturday morning radio address that he had vetoed legislation that would have prohibited the CIA from using waterboarding and other harsh interrogation tactics. He justified his veto by stating that the prohibitions "would take away one of the most valuable tools on the war on terror." And he added that "this is no time for Congress to abandon practices that have a proven track record of keeping America safe."[52] In other words, torturing terrorists and suspected terrorists remained part of Mr. Bush's "war on terrorism." Besides prohibiting torture altogether, the vetoed bill would have banned the following:

Forcing a prisoner to be naked, perform sexual acts or pose in a sexual manner.

Placing hoods or sacks over the head of a prisoner, and using duct tape over the eyes.

Waterboarding.

Using military working dogs.

Inducing hypothermia or heat injury.

Depriving a prisoner of necessary food, water or medical care.

On December 11, 2008, the Senate Armed Services Committee released the executive summary of its eighteen-month inquiry into the treatment of detainees held in U.S.-run prison facilities abroad. The committee found "that the authorization of aggressive interrogation techniques by senior officials was both a direct cause of detainee abuse and conveyed the message that it was okay to mistreat and degrade detainees in U.S. custody."[53] The detailed conclusions of the document (see box pages 219–222) attribute responsibility for the mistreating and, yes, torturing of detainees to President Bush, members of his cabinet (in particular Defense Secretary Donald Rumsfeld), the National Security Council, and military leaders. Addressing Abu Ghraib in particular, the Senate committee concluded that the abuse there was not just a case of "a few soldiers acting on their own" but rather the result of policies approved by "senior military and civilian officials."[54] Nevertheless, only a handful of the lowest-level soldiers were convicted for the mistreatment of detainees, while the only officer charged, a lieutenant colonel in charge of the interrogations at the Abu Ghraib prison, was acquitted by a military court.

If there were any heroes in this dark chapter, they were the lawyers in the military services who questioned proposed "aggressive interrogation" policy and defended and judged Guantanamo prisoners in a professional fashion. As David Cole noted,

[D]ocuments disclosed in the course of the [Senate] hearings now show that when the coercive measures were under consideration, top lawyers for every branch of the military— Army, Navy, Air Force, and Marine Corps—objected that the tactics might be illegal.[55]

But when the legal counsel to General Richard Myers, chairman of the Joint Chiefs of Staff, began to review the legal questions involved here, the general "ordered that the legal inquiry be quashed" at the request of the Defense Department's general counsel.[56]

Senate Armed Services Committee Conclusions on the Treatment of U.S.-Held Detainees

Conclusion 1: On February 7, 2002, President George W. Bush made a written determination that Common Article 3 of the Geneva Conventions, which would have afforded minimum standards for humane treatment, did not apply to al Qaeda or Taliban detainees. Following the President's determination, techniques such as waterboarding, nudity, and stress positions, used in SERE [Survival Evasion Resistance and Escape] training to simulate tactics used by enemies that refuse to follow the Geneva Conventions, were authorized for use in interrogations of detainees in U.S. custody.

Conclusion 2: Members of the President's Cabinet and other senior officials participated in meetings inside the White House in 2002 and 2003 where specific interrogation techniques were discussed. National Security Council Principals reviewed the CIA's interrogation program during that period.

Conclusion 3: The use of techniques similar to those used in SERE resistance training—such as stripping students of their clothing, placing them in stress positions, putting hoods over their heads, and treating them like animals—was at odds with the commitment to humane treatment of detainees in U.S. custody. Using those techniques for interrogating detainees was also inconsistent with the goal of collecting accurate intelligence information, as the purpose of SERE resistance training is to increase the ability of U.S. personnel to resist abusive interrogations and the techniques used were based, in part, on Chinese Communist techniques used during the Korean War to elicit false confessions.

Conclusion 4: The use of techniques in interrogations derived from SERE resistance training created a serious risk of physical and psychological harm to detainees. The SERE schools employ strict controls to reduce the risk of physical and psychological harm to students during training. Those controls include medical and psychological screening for students, interventions by trained psychologists during training, and code words to ensure that students can stop the application of a technique at any time should the need arise. Those same controls are not present in real world interrogations.

Conclusion 5: In July 2002, the Office of the Secretary of Defense General Counsel solicited information from the Joint Personnel Recovery Agency (JPRA) on SERE techniques for use during interrogations. That solicitation, prompted by requests from Department of Defense General Counsel William J. Haynes II, reflected the view that abusive tactics similar to those used by our enemies should be considered for use against detainees in U.S. custody.

Conclusion 6: The Central Intelligence Agency's (CIA) interrogation program included at least one SERE training technique, waterboarding. Senior Administration lawyers, including Alberto Gonzales, Counsel to

(continued)

Senate Armed Services Committee Conclusions on the Treatment of U.S.-Held Detainees *(continued)*

the President, and David Addington, Counsel to the Vice President, were consulted on the development of legal analysis of CIA interrogation techniques. Legal opinions subsequently issued by the Department of Justice's Office of Legal Counsel (OLC) interpreted legal obligations under U.S. anti-torture laws and determined the legality of CIA interrogation techniques. Those OLC opinions distorted the meaning and intent of anti-torture laws, rationalized the abuse of detainees in U.S. custody and influenced Department of Defense determinations as to what interrogation techniques were legal for use during interrogations conducted by U.S. military personnel.

Conclusion 7: Joint Personnel Recovery Agency (JPRA) efforts in support of "offensive" interrogation operations went beyond the agency's knowledge and expertise. JPRA's support to U.S. government interrogation efforts contributed to detainee abuse. JPRA's offensive support also influenced the development of policies that authorized abusive interrogation techniques for use against detainees in U.S. custody.

Conclusion 8: Detainee abuse occurred during JPRA's support to Special Mission Unit (SMU) Task Force (TF) interrogation operations in Iraq in September 2003. JPRA Commander Colonel Randy Moulton's authorization of SERE instructors, who had no experience in detainee interrogations, to actively participate in Task Force interrogations using SERE resistance training techniques was a serious failure in judgment. The Special Mission Unit Task Force Commander's failure to order that SERE resistance training techniques not be used in detainee interrogations was a serious failure in leadership that led to the abuse of detainees in Task Force custody. Iraq is a Geneva Convention theater and techniques used in SERE school are inconsistent with the obligations of U.S. personnel under the Geneva Conventions.

Conclusion 9: Combatant Command requests for JPRA "offensive" interrogation support and U.S. Joint Forces Command (JFCOM) authorization of that support led to JPRA operating outside the agency's charter and beyond its expertise. Only when JFCOM's Staff Judge Advocate became aware of and raised concerns about JPRA's support to offensive interrogation operations in late September 2003 did JFCOM leadership begin to take steps to curtail JPRA's "offensive" activities. It was not until September 2004, however, that JFCOM issued a formal policy stating that support to offensive interrogation operations was outside JPRA's charter.

Conclusion 10: Interrogation techniques in Guantanamo Bay's (GTMO) October 11, 2002 request for authority submitted by Major General Michael Dunlavey were influenced by JPRA training for GTMO interrogation personnel and included techniques similar to those used in SERE training to teach U.S. personnel to resist abusive enemy interrogations.

GTMO Staff Judge Advocate Lieutenant Colonel Diane Beaver's legal review justifying the October 11, 2002 GTMO request was profoundly in error and legally insufficient. Leaders at GTMO, including Major General Dunlavey's successor, Major General Geoffrey Miller, ignored warnings from DoD's Criminal Investigative Task Force and the Federal Bureau of Investigation that the techniques were potentially unlawful and that their use would strengthen detainee resistance.

Conclusion 11: Chairman of the Joint Chiefs of Staff General Richard Myers's decision to cut short the legal and policy review of the October 11, 2002 GTMO request initiated by his Legal Counsel, then-Captain Jane Dalton, undermined the military's review process. Subsequent conclusions reached by Chairman Myers and Captain Dalton regarding the legality of interrogation techniques in the request followed a grossly deficient review and were at odds with conclusions previously reached by the Army, Air Force, Marine Corps, and Criminal Investigative Task Force.

Conclusion 12: Department of Defense General Counsel William J. Haynes II's effort to cut short the legal and policy review of the October 11, 2002 GTMO request initiated by then-Captain Jane Dalton, Legal Counsel to the Chairman of the Joint Chiefs of Staff, was inappropriate and undermined the military's review process. The General Counsel's subsequent review was grossly deficient. Mr. Haynes's one page recommendation to Secretary of Defense Donald Rumsfeld failed to address the serious legal concerns that had been previously raised by the military services about techniques in the GTMO request. Further, Mr. Haynes's reliance on a legal memo produced by GTMO's Staff Judge Advocate that senior military lawyers called "legally insufficient" and "woefully inadequate" is deeply troubling.

Conclusion 13: Secretary of Defense Donald Rumsfeld's authorization of aggressive interrogation techniques for use at Guantanamo Bay was a direct cause of detainee abuse there. Secretary Rumsfeld's December 2, 2002 approval of Mr. Haynes's recommendation that most of the techniques contained in GTMO's October 11, 2002 request be authorized influenced and contributed to the use of abusive techniques, including military working dogs, forced nudity, and stress positions, in Afghanistan and Iraq.

Conclusion 14: Department of Defense General Counsel William J. Haynes II's direction to the Department of Defense's Detainee Working Group in early 2003 to consider a legal memo from John Yoo of the Department of Justice's OLC as authoritative blocked the Working Group from conducting a fair and complete legal analysis and resulted in a report that, in the words of then-Department of the Navy General Counsel Alberto Mora, contained "profound mistakes in its legal analysis." Reliance on the OLC memo resulted in a final Working Group report that recommended approval of several aggressive techniques, including removal of clothing, sleep deprivation, and slapping, similar to those used in SERE training to teach U.S. personnel to resist abusive interrogations.

(continued)

Senate Armed Services Committee Conclusions on the Treatment of U.S.-Held Detainees *(continued)*

Conclusion 15: Special Mission Unit (SMU) Task Force (TF) interrogation policies were influenced by the Secretary of Defense's December 2, 2002 approval of aggressive interrogation techniques for use at GTMO. SMU TF interrogation policies in Iraq included the use of aggressive interrogation techniques such as military working dogs and stress positions. SMU TF policies were a direct cause of detainee abuse and influenced interrogation policies at Abu Ghraib and elsewhere in Iraq.

Conclusion 16: During his assessment visit to Iraq in August and September 2003, GTMO Commander Major General Geoffrey Miller encouraged a view that interrogators should be more aggressive during detainee interrogations.

Conclusion 17: Interrogation policies approved by Lieutenant General Ricardo Sanchez, which included the use of military working dogs and stress positions, were a direct cause of detainee abuse in Iraq. Lieutenant General Sanchez's decision to issue his September 14, 2003 policy with the knowledge that there were ongoing discussions as to the legality of some techniques in it was a serious error in judgment. The September policy was superseded on October 12, 2003 as a result of legal concerns raised by U.S. Central Command. That superseding policy, however, contained ambiguities and contributed to confusion about whether aggressive techniques, such as military working dogs, were authorized for use during interrogations.

Conclusion 18: U.S. Central Command (CENTCOM) failed to conduct proper oversight of Special Mission Unit Task Force interrogation policies. Though aggressive interrogation techniques were removed from Combined Joint Task Force 7 interrogation policies after CENTCOM raised legal concerns about their inclusion in the September 14, 2003 policy issued by Lieutenant General Sanchez, SMU TF interrogation policies authorized some of those same techniques, including stress positions and military working dogs.

Conclusion 19: The abuse of detainees at Abu Ghraib in late 2003 was not simply the result of a few soldiers acting on their own. Interrogation techniques such as stripping detainees of their clothes, placing them in stress positions, and using military working dogs to intimidate them appeared in Iraq only after they had been approved for use in Afghanistan and at GTMO. Secretary of Defense Donald Rumsfeld's December 2, 2002 authorization of aggressive interrogation techniques and subsequent interrogation policies and plans approved by senior military and civilian officials conveyed the message that physical pressures and degradation were appropriate treatment for detainees in U.S. military custody. What followed was an erosion in standards dictating that detainees be treated humanely.[57]

Torture: The Public Debate

The shocking revelation that American soldiers had tortured Iraqi inmates in the U.S.-run Abu Ghraib prison forced the nation to face the uncomfortable truth that the "lesser evils" had spun out of control. Actually, the media had raised the issue of torture repeatedly in the months and years after 9/11 and long before the revelations of torture at the Abu Ghraib prison. Initially, the contextual frame was the hypothetical terrorist in the custody of U.S. authorities who could have information regarding the next terror strike. Once actual terrorists were in U.S. custody, the debate became more urgent. While expressing shock when they publicized the images of horrible torture scenes from the Abu Ghraib prison, the media—especially TV news programs—had earlier featured the proponents of torture far more frequently and prominently than the opponents. Several weeks after 9/11, *Newsweek* columnist Jonathan Alter wrote, for example,

> *Even as we continue to speak out against human-rights violations around the world, we need to keep an open mind about certain measures to fight terrorism, like court-sanctioned psychological interrogation. And we'll have to think about transferring some suspects to our less squeamish allies, even if that's hypocritical. Nobody said this was going to be pretty.*[58]

In a lengthy story in the *Atlantic Monthly*, Mark Bowden distinguished between hardcore torture and "torture lite," or what he suggested was "coercion." With respect to torture lite, Bowden wrote, "Although excruciating for the victim, these tactics leave no permanent marks and do no lasting physical harm."[59]

In an op-ed article, legal expert Henry Mark Holzer attacked the opponents of torture:

> *There are those among us—Jimmy Carter-like pacifists and Ramsey Clark-type America haters come to mind—who would probably stand by idly and endure an atomic holocaust. But most people would doubtless opt for torture, albeit reluctantly.*
>
> *These realists—and I suspect they are a large majority of the American public—would be correct. In approving the use of torture—or at least accepting it—they needn't suffer even a scintilla of moral guilt. Torture of whatever kind, and no matter how brutal, in defense of human rights and legitimate self-preservation is not only not immoral; it is a moral imperative.*[60]

There were far fewer voices categorically condemning torture in the leading print media. Editorials in the *Washington Post* and an op-ed piece by Jonathan Turley were among the exceptions. Turley wrote,

> *This week, West Virginia Sen. John D. Rockefeller actually encouraged the U.S. to hand over the recently arrested Al Qaeda suspect Khalid Shaikh Mohammed to another country for torture. Whatever legal distinction Rockefeller sees in using surrogates to do our torturing, it is hardly a moral distinction. As a result, we are now driving the new market for torture-derived information. We have gone from a nation that once condemned torture to one that contracts out for torture services.*[61]

Although he would prefer a total ban of torture, Alan Dershowitz recognizes that gross abuses of terrorism suspects will occur. He therefore pleads for legalized torture—if a judge can be convinced of a "ticking bomb" scenario, in which a detainee is believed to have knowledge of an imminent terrorist act and torture is seen as the only method to get the crucial information that would prevent the terrorist strike.[62] His colleague at Harvard Law School, Philip Heymann, rejected torture categorically, warning that the use of torture would drastically increase if there were "torture warrants" à la Dershowitz. According to Heymann, "Judges have deferred to the last fourteen thousand requests for national security wiretaps and they would defer here."[63] In contrast to Professor Dershowitz, who appeared frequently on television, Professor Heymann was not interviewed at all on network television on this matter.

When given the opportunity, average Americans showed an understanding of the complexity of the issue, took positions, and were mindful of opposing viewpoints. Two New Yorkers who participated in a town hall meeting on torture in New York City were a case in point. The following exchange occurred during an ABC News *Nightline* broadcast with Ted Koppel as host:

> MR. CASEY: I live down in Rockaway. And for those of you who know Rockaway, we lost 70 people from my little town in—in the Trade Center collapse. . . . The—you know, you talk about torturing them [terrorists]. If—if they could have gotten these people that flew those tra—planes into the World Trade Center and had been able to get that information from them beforehand, I think a lot of people around here would have been a lot happier, and we wouldn't have all the grief that we have here.
>
> KOPPEL: Well . . .
>
> MR. CASEY: And I—I don't—I—I feel there should be limits, but I—I think the limits should—I don't think it should be that extreme. I think there should be controls on it, but if you can get the information out of them, I think you should have to get it.
>
> MS. MARY FONTANA: Hi, my name is Mary Fontana. I lost my husband Dave, who was a firefighter in Brooklyn and he also—his father was a vet and his uncle was killed in the Battle of the Bulge. I think it's—we have to—it's a slippery slope to start think about our rights in this country, the rights that he died for and the rights that his father and uncle did. . . . So I think that, you know, you really have to be careful about who we begin to target because I think it will be—create prejudice, and it will start to become a witch hunt really—that's my concern that, you know, we all live in this country. My husband died for our rights to live together, and that we really have to be careful when we start talking about torturing people for information. It's frightening to me.[64]

These two town hall participants and others who spoke out during the event were mindful of the problems inherent in a trade-off between security and civil liberties. For the most part, the pro and con views expressed in letters to the editor were equally thoughtful and civil. Opinion polls showed that after 9/11, the American public was split down the middle on the question of torture.

That changed after the Abu Ghraib revelations. The administration and its supporters became very much part of the mass-mediated torture debate and either denied that Americans or surrogates in other countries were guilty of torturing detainees or justified "aggressive interrogation" as a means to national security ends. Their arguments seemed to carry more weight with the American public. Thus, in the years after the Abu Ghraib revelations only one of three Americans believed that torture was never justified, whereas a robust majority thought that torture was "sometimes," "rarely," or "often" justified. This attitude of the majority of Americans was shared by key actors at the highest level of the U.S. government outside the administration. In early 2008, Supreme Court Justice Antonin Scalia expressed these sentiments when he told the BBC that "it is far from clear that torture is unconstitutional and says that it may be legal to 'smack [a suspect] in the face' if the suspect is concealing information which could endanger the public."[65]

Notes

1. "Transcript of bin Laden's October Interview," with Al Jazeera correspondent Tayseer Alouni, www.cnn.com/2002/world/asiapcf/south/02/05/binladen.transcript/index.html.
2. Paul Wilkinson, *Terrorism versus Democracy: The Liberal State Response* (London: Frank Cass, 2001), 94, 95.
3. Marc A. Celmer, *Terrorism, U.S. Strategy, and Reagan Policies* (New York: Greenwood Press, 1987), 13.
4. www.wikipedia.org/wiki/counter-terrorism (retrieved January 30, 2005).
5. Peter J. Katzenstein, "West Germany's Internal Security Policy: State and Violence in the 1970s and 1980s." Occasional Paper number 28, published by the Center for International Studies, Cornell University, 1990.
6. John Yoo in his testimony before the Subcommittee on Homeland Security (Senate Appropriation Committee) September 18, 2006, 4; http://www.freerepublic.com/focus/f-news/1705339/posts
7. Ibid.
8. Ibid., 2.
9. David Cole and James X. Dempsey, *Terrorism and the Constitution* (New York: New York Press, 2002), 117.
10. Laura K. Donohue, "Fear Itself: Counter-Terrorism, Individual Rights, and U.S. Foreign Relations Post 9/11," paper presented at the Annual Meeting of the International Studies Association, March 24–27, 2002, in New Orleans.
11. Ibid.
12. Charles Doyle, "The USA PATRIOT ACT: A Sketch," Congressional Research Service, April 18, 2002.
13. Cole and Dempsey, 167.
14. Kevin Bohn, "Patriot Act Report Documents Civil Rights Complaints," CNN.com/Law Center, July 31, 2003.
15. Ibid.
16. Philip Shenon, "Report on USA PATRIOT ACT Alleges Civil Rights Violations," *New York Times*, July 21, 2003, 1.
17. Eric Lichtblau, "Despite a Year of Ire and Angst, Little Has Changed on Wiretaps," *New York Times*, November 25, 2006, http://select.nytimes.com/search/restricted/article?res=FA0A10F9385A0C768EDDA8099
18. President Bush's signing remarks are available at: http://www.whitehouse.gov/news/releases/2008/07/20080710-2.html (accessed December 31, 2008).
19. Senator Dodd's remarks are available at http://dodd.senate.gov/index.php?q=taxonomy/term/373 (accessed December 31, 2008).
20. For more on the ACLU legal action, see http://blog.aclu.org/2008/12/12/update-fisa-amendments-act-case/ (accessed December 31, 2008).
21. Ronald Dworkin, "Terror and the Attack on Civil Liberties," *New York Review of Books*, November 6, 2003.
22. Anthony Lewis, "The Justices Take on the President," *New York Times*, January 16, 2004, A21.
23. Michael Ignatieff, "Lesser Evils," *New York Times Sunday Magazine*, May 2, 2003. Available at http://www.nytimes.com/2004/07/25/books/review/25STEELL.html?scp=1&sq=Ignatieff%20the%20lesser%20evil&st=cse (accessed May 20, 2009).
24. Ibid.
25. Lewis
26. See *Rasul v. Bush*, No. 03–334. The 6–3 decision was announced on June 29, 2004.

27. See *Hamdi v. Rumsfeld*, No. 03–6696.
28. Ibid.
29. Since the Supreme Court handed down a rather narrow decision with respect to the foreign detainees at Guantanamo, cases on behalf of these "enemy combatants" continued to be heard.
30. Human Rights First, press release of June 17, 2004.
31. Ignatieff.
32. Chief Justice John Roberts, who had ruled against Hamdan while serving on the D.C. Circuit Court of Appeals, recused himself from the Supreme Court case.
33. Fereed Zakaria, "The Enemy Within," *New York Times*, December 17, 2006, http://query.nytimes.com/gst/fullpage.html?res=9E07E1DF1731F934A25751C1A9609C8B63
34. Neil A. Lewis, "Judge Sets Back Guantanamo Detainees," *New York Times*, December 14, 2006, 32.
35. Elizabeth White, "Obama Says Gitmo Facility Should Close," *Washington Post*, June 24, 2007, http://www.washingtonpost.com/wp-dyn/content/article/2007/06/24/AR2007062401046.html (accessed December 30, 2008).
36. For the text of the Executive Order, see http://www.whitehouse.gov/the_press_office/ClosureOfGuantanamoDetentionFacilities/ (accessed May 14, 2009).
37. For transcript of President Obama's declaration on the resurrection of military tribunals at Guantanamo, see http://www.whitehouse.gov/the_press_office/Statement-of-President-Barack-Obama-on-Military-Commissions/ (accessed May 20, 2009).
38. The decision is available at http://www.scotusblog.com/wp/wp-content/uploads/2009/04/jeppesendecision.pdf. accessed May 19, 2009.
39. Jane Mayer, "A Deadly Interrogation," *The New Yorker*, November 14, 2005. Article is available at http://www.newyorker.com/archive/2005/11/14/051114fa_fact (accessed May 20, 2009).
40. http://www.talkingpointsmemo.com/docs/mukasey-dems/?resultpage=1&
41. Philip Shenon, "Mukasey Will Not Rule Out Waterboarding," *New York Times*, January 31, 2008, http://www.nytimes.com/2008/01/31/washington/31justice.html (accessed February 2, 2008).
42. http://hrw.org/english/docs/2006/10/26/usdom14465.htm.
43. Ibid.
44. The Eighth Amendment of the U.S. Constitution's forbids the use of "cruel and unusual punishments," which is widely interpreted as a prohibition of the use of torture. The Uniformed Code of Military Justice forbids torture outside the United States.
45. Donald P. Gregg, "After Abu Ghraib; Fight Fire with Compassion," *New York Times*, June 10, 2004.
46. http://www.whitehouse.gov/news/releases/2006/10/20061017-1.html.
47. http://www.whitehouse.gov/news/releases/2006/09/20060906-3.html.
48. http://www.whitehouse.gov/news/releases/2006/10/20061024-7.html.
49. http://www.nytimes.com/2008/02/06/washington/06intel.html?scp=11&sq=waterboarding&st=nyt
50. Dan Fromkin, "We Tortured and We'd Do it Again," Washingtonpost.com, February 6, 2008, http://www.washingtonpost.com/wp-dyn/content/blog/2008/02/06/BL2008020602244_pf.html (accessed February 11, 2008).
51. David Stout and Scott Shane, "Cheney Defends the Use of Harsh Interrogation," *Washington Post*, February 7, 2008, http://www.nytimes.com/2008/02/07/washington/07cnd-intel.html?hp
52. Presidential radio address on March 8, 2008. http://www.whitehouse.gov/news/releases/2008/03/20080308.html (accessed March 9, 2008).
53. From U.S. Senator Carl Levin's news release, available at http://levin.senate.gov/newsroom/release.cfm?id=305735 (accessed December 28, 2008).
54. From the summary of the "Senate Armed Services Committee Inquiry into the Treatment of Detainees in U.S. Custody," available at http://armed-services.senate.gov/Publications/EXEC%20SUMMARY-CONCLUSIONS_For%20Release_12%20December%202008.pdf (accessed December 30, 2008).
55. David Cole, "What to Do About the Torturers?" *The New York Review of Books*, January 15, 2009, 22.
56. Ibid.
57. From the summary of the "Senate Armed Services Committee Inquiry into the Treatment of Detainees in U.S. Custody."
58. Jonathan Alter, "Time to Think About Torture," *Newsweek*, November 5, 2001, 45.
59. Mark Bowden, "The Dark Art of Interrogation," *Atlantic Monthly*, October 2003, 53.

60. Henry Mark Holzer, "Terrorism Interrogations and Torture," *Milwaukee Journal Sentinel*, March 16, 2003, 5J.
61. Jonathan Turley, "Rights on the Rack: Alleged Torture in Terror War Imperils U.S. Standards of Humanity," *Los Angeles Times*, March 6, 2003, B17.
62. Alan M. Dershowitz, *Why Terrorism Works* (New Haven, CT: Yale University Press, 2003).
63. Philip B. Heymann, *Terrorism, Freedom, and Security: Winning Without War* (Cambridge, MA: MIT Press, 2003), 111.
64. From ABC News, *Nightline*, March 8, 2002.
65. http://news.bbc.co.uk/2/hi/programmes/law_in_action/7238665.stm.

Homeland Security: Preparedness and Prevention

IN DECEMBER 2008, DURING A HEARING OF THE SENATE COMMITTEE ON Homeland Security and Governmental Affairs on the threat posed by weapons of mass destruction (WMD), Senator Susan Collins (R-Maine) said,

> Bioweapons are appealing to terrorists in part because we are unlikely to realize that an attack has occurred before it begins to kill many of its victims. In the early stages of an anthrax attack, for example, health care providers are likely to believe that they are simply seeing an outbreak of flu.
>
> That worldwide security has lagged behind the growth of this threat is sobering. Even within our own country, . . . we failed to secure potential biological weapons effectively. Thousands of individuals in the United States have access to dangerous pathogens. Currently, there are about 400 research facilities and nearly 15,000 individuals in the United States authorized to handle the deadly pathogens on what is called the "select agents list." Many other research facilities handle less strictly controlled yet still dangerous pathogens, with little or no regulation.[1]

After these sobering words, members of the bipartisan Commission on the Prevention of Mass Destruction Proliferation and Terrorism reported on their investigations and findings. Commission co-chairman and former U.S. Senator Bob Graham summarized what he called "the bad news" at the outset of his testimony:

1. the risks that we are facing, in spite of all that we have done in the Congress and in the executive branch, at state and local government, that our margin of safety is declining, that we are becoming more vulnerable;
2. the commission finds that it is more likely than not that between now and the end of 2013 a weapon of mass destruction will be used somewhere on the globe;

3. *we found that it was more likely that the attack would be by biological weapons rather than by a nuclear weapon;*

4. *We also found that in terms of intent, that the terrorists are just as intent to use weapons of mass destruction today as they were almost 20 years ago, when bin Laden first attempted to acquire nuclear material while still living in the Sudan. That effort to obtain and use has been described by bin Laden as a religious duty of al Qaeda.*[2]

More than a decade earlier, then Secretary of Defense William Cohen held up a five-pound bag of sugar during a prime-time TV interview to warn Americans how much anthrax—or, to be more precise, how little of the biological agent—it would take to kill all the people in Washington, D.C.[3] For the usually low-key Cohen, this was a shocking demonstration to dramatize the threat of weapons of mass destruction in the hands of terrorists or rogue states. But there were no indications that the message had been a wake-up call for the news media, the general public, or, more importantly, decision-makers in Washington. In October 2001, only weeks after the shock of 9/11, a smaller version of Cohen's nightmare scenario came true when letters containing anthrax spores were mailed to several media figures and politicians, killing several persons in the U.S. Postal Service in the process. The anthrax case was a chilling reminder that a far more devastating version of bioterrorism by one individual or a small group, whether sponsored by states or acting independently, was a real possibility.

Improving Homeland Security: New Department, New Cabinet Post

The Department of Homeland Security was created after 9/11 in one of the most comprehensive reorganizations of the executive branch. Under the first Secretary of Homeland Security, Tom Ridge, the controversial color-coded terrorism threat alert system was implemented. This picture shows Secretary Ridge during a news conference on July 8, 2004, when he warned of possible Al Qaeda attacks on the United States through the summer and up to Election Day in early November.

The dramatic event that separated these two very specific warnings of the likelihood of catastrophic terrorism and the urgent need for improved prevention and preparedness measures was, of course, the experience of September 11, 2001. Before that day, homeland security was, as the "2007 National Strategy for Homeland Security" correctly noted, "a patchwork of efforts undertaken by disparate departments and agencies across all levels of government."[4] There was no overall mission, no coherent strategy, and no unifying purpose and distinct institutional arrangement among federal agencies and departments or between the federal government and state, and local governments. Instead, there were turf battles and overlapping programs at the expense of equally or more important measures to prevent and prepare for terrorist strikes.

Recognizing that even the most elaborate and skillful preventative measures would not eliminate terrorist acts altogether, the federal government, states, and local communities in the United States—and the comparable authorities in many other countries around the world—intensified their efforts to improve the preparedness of emergency response professionals after 9/11. But when Hurricane Katrina devastated New Orleans and other areas along the Gulf coast in late August 2005 and caused many deaths and human tragedies, it became obvious that neither the federal government nor state and local emergency responders were adequately prepared to effectively deal with such a catastrophe. As Senator Joseph Lieberman pointed out in a stinging criticism of federal preparedness, Katrina should have been "a lesser challenge to the nation's emergency-management apparatus than the 9/11 attacks: It [the hurricane] was preceded by 72 hours of increasingly dire predictions."[5] Indeed, while the stunningly flawed or nonexistent preparedness measures before Katrina struck and the botched emergency response afterwards laid bare the soft underbelly of America's preparedness for predictable disasters, they did far more so with respect to unpredictable terrorist events.

This failure to prepare for and respond to a natural disaster was shocking to Americans and people around the globe. After all, homeland security had become the single most important objective in American domestic and foreign policy after 9/11. As Vice President Cheney put it when asked in an interview to identify his "highest moment [of] the last eight years,"

> Well, I think that the most important, the most compelling, was 9/11 itself, and what that entailed, what we had to deal with, the way in which that changed the nation and set the agenda for what we've had to deal with as an administration.[6]

But there were vastly different opinions on the choices in and effectiveness of the administration's agenda. Homeland security expert Stephen Flynn was highly critical of the Bush administration's approach to preventing further terrorism at home, writing in 2007,

> Rather than address the myriad of soft targets within the U.S. border, the White House has defined the war on terrorism to be managed by actions beyond our shores. The rallying cry of the Bush administration and its allies on Capitol Hill has been "We must fight terrorists over there so we don't have to fight them here!" What this ignores is that terrorists can still come here—and, worse yet, are being made here.[7]

Flynn asked, "How have we allowed our government to be so negligent? Who will keep your family safe? Is America living on borrowed time?"[8] But for the Bush administration and many of its supporters, the government's post–9/11 record on terrorism prevention was a stellar one. Vice President Cheney was far more positive, when he told Chris Wallace of *Fox News*, "I think the fact that we were able to protect the nation against further attacks from al Qaeda for seven-and-a-half years is a remarkable achievement."[9] Cheney was right in pointing out that there had not been an attack by Al Qaeda in the United States since 9/11, but he failed to mention that the group had not struck on American soil in the seven-and-a-half years before September 11, 2001 either. In a mixed review, security expert Charles Perrow wrote,

> There is no doubt in my mind that the nation is somewhat safer since the 9/11 attack. Suspects have been apprehended, the FAA has made changes, and so has the Immigration and Customs Enforcement. But the first two were made outside of the new Department of Homeland Security, and the third easily could have been made without its appearance. The department has had very limited success in making our vulnerable chemical and nuclear stockpiles more secure. Our borders are still so porous that it would be sheer luck if a guard happened on to a terrorist.[10]

In short, the administration's positive evaluation of its terrorism prevention efforts was disputed by independent security experts.

Assessments were even more negative when it came to terrorism preparedness and emergency response. Although government officials mentioned and the news media reported frequently about the seriousness of the terrorist threat in the post–9/11 years, this did not result in markedly improved preparedness among ordinary citizens and did not remedy major problems within and among emergency response agencies. Public opinion survey data revealed "a national state of unpreparedness for emergency events" in the post–9/11 years.[11] And the assessment of professional responders was just as grim, summed up in the conclusion that "[o]verall, the existing government response system is more accurately described as disarrayed, disconnected, uncoordinated, underfunded, and discredited."[12]

Other countries were plagued by similar preparedness and response problems. This became painfully clear after four suicide bombers struck London's transit system in July 2005. In a comprehensive report that was released nearly a year after the deadly terrorist attacks, a review committee listed a multitude of shortcomings in the response system, among them failures of communication between the emergency services, since police, fire, and emergency medical services used different radio systems. Also, there was "a lack of planning to care for survivors" and "of basic equipment, including stretchers and triage cards, and too few essential supplies such as fluids at the affected sites."[13]

In the United States, besides the adoption of a multitude of new counterterrorism laws the most striking response to 9/11 was a fundamental reorganization of the homeland security and intelligence areas.

Post–9/11 Reorganization of Homeland Security

For decades, the threat of terrorism and actual terrorist incidents inside the United States—in most cases, by homegrown perpetrators—were treated like potential and actual crimes. This meant that the FBI and local law enforcement were in charge of prevention efforts and investigations after the fact. Emergency responders on all levels of government prepared to handle the immediate aftermath of terror strikes in much the same way as they responded to other man-made or natural emergencies.

As a direct result of the two terrorist bombings in New York in 1993 and Oklahoma City two years later, the release of nerve gas in the Tokyo subway system in 1995, and intelligence about Al Qaeda's efforts to acquire biological, chemical, and nuclear weapons, the pertinent local, state, and federal agencies intensified their preparedness efforts before 9/11. These initiatives were typically undertaken by existing agencies. One of the exceptions was the establishment of twenty-seven Weapons of Mass Destruction Civil Support Teams within the National Guard following the Tokyo sarin gas attacks. Stationed across the country, these teams were trained to identify deadly agents that could be used in biological or chemical attacks.

But a piecemeal approach was no longer acceptable after the attacks of 9/11; instead, there was widespread agreement on the need to streamline anti- and counterterrorist efforts at home. The establishment of the Department of Homeland Security was a direct result of 9/11. The new department brought together, under one umbrella, twenty-two entities that had been either independent or part of larger departments and agencies. The idea was to avoid duplication and, most importantly, to improve cooperation and coordination horizontally within the federal government and vertically between the pertinent players on the local, state, and federal levels. Although the White House retained its own Office of Homeland Security, which was also charged with coordinating interagency activities, the Department of Homeland Security became the centerpiece of the post–9/11 antiterrorism reforms. Its four major directorates (besides a fifth one for management and personnel matters), each headed by an undersecretary, united a multitude of agencies under one roof:

The Border and Transportation Security Directorate (charged with border and transportation security) housed the Immigration and Naturalization Service, the U.S. Customs Service, the Federal Protective Service, the Transportation Security Administration, the Office for Domestic Preparedness, the Animal and Plant Health Inspection Service, and the Federal Law Enforcement Training Center.

The Emergency Preparedness and Response Directorate (charged with overseeing domestic preparedness and emergency response) included the Federal Emergency Management Agency, or FEMA; the Strategic National Stockpile and the National Disaster Medical System; the Nuclear Incident Response Team; the Domestic Emergency Support Teams; and the National Domestic Preparedness Office.

The Science and Technology Directorate (charged with utilizing all scientific and technological means to bolster homeland security) contained the CBRN (Chemical, Biological, Radiological, Nuclear) Countermeasure Programs, the Environmental Measurement Laboratory, the National BW (Biological Weapon) Analysis Center, and the Plum Island Animal Disease Center.

The Information Analysis and Infrastructure Protection Directorate (charged with analyzing intelligence that relates to homeland security and the protection of domestic infrastructure) included the Critical Infrastructure Assurance Office, the Federal Computer Incident Response Center, the National Communications System, the National Infrastructure Protection Center, and the Energy Security and Assurance Program.

Although not part of one of the directorates but remaining intact in their previous form, the Secret Service and the Coast Guard nevertheless became part of the Department of Homeland Security, with their heads reporting directly to the secretary of homeland security. The Central Intelligence Agency (CIA), the Federal Bureau of Investigation (FBI), the National Security Agency (NSA), and other intelligence agencies were not incorporated into the new department but were directed to work closely with the DHS, especially with the Information Analysis and Infrastructure Protection Directorate. In addition, other departments and a host of other agencies were involved in various aspects of homeland security, for example, the Department of Defense. In extraordinary cases of imminent terrorist threats or actual attacks, the Department of Defense would direct military missions in the air or conduct maritime defense operations. In cases of terrorist emergencies, the Defense Department would provide capabilities that are not available to the Department of Homeland Security or other departments and agencies. Other important players in the area of homeland security were the Centers for Disease Control and Prevention and the National Institute for Health (both part of the Department of Health and Human Services), as well as the Food Safety Inspection and Agricultural Research Services (part of the Department of Agriculture). Finally, the Department of Homeland Security made efforts to facilitate and streamline the interactions between localities and states on the one hand and the federal government on the other.

When the Department of Homeland Security (DHS) was established in 2002, it was the result of the most drastic reorganization since 1947, when the Department of Defense and the CIA were created. But such reforms make for turf battles and growing pains. In this particular case, the DHS's intelligence functions were resented from the outset by the CIA and the Department of Defense. There were also clashes between the DHS and the Department of Justice and their respective heads, Tom Ridge and John Ashcroft. According to one account, "The Defense Department simply pursued its own homeland-security programs, while the Justice Department absconded with D.H.S.'s authority to investigate terrorist financing."[14]

Moreover, from the outset there were doubts whether a megadepartment like DHS could strengthen and streamline preparedness and prevention effectively or would actually weaken some of its parts' effectiveness in those areas. These doubts became stronger after the disastrous FEMA response to hurricane Katrina in 2005. The Department of Homeland Security and the Federal Emergency Management Agency were the particular targets of harsh criticism following the Katrina fiasco. Experts questioned whether FEMA's absorption into the huge DHS had weakened its ability to effectively coordinate responses to terrorist attacks and natural disasters by federal, state, and local first responders. Putting an agency charged with preparedness and response under the same umbrella as those entities trying to prevent terrorism in the first place was seen as ill-advised by many critics.

When the DHS was reorganized by Secretary Chertoff, the Federal Emergency Management Agency remained under the department's roof but was no longer part of a multiagency directorate; instead, as Figure 13.1 shows, FEMA became a member agency with a direct line to the Secretary's office. The same changes were made with respect to four other agencies (Transportation Security Administration, Customs and Border Protection, Citizenship and Immigration Services, and Immigration and Customs Enforcement). As mentioned earlier, the U.S. Coast Guard and the U.S. Secret Service reported all along to the DHS Secretary from the outset and retained this status.

By 2008, the Department of Homeland Security had more than 200,000 employees and was the third largest behind the departments of Defense and Veterans Affairs. Given the range and difficulty of its charge, the size of its workforce, its links to states and local governments, and the responsibility for relevant research, the department

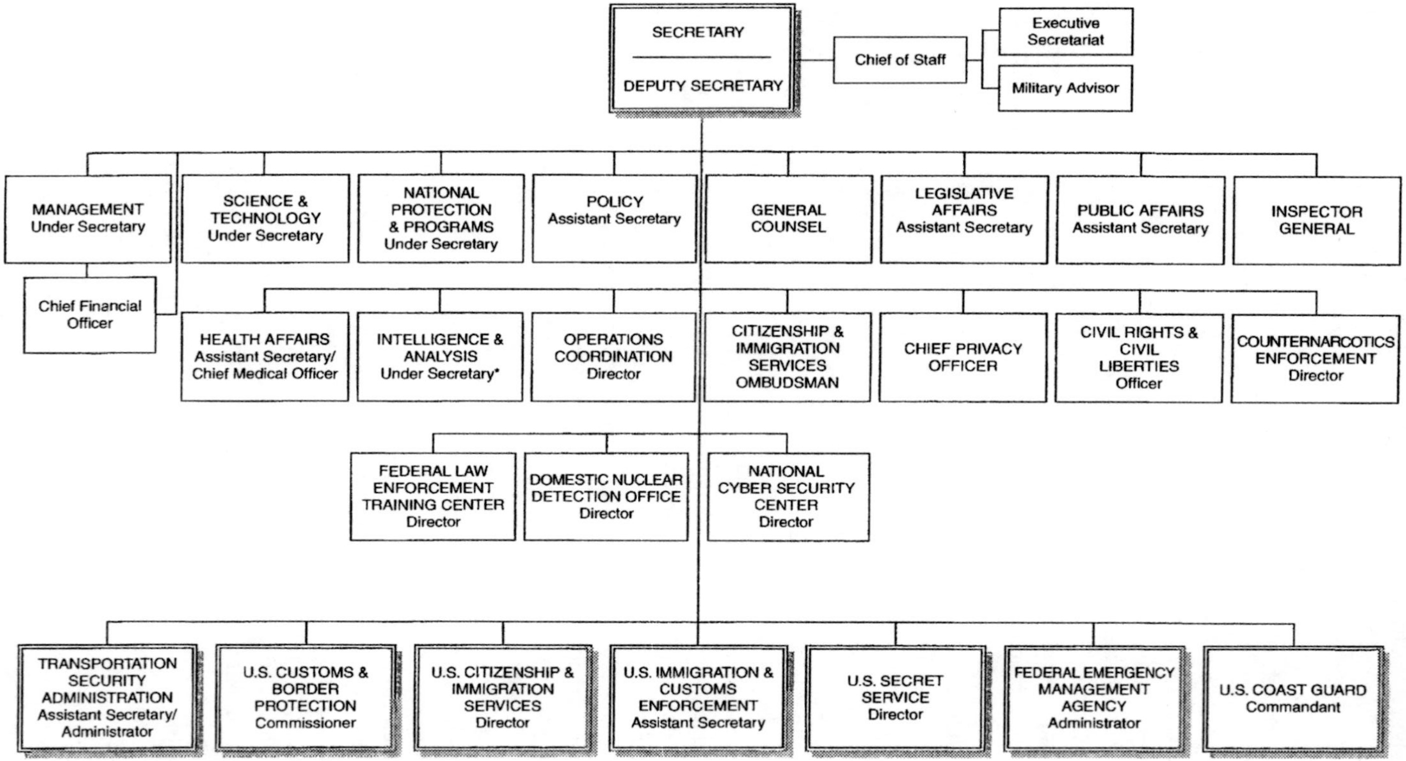

FIGURE 13.1 Organization of the Department of Homeland Security.

http://www.dhs.gov/xlibrary/assets/DHS_OrgChart.pdf

controlled a sizeable budget that grew from $31.4 billion in 2003 to a $50.5 billion request in the president's proposed budget for 2009. In 2008, the U.S. General Accountability Office (GAO) reported that since 2002 the DHS had distributed close to $20 billion in federal grants and thereby provided funding to public jurisdiction and private owners/operators "for planning, equipment, and training to enhance the nation's capabilities to respond to terrorist attacks and, to a lesser extent, natural and accidental disasters."[15]

Former Speaker of the House Thomas "Tip" O'Neill used to say that all politics is local. Terrorist attacks and other catastrophes tend to be first of all local and perhaps regional problems. Not surprisingly, local communities and states compete for federal funds earmarked for prevention and preparedness measures as they do for grants in other areas. From the outset, there was much controversy about the allocation of funds. When the 9/11 Commission issued its last report card on "emergency prepared-ness and response" in the fall of 2005, it gave the five pertinent prevention and pre-paredness areas two "C," one "D," and two "F" grades. But the commissioners were most critical of the unwillingness of Congress to allocate homeland security funds based on risk. As the bipartisan 9/11 Commission put it, "Congress has still not changed the underlying statutory authority for homeland security grants, or benchmarks to insure that funds are used wisely. As a result, homeland security funds continue to be distributed without regard for risk, vulnerability, or the consequences of an attack. . . ."[16] Even after protests led to an adjustment in the 2005 grant allocation scheme, states with small populations and a relatively low risk of becoming the targets of terrorism fared on a per capita basis better than larger states and high-risk urban area. Pointing out one such discrepancy, one report noted that "Wyoming, the state with the fewest resi-dents, once again will receive the most funding per capita to fight terrorism in fiscal 2005 . . . Wyoming will get $27.80 per person in anti-terrorism grants this year, down significantly from $40 a person last year. In contrast, New York, a victim of repeat ter-rorist attacks, will receive $15.54 per person in 2005, up from $10.13 last year."[17]

The Democratic majority in the 110th Congress took over with the campaign pledge that it would adopt the recommendations of the 9/11 Commission—including the allocation of federal funds on the basis of vulnerability of particular areas.[18] The result was the The 9/11 Commission Act of 2007 that directed the DHS to consider in the allocation of funds among states and high-risk urban areas the relative threat, vulnerability, and consequences from terrorist acts as well as the anticipated effec-tiveness of the proposed use of grants.[19] This was a giant step forward in correcting the inadequacies in the distribution of homeland security grants. In an assessment of the DHS's 2008 risk-based grants, the GAO noted that in general the department "has constructed a reasonable methodology to assess risk and allocate funds within a given fiscal year." But the report also pointed to remaining problems, and in partic-ular that

> the vulnerability element of the risk analysis model has limitations that reduce its value. Measuring vulnerability is considered a generally-accepted practice in assessing risk; however, DHS did not measure vulnerability for each state and urban area. Rather, DHS considered all states and urban areas equally vulnerable to a successful attack and assigned every state and urban area a vulnerability score of 1.0 in the risk model. Thus, as a practical matter, the final risk scores are determined by the threat and consequences scores. By not measuring variations in vulnerability, DHS ignores differences across states and urban areas.[20]

In other words, empirical and commonsensical evaluation measures on the likelihood of target areas' vulnerability to being struck by terrorists were still not established and not taken into consideration. But in the years after 9/11, the White House Office of Homeland Security and the Department of Homeland Security made efforts to establish a comprehensive homeland security strategy with specific assessments and objectives.

General and Specific Homeland Security Strategies

The 2007 "National Strategy for Homeland Security" defined homeland security as "a concerted national effort to prevent terrorist attacks within the United States, reduce America's vulnerability to terrorism, and minimize the damage and recover from attacks that do occur."[21] The DHS "Security Strategic Plan Fiscal Years 2008–2013" reflected this definition and devoted three of the five explicit strategic goal categories to the prevention of terrorism, one to preparedness, and one to the department's management and spirit. These are the stated DHS objectives and subgoals:

Goal 1 "Protect Our Nation from Dangerous People"
1.1 Achieve effective control of our borders;
1.2 Protect our interior and enforce immigration laws;
1.3 Strengthen screening of travelers and workers;
1.4 Improve security through enhanced immigration services

Goal 2 "Protect Our Nation from Dangerous Goods"
2.1 Prevent and detect radiological, nuclear attacks;
2.2 Prevent, detect, and protect against biological attacks;
2.3 Prevent and detect chemical and explosive attacks;
2.4 Prevent the introduction of illicit contraband while facilitating trade

Goal 3 "Protect Critical Infrastructure"
3.1 Protect and strengthen the resilience of the nation's critical infrastructure and key resources;
3.2 Ensure continuity in government communication and operations
3.3 Improve cyber security;
3.4 Protect transportation sectors

Goal 4 "Strengthen Our Nation's Preparedness and Emergency Response Capabilities"
4.1 Ensure preparedness;
4.2 Strengthen response and recovery

Goal 5 "Strengthen and Unify DHS Operations and Management"
5.1 Improve department governance and performance;
5.2 Advance intelligence and information sharing;
5.3 Integrate DHS policy, planning, and operations coordination

In the years following 9/11, the White House and the Homeland Security Department also developed a number of threat-specific strategies as well as detailed incident-management plans—sometimes in response to critics. For example, the 9/11 Commission and security experts criticized insufficient seaport security and the failure to inspect cargo before it arrived in U.S. ports. Some provisions in

"The National Strategy for Maritime Security" of 2005 dealt with these complaints by focusing on the protection of maritime-related population centers and on measures to prevent terrorists and/or weapons, particularly WMD, to be hidden on U.S.-bound ships or in cargo. To this end, the Maritime Security Strategy aimed at:

- Expanding the United States Government's capabilities to prescreen international cargo prior to loading;
- Adopting procedures for enforcement action against vessels entering or leaving a nation's port, internal waters, or territorial seas when they are reasonably suspected of carrying terrorists or criminals or supporting terrorist or criminal endeavor; and
- Adopting streamlined procedures for inspecting vessels reasonably suspected of carrying suspicious cargo and seizing such cargo when it is identified as subject to confiscation.[22]

In November 2008, a multipronged terrorist attack was carried out in the Indian city of Mumbai. The team of terrorists that killed 173 people and injured more than 300 had traveled by sea and used a small boat to land near its target sites. Ten months earlier, the Department of Homeland Security had completed its "Small Vessel Security Strategy" in recognition that terrorists could use small commercial vessels, such as small ferries or fishing boats, and recreational boats to enter the United States and/or bring weapons ashore.[23] It seems that officials in the Homeland Security Department were ahead of their foreign counterparts in focusing on small boat and seaport security and perhaps other threat areas.

Ultimately, success and failure depend largely on the implementation of the best laid plans and strategies. In 2003, President Bush's Homeland Security Presidential Directive charged the Secretary of Homeland Security with developing a National Incident Management System (NIMS) "to provide a consistent nationwide approach for Federal, State, and local governments to work effectively and efficiently together to prepare for, respond to, and recover from domestic incidents, regardless of cause, size, or complexity."[24] By early 2004, the DHS had a comprehensive mission and organizational plan in place and presumably ready for the implementation of an effective way to manage and coordinate major catastrophes. However, as previously mentioned, when Hurricane Katrina struck about eighteen months after the release of the detailed NIMS plan, what was supposed to be an effective, new crisis-management system failed.

It's the Intelligence, Stupid

There is widespread agreement that good intelligence is, as Grant Wardlaw has remarked, the "first line of defense against political terrorism."[25] Or, in the words of Marc Celmer, "The most important aspect of any nation's fight against domestic and international terrorism is current and accurate intelligence."[26] Without good and reliable intelligence there is little chance of preventing terrorists from carrying out their attacks. In the United States, a host of agencies comprise the intelligence community, most notably the Central Intelligence Agency (CIA), the Federal Bureau of Investigation (FBI), the National Security Agency (NSA), the Defense Intelligence Agency (DIA), the Department of State's Bureau of Intelligence and Research, and the intelligence units of the various branches of the armed services. The CIA is the backbone of foreign intelligence in the fields of both anti- and counterterrorism; the National Security Act forbids the Central Intelligence Agency from spying within the United States. The FBI is the lead investigative agency, with jurisdiction over surveillance in the areas of both domestic and international terrorism. However, as a result of anti-American terrorism in the 1980s, the FBI's traditional investigative and law enforcement jurisdiction was extended by Congress to reach beyond U.S. borders in cases in which international terrorists targeted Americans abroad. Other members of the intelligence community concern themselves with special tasks. The NSA, for example, collects vast amounts of electronic intelligence from around the globe; the intelligence units of the armed services focus naturally on possible threats to the military.

All of these agencies share one common goal: to gather information that reveals details about threats to the United States' national security—including terrorist plots. In many instances, one or more agencies get hold of suspicious nuggets of information that do not add up to definitive clues about specific terrorist threats. Or the available bits and pieces of information could reveal a terror plot—but are not put together within one particular agency or in the larger intelligence community. This was the case before 9/11, when various agencies possessed bits of intelligence that perhaps could have led to the discovery of the hijacking plot and its terrible consequences. After the attacks, there were revelations about problems within and among agencies. As Philip Heymann pointed out, "The FBI and the CIA were unwilling or unable to exchange information quickly and effectively; this applied even more to furnishing information to the Immigration and Naturalization Service [INS]. The INS did not learn from the CIA what identified terrorists were entering the United States and where they were."[27]

The FBI, on the other hand, seemed slow in tracking suspects inside the country when the CIA provided intelligence about their identity. Perhaps more shocking was the disclosure that higher-ups at the FBI headquarters in Washington ignored the leads and thwarted the investigations of FBI agents in field offices that should have led to the arrests of 9/11 plotters before they could strike. Agents in the field reported to their Washington superiors that foreign flight school students insisted on learning how to pilot commercial jetliners but were not at all interested in takeoffs and landing procedures. Coleen Rowley, an agent and lawyer in the Minneapolis field office of the FBI, testified before the Senate Judiciary Committee that she and her colleagues were frustrated because FBI headquarters had obstructed their efforts to investigate Zacarias Moussaoui, allegedly the designated twentieth hijacker in the 9/11 plot and one of the suspicious flight school students. According to one account, Rowley was particularly incensed because FBI headquarters rejected a warrant request to examine Moussaoui's computer. It was only after 9/11 that the FBI got the warrant and reportedly found information related to commercial planes and crop dusters on the computer's hard drive. The government grounded crop-dusting planes temporarily because of what it found.[28] Some observers concluded that the Minneapolis investigation, if not hampered by FBI higher-ups, could have produced evidence about the identity of foreigners and their suspicious interest in piloting commercial jets in flight. The likelihood of discovering the plot before it was too late should have been enhanced by an alert agent in the FBI's Phoenix field office whose memo informed superiors in Washington about several Arabs who were training in a flight school in Arizona. But again, officials at the FBI headquarters showed no particular interest.

Besides serious problems in the culture of individual agencies and turf battles between different agencies, a multitude of other deficiencies had been identified well before 9/11. In a June 2000 report to President Clinton titled "Countering the Changing

Threat of International Terrorism," the National Commission on Terrorism warned that its members had "identified significant obstacles to the collection and distribution of reliable information on terrorism to analysts and policymakers" and that "these obstacles must be removed."[29] Among the identified problems were the following:

- **Lack of information sharing.** The most glaring problem was the failure of the various members of the intelligence community to share information. "Law enforcement agencies are traditionally reluctant to share information outside of their circles so as not to jeopardize any potential prosecution. The FBI does promptly share information warning about specific threats with the CIA and other agencies. But the FBI is far less likely to disseminate terrorist information that may not relate to an immediate threat even though this could be of immense long-term or cumulative value to the intelligence community. . . . The problem is particularly pronounced with respect to information in the FBI's field offices in the United States, most of which never reaches the FBI headquarters, let alone other U.S. government agencies or departments."[30] An investigation by the staff of the 9/11 Commission came to the same conclusion: "The [intelligence] Community lacked a common information architecture that would help to ensure the integration of counterterrorism data across CIA, NSA, DIA, the FBI, and other agencies."[31]
- **Insufficient human intelligence.** The National Commission on Terrorism stated, "Inside information is the key to preventing attacks by terrorists. The CIA must aggressively recruit informants with unique access to terrorist plans. That sometimes requires recruiting those who have committed terrorist acts or related crimes, just as domestic law enforcement agencies routinely recruit criminal informants in order to pursue major criminal figures."[32] Therefore, the Commission recommended, the CIA must act on the recognition that "the aggressive recruitment of human intelligence sources on terrorism is one of the intelligence community's highest priorities."[33]
- **Lack of state-of-the-art information technology.** One reason why the FBI and other intelligence agencies failed in the past to connect the dots of the available intelligence to pinpoint the connections between suspected terrorists and the targets of terrorist plots was the lack of state-of-the-art information technology—although, as the National Commission on Terrorism concluded well before 9/11, "The ability to exploit information collected—process it into understandable information and prioritize it—is essential to an effective global counterterrorism program."[34] The lack of sufficient financial resources delayed the modernization of information technology in literally all intelligence agencies. As far as the FBI was concerned, its "ability to exploit the increasing volume of terrorism information has been hampered by aging technology."[35] At the CIA, the Counterterrorism Center in particular was "suffering from inadequate resources" and therefore "had to cut back or eliminate plans for an increased operational tempo to meet the globalization of terrorism and for development and acquisition of technology designed to assist in combating terrorists."[36] With respect to the National Security Agency, the National Commission on Terrorism concluded that the NSA, because of its inability to "keep pace with the information revolution . . . is losing its capability to target and exploit the modern communication systems used by terrorists, seriously weakening the NSA's ability to warn of possible attacks."[37]

The FBI's Inadequate Computer System

Even when generous funding became available, the FBI failed to build a state-of-the-art information system within a reasonable time frame. In early 2005, the Justice Department's inspector general concluded that the failure to upgrade its computer system hampered the FBI's "ability to prevent terrorism and combat other serious crimes."[38] More than three years after 9/11, it was clear that Trilogy, a $581 million three-pronged program to bring the FBI's information system into the twenty-first century, was far from becoming reality. One part of the $170 million effort to establish a so-called Virtual Case File (VCF) program that agents could access via computers was not performing as needed.

During a U.S. Senate Appropriation Subcommittee hearing on February 3, 2005, in which FBI Director Robert S. Mueller testified, Senator Patrick J. Leahy (D-VT) made the following remarks with respect to the FBI's lagging information and communication ability:

It is unbelievable, given the years that have gone by, the advances in technology that have marched on in the meantime, that we're here today to discuss whether or not to completely scrap a key component of the Trilogy Project, the long anticipated Virtual Case File.

This unraveling of the Trilogy Project or—as some FBI agents have told me privately, the Tragedy Project—bringing the FBI's information technology into the 21st century, that shouldn't be rocket science.

We have a classic example of too many cooks with unpredictable results. The initial contract for VCF was modified 36 times. During this period, the FBI had five different chief information officers; I am told, 10 different project managers.

We have to protect the American people. To do this effectively, the FBI has to have state-of-the-art technology that works. It's a vital task.

Now, we're going to have to spend more money to buy what we thought we had bought.[39]

A few weeks later, in early March 2005, the FBI officially abandoned its $170 million Virtual Case File project that had been considered critical to assisting agents in investigating terrorism. The agency aimed at developing a new software system within three-and-a-half years that would satisfy the needs of the agency. But in late 2008, the Justice Department's inspector general revealed that the new system, named Sentinel, would cost $451 rather than the projected $425 million and be completed by June 2010 rather than in late 2009 as earlier promised.

- **Shortage of linguists.** The NSA in particular but the rest of the intelligence community as well "face a drastic shortage of linguists to translate raw data into useful information."[40] At a time when the global network of terrorists presided over or inspired by bin Laden represents the most serious terrorism threat to the United States, the NSA collects vast amounts of raw data in a multitude of languages and even unique dialects. Without qualified linguists translating this material into English, intelligence of this kind is not at all useful for analysts and policy-makers. But since the translation of highly sensitive intelligence information can only be entrusted to persons eligible for the highest level of security clearance, the hiring of additional linguists has been slow—even after 9/11.

Taken together, the hearings and staff investigations of the 9/11 Commission affirmed all of these major problems. But perhaps the most critical conclusion was that the intelligence community lacked one single leader with decision-making powers over the whole community. According to one staff report,

> The DCI [Director of Central Intelligence who heads the CIA] labored within—and was accountable for—a Community of loosely associated agencies and departmental offices that lacked the incentives to cooperate, collaborate, and share information. Like his predecessors, he focused his energies on where he could add the greatest values—the CIA, which is a fraction of the nation's overall intelligence capability. As a result, a question remains: Who is in charge of intelligence?[41]

Perhaps all of these problems were not aggressively attacked before 9/11 because, as Heymann has pointed out, terrorism "posed a minimal risk at home."[42] The result was complacency. "We were focused on attacks on Americans abroad, although we should have been able to imagine terrible attacks at home, even of the sort that took place [on 9/11]."[43]

The Bush administration and Congress decided that changes in gathering, coordinating, and analyzing intelligence were needed. Following the adoption of the Intelligence Reform and Terrorism Prevention Act of 2004 (PL-108-458), there was indeed the most drastic reorganization of the intelligence community since the implementation of the National Security Act of 1948.

Reorganization of the Intelligence Community

Following the recommendations of the 9/11 Commission, the Intelligence Reform and Terrorism Prevention Act of 2004 created the new position of director of national intelligence (DNI) to head up and coordinate the various intelligence agencies that continued to exist in their previous forms. The director of central intelligence was to report to the director of national intelligence. When President George W. Bush nominated John Negroponte as the first DNI, he characterized the new office and its occupant's role this way:

> John will lead a unified intelligence community, and will serve as the principle [sic] advisor to the President on intelligence matters. He will have the authority to order the collection of new intelligence, to ensure the sharing of information among agencies, and to establish common standards for the intelligence community's personnel. It will be John's responsibility to determine the annual budgets of all national intelligence agencies and offices and direct how these funds are spent. Vesting these authorities in a single official who reports directly to me will make our intelligence efforts better coordinated, more efficient, and more effective.[44]

In addition to creating the DNI position and that of a deputy DNI as well, the law prescribed the establishment of a National Counterterrorism Center. Staffed by analysts from all intelligence agencies, the new center was charged with planning intelligence missions and, most importantly, coordinating information on terrorism threats and responses.

Given the perennial turf battles among various agencies and departments, however, it proved difficult for the DNI and the head of the new Counterterrorism Center to discharge their awesome responsibilities. It was probably no coincidence that President Bush selected a longtime diplomat, John Negroponte, as the first director of national intelligence and a career Air Force intelligence officer and director of the National Security Agency, Lt. General Michael Hayden, as deputy DNI. Their most crucial task was clear—to unify the intelligence community and keep it unified. The Department of Defense in particular resented a strong director of national intelligence who would be able to meddle in its several intelligence agencies. This reaction was hardly surprising. The Pentagon, after all, receives and controls 80% of the total funds allotted to the intelligence community. Without authority over the total intelligence budget and personnel decisions, the DNI would be impotent and unable to effectively oversee an integrated intelligence system. But when the new position was created as a result of the Intelligence Reform and Terrorism Prevention Act of 2004, it was far from certain what authorities the DNI would really have. Although the president said that the director of national intelligence would have centralized intelligence-gathering and budgetary authorities, he seemed to assure others in the intelligence community, especially the civilian and military leadership in the Department of Defense, continuity rather than change when he said,

> The law establishing John's [i.e., John Negroponte's] position preserves the existing chain of command and leaves all our intelligence agencies, organizations, and offices in their current departments. Our military commanders will continue to have quick access to the intelligence they need to achieve victory on the battlefield.[45]

Negroponte, a career diplomat with no previous experience in any of the intelligence agencies, left his cabinet-level post in early 2007 after only nineteen months to become deputy secretary of state—a subcabinet position. At the time, observers in Washington wondered,

> whether Mr. Negroponte was there long enough to lay the foundation of real change and whether his transfer suggested that the Bush administration was less committed than it claimed to be to an intelligence overhaul that President Bush had billed as the most significant restructuring of American spy agencies in half a century.[46]

Also, the verdict was still out on the power struggle between the director of national intelligence and the Department of Defense, with some observers claiming that the diplomat Negroponte had not been aggressive enough in "bringing the Pentagon's intelligence budget under his control."[47] Nor was it clear whether the creation of a national intelligence czar and a National Counterterrorism Center for the analysis and evaluation of intelligence information from all spy agencies had strengthened the counterterrorism capabilities or simply added another layer to a massive bureaucracy he was supposed to streamline for the sake of greater cooperation and effectiveness. It was telling, however, that President Bush nominated an experienced intelligence specialist to succeed Negroponte as director of national intelligence: retired admiral Mike McConnell, a former director of the National Security Agency.

As far as the 9/11 Commission was concerned, in many respects the intelligence community was slow to enact important reforms. The Commission's final assessment mentioned little or modest progress in the enactment of the following recommendations:

- **Create FBI national security workforce.** The FBI's shift to a counterterrorism posture is far from institutionalized, and significant deficiencies remain. Reforms are at risk from inertia and complacency; they must be accelerated, or they will fail.

- **New missions for CIA Director.** Reforms are underway at the CIA, especially of human intelligence operations. If the CIA is to remain an effective arm of national power, Congress and CIA leadership need to be committed to accelerating the pace of reforms.
- **Incentives for information sharing.** Changes in incentives, in favor of information sharing, have been minimal. The office of the program manager for information sharing is still a start-up, and is not getting the support it needs from the highest levels of government. There remain many complaints about lack of information sharing between federal authorities and state and local level officials.
- **Government-wide information sharing.** Designating individuals to be in charge of information sharing is not enough. They need resources, active presidential backing, policies and procedures in place that compel sharing, and systems of performance evaluation that appraise personnel on how they carry out information sharing.
- **Homeland airspace defense.** Situational awareness and sharing of information has improved. But it is not routine or comprehensive, no single agency currently leads the interagency response to airspace violations, and there is no overarching plan to secure airspace outside the National Capital region.[48]

Following the reorganization, the national intelligence community has sixteen member agencies (see Figure 13.2). Unlike all other members, the Office of the Director of National Intelligence and the Central Intelligence Agency (CIA) are the only ones not part of a cabinet department. The Department of Defense has by far the largest number of intelligence agencies under its umbrella: the Defense Intelligence Agency (DIA), the National Security Agency (NSA), the National Reconnaissance Office, the National Geospatial Intelligence Agency, and the intelligence arms of each of the four military branches. In other words, eight of the sixteen members of the intelligence community are parts of the Department of Defense.

FIGURE 13.2

Members of the U.S. Intelligence Community

Director of National Intelligence (DNI) and Office of the DNI Principal Deputy Director of National Intelligence **Undersecretary of Defense for Intelligence**	
Member-Agencies and Member–Departments	
Air Force Intelligence	Coast Guard Intelligence
Army Intelligence	Central Intelligence Agency
Defense Intelligence Agency	Department of Energy
Marine Corps Intelligence	Department of Homeland Security
National Geospatial-Intelligence Agency	Department of State
National Reconnaissance Office	Department of the Treasury
National Security Agency	Drug Enforcement Administration
Navy Intelligence	Federal Bureau of Investigation

Source: United States Intelligence Community.

For this reason, the undersecretary of defense for intelligence is a member of the intelligence community since he "provides oversight and policy guidance for all DoD intelligence activities."[49]

Given the strong representation of Defense Department agencies in the intelligence community, it is hardly surprising that leading and coordinating is not an easy task for any director of national intelligence. However, the office-holder tends to have a close relationship with the president and other high officials in the White House because he acts as the principal advisor to the president, the National Security Council, and the Homeland Security Council for intelligence matters related to national security besides overseeing and directing the implementation of the National Intelligence Program.

International Cooperation

Intelligence is essential not only in the prevention of terrorism but also in law enforcement agencies' efforts to hunt down the perpetrators of terrorism, the architects of terrorism, and the supporters of terrorist groups. While one objective here is to bring terrorists to justice, an even more urgent goal is to get arrested terrorists to reveal information about planned terror plots, accomplices, financial resources, and weapon suppliers. In cases of international terrorism, successful investigations require close and continued transnational cooperation between intelligence and law enforcement agencies. After 9/11, most Americans associated efforts to prevent further terror strikes with the military actions in Afghanistan against Al Qaeda and the Taliban and in Iraq against Saddam Hussein's regime. But the work of the domestic intelligence and law enforcement agencies and extraordinary international cooperation were equally—or more—important.

Two years after 9/11, more than 3,000 terrorism suspects had been arrested. Although hundreds were captured during the Afghanistan war, most of the leading figures of Al Qaeda and their followers were caught as a result of cooperation between American police and intelligence agencies and their counterparts abroad. This resulted in many arrests in Pakistan and other countries in the region. But, as the Department of State's report on "Patterns of Global Terrorism" for 2002 detailed, success stories were also reported from other parts of the world, especially Western Europe, because of bilateral and multilateral cooperation efforts.[50] These trends continued during the following years. Moreover, the 9/11 strike and subsequent terrorist attacks shocked international and regional organizations into focusing more on their antiterrorism capabilities and expanding them:

- The United Nations adopted resolutions that obligate member states to take specific actions to combat terrorism, especially in the area of interrupting the financing of terrorism. The UN established the Counterterrorism Committee and a mechanism to oversee the implementation of the agreed-upon measures.
- INTERPOL, the International Police Organization (with 181 member countries), strengthened its efforts in information sharing and law enforcement with respect to anti- and counterterrorism significantly. In particular, the new Fusion Task Force, established in 2002, can assist member countries in their terrorism investigations. "Project Tent," part of the Fusion Task Force, collects information on individuals known to have attended terrorist training camps.
- Europol, the European version of INTERPOL, and Eurojust, a transnational investigative body within the European Union, established policies and mechanisms to ensure increased information sharing and cross-border law enforcement in order to combat terrorism.

- The Southeast European Cooperative Initiative (SECI), with a SECI Center in Bucharest; the Southern African Development Community (SADC); and the Southern Africa Regional Policy Cooperative Organization (SARPCO) are efforts to function in their respective regions along the Europol and Eurojust models.
- Project Pacific, the result of an Asian regional conference in Sri Lanka, aims at increasing member states' proactive and operational cooperation in order to combat terrorism.

Given that Western democracies are the special targets of Al Qaeda and like-minded organizations, cells, and even lone wolves, cooperation between the United States and European countries is of great importance. In a policy paper on post–9/11 transatlantic cooperation, a group of distinguished experts wrote that despite fundamental differences in counterterrorism approaches,

> the United States and the European Union have shared a commitment to making their evolving collaboration against terrorism a success. During the past three years, they have reached agreement on many new arrangements, such as the Container Security Initiative and Passenger Name Records (PNR), but also on terrorist financing, sharing of evidentiary information, extradition of suspected terrorists, and many others. They have built close ties between parts of their bureaucracies that had rarely been in contact before, and involving officials from working level to Cabinet secretary and European commissioner.
>
> The question now before the United States and the EU is whether and how to build on the cooperation achieved thus far and ensure that this post–9/11 partnership continues into the future. This will not be easy. Legislation and other agreements must be implemented and enforced. Existing areas of cooperation must be extended, and collaboration in new areas must be explored and developed. The good news is that the United States and the European Union have established basic mechanisms for building cooperation through regular consultations and have successfully concluded some basic agreements.[51]

Since the greatest threat of international terrorism of our time will not be defeated nor contained unilaterally, more bilateral and multilateral cooperation must be established and existing ties strengthened.

Congress Resists Change

Resistance to change did not come only from intelligence agencies and their parent organizations in the executive branch; the hardest nut to crack according to the 9/11 Commission was Congress. Pointing out that eighty-eight congressional committees and subcommittees were involved in overseeing one or another aspect of homeland security, the Commission recommended the drastic streamlining of oversight in the areas of intelligence and counterterrorism within Congress. In the 9/11 Commission's words,

> Congressional oversight for intelligence—and counterterrorism—is now dysfunctional. Congress should address this problem. We have considered various alternatives: A joint committee on the old model of the Joint Commission on Atomic Energy is one. A single committee in each house of Congress, combining authorizing and appropriation authorities, is another.[52]

If enacted, this recommendation would result in Congress's ability to effectively discharge its oversight responsibilities and free homeland security and intelligence personnel from testifying in front of several dozen committees. But while the U.S. House of

Representatives and the U.S. Senate legislated reforms in the executive branch, there were no signs that an equally important reform along the lines of the 9/11 Commission's recommendation of a joint committee or single committee in each chamber was seriously considered. At best, there was some tinkering with the existing structures. Republicans and Democrats alike were not willing to make such drastic changes.

By late 2008, nothing had changed. As the Commission on the Prevention of WMD Proliferation and Terrorism wrote, "That Congress has yet to adequately organize itself to cope with the nuclear age, much less the post-9/11 era, is deeply troubling and demands action."[53] The commissioners noted that in the House, still 16 committees and 40 subcommittees had jurisdiction over the Department of Homeland Security and that in the Senate 14 full committees and 18 subcommittees shared oversight responsibilities.

Only time will tell whether the adopted reforms and reorganizations and the creation of new offices and systems will achieve the ambitious objectives in prevention and preparedness. Recognizing and legislating changes in preparedness and prevention were important steps; the crucial part will be to continue commonsensical reforms and press for their implementation.

Notes

1. From Senator Susan Collins' remarks as contained in the Federal News Service transcript of the Senate Committee on Homeland Security and Governmental Affairs hearing on December 11, 2008, available at the Lexis/Nexis electronic archives.
2. Ibid.
3. Mentioned in Lawrence Freedman, ed., *Superterrorism: Policy Responses* (Malden, MA: Blackwell Publishing, 2002), 21.
4. Office of Homeland Security, "National Strategy for Homeland Security," July 2002, 3. The text is available at http://www.whitehouse.gov/infocus/homeland/nshs/NSHS.pdf (accessed January 5, 2009).
5. http://www.nola.com/katrina/pdf/hs_katrinarpt_lieberman.pdf
6. Vice President Cheney made the remark in his interview with Chris Wallace on *Fox News Sunday*, December 21, 2008.
7. Stephen Flynn, *The Edge of Disaster: Rebuilding a Resilient Nation* (New York: Random House, 2007), 4.
8. Flynn, from text on dust jacket.
9. Chris Wallace interviewed Vice President Cheney on *Fox News Sunday*, December 21, 2008.
10. Charles Perrow, "The Disaster after 9/11: The Department of Homeland Security and the Intelligence Reorganization," *Homeland Security* 2:1 (April 2006): 27–28.
11. Irwin Redlener and David A. Berman, "National Preparedness Planning: The Historical Context and Current State of the U.S. Public's Readiness, 1940–2005," *Journal of International Affairs* 59:2 (Spring/Summer 2006): 87.
12. Sang Ok Choi, "Emergency Management: Implications from a Strategic Management Perspective," *Journal of Homeland Security and Emergency Management* 5:1) (2008): Article 1, 7.
13. BBC News, "London Assembly report on 7/7," June 5, 2006, http://news.bbc.co.uk/2/hi/uk_news/england/london/5048806.stm
14. William Finnegan, "Homeland Insecurity," *New Yorker*, February 7, 2005. The article is available at http://www.newyorker.com/archive/2005/02/07/050207ta_talk_finnegan, accessed May 20, 2009.
15. Report is available at http://www.gao.gov/new.items/d08852.pdf (accessed December 31, 2008).
16. The 9/11 Commission's final scorecard is available at http://i.a.cnn.net/cnn/2005/images/12/05/2005-12-05_report.pdf (accessed May 19, 2009).
17. Kathleen Hunter, "Per Capita, New Anti-terror Funds Still Favor Wyoming," available at Stateline.Org: http://www.stateline.org/live/ViewPage.action?siteNodeId=136&languageId=1&contentId=15873 (accessed December 30, 2008).
18. In early January 2007, Secretary of Homeland Security Michael Chertoff designated for the first time six high-risk urban areas—New York and northern New Jersey, the Washington region, Los Angeles–Long Beach, Chicago, the San Francisco Bay area, and Houston—to compete for

$411 million, or 55%, of the so-called Urban Area Security Initiative (UASI) funds. But by joining major cities and suburban areas and decreasing the funding of the program, Chertoff's initiative was met by skepticism and criticism in New York and other big cities.

19. For a summary of the act, see http://www.govtrack.us/congress/bill.xpd?bill=h110-1&tab=summary (accessed January 3, 2008).
20. http://www.gao.gov/new.items/d08852.pdf
21. The White House Office of Homeland Security, "National Strategy for Homeland Security," July 2007, available at http://www.whitehouse.gov/infocus/homeland/nshs/NSHS.pdf (accessed January 3, 2009).
22. The text of The National Strategy for Maritime Security is available at http://www.whitehouse.gov/homeland/maritime-security.html (accessed January 6, 2009).
23. The text of the Small Vessel Security Strategy is available at http://www.dhs.gov/xlibrary/assets/small-vessel-security-strategy.pdf (accessed January 5, 2009).
24. Cited in the Department of Homeland Security's plan for the "National Incident Management System." The text is available at http://www.fema.gov/pdf/emergency/nims/nims_doc_full.pdf (accessed January 4, 2009).
25. Grant Wardlaw, *Political Terrorism: Theory, Tactics, and Counter-Measures* (New York: Cambridge University Press, 1989), 136.
26. Marc A. Celmer, *Terrorism, U.S. Strategy, and Reagan Policies* (New York: Greenwood Press, 1987), 85.
27. Philip B. Heymann, *Terrorism, Freedom and Security: Winning without War* (Cambridge, MA: MIT Press, 2003), 64.
28. "Whistle-Blower Testifies," www.ABCNews.com (retrieved October 21, 2003).
29. Report from the National Commission on Terrorism, *Countering the Changing Threat of International Terrorism*, June 2000, 7.
30. Ibid., 15, 16.
31. 9/11 Commission, "The Performance of the Intelligence Community," Staff Statement no. 11, 12.
32. Report from the National Commission on Terrorism, 8.
33. Ibid.
34. Ibid., 13.
35. Ibid., 14.
36. Ibid.
37. Ibid.
38. Dan Eggen, "Computer Woes Hinder FBI's Work, Report Says," *Washington Post*, February 4, 2004, A15.
39. Federal News Service, February 3, 2005.
40. Ibid.
41. 9/11 Commission, 12.
42. Heymann, 4.
43. Ibid., 64.
44. President Bush's remarks were made during a White House press conference on February 17, 2005.
45. From President Bush's remarks during a White House press conference on February 17, 2005.
46. Mark Mazzetti and David Sanger, "Spy Chief's Choice to Step Back Feeds Speculation," *New York Times*, January 5, 2007, http://www.nytimes.com/2007/01/05/washington/05intel.html?_r=1&oref=slogin
47. Ibid.
48. 9/11 Public Discourse Project, "Final Report on 9/11 Commission Recommendations," December 5, 2005, http://www.9-11pdp.org/press/2005-12-05_report.pdf
49. From the United States Intelligence Community web site, available at http://www.intelligence.gov/1-members.shtml (accessed January 4, 2009).
50. U.S. Department of State, "Patterns of Global Terrorism 2002," www.state.gov/s/ct/rls/pgtrpt/2002/html
51. David L. Aaron et al., "The Post 9/11 Partnership: Transatlantic Cooperation against Terrorism," Policy Paper, The Atlantic Council of the United States, December 2004, http://se2.isn.ch/serviceengine/FileContent?serviceID=PublishingHouse&fileid=314CA3A0-B359-B009-DA3B-9D9FA889FBEE&lng=en
52. *The 9/11 Commission Report* (New York: W.W. Norton, 2004), 420.
53. Commission on the Prevention of Weapons of Mass Destruction, Proliferation and Terrorism, *World at Risk* (New York: Vintage Books, 2008), 89.

PART 3

The Media and the Public

CHAPTER 14

Terrorist Propaganda and the Media

AUGUST 19, 2003: ANOTHER SHOCKING SUICIDE BOMBING SINCE the beginning of the second Palestinian intifada, or uprising. A city bus packed with families returning from Judaism's holiest site, the Western Wall, is ripped to pieces by a powerful explosion. It is an unspeakable scene of carnage. Twenty people, among them six children, are killed. More than a hundred are injured. Traumatized survivors and witnesses. Disheartened rescuers. Shortly after the blast and well before the dead and critically injured men, women, and children are identified, a cell of the Palestinian Hamas group releases a written press statement claiming responsibility for the attack and a pretaped video of the "martyr" explaining his deed. The videotape shows twenty-nine-year-old Raed Abdul Hamid Misk holding a rifle in one hand and a Qu'ran in the other. The father of two young children with a pregnant wife, and the imam of a Hebron mosque, justifies his attack on innocents partially in Arabic and partially in English. His wife does not seem surprised when she says, "All his life he was saying, 'Oh God, I wish to be a martyr.'"[1]

By making the videotape available to the media nearly simultaneously with the explosion, the terrorists calculated correctly that the news media would pay a great deal of attention to Misk. He did not fit the profile of Palestinian suicide bombers—not in terms of his profession, age, or family status. This assured him and his act special media attention around the world when details about his victims were not yet available. During the following days, the media's interest in this unlikely terrorist remained high. Five days after the attack, for example, the New York Times illustrated a general story on suicide attacks with a huge color photograph of Misk; taken three days before he killed himself in order to kill others, the photograph showed the smiling father with his three-year-old son and two-year-old daughter in his arms. Here was a compelling image that made people wonder what conditions could drive such a man to become a human bomb. This was precisely the effect that terrorists hope for. In this particular case, the news added up to an utterly successful publicity campaign that couldn't have been better orchestrated by the best experts on Madison Avenue.

The same was true for an earlier case that unfolded in Russia's capital. Soon after heavily armed Chechen separatists seized a theater in Moscow on October 21, 2002, their accomplices delivered videotapes to the Moscow bureau of the Arab satellite news network Al Jazeera. They explained that they had chosen to die on "the path of struggling for the freedom of the Chechen."[2] The videotape was played by TV networks and stations around the world. As many of the hundreds of hostages inside used their cellular phones to communicate with families and friends, some of them conveyed the chilling messages of their captors to the Russian public and especially to Russian President Vladimir V. Putin. The hostage-holders left no doubt that they would blow up the building and kill hundreds of innocent people unless the Putin government ordered the withdrawal of Russian troops from Chechnya. At the height of the siege, one of the captors grabbed the cell phone from a hostage who was speaking to a local radio station and delivered a tirade against Russia's war against the Chechen people.

Although local politicians noted how media savvy these hostage-takers were, the Chechens did not break new ground. During the Iranian hostage crisis of 1979–1981 and subsequent hostage situations in and around Beirut throughout the 1980s, the captors repeatedly produced videotapes that depicted the plight of their American hostages. Such tapes were made available to Western news organizations—in some instances with the mutual understanding that the material would be aired unedited.

Devoted Father Turned Suicide Bomber

Before Raed Abdul Hamid Misk went on his deadly suicide mission that killed twenty Israelis, he posed with his two young children for a picture to be made available to the press after he had killed himself to kill others. Because the imam of a mosque in Hebron and devoted family man did not fit the profile of a suicide terrorist, he, his deed, and his pregnant widow received a great deal of media attention.

Similarly, terrorists have used cell phones for as long as they have been available to communicate their demands and grievances to their target audiences. Thus, the Abu Sayyaf, Muslim separatists in the southern Philippines utilized cellular phones to contact radio stations and communicate their demands for the release of their Western and Asian hostages.

Former British Prime Minister Margaret Thatcher was right when she said that publicity is the oxygen of terrorism. Terrorists at all times understood this and acted accordingly. Nearly 2000 years ago and long before Johannes Gutenberg invented the printing press, the Sicarii, an extremist sect active in the Jewish Zealots' struggle in Palestine, attacked the Roman occupiers of their land (and fellow Jews who did not share their agenda) on religious holidays at the most crowded places. This way, the Sicariis made sure that eyewitnesses would spread the word of their violence. The anarchists of the nineteenth century explained their political violence as "propaganda of the deed" and thereby indicated that their terror strikes were designed to get their messages across to their targets: the governments they opposed and the publics they wanted to shock and turn against the existing regimes.

Contemporary terrorists, too, commit violence in order to spread their propaganda, but modern communication technology has equipped today's terrorists far better than their predecessors. Well aware of the news media's appetite for featuring violence-as-crime and violence-as-terrorism, terrorists have staged increasingly shocking and deadly acts with the knowledge that the resulting news coverage will further their goals. They believe that the most spectacular and the most bloody events will result in the most extensive media coverage.

Whenever possible, terrorists do not depend on the media's gatekeepers to facilitate their desire for publicity, but rather try to convey their messages directly. This was also true for earlier terrorists. Thus, using his anarchist newspaper *Freiheit* as a platform, John Most urged his comrades to prepare posters in advance of their terrorist actions in order to explain their motives rather than depend on hostile newspapers to carry their message. More recent terrorists have utilized copying machines, mobile radio transmitters, their own television stations, cellular phones, audiotapes, videotapes, and, most of all, the Internet. But the traditional mass media—namely, newspapers, newsmagazines, radio, and television—remain the most important targets in the terrorist publicity scheme because they are still the predominant sources of information. Because they guarantee freedom of expression and press freedom, liberal democracies have been especially susceptible to terrorist messages; the fundamental civil liberties in democracies play into the terrorists' appetite for publicity. But the recent proliferation of global television networks has increased terrorists' opportunities to address audiences in those parts of the world where governments curb the domestic press.

Publicity: The Universal Terrorist Goal

Although publicity is what one may call a universal goal of terrorists, it is never their only and ultimate objective. As described in Chapter 8, terrorists have short-term and long-term political ambitions and goals. But they are well aware that publicity is the absolutely necessary means to their ultimate political ends. Governments could simply ignore terrorists and their violence—or at least many of such deeds—and they would probably do so were it not for news coverage and its real or anticipated effects on the general public. According to Bruce Hoffman, all terrorists share one trait: Each group wants "maximum publicity to be generated by its [terrorism's] actions."[3] Thus, although terrorists differ with respect to their specific short-term and long-term political goals, they all understand that their most important political objectives are not obtainable without getting their messages across to a larger audience or, in other words, without receiving publicity via the mass media. In their writings and in interviews, terrorists have revealed that they understand the importance of publicity in their scheme. Take the case of Leila Khaled, who, as a member of the Popular Front for the Liberation of Palestine, participated in hijacking operations. In 2000, thirty years after a quadruple hijacking coup that made her famous, she revealed in an interview that she had to be pushed by the PFLP leadership to meet with media representatives and explain the group's causes. She said that she told Dr. George Habash, the PFLP's leader, that she was afraid of talking to reporters. Habash thought it strange that this woman was not afraid to hijack airplanes but balked at meeting the press. He told her that she had participated in the hijacking to tell the whole world about the Palestinian cause and that she had to speak for her comrades who were in jail. And Khaled obeyed and faced the press.

Terrorists have demonstrated time and again that they understand the importance of the mass media by the way they have acted during and after terrorist incidents. Reporting from Tehran during the Iran hostage crisis in 1979, CBS correspondent Tom Fenton recognized that the captors, who claimed to be students but may have been part of the Revolutionary Guards, were very resourceful in getting the press to report their side of the story. According to Fenton,

> It did not take them long to realize that this is a media event. The students have even attempted to buy off television networks by offering an unpublished American embassy secret document in return for five minutes unedited air time.[4]

The Red Army faction in West Germany and its successor cells timed their terrorist attacks so that the news coverage would be particularly generous: They struck on days when the news holes in newspapers were larger than on other days. Reporters who covered the TWA hijacking ordeal in 1985 noted that the hijackers and their Hezbollah supporters in Beirut were well aware of the geographic reach of the American media, the audience size of different media types, the working of press pools, and the advantages of scheduling live interviews during TV networks' popular morning and early evening news broadcasts. According to some reports, graduates of media studies and communications programs at American universities acted as advisors to the hijackers and those who negotiated on the terrorists' behalf. Following these experts' advice, the militants granted television reporters preferential treatment for the sake of reaching the largest audiences. But there was another reason for favoring television over print: Terrorists were aware that visual images affect audiences far more deeply and for longer periods of time than the spoken or written word. In other words, terrorists knew in the past, as they know today, that one picture is worth a thousand words—and probably more.

In a real sense, then, the immediate victims of bombings, hijackings, kidnappings, and other terrorist acts are simply pawns in the plays that terrorists stage in order to engage their domestic and international audiences. But unlike the producers who stage a drama on Broadway or in theaters elsewhere, terrorists cannot reach their intended audiences unless they generate a great deal of news coverage.

The most lethal and shocking terrorist attacks always result in massive news reporting, but minor terrorist activities often trigger extraordinary media attention as well, if they are staged cleverly at the right place and at the right time. A good example was a meeting of the World Trade Organization (WTO) in Seattle, Washington, in late 1999. Even before delegates from all over the globe had met for their opening session, violence broke out. While an estimated 40,000 union members, environmentalists, and other antiglobalization activists demonstrated peacefully against WTO policies, a rather small number of masked protesters in fatigues pulled hammers, baseball bats, M-80 firecrackers, and spray cans out of their knapsacks and vandalized a number of well-known store chains, such as Starbucks, Nike, and Old Navy. The activities of the self-described anarchists and their subsequent clashes with police amounted to little more than a nuisance. But the news media headlined these occurrences as "the Battle of Seattle" and devoted a stunning amount of coverage to the doings of a handful of amateur terrorists, while reporting little—or nothing—about the legitimate protests and WTO proceedings. This was precisely what the anarchist clique had in mind; as sympathizers explained, they had not committed "mindless and adolescent vandalism—it was done for political reasons."[5]

Indeed, the tiny minority that had planned and carried out the violent actions received a great deal of news coverage, which introduced its rationale to the public. In the ten days following the disturbances in Seattle, the English-language wire services available in the LexisNexis database carried twenty-three dispatches that dealt specifically with the causes of these "anarchists." Thus, an Associated Press dispatch from December 3, 1999, explained why a group of anarchists was occupying a Seattle warehouse: "The occupation is a protest against the WTO because big business worldwide is a major cause of rising housing costs and homelessness."[6] Another AP story reported on the views of anarchists in Eugene, Oregon, and why they were involved in the violence at the WTO meeting in Seattle. According to the story, one Eugene resident explained, "People feel angry and alienated, unable to achieve change through conventional means. Peaceful protest just doesn't seem to work. So people are taking the Wild West approach, which is breaking windows, throwing rocks and sabotage."[7] Newspapers represented in the LexisNexis archive published eighty articles altogether about the role of these "anarchists," their ideology, and their opposition to the globalization stance of the WTO. None of the publications called the anarchists involved "terrorists" or their violence "terrorism." Newspapers were not the only media organizations that paid attention to the beliefs of these antiglobalization terrorists. ABC News reported in four news programs, NBC News in two, and CBS News and CNN in one news program each on the causes of this particular group.

Given this media attention, one must conclude that the publicity rationale undergirding political violence worked superbly. The anarchists themselves had made efforts to cultivate their media image. Some reporters who tried to interview the anarchists were advised to contact the group's "publicist." Although chiding the "corporate media" for biased reporting, the group, said to share Unabomber Theodore Kaczynski's antitechnology, anticonsumerism views, recognized the value of nonstop media attention. "The WTO protests are a watershed," followers proclaimed on one web site, predicting that "after the Battle of Seattle the anarchists will no longer be ignored."[8]

With the huge media success of Seattle as a feather in their cap, antiglobalization extremists upstaged their far more numerous nonviolent brethren at subsequent international forums with antiglobalization terrorism that became increasingly violent. In April 2001, for example, black-clad anarchists with ski masks or handkerchiefs over their mouths led the charge against the Summit of the Americas in Quebec City, Canada. There was no doubt the much-publicized violence in Seattle had been the fuse that had ignited more serious political violence during meetings of the International Monetary Fund, the World Bank, and other international organizations. The radical organizers mentioned the Seattle model on their web sites and on the streets of Quebec City, Prague, Nice, and wherever else they staged their violence. As one masked demonstrator said, "If we can pass our message, we have gone in a good direction."[9]

An Alternative View: Contemporary Terrorists Do Not Need Publicity

When terrorists struck in the 1970s and 1980s, they typically claimed responsibility for their deeds and communicated their motives. But more recently, the perpetrators of major terrorist attacks have often failed to claim responsibility in an explicit and timely fashion. Some experts in the field concluded, therefore, that a new "terrorism of expression" or "expressive terrorism" had emerged. Typically committed by religious or pseudoreligious fanatics, the new "faceless" superterrorism is said to have no publicity goals. According to Avishai Margalit, these terrorists "lack clearly defined political ends" but give vent to "rage against state power and to feelings of revenge." They want to inflict the greatest amount of pain on their targets.[10] But this argument has weaknesses. Proponents of the expressive terrorism theory point to the first World Trade Center bombing in 1993 as a milestone. But this case was in reality one in which the perpetrators did claim responsibility and explained their grievances against the United States in a typewritten letter mailed to the *New York Times*. The FBI determined that the letter was authentic and found the typewriter on which it had been written in the possession of a man who turned out to belong to the group that had plotted the bombing.

In other instances, terrorists left important clues that revealed their motives. Timothy McVeigh and his accomplice Terry Nichols did not contact news organizations to claim responsibility for the Oklahoma City bombing. However, by detonating their destructive bomb on the second anniversary of the FBI's and other federal agents' ill-fated actions against a heavily armed group of religious extremists, the Branch Davidians, in Waco, Texas, the duo ensured that the media would figure out their motive—revenge for Waco. McVeigh wanted the greatest amount of news coverage for his act of terrorism. Before he was executed in June 2001, he said in an interview, "I don't think there is any doubt the Oklahoma City blast was heard around the world." McVeigh said furthermore that he had attacked the Alfred P. Murrah Federal Building in Oklahoma City because it had "plenty of open space around it, to allow for the best possible news photos and television footage." He left no doubt that he wanted to "make the loudest statement . . . and create a stark, horrifying image that would make everyone who saw it stop and take notice." Anticipating that he might be killed or arrested after fleeing the bombing site, McVeigh left an envelope filled with newspaper articles and documents in his getaway car to make sure that the world would be informed of his motives.[11]

Following the simultaneous bombings of the U.S. embassies in Kenya and Tanzania in August 1998, Osama bin Laden was covered as the likely architect of these terrorist strikes—although there was no immediate claim of responsibility. But two months earlier, the Saudi exile had told journalists that Americans were "easy targets" and that this would be obvious "in a very short time."[12] Michel Wieviorka has pointed out that some terrorists do not seek media attention. But he nevertheless recognized that the perpetrators of political violence will get news coverage—regardless of whether they seek it or not.[13]

It is likely that terrorists who make no claims would be pleased when their deeds are highlighted in the news. For this reason, Dale Van Atta has rejected the notion of the media's diminished role in the terrorist calculus, arguing that the "very act of intending to kill hundreds in airplane and building explosions means they [terrorists] seek sensational coverage for their deeds. . . . Like it or not, the media is still an integral part of achieving the terrorist's aim—and therefore must be as judicious and responsible as possible in its reportage."[14] Thomas Friedman, the Pulitzer Prize–winning *New York Times* columnist, has suggested that bin Laden transcends the scope of a mere terrorist because of his geopolitical aspirations and that the Al Qaeda leader employs "violence not to grab headlines but to kill as many Americans as possible to drive them out of the Islamic world and weaken their society."[15] But bin Laden and his associates contradict this conclusion. Thus, an Al Qaeda training manual advised recruits to target "sentimental landmarks" such as the Statue of Liberty in New York, Big Ben in London, and the Eiffel Tower in Paris because their destruction would "generate intense publicity."[16] In the Al Qaeda training camps in Afghanistan, a video production crew produced propaganda material that was peddled to the Arab TV network Al Jazeera. Even when Al Qaeda's leaders were on the run, there were, thanks to Arab TV networks, frequent mass-mediated communications.

Terrorism and the Triangle of Communication

To be at least partially successful, terrorists calculate that they need and will get access to what one might call the triangle of political communication. The mass media, governmental decision-makers, and the public constitute the corners of this triangle (see Figure 14.1). By staging horrific spectaculars, terrorists gain instant access to the

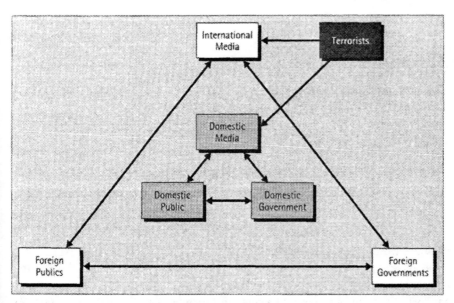

FIGURE 14.1 Terrorists and the Triangle of Communication
Source: Author.

communication triangle: The media report—and overreport—the public watches, and decision-makers pay attention to both the media's frenzy and the public's fearful reactions. Terrorists are first of all interested in accessing the domestic communications links, but they are also interested in tapping into the international or global triangle. Although the history of terrorism is littered with failures as far as the ultimate or long-term objectives of terror movements are concerned, terrorists are stunningly successful in spreading their "propaganda by the deed," and they harm their target societies in many different ways. Of course, as described later in Chapter 16, when public officials respond to terrorism, they, too, can and do exploit the triangle of communication for their purposes.

Media-Related Goals

Walter Laqueur has suggested that a terrorist strike without news coverage "would defeat the whole purpose of the exercise—the deed would pass unheralded and unrecognized."[17] This is reminiscent of a famous cartoon by Robert Mankoff that the *Saturday Review* published many years ago. The drawing depicts a father and his son. "Dad," the son asks, "if a tree falls in the forest, and the media are not there to report it, has the tree really fallen?" If one imagines for a moment that no newspaper, no newsmagazine, no radio station, no television network, and no Internet site reports on a terrorist act, the result would be nearly as if the violent deed did not happen at all. But what is imaginable in cartoons is unimaginable in reality. As a general rule, terrorist incidents further the perpetrators' universal or media-related goals—regardless of whether they also advance their short-term or long-term political objectives. There are three goals in particular that terrorists tie to news coverage and other forms of communication: (1) They want attention; (2) they want their grievances, demands, and objectives recognized; and (3) they want to win respect and even gain legitimacy in some circles, countries, or regions. The obvious question is, of course, to what extent do media organizations facilitate these objectives?

The Attention-Getting Goal

The most fundamental role of a free press is to fully inform the public. Thus, the issue here is not whether the media should cover terrorist events, but rather how much and what kind of coverage should be devoted to terrorist incidents. Violence has always been an attractive topic for the press, regardless of whether it is criminal or political in nature. News organizations tend to overcover terrorist strikes when they are especially dramatic and shocking and offer plenty of human interest. The 444 days of the Iran hostage crisis were a case in point in that the three television networks—ABC News, CBS News, and NBC News—respectively devoted during November and December 1979 54%, 50%, and 48% of their evening news broadcasts to the incident. Although the volume decreased in the following twelve months, the hostage situation remained the number-one news story throughout its duration—even though not a single hostage was killed. During the two weeks of the TWA hijacking crisis in 1985, about two-thirds of the networks' evening news broadcasts were filled by reports on the drama in Lebanon and its effects elsewhere. Media expert Benjamin Bagdikian called the coverage of the TWA incident "excessive for strictly self-serving, competitive reasons" and complained that as a result, other important news had been obliterated.[18] Although the print press has escaped similar criticism, newspapers and newsmagazines displayed the same appetite for terrorist dramas as the television networks. During the 1985 TWA hijacking situation, for example, the *New York Times* devoted an average of 19%, the *Washington Post* 18%, and the *Los Angeles Times* 15% of their total national/international news coverage to this incident. However, unlike the television networks with their limited airtime for newscasts, newspapers tend to have enough space to report on other news developments as well.[19] And while the broadcast networks and the print media overemphasize reporting on terrorism, their coverage pales in comparison to that of the all-news cable and satellite networks.

There was, however, one shocking incident in the early 1970s that received an up-to-then unprecedented amount of news coverage: the assault on members of Israel's national team during the 1972 Olympic Games in Munich by the Palestinian Black September group. The architects of the assault had chosen this site to take advantage of the international media present in Germany to report on the sports competition. It was estimated at the time that between 600 and 800 million people around the globe watched the deadly drama in Munich. Nearly three decades after the Munich ordeal, cable and satellite television and a multitude of specialty channels have joined the broadcast networks. CNN and other truly global networks are watched around the world. As a result, one can assume that far more people saw the horrific images of 9/11 than those of the events in Munich. In the United States, television and radio reported virtually nothing else in the days and nights following the 9/11 attacks. Not even commercials were aired. Most sports and entertainment channels switched to crisis news, many of them carrying the coverage of one of the networks; others suspended their programming altogether and simply showed the American flag on the screen. Newspapers and magazines devoted all or most of their news to the crisis. The media abroad, too, dedicated an extraordinary amount of time and space to the terrorist strikes in the United States.

Literally all Americans were aware of the 9/11 attacks. Opinion polls showed that 99% of the American public followed the news of the terrorist attacks by watching television or listening to the radio. Most adults identified television and radio as their primary sources for crisis information, but nearly two-thirds also mentioned the Internet as one of their information sources.[20] This initial universal interest in terrorism news did not weaken quickly. Probably affected by the news of anthrax attacks along the U.S. east coast, more than 90% of the public kept on watching the news about terrorism "very closely" or "closely" nearly six weeks after the events of 9/11.[21] For the architects of the 9/11 terror, this was a perfect score with respect to their desire to get attention. Moreover, foreign audiences were just as aware of the horrible events in the United States as were Americans.

By getting the attention of their target audience, terrorists achieve another objective: They intimidate their target society and spread fear and anxiety in the population. After all, terrorism is psychological warfare. The perpetrators of this sort of violence want to get to the psyche of the society they target. Public opinion surveys taken in the weeks after 9/11 revealed that many Americans were traumatized and feared that they or their loved ones could become the victims of future terrorism. Many suffered from depression and were unable to sleep. In some other countries, especially in Europe, the public expressed similar fears and anxieties. These feelings did not evaporate in the following months and even years—especially not in the United States. One month before the second anniversary of the 9/11 attacks, for example, 34% of New Yorkers

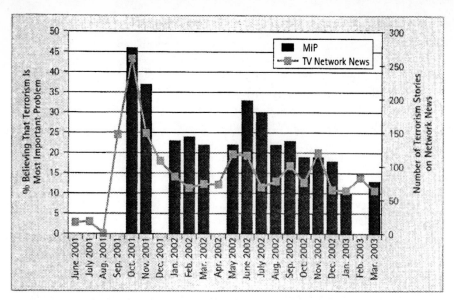

FIGURE 14.2 Volume of Terrorism News and Public Opinion on Terrorist Threat
Source: Pippa Norris, Montague Kern, and Marion Just, *Framing Terrorism: The News Media, the Government, and the Public* (New York: Routledge, 2003).

were "very concerned" and 47% were "concerned" that there would be more terror attacks in the United States. At the same time, 22% of Americans across the country were "very concerned" and 54% "concerned" that terrorists might strike again within U.S. borders.[22] As one would expect, the public's concerns reflected the volume of the news devoted to terrorism and to the events of 9/11 in particular. In the months preceding 9/11, when Americans were asked about the most important problem their country faced, terrorism was not mentioned at all. As Figure 14.2 shows, after the strikes in New York and Washington, terrorism ranked high in the public's perception of what was the most important problem for the United States. As the volume of terrorism news declined somewhat during the following months, the public's ranking of the terrorism threat subsided similarly.

The Recognition Goal

The leader of the Popular Front for the Liberation of Palestine, Dr. George Habash, once explained that by committing political violence, his group forced people to ask, "What is going on?"[23] A member of the Japanese Red Army who had participated in an attack on a large crowd at Tel Aviv airport in 1972 explained his motives after his arrest: He and his comrades had killed twenty-eight innocent people in order to propel the Palestinian cause onto the world stage. This was also the rationale behind Black September's attack on Israeli athletes that same year during the Olympic Games. During this hair-raising incident, many people around the world learned for the first time about this group and similar organizations, and—more importantly—they learned about the grievances and demands of these terrorists. During the Iran hostage crisis, the Iranian captors granted interviews to U.S. correspondents in order to air their grievances against the United States. CBS News correspondent Tom Fenton reported about a meeting with the young hostage-holders:

> They spoke bitterly about corruption and murder under the deposed Shah's regime, America's role in supporting him, their deep resentment when he was allowed to enter the United States, and their fear that the American government is trying to topple the new Iranian regime.[24]

Terrorists also get hostages to speak out in support of their causes, grievances, and demands—sometimes by force, sometimes by persuasion, and sometimes by exposing their captives to situations in which the so-called Stockholm syndrome kicks in: the tendency of some hostages to identify with their captors. During the 1985 TWA hijacking crisis, one of the hostages said during a news conference his captors had staged, "We understand that Israel is holding as hostage [sic] a number of Lebanese people who undoubtedly have as equal a right and as strong a desire to go home as we do." He called on the governments and people involved in the negotiations to free him and the other American hostages to "allow justice and compassion to guide their way."[25]

Government officials are critical of the media's willingness, if not eagerness, to give terrorists a public platform to articulate their motives. Former National Security Advisor Zbigniew Brzezinski, for example, criticized television news in particular for permitting terrorists to appeal directly to the American public.[26] But journalists and others in the news media consider it part of their responsibility to present all important views and put the news about terrorist incidents into a larger political context. Tom Brokaw once said,

> Terrorism often does have political roots and we have to deal with these political roots. It is not always, although it appears that way, a mindless act of sheer terrorism for the sake of terrorism. There is generally some political context as well and I think we have to work harder at putting it into some kind of political context, however strong or weak that context might be.[27]

A content analysis of news reports on terrorism aired by the three TV networks (as mentioned, ABC News, CBS News, and NBC News) from 1981 through 1986 found that 74% were predominantly "episodic" (focusing on individual acts of terrorism and their effects) and 26% "thematic" (framing terrorism in the larger context of a political problem). This means that a surprisingly large proportion of the news on terrorism—more than a quarter of the total reporting—described, articulated, or commented on the root causes of terrorist violence. In contrast, this same study found that only 11% of all domestic crime stories during this six-year period were "thematic" in nature.[28]

Before the 9/11 terror attacks, the vast majority of American news organizations reported far less from abroad than their European counterparts. Moreover, foreign news reporting was predominantly episodic and concentrated on a particular case at hand, rather than thematic and focusing on underlying conditions, developments, and attitudes. After 9/11, there was far more thematic or contextual coverage of Arab and Muslim countries than before the attacks. By striking hard at the United States, the terrorists enticed the media to explore their grievances in ways that transcended by far the quantity and quality of the precrisis coverage. This had an impact on the public in the United States and elsewhere in the West. Suddenly, people wanted to know why people in faraway countries wanted to kill Americans. Nobody seemed

In Holland, at one of the centers, the number of people who accepted Islam during the days that followed the operations [of 9/11] were more than the people who accepted Islam in the last eleven years.

I heard someone on Islamic radio who owns a school in America say: "We don't have time to keep up with the demands of those who are asking about Islamic books to learn more about Islam." This event made people think, which benefited Islam greatly.[29]

There are no data on conversions to Islam in the West on the heels of the 9/11 attacks, but universities and adult education programs added courses on Islam and the Middle East because of the increased demand. News coverage helped kindle this sudden interest. One comprehensive content analysis of religious news in ten American daily newspapers, nine newsmagazines, and one wire service (the Associated Press) found that stories on Islam and Muslims dominated this coverage in the weeks following the events of 9/11. Indeed, 70% of the stories fully devoted to religion concerned Islam and Muslims, and the remaining 30% dealt with Christianity and Christians, multifaith issues, Judaism and Jews, nondenominational issues, and Buddhism and Buddhists.[30]

It is certainly understandable that after 9/11 the media devoted an extraordinary amount of column inches and airtime to Muslims, Arabs, and the religion of Islam at home and abroad. But one would have wished that the press had paid more attention to the sentiments among Arabs and Muslims in the years and decades before 9/11— not as a direct result of an act of terrorism. If one accepts the notion that terrorists strike in order to publicize their grievances, bin Laden and Al Qaeda were extraordinary successful in realizing this objective.

The Respectability/Legitimacy Goal

On September 26, 1990, during the buildup to the first Persian Gulf War in 1991, Dr. George Habash of the Popular Front for the Liberation of Palestine was interviewed by Ted Koppel on the ABC News *Nightline* program. Habash threatened a wave of terrorism against American targets if the United States made a military move against Iraq. Saudi Arabia's ambassador to the United States, Prince Bandar bin Sultan, was another guest on the program. Koppel made no distinction between his two guests. Thus, it is not unreasonable to conclude that an appearance by an acknowledged terrorist side-by-side with an accredited diplomat bolstered the status of Habash. Or take the case of antiabortion terrorist Paul Jennings Hill, who was executed in Florida in September 2003—nine years after he had killed a physician and his security guard outside an abortion clinic in Pensacola. Before he targeted Dr. John Britton in 1994, Hill had promoted the killing of abortion providers by comparing them to Adolf Hitler; he condemned women who had abortions as "accessories to murder." The news media gave Hill, a former Presbyterian minister, plenty of opportunities to promote his crusade. According to the *New York Times*,

Even before his crimes, Mr. Hill was known for advocating violence against abortion providers and his extreme views had won him a high profile. With a serene voice and smile, he became a spokesman for the cause after another doctor, David Gunn, was shot

to death by Michael Griffin at Pensacola's other clinic in 1993. . . . In the months following Dr. Gunn's murder, Mr. Hill appeared on television shows like "Nightline" and "Donahue," where he drew parallels between killing an abortion doctor and killing Hitler. Mr. Hill insisted that murdering abortion providers was "justifiable homicide," a defense he attempted to use in his trial but that the judge would not allow.[31]

John O'Sullivan has correctly argued that the media, and especially television, bestow respectability and perhaps even legitimacy upon terrorists—simply by interviewing them the same way legitimate political actors are interviewed.[32] The same can be said about reporters who attend the news conferences staged by terrorist groups or about reports that refer to the "spokespersons" of terrorist organizations and the "communiques" they release. Osama bin Laden and his associates did not give interviews and did not hold news conferences after 9/11, but they communicated via fax messages, audiotapes, and videotapes. In the months following the attacks of 9/11, TV audiences found it impossible to miss the image of Osama bin Laden when channel surfing. This prominence in the news made bin Laden a household name around the world. To be sure, in the United States and many other countries, the Al Qaeda leader did not win the hearts and minds of the people. Instead, he became the evildoer-in-chief. But this played into his hands as well. After all, terrorists do not want to be loved by their targets; they want to be feared. This is especially true when they strike on the territory of a foreign enemy. But bin Laden became a larger-than-life hero in countries and regions where he wanted to establish or broaden his popular support. These gains in public esteem for bin Laden in the Arab and Muslim world were not short-lived. In 2003, when asked by pollsters about their confidence in "world figures" to do the right thing, Palestinians placed bin Laden first and Yassir Arafat second. In Jordan, Morocco, and Pakistan, bin Laden placed second; in Indonesia, third. In short, in some countries and regions, the Al Qaeda leader gained a tremendous amount of respectability and legitimacy precisely because of his association with the events of 9/11.

Bedfellows in a Marriage of Convenience

All in all, then, terrorists are very successful in realizing their three media-dependent objectives in that they receive news coverage that assures them a great deal of public and elite attention, spells out their causes and grievances, and earns them respect and even legitimacy in some circles. This is not to say that the media in countries plagued by domestic and/or foreign terrorism are wittingly supporting groups and individuals that perpetrate political violence. Take the case of the United States. The American media and terrorists are not accomplices. However, they are involved in a symbiotic relationship in that they feed off each other: The media want dramatic, shocking, disconcerting news that keeps readers, listeners, and viewers captivated and that bolsters the circulation of the print press and the ratings of the electronic media. Terrorists need to spread their propaganda to further their ultimate political objectives. To put it differently, the news media and terrorists are not involved in a love story; they are strange bedfellows in a marriage of convenience.

Following the Iran hostage crisis, Gary Sick observed that the situation "was the longest running human interest story in the history of television, in living colors from the other side of the world. Commercially it was a stunning success." Furthermore, he wrote, "It may never be known how many pairs of pantyhose and how many tubes of toothpaste were sold to this captive audience as a direct result of the hostage crisis, but the numbers are substantial."[33] Much has changed in the media landscape since the Iran hostage crisis ended in early 1981. Financial considerations became far more pressing in news organizations because of increasingly fierce competition caused by the proliferation of television channels, the emergence of the Internet as an increasingly attractive news source, and the creation of megamedia corporations with more commitment to profits than to serious news.

Under these circumstances, it is unrealistic to expect the media to curb their appetite for the news that terrorists provide. One wonders whether there could be an altogether different approach to prevent terrorism in the first place—with the assistance of media organizations. If terrorists strike primarily in order to force the media to publicize their deeds and their motives, why not cover the grievances of groups and individuals before they resort to terrorism? As desirable as the solution seems at first sight, it may be unrealistic to believe that the news media could grant terrorists a degree of access and coverage that would satisfy their appetite for front-page news.

Years ago, the widely respected journalist David Broder suggested that "the essential ingredient of any effective antiterrorist policy must be the denial to the terrorist of access to mass media outlets. The way by which this denial is achieved—whether by voluntary means of those of us in press and television, self-restraint, or by government control—is a crucial question for journalists and for all other citizens who share our beliefs in civil liberties."[34] While many in the American media would agree that the fourth estate, as the press is sometimes called, would be well advised to exercise self-restraint with respect to terrorism coverage, few would wish for government-imposed restrictions. In the past, some liberal democracies—for example, the United Kingdom, Germany, and Greece—adopted press laws that restricted news coverage during terrorist incidents and especially during hostage situations. These laws were enacted in response to domestic terrorism. But given the strong commitment to the First Amendment's constitutional guarantee of a free press, government censorship is less likely in the United States and is certainly not a desirable solution. The late publisher of the *Washington Post*, Katharine Graham, once said,

> Publicity may be the oxygen of terrorists. But I say this: News is the lifeblood of liberty. If the terrorists succeed in depriving us of freedom, their victory will be far greater than they ever hoped and far worse than we ever feared. Let it never come to pass.[35]

Terrorism and the Global Media

The problems surrounding terrorism coverage and possible restrictions are different today than in the past because of the emergence of global news networks. Today, neither government censorship nor self-censorship in the media prevents citizens from getting access to uncensored news. If such news is not offered by any of the global TV and radio networks, there is always the Internet. The Russian government learned this lesson in the fall of 2002, when Chechen separatists seized a Moscow theater and held hundreds of hostages. Although the Russian government was quite successful in preventing the news media—especially broadcasters—from reporting extensively on the crisis, the Russian public was well informed, thanks to global TV networks and the World Wide Web.

Defending the Media

Those who defend the media in this context point to terrorist situations in which reporters withheld sensitive information for fear that the news could harm American citizens. For example, a number of reporters learned that several Americans had escaped from the U.S. embassy in Tehran when it was taken over by militants in late 1979 and that these people had taken refuge in the Canadian embassy. Not one word was publicized until the Americans had left Iran. Other observers mention prudent intraorganizational guidelines that specify how to report and how not to report terrorist incidents, especially hostage situations. Indeed, most news organizations have adopted such guidelines. The problem is that these guidelines are not adhered to in the face of actual terrorist incidents.

The best case in defense of the media is based on their public-service role during terrorist situation. News organizations, especially radio and television networks and stations, are as essential for the management of a terrorist attack as they are during and after devastating earthquakes, floods, hurricanes, riots, or other natural and man-made disasters. This is particularly true of local and regional media outlets. In the case of the Oklahoma City bombing, for example,

> The local broadcast and cable stations functioned as conduits of communication between public officials and citizens in the affected city and region. For example, by disseminating officials' appeals to donate blood for the injured victims at specific locations, not to enter the immediate disaster area, or to contribute warm clothing for rescue workers, the media provided an excellent public service. Since many officials, who were involved in managing the crisis, followed the news about the disaster, the stations facilitated also the difficult task of coordinating emergency services that involved a great number of organizations and individuals.[36]

The media performed in an equally exemplary way in the hours and days following the terrorist attacks of 9/11 in New York, Washington, and Pennsylvania. According to one account,

> For crisis managers, the mass media offered the only effective means to tell the public about the immediate consequences of the crisis—what to do (donate blood of certain types, where to donate and when) and what not to do (initially, for example, not trying to drive into Manhattan because all access bridges and tunnels were closed). In this respect, the media served the public interest in the best tradition of disaster coverage.[37]

When people are directly or indirectly affected by an emergency, they immediately turn to the news media for information. If there is no electric power, battery-powered radios may be available. At no other times are radio and television audiences larger than during and after major disasters. According to one media scholar, the reasons for this demand are obvious:

> Information about [a] crisis, even if it is bad news, relieves disquieting uncertainties and calms people. This mere activity of watching or listening to familiar reporters and commentators reassures people and keeps them occupied. It gives them a sense of vicarious participation, of "doing something."
>
> News stories [also] serve to reassure people that their grief and fear are shared.[38]

Television and radio offer crisis managers the opportunity to directly address the public whenever they desire. About two hours after the first plane had hit one of the

World Trade Center towers, Mayor Rudy Giuliani was in the studio of New York 1, an all-news cable channel in New York City, to urge New Yorkers to remain calm and to evacuate lower Manhattan. But while the mayor was collected, decisive, and cool, he did not minimize what had happened but spoke of "a horrible, horrible situation."[39] By providing a public meeting place literally around the clock, whether via broadcasting, cable, or print, news organizations served the public's interest well in the hours and days after the terrorists struck New York and Washington. Perhaps that was the most important reason why the American public looked far more favorably upon the news media in the weeks after 9/11 than before the shocking events. However, these newly found public sympathies for the media were short-lived and soon replaced by far more critical public attitudes toward the press.

Treason or Public Service?

In mid-2006, when the *New York Times* revealed that the Bush administration monitored the flow of money through banking systems, including Swift, the Belgian-based banking consortium, in order to discover money trails to terrorist groups, administration officials and others condemned the paper for obstructing counterterrorist efforts and thereby helping terrorists. President Bush said, "We're at war with a bunch of people who want to hurt the United States of America, and for people to leak that program, and for a newspaper to publish it, does great harm to the United States of America."[40] There were similar condemnations, even charges of treason, after media organizations published reports on illegal electronic surveillance by the National Security Agency, the existence of secret CIA prisons for terrorist suspects abroad, and the CIA's practice of rendering alleged terrorists captured by American agents abroad to "third countries, countries with notorious reputations for political prisoners, such as Egypt, Syria, Morocco, and Uzbekistan."[41] Even local revelations resulted in controversies about the limits of press freedom. In December 2006, for example, the *New York Times* published a prominently placed report revealing that "the PATH train tunnels under the Hudson River are far more vulnerable to a bomb attack than previously thought, and that a relatively small amount of high explosives could cause significant flooding of the train system within hours."[42] In all of these cases—and many other stories about vulnerable and ill-protected possible terrorist targets, the crucial question is always whether such revelations harm American national security or actually help to alleviate wrongs and shortcomings in counterterrorism and homeland security efforts.

It is far from easy to decide whether to publicize or withhold sensitive material. With respect to the PATH tunnels' vulnerability to even a small bomb blast, one wonders whether the *New York Times'* public revelation, followed by similar stories in the *Los Angeles Times* and the *Wall Street Journal*, was the only and the best choice. The motive of the person who leaked the information to the news media was to force the responsible higher-ups in the Port Authority of New York and New Jersey to address the problems. It is entirely possible that an editor could have alerted the governors of New York and New Jersey to the Hudson tunnels' vulnerability and thereby assured action—without publicizing the material. Although it is well known that terrorists are well informed about the vulnerabilities of all kinds of sites in all kinds of target countries, why point them to particularly problematic venues? As for the controversial revelations of eavesdropping, the "outsourcing" of torture to countries some of which are listed by the U.S. Department of State as human rights violators, and other counterterrorist practices contrary to domestic and international laws and precious American values, they are condemned by some and defended by others—depending on one's feelings about what should and what should not be done in the name of national security in the "war on terrorism."

Notes

1. These quotes were published in many reports both in the print and broadcast media.
2. Michael Wines, "Hostage Drama in Moscow: The Moscow Front; Chechens Kill Hostage in Siege at Russian Hall," *New York Times*, October 25, 2002, A1.
3. Bruce Hoffman, *Inside Terrorism* (New York: Columbia University Press, 1998), 131.
4. Fenton reported this on the CBS *Evening News* on December 6, 1979. Similar observations were made by other broadcast and print correspondents during the long hostage crisis.
5. "Black blocs for dummies," www.infoshop.org/blackbloc.html
6. Nicholas K. Geranios, "Anarchists Occupy Building to Protest WTO," Associated Press, December 3, 1999, AM cycle.
7. Jeff Barnard, "Eugene Anarchists Long for a Simpler World," Associated Press, December 12, 1999, AM cycle.
8. The statement was posted at www.chumba.com/_gospel.htm.
9. Quoted in Robin Wright, "Bush Says Free Trade Is Key to Meeting Needs of the Poor," *Los Angeles Times*, April 22, 2001, www.latimes.com/cgi-bin/print.cgi
10. This argument is made, for example, by Avishai Margalit, "The Terror Master," *New York Review of Books*, October 5, 1995, 19.
11. McVeigh revealed a great deal about his right-wing ideology, his motives, and his desire for publicity in interviews with a reporter from the *Buffalo News*. Interview with Lou Michel, April 2001. See also Lou Michel and Dan Herbeck, *American Terrorist: Timothy McVeigh and the Oklahoma City Bombing* (New York: Regan Books, 2001), esp. pp. 168, 169, 227, 245, 382.
12. Based on what bin Laden said in this particular news conference as well as in other communications, it was not difficult to pinpoint him as the driving force behind the bombings in East Africa. The quotes from his news conference in Khost, Afghanistan, are from Dale Van Atta, "Carbombs and Cameras: The Need for Responsible Media Coverage," *Harvard International Review* (Fall 1998): 66.
13. Michel Wieviorka, *The Making of Terrorism* (Chicago: University of Chicago Press, 1993), 46, 47.
14. Van Atta, 68.
15. Thomas L. Friedman, "No Mere Terrorist," *New York Times*, March 24, sec. 4, 15.
16. Hamza Hendawi, "Terror Manual Advises on Targets," http://story.news.yahoo.com/ (retrieved February 11, 2002).
17. Walter Laqueur, *The Age of Terrorism* (Boston: Little, Brown, 1987), 123.
18. Bagdikian's testimony before a congressional committee was mentioned in "Closer Look at Network Coverage of TWA flight 847," *Broadcasting*, August 5, 1985.
19. For more on the coverage of terrorist incidents in the 1980s and early 1990s, see Brigitte L. Nacos, *Terrorism and the Media* (New York: Columbia University Press, 1994).
20. According to a *Los Angeles Times* telephone poll on September 13–14, 2001, 83% of the respondents said they watched the news "very closely," 15% "closely," and 2% "not too closely." Nobody chose the response option "not closely at all." The Gallup Organization found in a survey conducted on September 14–15, 2001, that 77% of the public followed the news "very closely," 20% "somewhat closely," 2% "not too closely," and 1% "not at all." An ABC/*Washington Post* poll on September 11, 2001, found that 99% of the public followed the news on television and radio. Polling online adults on September 11 and 12, 2001, Harris Interactive found that 93% identified television and radio as their primary news source, and 64% mentioned the Internet as one of their primary sources.
21. According to a survey conducted by the Pew Research Center for the People and the Press on October 17–21, 2001, 78% of the respondents said they watched terrorism news very closely,

22% watched closely, 5% not closely, and 1% gave no answer. This was about the same level of interest as in mid-September (13–17), when 74% of survey respondents revealed that they watched terrorism news very closely, 22% closely. In fact, more Americans watched this kind of news very closely in the second half of October than in mid-September.

22. The poll was conducted by the Marist College Institute for Public Opinion from August 5 to 20, 2003.
23. Habash is quoted in Martha Crenshaw, "The Logic of Terrorism," in Walter Reich, ed., *Origins of Terrorism* (New York: Cambridge University Press, 1990), 18.
24. Nacos, *Terrorism and the Media*, 61.
25. Ibid., 62.
26. Neil Hickey, "The Impact of Negotiations: What the Experts Say," *TV Guide*, September 21, 1985.
27. Brokaw made his remarks during a seminar on "The Media and Terrorism," organized by the Center for Communications, Inc., October 23, 1985.
28. Shanto Iyengar, *Is Anyone Responsible? How Television Frames Political Issues* (Chicago: University of Chicago Press, 1991), ch. 4.
29. From a bin Laden videotape presumably made in mid-November 2001.
30. "A Spiritual Awakening: Religion in the Media, Dec. 2000–Nov. 2001," study prepared by Douglas Gould & Co. for the Ford Foundation.
31. Abby Goodnough, "Florida Executes Killer of an Abortion Provider," *New York Times*, September 4, 2003, A16.
32. John O'Sullivan, "Media Publicity Causes Terrorism," in Bonnie Szumski, ed., *Terrorism: Opposing Viewpoints* (St. Paul, MN: Greenhaven, 1986), 73.
33. Gary Sick, *All Fall Down: America's Tragic Encounter with Iran* (New York: Penguin, 1986), 258–59.
34. Broder made his remarks during a seminar on "The Media and Terrorism," sponsored by the Center for Communication, Inc., October 23, 1985.
35. Katharine Graham, "The Media Must Report Terrorism," in Szumski, 81.
36. Brigitte Nacos, *Terrorism and the Media: From the Iran Hostage Crisis to the Oklahoma City Bombing* (New York: Columbia University Press, 1996), xiii, xiv.
37. Brigitte L. Nacos, *Mass-Mediated Terrorism: The Central Role of the Media in Terrorism and Counterterrorism* (Lanham, MD: Rowman & Littlefield, 2002), 51.
38. Doris Graber, *Mass Media and American Politics* (Washington, DC: Congressional Quarterly Press, 1997), 143.
39. For more on the media and crisis management, see Nacos, *Mass-Mediated Terrorism*, ch. 6.
40. Sheryl Gay Stolberg, "Bush Condemns Report on Sifting of Bank Records," *New York Times*, June 27, 2006, http://select.nytimes.com/search/restricted/article?res= F50610FB3C540C748EDDAF0894DE404482
41. Raymond Bonner, "The CIA's Secret Torture." *The New York Review of Books*, January 11, 2007, 28.
42. William K. Rashbaum and William Neuman, "Path Tunnels Seen as Fragile in Bomb Attack, *New York Times*, December 22, 2006, http://select.nytimes.com/search/restricted/article?res= F2071EFC3A550C718EDDAB0994DE404482

CHAPTER 15

Terror and Hate in Cyberspace

IN THE FALL OF 2002, SECRET MESSAGES ATTRIBUTED TO Osama bin Laden and meant for his followers only were hidden on senobite.com, a site started by a fan of science fiction writer Clive Barker. Other web sites were used for the same purpose. According to experts, the operators of these sites had no idea of the uninvited posts because the data were in a hidden file that could only be accessed by entering a code. For this reason, one Internet security expert called the intrusion a "parasite attack." A few months before these parasitic activities began, a Maryland-based hacker had successfully hijacked the alneda.com site known for carrying pro–Al Qaeda propaganda. The seemingly harmless exchanges on alneda.com's message board were believed to contain coded communications between members of the terrorist organization. Azzam.com, another web site devoted to militant Islamicist propaganda, was repeatedly bumped by Internet service providers (ISPs) and attacked by hackers. In September 2003, for example, the Azzam.com site carried the message "Hacked, tracked, and NOW owned by the U.S.A." Azzam News, which is based in the United Kingdom, switched to a site called IslamicAwakening.com, where it was welcome to post its material, according to Azzam News, "so long as it is within the regulation of the British law." But in one of Azzam News' discussion boards, a poster urged believers to use the Internet for the cause of Allah. Another discussant recommended the utilization of computers and other electronic devices—albeit in a careful manner—because "they can be tracked." Suggesting computer hacking, the poster specified,

> *Among the targets of hacking should be military installations, intelligence departments such as NSA, CIA, FBI, MI5, Mossad, NASA, civilian police forces and national guards, so called "united nations peace keeping troops" which are none other than the army of democracy and America and any and every disbelieving organization responsible for military and economic support against the muslims.*[1]

Al Qaeda and other extreme Muslim groups and individuals are not the only ones that have incorporated the Internet into their strategy of hate and terror. Religious and secular groups and individuals of all ideological bents utilize all aspects of high-tech communication technology, especially the Internet. In 2000, for example, Israeli hackers and their supporters abroad launched electronic attacks against Islamic militants' web sites, while Palestinians and their supporters in the Middle East, the United States, and elsewhere targeted sites in Israel and in the United States. At one point, a picture of the Israeli flag occupied the web site of Hezbollah's television station, Al-Manar, for twelve hours and Israel's national anthem was heard whenever someone accessed Hezbollah's site. While this seemed like a coup in the struggle for propaganda supremacy, an attack on the site of the American Israeli Public Affairs Committee, a lobbying organization based in the United States, had far more serious consequences: Besides plastering the site with anti-Israeli slogans, a Pakistani hacker accessed thousands of e-mail addresses and credit card numbers stored in the organization's computers, sent anti-Israeli messages to these addresses, and published the stolen credit card data on the Internet.

It was never learned whether Israeli or Arab individuals threw the first cyber bomb in this electronic tit-for-tat exchange: Both sides invaded hostile web sites and/or swamped them with so much e-mail that they became hopelessly overloaded and completely incapacitated. Israeli hackers put the sites of the Palestinian National Authority, Hezbollah, and Hamas temporarily out of commission; Arab militants and Muslim sympathizers elsewhere hit Israeli sites just as hard by taking down those of the foreign ministry, the Israeli Defense Forces, the prime minister, the Knesset (Parliament), the Bank of Israel, and the Tel Aviv Stock Exchange. Appeals on both sides drew a large number of supporters who participated in the campaigns. By simply clicking their mouse, visitors to the respective sites triggered automated e-mail

The Internet as Terrorists' Best Friend

Like most terrorist groups in the United States and around the world, the World Church of the Creator, a white supremacy organization, used its web site as its most effective recruiting tool and propaganda organ. The picture shows Matt Hale, the now-imprisoned leader of the group, as he worked on the organization's web site at his home in Peoria, Illinois.

systems that sent out messages on their behalf. Hezbollah attributed the crashing of its site, which normally got between 100,000 and 300,000 hits a day, to "nine million hits per day, mainly from Israel, the United States, and to a lesser degree from Canada and South Africa."[2]

What the Palestinians came to call "Internet intifada" and Islamic extremists termed an "e-jihad" bolstered their hope that the Internet offered them a level playing field. Hezbollah's webmaster, Ali Ayoub, quoted the late Ayatollah Ruhollah Khomeini of Iran, who once hypothesized that if every Arab threw a bucket of water on Israel, the Jewish state would drown. According to Ayoub, "This is exactly what happened, supporters of the resistance from all over the world, both Arabs and foreigners, are contributing."[3]

These cyberattacks changed nothing in the actual Middle East conflict, but they did reward both sides with attention in the conventional news media. In this sense, the electronic attacks and counterattacks represented another dimension of terrorism—with a comforting twist: No human life was lost, no human being was injured, and the material and psychological damages were minor in comparison to real terror strikes. In the real world, only a limited number of extremists commit and actively promote mass-mediated political violence; in cyberspace, far more sympathizers are willing to click the mouse and participate in cyberattacks.

Luring an innocent teenager simply because of his religion and nationality into a prearranged ambush under the pretense of a passionate romance qualifies as an act of terrorism. But while the fate of Ofir Rahum (see box on the following page) is a unique case—for the time being, that is—the use of the Internet by terrorists and their sympathizers for the purpose of hate is very common.

Terrorists and the Newest Communications Technologies

Terrorists have always embraced the newest communications technologies and added them to the previously available media. For example, the Brazilian Marxist revolutionary Carlos Marighella, who became the idol of many left-wing terrorists far beyond Latin America, recommended in the post–World War II period the use of copying machines to produce large numbers of propaganda pamphlets and manifestos. As broadcasting transmitters became lighter and easy to transport, groups with direct or indirect involvement in terrorism established their own radio and television facilities. In the early 1990s, the Lebanon-based Hezbollah organization started its own television station, Al-Manar. Al-Manar's satellite channels became popular in Palestinian homes on the West Bank and Gaza and in several Arab countries. In Colombia, left- and right-wing terror groups have utilized mobile radio transmitters. The Revolutionary Armed Forces of Colombia (FARC) has broadcast over an increasingly large number of channels. Disc jockeys tend to play popular songs, such as "Guerilla Girls" or "Ambush Rap," with lyrics adapted to the FARC cause. This light diet is always served with frequent doses of direct propaganda. As one disc jockey explained, "We're doing the shooting from the radio."[4]

Today all other means of communication, print and broadcasting included, pale in comparison to the opportunities that the Internet offers terrorists and hatemongers. The Internet is an ideal vehicle to disseminate terrorist propaganda and hate speech, glorify the "heroes" and "martyrs" of the movement's cause, facilitate

Internet "Love Story" as Terrorist Trap

In at least one case, the Internet was used to lure an unsuspecting teenager into a terrorist trap. Ofir Rahum, a sixteen-year-old Israeli living with his parents in Ashkelon, was in love. He met his twenty-five-year-old girlfriend, Sali, in an Internet chat room. She had told him she was an Israeli of Moroccan descent living in Jerusalem. Ofir and Sali corresponded nonstop via e-mail. "You don't know how much I am waiting for Wednesday," Ofir wrote Sali in the middle of January 2001. Wednesday was the day they would finally have a personal meeting. Sali had asked Ofir to meet her in Jerusalem for a romantic encounter in her girlfriend's apartment. She had urged him not to inform his parents of his plans, and he had promised to keep their secret. On the morning of January 18, 2001, instead of going to school, Ofir traveled by bus to Jerusalem, where Sali met him at the central bus terminal. They took a taxi to her car that she had parked north of the city. Together they drove toward Ramallah—although Ofir was probably unaware of their destination. After Sali stopped her car rather suddenly, a man with a Kalashnikov appeared from nowhere, ordering Ofir out of the car. When the teenager refused, the man shot him. The killer drove off with the body. Sali left the scene to meet a girlfriend for lunch.

Three days later, Sali was arrested by Israeli police officers, who began to shed light on what turned out to be a terrorist kidnapping via the Internet. Sali turned out to be Amana Mona, a Palestinian woman from Bir Naballah who worked as a journalist and was a member of the Al Fatah organization. She explained that she decided to strike after covering the funerals of many Palestinians who were killed in the conflict with Israel, and that she wanted to inflict pain on an Israeli family. According to her mother, "Seeing mothers crying all the time gave her the idea."[5] After her arrest and first appearance in a Jerusalem court, *Newsweek* wrote that this young woman from a middle-class family in the West Bank "hardly fits the profile of a terrorist."[6] But whether she fit the stereotype of a Palestinian terrorist or not, Amana Mona did not have any regrets. She told journalists that she was proud of her actions and that she had acted for the Palestinian people.

Mona was sentenced to life in prison. According to Israeli sources, she led a revolt by two dozen female Palestinian inmates in Israel's Neve Tirza prison in July 2002. According to *Yediot Aharonot*, an Israeli newspaper,

> Mona had her own "personal army" in the Neve Tirza prison, and had con-
> trolled activities of the Palestinian women, as well as those of the Israeli Arab
> women serving time there. During morning breaks outdoors, Mona would
> organize the women in marching drills, the singing of nationalist songs and
> paramilitary exercises.[7]

But eventually, when the female Israeli Arab inmates refused to obey Mona's orders, the two groups attacked each other and had to be separated by prison officials. Mona was transferred to another prison.

communications between members and sympathizers, plot terrorist acts, retrieve strategic and tactical information, recruit new members, and, finally, raise funds. Unlike any other communication means, the Internet's global reach allows like-minded organizations and like-minded people in any country around the world to learn of each other's existence and communicate with each other. The Internet combines the characteristics of all information technologies—text, audio, and video—and terrorist organizations and hate groups exploit all of these opportunities for their purposes.

Propaganda and Hero Worship

Terrorists who fight modernity in many ways have nevertheless embraced modern information and communication technology—most of all the Internet. Bin Laden, Al Qaeda, and similar people and groups may be traditional in many ways, but they rely heavily on the Internet to spread their propaganda. Unlike many other terrorist organizations, Al Qaeda never established its own web site but has depended on sympathetic individuals and groups to carry its propaganda. Take the above-mentioned sites of Azzam Publications and Islamic Awakening, where the posted material could not be more pro–bin Laden if it were personally written or selected by the Al Qaeda boss. A lengthy "communique" claimed responsibility for the massive power failure in the American Northeast in 2003. Allahu Akbar, the poster, wrote,

> In compliance with the order of the Commander of the Mujahids, Usamah bin Ladin (may God preserve him), to strike America's economic links, the Abu al-Misri Brigades struck at two important electricity generating targets in the region of the American East, including the most important cities of America and of Canada.
>
> The soldiers of God cut off the power to the above named cities, plunging the lives of Americans into darkness, just as the criminals had plunged the lives of the Muslim peoples of Iraq, Afghanistan, and Palestine into darkness.
>
> We say to the Muslims that this is not the strike that has been expected. This is something called a war of skirmishes (to wear down the enemy).
>
> We say to the people of Afghanistan and Kaschmir that the gift of the Shaykh of the Mujahids, Usamah bin Ladin, is on its way to the White House.[8]

Although there was no evidence that the blackout was the work of terrorists, the poster seized the opportunity to spread propaganda à la bin Laden. Azzam Publications' message boards included the latest articles and audio messages from known Al Qaeda leaders and their sympathizers. Thus, on September 14, 2003, there was a posting attributed to bin Laden's right-hand man Ayman Al-Zawahiri. A few days later, the "Jihad" board carried a lengthy message under the headline "Why I support Sheikh Usama bin Laden." There were ample articles and messages posted for women that explained, for example, why women should encourage their husbands to join the jihad. Typically, such message boards contain links to similar sites and resources. For example, one mouse click on one of the Azzam boards produced the JihadFiles site. Its operators assured that they did not promote terrorism and did not hate the United States, but the material available in such categories as "Shayk Usama Files," "Taliban Truth," or "Martyrdom Operations 'suicide bombing' " told another story.

Although the web sites of many terrorist groups are regularly dropped by ISPs or hacked, there is never a lack of sites that support terrorism for all kinds of causes.

German extremists of the left and right variety have used Internet sites, discussion boards, and e-mail correspondence for many years to spread their hate propaganda. These German groups and individuals have always managed to circumvent their country's tough laws against hate speech and the glorification of Hitler's worldview by using ISPs abroad. Principals on German left- and right-wing sites operate anonymously and hide behind the firewalls of encrypted messages, electronic boards, and mailboxes that are accessible only to trusted comrades with confidential passwords. The neo-Nazi *Thule-Netz* (in English, Thule-Net) was one of the sites that advised their e-visitors on the benefits of encryption and recommended software. When linked to neo-Nazi sites and discussion forums abroad, Germans were often denied access—and still are—because of the actions taken by law enforcement authorities in the Federal Republic. In the summer of 2003, for example, a poster on the U.S. board of the neo-Nazi organization Stormfront complained that the "stupid" actions of the German police had shut down the "auf Deutsch" forum—the German part of the discussion board.

Over the years, German authorities threatened and in some cases took legal actions against ISPs that allowed Germans to access neo-Nazi web sites. In France, too, two interest groups (the Union of Jewish Students in France and the League Against Racism and Anti-Semitism) won a court judgment against the Internet portal Yahoo! that ordered the U.S. company to deny French web surfers access to e-auctions of Nazi memorabilia. Threatened with a fine of $15 million, Yahoo! removed the controversial items from its web site altogether, saying that it was impossible to filter out just the users from one particular country. But that was not the end of the case, in that Yahoo! sued the two French interest groups in U.S. District Court for the Northern District of California in an effort to have the French verdict declared unenforceable in the United States since it violated the First Amendment right of free speech. The District Court decided in favor of Yahoo!, but the Ninth U.S. Circuit Court of Appeals ruled in favor of the French groups. Yahoo!'s effort to have the U.S. Supreme Court decide failed: In May 2006 the highest court declined to hear the case.

A number of ISPs have also denied service to the most offensive among the many hundreds of hate sites originating in the United States and Canada. Thus, one U.S.-based neo-Nazi voice on the Internet complained that Geocities and other web hosting services, as well as America Online, "adopted policies censoring pro-White pages as soon as they can find them."[9] Kahane.org, the U.S.-based web site of the extremist Jewish Kahane movement, whose political organizations Kach and Kahane Chai are on the U.S. State Department's list of foreign terrorist organizations, was dropped by its American server as well.[10] But the rejects generally find alternative servers. In the past several years, many of these sites disappeared when their content happened to catch the eyes of watch groups, then reappeared with new domain names. Many hate sites have proven clever enough to refrain from direct calls for political violence. Yet, one can easily imagine what damage even the cleaned-up tirades against particular groups might cause in confused minds. Here are just a few examples from Internet sites that speak of deep-seated hate against members of different racial, ethnic, or religious groups.

For years, the white supremacy Vanguard News Network (VNN) has posted news as well as movie, book, and music reviews that are unspeakably hateful vis-à-vis the declared enemies, especially Jews, Mexican and other Latino "invaders," and blacks—the latter always described by using the "n" word. In September 2003, the site proclaimed that "there are no good niggers, except dead ones." The previous year, an article was written about "spitting rocks, dogs and empty cases of Corona: the mestizo 'culture' that's driving out ours. Until Whites unite and shit on Mexicans and Puerto Ricans the way they do on us, nothing changes." And in another posted text, it was argued that "the

Jewish media are holding our hands back to prevent our doing what needs to be done.... Jews are nation-killers. It doesn't matter if they present themselves as conservatives or liberals, they are bent on destroying our race to further theirs. Whites must unite and treat the Jew justly before he destroys us." There was also a vicious rhetorical attack on Chinese under the headline "What Chinks do when they are not eating dogs."[11]

An extreme antiabortion web site celebrated the second anniversary of Dr. Barnett Slepian's murder by James C. Kopp by condemning the victim and praising the terrorist killing. In particular, the site's text stated,

> *On this second anniversary we remember that abortionist Barnett Slepian reaped what he sowed. Abortionist Slepian was told he was murdering children, but he did not care that he was taking the lives of innocent babies. Someone stopped serial murderer Slepian from murdering any more children. A cause to celebrate.*
>
> *We as Christians have a responsibility to protect the innocent the same way we would want someone to protect us if we were about to be killed.*[12]

It is not difficult to find these sites. Accessing one means in many instances that you are provided with many links to like-minded sites at home and abroad both in English and in other languages. The oldest of the American neo-Nazi sites is Stormfront.org, founded in 1995 by Don Black, formerly a leader of the Knights of the Ku Klux Klan.[13] The frequently updated site has provided the e-addresses of Internet mailing lists, links to "newsgroups of interest to White Nationalists," dial-in bulletin board systems, and alphabetically listed "White Nationalism/White Patriotism" sites that add up to a Who's Who of the cyberworld's most extreme and most hateful white supremacy, neo-Nazi, and Christian Identity groups. For a while, Stormfront offered a "White Singles" site that was described as follows: "Formerly known as the Aryan Dating Page, this is a Free service available to single White women and men. Arrange dates for friendship or love." At times, some of the features disappear or are simply not accessible for unexplained reasons.

It is ironic that the most blatant racist views of the neo-Nazi/white supremacy sites have been mirrored on the web pages of the most extremist Jewish groups and/or on the discussion boards of these sites. The most extreme of these sites, that of the Jewish Task Force (JTF), is located in New York. The group has described itself as the "torchbearer of the magnificent legacy of the spiritual giant of our generation, HaRav (The Rabbi) Meir Kahane" and as fighting "to save America's whites and Israel's Jews from the Third World hordes."[14] Unlike Christian Identity groups and groups in the neo-Nazi, white supremacy movements, the JTF lumps Jews and Christian European whites together but otherwise unleashes the same hate tirades against the same targets as do the most extremist of the Jew-bashing white supremacy groups. According to the JTF site, the organization demands an end to foreign immigration and U.S. withdrawal from the United Nations. In the fall of 2003, the site contained texts that called the Qu'ran "Islam's terrorist bible," President George W. Bush "George Wahabi Bush," Senator Joseph Lieberman "the vile Jewish anti-Semite," and the *New York Times* the "New York Nazi Times." The Reverends Jesse Jackson and Al Sharpton were labeled "black Hitlers." According to the site,

> *The Statue of Liberty is a white woman. Can you imagine if she were a schvartze with a big nose and kinky hair? Or an Arab with a veil over her ugly face and a full length dress covering her body and what was left of her clitoris that her father chopped off when she was six years old?*[15]

Actually, whoever looks for hatemongers on the web will find them even without knowing the name of a single hate group. Just typing a racist slur into the search box of a search engine will produce such hate sites.

The obvious question here is whether hate speech and calls for action influence visitors to these web sites to actually resort to violence. It is entirely logical to suspect that the proliferation of hate sites and the large number of people online infect more people with the virus of hate than did the traditional media in the pre-Internet era. This was precisely the point of *Hate.com: Extremists on the Internet*, an HBO documentary produced in association with the Southern Poverty Law Center, a nonprofit group that tracks hate groups in the United States. The program contained an interview with Joseph Paul Franklin, a convicted killer and follower of the late neo-Nazi/white supremacist leader William Pierce. Pierce wrote several best-selling books, among them *Hunter*, about a white supremacist who fights for the purity of his race. Franklin turned out to be the real-life "Hunter." He told interviewers about two female hitchhikers he picked up and killed after one revealed that she was dating a black man. Books like *Hunter* and *The Turner Diaries*, another volume authored by Pierce and published under the pseudonym Andrew MacDonald, are prominently displayed and offered for sale on white supremacy web sites. *The Turner Diaries* describes how white American supremacists plot and fight an all-out war against nonwhite minorities and the "Jewish-controlled Federal Government." It is no secret that the Oklahoma City bomber, Timothy McVeigh, read *The Turner Diaries* and used the described destruction of the FBI's headquarters in Washington as a blueprint for bombing the Alfred P. Murrah Federal Building in Oklahoma. One of the three white Texans who beat and decapitated James Byrd, Jr., an African American man, as he was dragged on a chain by their pickup truck said at the time, "We're starting The Turner Diaries early."[16] It was also revealed that McVeigh's accomplice, Terry Nichols, possessed a copy of *Hunter*. Both *Hunter* and *The Turner Diaries* are fiction, but they are exclusively about hateful ideas that Pierce and other right-wing extremists spread via the Internet.

Many of these sites keep track of the number of their visitors. In the summer of 2003, for example, messages on the Stormfront discussion board celebrated the alleged record increase in people who posted messages on the American site as well as on the organization's main boards in France, Ireland, Britain, Latin countries, Canada, South Africa, the Baltic/Scandinavian countries, Australia, Russia, and Serbia. The only board that did not grow was that of the German Stormfront.

The founding father of the United States' right-wing web of hate, Don Black, explained his enthusiasm for the Internet when he said, "I am tired of the Jewish monopoly over the news media and the entertainment media, and I'm working very hard to provide an alternative to that, and the Internet is that opportunity we've been looking for."[17] The sites mentioned above are not the only domains in cyberspace that offer the opportunities that people like Black are seeking. Electronic message boards established by media organizations and Internet portals with the well-meaning intent of enhancing public debate are often misused by individuals and groups. On September 17, 2003, for example, Yahoo! opened a discussion board about the news that more than fifty black customers had sued a restaurant chain because of discrimination. Five days later, more than 1,300 messages had been posted—many of them crude racist attacks on African Americans. The customer review sections of online booksellers, too, are utilized by extremists. A customer who gave *The Turner Diaries* five stars, the best grade, began and ended his review with the white supremacist greeting "RAHOWA" (for Racial Holy War) and praised Pierce for "a brilliant book that graphically captures the inevitable race-war we'll soon face."[18] It is impossible to estimate how many of the positive "customer reviews" for books like *The Turner Diaries* came from the right-wing extremist core and even from the National Alliance, the group that Pierce led until his death in 2002. It is known, however, that the leaders of some of these groups encourage their followers to bring their propaganda to as many chat rooms and discussion boards as possible. In early 2001, for example, the World Church of the Creator group, now called the Creativity Movement, declared on its web site an "Internet Blitzkrieg" and asked its members to join the battle because "the Internet has the potential to reach millions of White people." In particular, the call to e-arms urged "White Racial Loyalists" to "go to chat rooms and debate with 'new people,' " not those who "already know about the Jewish menace," and to "register their group's domain name to as many search engines as possible."[19] One of the twenty-two suggestions given under the headline "Nonviolent Tactics" on the women's page of Stormfront was the following:

> Go out on the internet Newsgroups, bulletin boards, and chat rooms and contact potential White sympathizers. Unfortunately, Jews, Feds, and other non-white operatives tend to "flood" chat rooms, scroll, and engage us in pointless dialogue with "decoys." Watch for these tactics and make White onlookers aware of them. Keep your chat room discussions in the rooms so that White onlookers can see what you have to say.[20]

The preachers of hate know full well that young minds are especially vulnerable to being indoctrinated by their propaganda. Several groups offer special web pages for kids. The son of Stormfront leader Don Black introduced himself as the webmaster of Stormfront.org for Kids and wrote,

> White people are taught in school to be ashamed of their heritage. Teachers cram as many politically correct ideas as they can into your head in 180 days. All the great white accomplishments throughout history are diminished. Therefore, I think that now is the time that all the white people across the globe should rise above the lies, and be proud of who we are. To take back our freedom and win for all to see our heritage in its greatest glory.[21]

These types of e-pages for children offer games, music, and material that glorify the white race as supreme. Discussion boards for teenagers contain typically outrageous postings that are filled with profanities directed at the members of other races and religions. Like the boards designed for adults, these youth boards have an international character in that "visitors" from abroad participate in the exchanges. Eric Harris and Dylan Klebold, high school students in Littleton, Colorado, who in the spring of 1999 killed twelve of their fellow students and a teacher before they took their own lives, had used the Internet to fuel their obsession with neo-Nazi ideology and with Adolf Hitler.[22] They could have gotten the same material from books, magazines, CDs, and movies. But the fact is that the Internet allows people of all ages to access whatever material they prefer in privacy. Harris and Klebold left several videotapes that documented and explained their motives.

To the extent that hateful computer games are available on the Internet, the young are also a major target. After clicking on the "Games" button on the Kahane organization's web site, visitors were invited to target doves among Israel's leaders as well as former Palestinian leader Yassir Arafat. In "Escape of the Oslo Criminals," for example, the "insane and dangerous Oslo Architects," former Prime Minister Ehud Barak and his Labor Party colleagues Shimon Perez and Yossi Beilin, escaped their prison in the year 2010 and were running for safe houses in the territory controlled by the Palestinian Authority. Players were urged to "capture" the criminals before they reached their Palestinian friends or were lynched by fellow Israelis. But in reality, the game came down to the virtual assassination of the pop-up pictures of the three political leaders. "Barakula" was another violent game targeting Ehud Barak, who was described as "a demented demonic beast." Players were urged to "knock this creature back to the abyss it came from." Arafat was the enemy in another game in which players were to "welcome our friend and partner to Peace of the Brave Abu-Amar (Arafat) to Kahane Land." Arafat's fate was not decided by a hug but by a revolver and a bullet.[23]

In the early 1990s, Leonard Eron said the following in his testimony on behalf of the American Psychological Association before the Senate Committee on Governmental Affairs:

> There can no longer be any doubt that heavy exposure to televised violence is one of the causes of aggressive behavior, crime, and violence in society. The evidence comes from both the laboratory and real-life studies. Television violence affects youngsters of all ages, of both genders, at all socio-economic levels and all levels of intelligence.[24]

In her revealing study on what she calls "media violence," Sissela Bok not only points to violence in television entertainment and news and in motion pictures but mentions computer games and the Internet as well.[25] There is no reason to believe that the propaganda of hate has no effect. On the contrary, one would suggest that this sort of indoctrination affects some people, not only the young, to the extent that they plot and commit violence.

The Internet as a Tool to Plan Terrorist Operations

Terrorists utilize computer technology and the Internet to plan and coordinate their violent actions. Former FBI Director Louis J. Freeh told the Citizens Crime Commission of New York, "When Ramzi Yousef [the mastermind of the World Trade Center bombing] was being tracked in the Philippines, he left behind a laptop computer that itemized plans to blow up [11] U.S. airliners in the Western Pacific on a particular day. All of the details and planning were set forth in that laptop computer."[26] Part of the information was encrypted and difficult to decode, but it revealed for the first time how sophisticated terrorists utilized computers for planning their operations. Even before the 9/11 attacks, U.S. intelligence agencies knew that Al Qaeda operatives used the Internet to communicate with each other. According to one account,

> Hidden in the X-rated pictures of several pornographic Web sites and the posted comments on sports chat rooms may lie the encrypted blueprints of the next terrorist attack against the United States or its allies. It sounds farfetched, but U.S. officials and experts say it's the latest method of communication being used by Osama bin Laden and his associates to outfox law enforcement.[27]

U.S. officials disclosed that bin Laden and others were "hiding maps and photographs of terrorist activities on sports sites, chat rooms, pornographic bulletin boards and other web sites."[28] It has become increasingly difficult to unlock the encrypted messages and images, and it is even harder finding them in the first place among the many millions of sites, boards, and chat rooms on the World Wide Web.

According to Timothy L. Thomas, "The Internet is being used as a 'cyberplanning' tool for terrorists. It provides terrorists with anonymity, command and control resources, and a host of other measures to coordinate and integrate attack options."[29] American law enforcement specialists found evidence that the 9/11 terrorists used the Internet to coordinate their operation. Their e-mail messages contained code words and never mentioned what they were really up to in plain language. According to one terrorism expert, "They knew exactly what to do. I mean, they went to Internet cafes and libraries, they erased the hard drives."[30] Al Qaeda's chief of operations, Abu Zubayda, used the Internet to keep in touch with the men who actually carried out the mission. The extent of Al Qaeda's dependence on cyberspace communication was discovered when several of the group's computers were found in Afghanistan and after Zubayda was arrested in Pakistan in early 2002. Effective command and control would be far more difficult to establish and maintain for Al Qaeda's terrorism network without the advantages of the Internet. As Thomas has noted, "The Internet's potential for command and control can vastly improve an organization's effectiveness, if it does not have a dedicated command and control establishment, especially in the propaganda and internal coordination areas." Noting that Internet chat rooms are one vehicle for command and control, the same expert explained that one particular web site, "alneda.com, has supported al Qaeda's efforts to disperse forces and enable them to operate independently, providing leadership via strategic guidance, theological arguments, and moral inspiration."[31]

Shocking Display of Digital Terrorism

The team that attacked ten sites in Mumbai, India, in November 2008 held hostages in several locations, caused the death of 173 and injured several hundred persons, utilized an unprecedented range of digital-age information and communication technology. They carried BlackBerrys and cell phones with exchangeable SIM cards that made it difficult to track them; they navigated from Karachi to Mumbai with the guidance of a Global Positioning System, and they carried CDs with high-resolution satellite images of their target sites. They communicated with their operation bosses and with each other via e-mail and satellite telephone, and they followed live TV coverage as security forces tried to respond to the hostage situations in several locations. (For excerpts from their conversations, see the box on page 280).

Talking about the lessons learned from the Mumbai attacks before the U.S. Senate Committee on Homeland Security & Governmental Affairs, New York's Police Commissioner Raymond Kelly said that the handlers of the Mumbai terrorists directed the operations from outside the attack zone using cell phones and other portable communications devices. As Kelly said, "This phenomenon is not new. In the past, police were able to defeat any advantage it might give hostage takers by cutting off power to the location they were in. However, the proliferation of handheld devices would appear to trump that solution."[32]

Excerpts from Conversations Between Mumbai Terrorists and Operation Leaders During the Hostage Situation in November 2008

Hotel Taj Mahal, Nov. 27, 2008: 0310 hrs

RECEIVER: Greetings!

CALLER: Greetings! There are three Ministers and one Secretary of the Cabinet in your hotel. We don't know in which room.

RECEIVER: Oh! That's good news! It is the icing on the cake.

CALLER: Do one thing. Throw one or two grenades on the Navy and police teams, which are outside.

RECEIVER: Sorry, I simply can't make out where they are.

Nariman House, Nov. 27, 2008: 2226 hrs

CALLER: Brother, you have to fight. This is a matter of prestige of Islam. Fight so that your fight becomes a shining example. Be strong in the name of Allah. You may feel tired or sleepy but the Commandos of Islam have left everything. Their mothers, their fathers. Their homes. Brother, you have to fight for the victory of Islam.
Be strong.

RECEIVER: Amen!

Oberei Hotel, Nov. 27, 2008: 0353 hrs

CALLER: Brother, Abdul. The media is comparing your action to 9/11. One senior police officer has been killed.

ABDUL REHMAN: We are on the 10th and 11th floor. We have five hostages.

CALLER 2: Everything is being recorded by the media. Inflict the maximum damage. Keep fighting. Don't be taken alive.

CALLER: Kill all hostages, except the two Muslims. Keep your phone switched on so that we can hear the gunfire.

FAHADULLAH: We have three foreigners including women. From Singapore and China.

CALLER: Kill them.

(Voices of Fahdulla and Abdul Rehman directing hostages to stand in a line, and telling to Muslims to stand aside. Sounds of gunfire. Cheering voices in background, Kafka hands telephone to Zarar)

ZARAR: Fahad, find the way to go downstairs.

Nariman House November 27, 2008: 1945 hrs

WASSI: Keep in mind that the hostages are of use only as long as you do not come under fire because of their safety. If you are still threatened, then don't saddle yourself with the burden of the hostages, immediately kill them.

RECEIVER: Yes, we shall do accordingly, God willing.

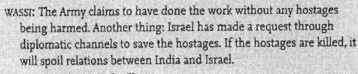

WASSI: The Army claims to have done the work without any hostages being harmed. Another thing: Israel has made a request through diplomatic channels to save the hostages. If the hostages are killed, it will spoil relations between India and Israel.

RECEIVER: So be it, God willing.

WASSI: Stay alert.

Source: *The New York Times.*[33]

Devastating Cyberterrorism

Several years ago, *New York Times* columnist Thomas Friedman outlined the following horror scenario:

> *In five years, with the Internet being used to run more and more systems, if someone is able to knock out the handful of key Internet switching and addressing centers in the U.S. (until recently, a quarter of all Internet traffic passed through one building in Tyson's Corner, Va., next to Morton's steak house), here's what happens: many trains will stop running, much air traffic will grind to a halt, power supplies will not be able to be shifted from one region to another, there will be no e-mail, your doctor's CAT scanner, which is now monitored over the Internet by its manufacturer, won't work if it breaks.*[34]

But this would not be the worst-case scenario that security experts inside and outside the U.S. government have come to fear. American analysts have seen enough evidence on Al Qaeda's computers to conclude that "terrorists are at the threshold of using the Internet as a direct instrument of bloodshed. The new threat bears little resemblance to familiar financial disruptions by hackers responsible for viruses and worms. It comes instead at the meeting point of computers and the physical structures they control."[35] No evidence exists for the above-mentioned claim that the power blackout in the American Northeast in August 2003 was the result of cyberterrorism. But attacks on power grids are among real threats that counterterrorism experts have warned of. During a 2002 conference for security experts, the participating experts admitted "that they had no idea how the [American electrical] power grid would respond to a cyber attack."[36] Worse yet, security experts foresee any number of horror scenarios likely to kill many people. Among the potential acts of cyberterrorism that Barry C. Collins has described are the following:

> A CyberTerrorist will remotely access the processing control systems of a cereal manufacturer, change the levels of iron supplement, and sicken and kill the children of a nation enjoying their food. That CyberTerrorist will then perform similar remote alterations at a processor of infant formula. The key: the CyberTerrorist does not have to be at the factory to execute these acts.
>
> A CyberTerrorist will place a number of computerized bombs around a city, all simultaneously transmitting unique numeric patterns, each bomb receiving each other's pattern. If bomb one stops transmitting, all the bombs detonate simultaneously. The keys: 1) the CyberTerrorist does not have to be strapped to any of these bombs; 2) no large truck is required; 3) the number of bombs and urban dispersion are extensive; 4) the encrypted patterns cannot be predicted and matched through alternate transmission; and 5) the number of bombs prevents disarming them all simultaneously. The bombs will detonate.

> *A CyberTerrorist will remotely alter the formulas of medication at pharmaceutical manufacturers. The potential loss of life is unfathomable.*
> *The CyberTerrorist may then decide to remotely change the pressure in the gas lines, causing a valve failure, and a block of a sleepy suburb detonates and burns. Likewise, the electrical grid is becoming steadily more vulnerable.*[37]

Suggesting that cyberterrorism can prevent a nation from eating, drinking, moving, and living, Collins emphasized that he did not describe scenarios that were borrowed from the realm of science fiction, but that all of these catastrophes could be triggered today—in the real world.

The Web and the Retrieval of Valuable Information

Even the most sophisticated terror organizations know that they can find a great deal of useful information on the Internet. In a training manual that Al Qaeda left behind in Afghanistan, recruits were instructed to use open sources (libraries, journals, government documents, Internet sites, and the like) because, as the text revealed, 80% of the information about the vulnerabilities of the enemy are publicly available. The group's leaders were also aware that the bulk of this information could be accessed on the Internet. On the hard drive of an Al Qaeda computer, also found in Afghanistan, U.S. experts discovered that it had been used to access a French site that posts a "Sabotage Handbook" with "sections on tools of the trade, planning a hit, switch gear and instrumentation, anti-surveillance methods and advanced techniques."[38] In the past, chat room participants discussed potential targets for cyberterrorism attacks. According to one account, "Targets that terrorists have discussed include the Centers for Disease Control and Prevention in Atlanta; FedWire, the money-moving clearing system maintained by the Federal Reserve Board; and facilities controlling the flow of information over the Internet."[39]

Online Recruitment

The Internet has become the most effective recruiting tool for terrorist and hate groups. Simply by making their propaganda material available online, by glorifying those who have committed political violence against civilians, and by urging visitors to their web sites to join the cause, these groups attract new followers. How this works is sometimes described on the message boards or e-mail selections posted on these sorts of sites. Thus, the "Letters from Browsers" on the National Alliance's web site affirmed the effectiveness of the Internet as a means to recruit new supporters. One recruit wrote, "I found this website April 24, 1999. Listening to the broadcast, 'New World Order,' led me to listen to all on the page. Never heard these issues explained so simply and in such an easy to understand manner. Every word you spoke: Absolute truth!" An unnamed fan from Norway e-mailed that he or she was listening in on the National Alliance through the Internet radio and revealed that his or her awakening came when studying sites on the net. A writer who identified himself as a "part-time college professor" and asked for anonymity for fear of losing his job thanked National Alliance leader Pierce for making his radio broadcasts accessible on the web and added, "I tell all those that will listen to visit the site." And "a public school teacher" from California wrote, "Since I have just purchased a computer I was able to tune into to [sic] your radio program. Dr. Pierce's message, politically and philosophically, was forceful, inspiring, and honest."[40]

Fund-Raising via the Net

Literally all terrorist and hate groups use the Internet to raise money for their activities. Even the well-funded Al Qaeda network utilizes web sites to solicit contributions. For this purpose, some web sites have publicized account numbers at particular banks specifically set up for fund-raising. Jessica Stern found that the Lasch-I-Taiba, or Army of God, in Pakistan utilized the World Wide Web to raise funds for its radical activities. Indeed, "Laschkar and its parent organization, Markaz ad-Da'wa Irshad (Center for Islamic Invitation and Guidance) have raised so much money, mostly from sympathetic Wahhabis in Saudi Arabia, that they are reportedly planning to open their own bank."[41] If they do not dare to direct their own fund-raising operations or aim at targeting larger audiences to solicit contributions, terrorist groups are content to have front organizations collect donations via the Internet. Terrorists have also resorted to criminal activities in cyberspace to finance their activities, with credit card fraud first on the list of their offenses. According to a leading French antiterrorism investigator, "Many Islamist terror plots in Europe and North America were financed through such criminal activity."[42]

Whatever their causes, international and domestic terrorist and hate groups try to raise funds online. In most instances, these appeals target people of modest means in the hope that they will sacrifice for the cause. The Internet publishers of the so-called Nuremberg Files, which identify abortion providers and their supporters, promise holy rewards for donations in that "the Living God will receive your donation as a sweet smelling savor arising to His nostrils and will bless you accordingly."[43] According to the Jewish Task Force's web site, the group looked in particular for "a wealthy Jew or a righteous Gentile with the needed millions of dollars" to push the group's agenda on a larger scale.[44]

All told, the Internet, like many other technological advances, can be used in positive and negative ways. Terrorists and hate groups have seized cyberspace rather quickly for their sinister purposes.

Notes

1. Posted in the "jihad" category of the discussion section of IslamicAwakening.com, www.as-sahwah.com/discus/ (retrieved September 12, 2003).
2. This is a quote from a Reuter dispatch of October 20, 2000, "Hizbollah Says Pro-Israelis Damaged Its Web Site," www.dailynews.yahoo.com/h/nm/20001020/wr/mideast_hizbollah_d_l.html
3. Ayoub was quoted in Ranwa Yehia, "Hizbollah: Arabs Have 'Tremendous Power to Fight' on New Cyber Front," (Beirut) Daily Star On Line, www.dailystar.com.lb/30_10_00/art2.htm (accessed October 30, 2000).
4. Karl Prenhaul, "Colombia's Rebels Hit the Airwaves," Newsday, December 24, 2000, A20.
5. The quote is from Dan Ephron and Joanna Chen, "Ofir's Fatal Attraction," Newsweek, April 2, 2001, 39.
6. Ibid. For my account of this case of terrorism, I drew from many media accounts, among them the mentioned story in Newsweek and Deborah Sontag, "Israelis Grieve as Youth Who Was Lured to His Death on the Internet Is Buried," New York Times, January 20, 2001, www.nytimes.com/2001/01/20/technology/20MIDE.html?pagewanted=all
7. http://webisraelinsider.com/Articles/Security/1295.htm (retrieved April 14, 2005).
8. http://as-sawah.com/discus/ (retrieved September 12, 2003).
9. See "Links to Other Web Sites," www.stormfront.org
10. While site server Scorpion Communications cancelled its contract with the Kahane organization, another firm, McMurtrey/Whitaker & Associates, struggled with the decision of whether to

let Kahane.org use its software to sell merchandise on its site. See Dean E. Murphy, "Ugliness Online Isn't Terrorism," *New York Times*, January 7, 2001, Week in Review section.

11. From www.vanguardnewsnetwork.com. In the summer of 2001, the site carried an ad for a Visa Nextcard.

12. From www.freespeech.org/paulhill/PressRelease.html

13. See "Links to Other Web Sites," www.stormfront.org

14. See www.jtf.org

15. The three quotes are from www.jtf.com

16. According to a report on Court TV. The brutal killing occurred in June 1998 in Jasper, Texas. See www.courttv.com/trials/berry/102599_ctv.html

17. Quoted in Julie Salamon, "The Web as Home for Racism and Hate," *New York Times*, October 23, 2000, E8.

18. From one customer review of *The Turner Diaries* as posted on www.amazon.com (accessed on September 21, 2003).

19. From "Creativity Internet Blitzkrieg," www.creator.org/internet.html

20. www.stormfront.org (accessed September 24, 2003).

21. From www.kids.stormfront.org

22. Many news sources reported about the two teenagers' heavy usage of the Internet and the reactions of parents and Americans in general to the possible role of the web in the massacre. See, for example, Amy Harmon, "Parents Fear That Children Are One Click Ahead," *New York Times*, April 20, 1999, A24; and Lawrence H. Tribe, "The Internet vs. the First Amendment," *New York Times*, April 28, 1999, A29.

23. See www.kahane.net/games/ (accessed at various times in 2000 and 2001).

24. Eron is cited in Sissela Bok, *Mayhem: Violence as Public Entertainment* (Reading, MA: Merloyd Lawrence, 1998), 47.

25. Ibid., in "Introduction."

26. Freeh's speech was published in *Vital Speeches of the Day* on October 1, 1999. The transcript contained a typing error that Freeh referred to a plan to attack "1 U.S. airliners" simultaneously; the correct number was eleven airliners. See also Simon Reeve, *The New Jackals* (Boston: Northeastern University Press, 1999), ch. 4, for details about this foiled plan.

27. Jack Kelley, "Terror Groups Hide Behind Web Encryption," *USA Today*, February 6, 2001, 7A.

28. Ibid.

29. Timothy L. Thomas, "Al Qaeda and the Internet: The Danger of 'Cyberplanning,'" *Parameters* (Spring 2003): 112–23, http://carlisle-www.army.mil/usawc/Parameters/03spring/thomas.htm

30. Steve Emerson made this remark during a conversation with Chris Matthews on CNBC's *Hardball with Chris Matthews*, March 2, 2002.

31. Thomas,

32. http://hsgac.senate.gov/public/_files/010809Kelly.pdf

33. The document is available at http://graphics8.nytimes.com/packages/pdf/nyregion/city_room/20090109_mumbaitranscripts.pdf (accessed January 14, 2009).

34. Thomas Friedman, "Digital Defense," *New York Times*, July 27, 2001, A19.

35. Barton Gellman, "Cyber-Attacks by Al Qaeda Feared: Terrorist at Threshold of Using Internet as Tool of Bloodshed," *Washington Post*, June 27, 2002, A1.

36. Ibid.

37. Barry C. Collins, "The Future of Cyber Terrorism: Where the Physical and Virtual Worlds Converge," speech delivered at the 11th Annual International Symposium on Criminal Justice Issues, http://afgen.com/terrorism1.html (accessed September 17, 2003).

38. Gellman.

39. Thomas, 118.

40. The excerpts were taken from the "Letters from Browsers" section at www.natall.com/letters/letters16.html (accessed April 1, 2002).

41. Jessica Stern, "Pakistan's Jihad Culture," *Foreign Affairs* (November–December 2000): 120.

42. Timothy L. Thomas identified Jean-François Richard as the French investigator he quoted.

43. According to the Nuremberg Files web site, www.tcrparty.com/atrocity/aborts.html

44. According to the group's web site, www.jtf.org

CHAPTER 16

Anti- and Counterterrorism in the News

IN DECEMBER 2003, FOUR DAYS BEFORE CHRISTMAS, THE BUSH administration raised the terrorism alert status to the second-highest level, "orange," for "high." Intelligence suggested that international terrorists planned another attack inside the United States. Appearing in droves on TV news programs, officials in Washington and throughout the country told the public to be both vigilant and calm. The media did not allow Americans to go about their normal lives; they unleashed a reporting frenzy as if an attack was imminent. Standing in airports, on street corners, or near the famous Times Square in New York, network reporters and their brethren from local stations assured their audiences that they would keep them informed of new developments—as if they expected to personally witness the terror attack.

To be sure, the news media should inform the public when government officials issue threat warnings and explain the security concerns of the intelligence community. But intensive coverage of this and previous threat-level alerts seemed designed to scare the hell out of the general public and keep people glued to their TV sets. Research revealed that between October 1, 2001, and December 31, 2004, the three television networks, ABC, CBS, and NBC, aired a total of eighteen news reports on the Bush administration's decision to raise the nationwide terror alert and fifteen segments on the lowering of the color-coded alarm. In addition, the networks reported three times on raised terror alerts for New York and two times for other cities, while two newscasts mentioned the lowering of regional alerts. True to the media's tendency to highlight shocking, sensational, disconcerting news, all twenty-three announcements of increases in the national or local terrorism alerts were reported on top of newscasts. Conversely, *ABC News*, *CBS News*, and *NBC News* reported decreases in the threat alert levels far less prominently, airing only 13% of such announcement as lead stories and 87% further down in their particular broadcasts.

When the Bush administration raised nationwide terrorism alerts, the networks devoted on average 5 minutes and 20 seconds to such reports; when the national terror alert was lowered, the average news segment lasted only 1 minute and 34 seconds. In some instances, the de-escalation of the official terrorism threat was not reported at all by one or the other network.[1]

Terrorist strikes and threats are always the stuff of massive news coverage, while important information on antiterrorism and preparedness measures seems of little interest to most media organizations. The problem is that broadcasters prefer sound bites and the print media prefer short stories—coverage patterns that are ill-suited to explaining rather complex problems and remedies. Thus, the general threat of catastrophic terrorism, especially the danger of biological and chemical attacks, made the news before 9/11. On the one hand, in exceptional cases these stories were based on investigative work, interviews with experts in the field, and excellent reporting.[2] But on the other hand, there was little or no media attention paid to information about problems in the areas of prevention and preparedness, as the following examples demonstrate.

In 1999, the U.S. Congress appointed an expert commission to "review the laws, regulations, directives, policies, and practices for preventing and punishing terrorism directed against the United States, assess their effectiveness, and recommend changes."[3] About three months before the kamikaze attacks on the World Trade Center and the Pentagon, the National Commission on Terrorism wrote in the executive summary of its report,

> *Not all terrorists are the same, but the groups most dangerous to the United States share some characteristics not seen 10 or 20 years ago: They operate in the United States as well as abroad. Their funding and logistical networks cross borders, are less*

President George W. Bush as Post–9/11 Crisis Manager

During severe crises, Americans tend to rally around their presidents. This reaction assures presidents of public support for their crisis management. This was particularly obvious in the days, weeks, months, and even years after 9/11, when President George W. Bush addressed the nation repeatedly to enlist support for his counterterrorist measures—including military actions in Afghanistan and Iraq.

dependent on state sponsors, and are harder to disrupt with economic sanctions. They make use of widely available technologies to communicate quickly and securely. Their objectives are more deadly. This changing nature of the terrorist threat raises the stakes in getting American counterterrorist policies and practices right.[4]

Instead of reporting on the eye-opening document and the deficiencies in America's anti- and counterterrorist efforts, most news organizations did not deem the commission's findings newsworthy. According to the LexisNexis archives, of the hundreds of U.S. newspapers across the country, only forty-three items mentioned the commission's report—many of them reducing it to a few lines. The *Daily News* in New York, for example, devoted just two sentences to the commission report. Of the newspapers that did pay more attention, most focused on some details identified as most likely to cause controversies, namely, the commission's recommendation to add Greece and Pakistan to the list of countries that were not fully cooperating in the battle against terrorism, to curb terrorist fund-raising in the United States, to monitor foreign students, and to use military forces in the event of a major terrorist attack on the United States. An editorial in the *Omaha World-Herald* suggested that the National Commission on Terrorism had "envisioned a level of evil more pervasive than common sense and experience suggest actually exists."[5]

This editorial seemed to explain the media's lack of interest: Most news organizations simply did not buy the premise that international terrorism was a major threat unless there were specific government alerts, as was the case with the Y2K predictions.[6] Television and radio news organizations showed no interest either. ABC's *World News Tonight* and CBS's *Evening News* mentioned criticism of the commission's recommendations once, as did the four stories aired by CNN. NBC's *Today Show* and *Meet the Press* devoted more airtime to the report than their competitors. When another blue-ribbon panel, the U.S. Commission on National Security in the 21st Century, released its comprehensive report in early 2001, its terrorism warnings and response proposals received, according to the *Financial Times*, "scant attention."[7] While the cochairs of the bipartisan panel, ex-Senators Gary Hart and Warren Rudman, as well as former U.S. Representative Newt Gingrich, a commission member, gave testimony before several congressional committees, most news organizations ignored the report completely. CNN's *The Point with Greta van Susteren* was the only program on the major TV broadcast and cable networks that reported the commission's findings at length.[8]

It was only after the events of 9/11 that a few members of the fourth estate recognized the media's lack of vigilance. In a column titled "The Terrorism Story—and How We Blew It" Richard Cohen wrote, "We [in the media]—and I mean most of us—were asleep."[9] He acknowledged that he and his colleagues had clues and should have reported about the terrorist threat and the weaknesses in the government's counterterrorist approaches. The media showed even less interest in the state of preparedness in the event of a terrorist attack inside the United States. In the five years from January 1996 through December 2000, the major TV networks (ABC, CBS, NBC, and CNN) and National Public Radio combined aired a total of forty-eight stories on preparedness. Most of these reports were triggered by drills that simulated worst-case scenarios in order to test the readiness of emergency response specialists. Whether on television, radio, or in print, the news was grim. Thus, NBC News anchor Tom Brokaw said in one newscast, "There is a quiet fear among many of the nation's highest ranking law enforcement officers that this country is grossly unprepared for what could be the greatest terrorist threat of the times, that's biological warfare."[10] In the *New York Times* Judith Miller reported, "At a time of growing fear of terrorism within America's borders, senior state and local officials say the Federal Government still has no coherent system for deterring or responding to it."[11] With few exceptions, however, these stories in the mainstream media focused on specific problems that surfaced during these drills but not on the underlying problems and issues in the politics of preparedness policies.

In the spring of 2001, a small political magazine, the *Washington Monthly*, published a revealing article under the headline "Weapons of Mass Confusion: How Pork Trumps Preparedness in the Fight against Terrorism." Writer Joshua Green reported that "the billions of dollars spent to prepare for an attack has only created an expensive and uncoordinated mess."[12] According to Green,

> *A bidding war in Congress quickly ensued. "There was a rush on Capitol Hill," says a senior researcher in a nonpartisan national security think tank. "There were literally dozens of agencies whispering in lawmakers' ears that their organizations could do the job and, in turn, make that congressman look good for choosing them."*[13]

The article did not alarm the large news organizations into following Green's lead. While always interested in controversy and wrongdoing, especially when public officials are involved, the mass media are far more likely to delve into questionable practices and outright missteps, when the facts—or rumors—are simple and easily told. The cumbersome politics surrounding highly technical and multiagency programs are not easily told in a few seconds by organizations that strive to entertain news consumers rather than fully inform citizens about important public affairs.

It is equally instructive to examine the news coverage of the antiterrorism legislation adopted within weeks of 9/11. Although the USA PATRIOT Act of 2001 in particular and other enacted laws curbed individual liberties, there was no intensive coverage of the difficult balancing act between the need for security and the protection of civil liberties. Television newscasts often did not provide any coverage at all on the important provisions of the proposed legislation. Somewhat longer broadcast segments and print stories focused typically on the political infighting between the backers and opponents of such measures. In other words, to the extent that the news reported on these at all, the stories were predominantly strategic in that they dwelt on the political calculations of supporters and opponents at the expense of explaining the substance of the proposed and eventually adopted measures.

Reasonable people can and do disagree on the trade-offs between civil liberties and national and personal security. But only if a free and responsible press reports fully on important public issues can citizens understand the pros and cons of important policy decisions and make educated judgments. In this case, most news organizations did not discharge their responsibility to the public.

A Model for Public Deliberation

Recognizing that public deliberation "is essential to democracy in order to ensure that the public's policy preferences—upon which democratic decisions are based—are informed, enlightened, and authentic," Benjamin Page assigns a central role to "professional communicators" in the mass-mediated deliberations of modern mass societies.[14] Since staffers write a newspaper's editorials, one wonders whether a newspaper's editorial opinion affects the selection of the letters to the editor and of op-ed pieces that are not written by regular columnists, or whether the editors in charge strive for a wide range of views.

Immediately after the 9/11 attacks, some astute Americans recognized that the event would force Americans to deal with "security versus liberty" issues. Some of those ordinary citizens who expressed their views in letters to the editor spoke out for or against curbs of civil liberties. Another topic that the writers readily addressed was the question of military retaliation in response to 9/11. One of the newspapers that facilitated readers' expression of a wide range of views in letters to the editor sections was the *New York Times*.

On September 12, 2001, the day after the terror strikes, several letters to the editor in the *New York Times* took positions on two questions that would soon emerge as major post–9/11 policy issues: (1) whether to retaliate militarily, and (2) whether to curb civil liberties for the sake of greater security. A reader from Tennessee demanded, "Now America must wield the sword in defense of liberty." But a letter writer from Pittsburgh appealed for restraint, pleading, "Violence does not deter the violent.... The only sane and civilized way to settle international disputes is by international negotiations." A reader from Bethesda, Maryland, worried about the protection of civil liberties in the aftermath of the terror attacks and cautioned, "The inevitable temptation to change fundamentally the nature of our society, by attacking the civil rights and civil liberties of any individual or group, must be resisted."[15] The same day, *Times* columnist William Safire wrote on the op-ed page, "When we reasonably determine our attackers' bases and camps, we must pulverize them—minimizing but accepting collateral damage—and act overtly or covertly to destabilize terror's national hosts."[16] His colleague Anthony Lewis cautioned that "one danger must above all be avoided: taking steps that in the name of security would compromise America's greatest quality, its open society."[17] In an editorial, the *New York Times* touched on both reprisal and civil liberties, writing that "retaliation is warranted" once the architects of the horror are identified and warning that "Americans must rethink how to safeguard the country without bartering away the rights and privileges of the free society that we are defending."[18]

The views expressed in the letters that the *Times* published in the following weeks and months were more diverse than the opinions on the op-ed page and often more timely than the editorials with respect to civil liberties issues. In the three months from September 12, 2001, to December 12, 2001, all pertinent editorials in the *New York Times* and eighteen of nineteen op-ed pieces expressed opposition to post–9/11 actions and antiterrorist measures at the expense of civil liberties; in the letters to the editor section the published letters ran 45–25 against curbing civil liberties, but these opposing views were expressed far more frequently than in editorials and op-ed page opinion pieces.

During the same time period, the *New York Times* presented its readers with opinions about the use of the U.S. military in the fight against terrorism in general and/or in Afghanistan. Except for an editorial in which the newspaper wrote that the "Bush administration would make a serious mistake by moving to wage war in Iraq,"[19] the rest of the relevant editorials were supportive of the administration's military plans and actual deployments. On the op-ed page, opinion pieces in support of military actions had a 6–3 advantage over the opponents. On this matter, the letters to the editor section resembled a vivid marketplace of ideas: Forty of the letters were in support of military responses, twelve were against, and thirteen were ambiguous. To the newspaper's credit, there was no sign at all that its editorial positions on the two issues influenced the selection of viewpoints that were published in the letters to the editor sections. In this case, the "professional communicators" did not shape according to their own viewpoints and preferences the public discourse as presented in the letters section.

The Media and Military Responses to Terrorism

While overcovering even minor terrorist incidents and terrorist threats, the news media undercover anti- and counterterrorist measures—unless the latter involve military action or at least the threat of military reprisal or preemption. Military reprisal and preemption in response to international terrorism have been rare. There have been only five such instances thus far that involved the United States: the bombing of Libya in 1986 in retaliation for Libya's role in the bombing of the La Belle disco bar in Berlin that was heavily frequented by American GIs, the 1993 bombing of Iraq's intelligence headquarters as punishment for an Iraqi plot to assassinate former President George H. W. Bush during his visit to Kuwait earlier that year, the 1998 missile strikes against targets in Afghanistan and Sudan following the bombing of U.S. embassies in Kenya and Tanzania, the massive military action against Al Qaeda and Taliban targets in Afghanistan in response to 9/11, and the invasion of Iraq in the spring of 2003. How did the news media cover these military measures?

The Bombing of Libya (1986)

In early 1986, after years of anti-American terrorism abroad, the Reagan administration was poised to respond. In the 1980s, Libya's Muammar Qaddafi was for President Reagan what Osama bin Laden became for President George W. Bush in 2001: the world's number-one terrorist and the United States' number-one enemy. The opportunity to demonstrate Washington's determination to set an instructive counterterrorist example arose in April 1986 when a bomb went off in Berlin's La Belle disco, killing two U.S. servicemen. Once intelligence sources abroad confirmed that Libyan agents were involved in the Berlin bombing, the Reagan administration claimed to have the smoking gun that justified the "swift retaliation" the president had promised when he entered the White House.

As the rhetoric in Washington heated up amidst leaks that military strikes were imminent, American media organizations beefed up their presence in the Libyan capital. As a result, Americans learned of the bombing raids against targets in Tripoli and Benghazi from media reports immediately after the attacks began and well before the administration informed the public. In the middle of the *CBS Evening News* broadcast on April 14, for example, correspondents Jeffrey Fager and Allen Pizzey reported over the telephone from Tripoli that the bombing raids had commenced. "Dan—Dan," Fager said, "if you can hear that in the background, there's a little bit of—a few blasts going off right now. The attack—the actual attack has been going on for ten minutes now."[20]

Although the media images and descriptions of innocent victims and massive damage to civilian areas were disturbing to many viewers, readers, and listeners, the overwhelming majority of Americans supported the strikes—including those in the news media. The sentiments were summed up when the *New York Times* wrote in an editorial that "even the most scrupulous citizen can only approve and applaud the American attack on Libya."[21]

Bombing of Iraq's Intelligence Headquarters (1993)

On June 26, 1993, the U.S. military launched a missile attack on Baghdad targeting the Iraqi intelligence headquarters. Shortly after dozens of Tomahawk missiles had hit Iraq's capital in what was a surprise attack, President Bill Clinton explained in a televised address to the nation that the actions had been taken in response to an Iraqi plot to assassinate former President George H. W. Bush during his visit to Kuwait in April 1993. According to the president, there was "compelling evidence" that "this plot—which included the use of a powerful bomb made in Iraq—was directed and pursued by the Iraqi intelligence service."[22] But Clinton did not enjoy the solid press support that Reagan received after the bombing of Libya. Tom Jerrol of *ABC News* wondered about political motives behind the decision to hit Baghdad, asking, "Should this enhance his political image here at home? That's always a consideration that we have to think of when action like this is taken."[23] Although approving the missile attack, the *Washington Times* did not consider the response strong enough. According to one of the newspaper's editorials, "The principle behind the choice of target was, Mr. Clinton stated, proportional. But is destroying an empty building proportionate to the attempted murder of an American leader?"[24] While recognizing the very limited effect of the missile strikes, the *Washington Post* supported Clinton in that he "did what a chief executive had to do in retaliating against Iraq's failed effort to assassinate former president Bush last spring."[25] But the same editorial suggested that Clinton's unilateral decision countered criticism of his preference for "multilateralism" in his foreign policy. In an editorial, the *New York Times* posed the question, "Was this strike necessary?"[26] According to the editorial page, there was not enough evidence to answer in the affirmative. Instead, the newspaper's editorial suggested that "the American people need more information about the reasons for and propriety of Mr. Clinton's action."[27] Finally, the *Times* questioned the president's motive, stating, "Any time a chief executive who is in political difficulty at home undertakes a dramatic military action, he or she must be prepared to face questions whether that action is intended to divert public attention and bolster support for the President."[28]

Missile Strikes in Afghanistan and Sudan (1998)

On August 7, 1998, terrorists drove car bombs into the U.S. embassies in Kenya and Tanzania, killing nearly 300 people, 12 of them Americans, and injuring several thousands. About two weeks later, on August 20, the U.S. military launched some seventy-nine Tomahawk missiles against Al Qaeda training grounds in Afghanistan and against what President Clinton called a "chemical weapons-related facility."[29] The counterterrorist strikes came only three days after the president had publicly acknowledged that he had had an affair with White House intern Monica Lewinsky. Not surprisingly, some staunch Clinton critics as well as reporters, editorial writers, and TV anchors questioned whether the president had ordered the attacks for selfish political reasons. During a Pentagon press briefing following President Clinton's short announcement of the counterterrorist actions, Secretary of Defense William Cohen was asked whether he was familiar with *Wag the Dog*, a movie in which a U.S. president cooks up an imaginary war for the purpose of deflecting interest away from his sexual encounter with a teenage girl. This exchange occurred during the briefing:

> *Question: Some Americans are going to say this bears a striking resemblance to "Wag the Dog." Two questions: Have you seen the movie? And second, how do you respond to people who think that?*
>
> *Cohen: The only motivation driving this action today was our absolute obligation to protect the American people from terrorist activities.*[30]

Washington Post staff writers faulted officials in the Clinton administration for not providing "information to substantiate their assertion that the exiled Saudi million-aire [Osama bin Laden] masterminded the recent bomb attacks on two U.S. embassies in Africa,"[31] but the newspaper's editorial page did not question the actions or Clinton's motive.[32] In stark contrast, the *New York Times* mentioned the Lewinsky case and called on the president to "dispel any lingering doubts about his motivation by providing the House and Senate intelligence committees with a complete briefing on the bin Laden information and instructing his aides to fill out the partial accounts they have given about the raids."[33] On NBC's *Nightly News*, anchor Brian Williams pointed to Clinton's "dual dilemmas, one a national security matter this week, one a domestic crisis that couldn't be more personal."[34] CNN's *Late Edition with Wolf Blitzer* took a "look at the presidency with attention split between the sex scandal in the White House and the military strikes aimed at the terrorists responsible for the U.S. embassy bombings."[35]

Most news organizations and their sources accepted the strikes against bin Laden's bases in Afghanistan, but many expressed doubts that the Al Shifa plant struck in Sudan had, as the administration claimed, produced chemicals for use in weapons of mass destruction. Although administration officials provided reporters with some sensitive intelligence to prove their case, journalists seemed more inclined to believe the claims by Sudanese officials, who denied any sinister purpose of the plant. Journalists do not like to revisit their earlier reporting and judgments when new information becomes available. In this particular case, a key witness in the trial against participants in the East African bombings corroborated the Clinton administration's claims about chemical weapon production in a Khartoum facility a few miles away from the Al Shifa plant and at the time of Clinton's counterterrorist strikes. But the news media all but ignored the revelation while reporting on other aspects of the testimony; only two newspaper articles mentioned the testimony in passing.[36]

Military Action Against Al Qaeda and the Taliban (2001)

On October 7, 2001, President George W. Bush told the nation in a live TV broadcast from the White House that the U.S. military had "begun strikes against Al Qaeda ter-rorist training camps and military installations of the Taliban regime in Afghanistan. "The president mentioned "war" only once in this speech, explaining that the military action was "part of our campaign against terrorism."[37] There was no need to define the actions against Al Qaeda and the Taliban as war, because the news media had invoked this metaphor endlessly since the 9/11 attacks on New York and Washington, D.C. Television, especially the all-news networks, had shown day in, day out on-screen banners with slogans like "America's New War" or "War against Terrorism." In addi-tion, ABC News had broadcast 86 stories that contained the terms "war" and "terror-ism," CBS News aired 96 such segments, NBC News 133, CNN 316, and National Public Radio 166. The U.S. print press available in the LexisNexis archive published a total of 5,814 articles that mentioned both "terrorism" and "war."

In response to the bombing of targets in Afghanistan, angry antiwar protests—some accompanied by violence—erupted in several Arab and Muslim countries. The American news media reported about these demonstrations, and they should have. But by excessively replaying the images of these protests, television in particular conveyed the impression that these regions of the world were in constant uproar against the United States. This was not the case, as one Middle East expert, Martin Indyk, established by keeping track of these demonstrations in twenty-one Arab countries, beginning with the first attack on Afghan targets. According to this survey, there were altogether nine anti-American demonstrations in week one, three in the second week, one in the third week, two in week four, zero in week five, and one in week six.[38] But while overcovering the protests abroad, domestic protests against military retaliation were largely ignored or criticized in the mainstream media. National Public Radio was among the few news organizations that reported at some length on a "burgeoning" or "fledgling" antiwar movement and the intolerant reaction it met inside and outside university campuses.[39]

Initially, the American media covered the war in Afghanistan mostly from a distance because the Taliban granted the Western media only selected access to whatever they wanted to showcase of the damage caused by real or alleged U.S. attacks. But the Arab TV network Al Jazeera reported extensively from Afghanistan and provided the U.S. media with reports American reporters could not provide. Based on some of these reports, American journalists were able to ask questions during Pentagon briefings. But given the broad media and public support for the actions in Afghanistan, there were few persistent inquiries by reporters. For many months, the media portrayed Afghanistan as a clear victory for the U.S.-led coalition—although neither bin Laden nor the leading Taliban figures had been captured and significant parts of the country remained under the control of warlords.

The Invasion of Iraq (2003)

In 2002, when President Bush and others in his administration shifted their attention from bin Laden (who was alive and well and hiding somewhere) to Saddam Hussein, the news media followed suit. Whereas Bush and other Washington officials mentioned bin Laden far more frequently than Saddam Hussein in the six months from October 1, 2001, to May 1, 2001, they referred to Iraq's dictator far more frequently in the six months from May 1, 2002, to October 31, 2002. During these periods, the leading news organizations followed the president's lead in that they reported far more often on bin Laden in the first time period and far more often on Saddam Hussein in the second time period. Of course, this coverage pattern speaks to the news media's practice of facilitating presidents when they use the bully pulpit during acute and even lingering foreign crises. But far from simply providing the chief executive with the stage for communicating with the American people, as one would expect, the media allowed President Bush to set the news agenda so that it changed drastically from first focusing on bin Laden as the number-one "evildoer" to shifting attention to Saddam Hussein as the United States' greatest threat. Just as terrorists use the media to further their propaganda goals (see Chapters 14 and 15), presidents and other leaders in targeted societies also take advantage of the mass media to push their agenda.

In the run-up to the Iraq war, the media, and television in particular, stirred the war sentiment. On-screen banners reminded audiences most of the time of the United States' "Showdown with Iraq" or "Showdown with Saddam." Reports described military preparations and the heartbreaking stories of soldiers getting ready to leave their families to fight the war against terrorism. Popular TV personalities traveled to the Persian Gulf region and anchored their programs from Kuwait and other countries in the vicinity—although such changes of venue did absolutely nothing to enhance their audiences' understanding of the anticipated invasion. But the close-to-the-action backdrops offered media celebrities the opportunity to appear without jacket and tie and tell their audience the same stories as they had earlier from their studios back in the United States. When Washington increased the terrorism alert at home to "high," CNN's Aaron Brown seemed exasperated as he stood in Kuwait to dramatize the coming war and realized that the "breaking news" was right then back home. In addition to such tricks of the trade as hyping venues close to the prospective theater of war, conducting instant "polls," and imposing countdowns to more or less important dates and deadlines, newscasters were preoccupied with stories about the movement of troops and their equipment into the neighborhood of Iraq and with quizzing an army of retired generals as experts on real or imagined developments. Taken together, this sort of news, especially on the all-news networks, conditioned the public to perceive the war against Iraq as inevitable.

Unlike the protests against the Afghan intervention, the antiwar demonstrations of early 2003 in the United States and abroad were massive. This time around, the American news media did pay a good deal of attention to these events, with front-page stories in print and lead stories on TV network news. Although always eager to invoke the First Amendment when defending the press's constitutional right of free expression, many commentators and columnists were quick to condemn antiwar protesters as supporting Saddam Hussein. Michael Kelly, for example, wrote in his column in the *Washington Post*, "It is a march for the furtherance of evil instead of the vanquishing of evil."[40] Hosts and guests on cable television characterized demonstrators frequently as communists, traitors, crazies, un-American, and not patriotic. Ex-President Jimmy Carter, a winner of the Nobel Peace Price, was singled out for harsh criticism after he spoke out against the invasion. Typically, these critics described Carter's presidency as a "failure" and condemned him for violating the unwritten rule whereby ex-presidents do not disagree publicly with an incumbent president. Few voices in the media defended the fundamental right of free speech and assembly in the United States for antiwar protesters also.

For the television networks and especially cable, the prospect of a conflict with Iraq was a two-edged sword. On the one hand, they saw an opportunity to increase their audiences—just as CNN had done during the buildup to and throughout the Gulf War in 1990–1991. But on the other hand, these organizations spent large amounts of money to prepare for the Iraq war, and they feared the loss of advertising revenue during their coverage of the war, when advertisers were expected to refrain from plugging their products. In the end, the investments in the anticipated war coverage were so substantial that television needed the war to attract larger audiences.

Once hostilities began, the "embedded media" model was put into place: Reporters, photographers, and TV crews were attached to specific military units as they invaded Iraq and won a quick victory. Beginning with the invasion of Grenada in 1983 and during the invasion of Panama in 1987 and the Gulf War in 1991, the U.S. military had directly or indirectly denied reporters access to witness the initial military deployments. By embedding correspondents within units, the Pentagon came up with and the media embraced a solution that made for often dramatic war coverage. The other side of the coin was that "embedded" correspondents got only a glimpse of the full theater of war and bonded with the men and women of "their" units. To identify with the soldiers who protected them meant also that many members of the fourth estate were reluctant to report on all aspects of this war—especially when it meant criticizing the U.S. military.

News reporting was far more critical of the difficulties in the U.S.-led efforts to restore law and order in Iraq and install a democratic system in place of Saddam

Hussein's reign of terror. In the fall of 2003, administration officials embarked on a public relations campaign to counter what they described as biased news from Iraq. Critics inside and outside the Bush administration charged that the media did not report at all, or did not report enough, on the significant progress made in returning life to normal in Iraq. President Bush told an interviewer, "There's a sense that people in America aren't getting the truth. We're making great progress about improving the lives of the people there in Iraq."[41] There is no doubt that the media during this period reported far more prominently about the daily attacks on members of the U.S.-led military coalition, on gas pipelines, and on soft targets such as hotels, embassies, the United Nations headquarters, and other civilian facilities in Iraq than on restored electrical power lines, reopened schools, and well-functioning hospitals. Critics were right at the time to complain that the news about Iraq overemphasized the violence and paid little attention to improvements in various areas, but such criticism was no longer justified once lethal attacks by homegrown insurgents and mostly foreign terrorists increased dramatically and pushed Iraq into a bloody civil war. As ever more Americans and Iraqis became day-in and day-out the victims of the violent clashes between Shi'ites and Sunnis, no one should have expected the news media to downplay the worsening conditions and the failure of American-led coalition forces and the Iraqi military and police units to take control and restore order. By late 2006, President Bush acknowledged that things were bad in Iraq, replaced Secretary of Defense Donald Rumsfeld, and worked on a new strategy to turn things around. Yet First Lady Laura Bush blamed the news media's slanted Iraq coverage for her husband's low public approval ratings. As the NBC Nightly News reported,

BRIAN WILLIAMS, ANCHOR: First lady Laura Bush had something to say about Iraq today. It was during an appearance on MSNBC. Mrs. Bush was asked by Norah O'Donell why she thinks only 2 out of 10 Americans in our latest NBC News/Wall Street Journal poll said they approved of the president's handling of the war in Iraq. Mrs. Bush placed the blame squarely on the news media.

MS. LAURA BUSH: I do know that there are a lot of good things that are happening that aren't covered, and I think the drumbeat in the country from the media, from the only way people know what's happening unless they happen to have a loved one deployed there, is discouraging.

WILLIAMS: Mrs. Bush went on to say she hopes for what she called more balanced coverage in the future. The recent report from the Iraq Study Group, however, specifically found that there has been significant under-reporting of the violence in Iraq.[42]

By and large, however, the focus on the most shocking, sensational, and threatening incidents is symptomatic of the way the news media cover, overcover, and undercover the responses to terrorism at home and abroad. Often, these reporting tendencies prove helpful to presidents as they pursue anti- and counterterrorist policies; but at other times, these same coverage patterns ignore, weaken, and contradict the messages that presidents want to get across to the American people. Just as the news media overemphasize the episodic and most lethal, shocking, and spectacular aspects of terrorism, anti- and counterterrorism news, too, is tilted in favor of the most dramatic, deadly, and troubling events, developments, and messages.

The Iraq War: Different News Coverage Abroad

Whether because of the 9/11 experience or as a consequence of different traditions of the media in the United States and western Europe, the news coverage before and during the 2003 Iraq War was markedly different in leading news organizations in the United States and in the United Kingdom, Germany, and other western European democracies. Ingrid Lehmann found, for example, that during the run-up to the Iraq invasion the German elite newspaper *Frankfurter Allgemeine* published "little to discredit or undermine the [United Nations arms] inspection process," while the *New York Times* was "more critical of the inspections."[43] Whereas the German news media may have been influenced by the German government's criticism of U.S. Iraq policy and its refusal to join the American-led coalition, the situation was very different in the United Kingdom, where Tony Blair was from the outset a strong supporter of the Bush administration's Iraq stance and British troops participated in the invasion and occupation of the country. A study of the web sites of news organizations in forty-eight countries around the world found that the news about the Iraq invasion was more positively framed in countries that officially supported the action than in those opposing the war.[44] Yet reporting in the British elite press was far less uniform than in the comparable U.S. media. One study found, for example, that "*The Independent* seemed more critical of the war, while *The Times* tended to support the British government position."[45] Similarly, the BBC broadcasts were "not patriotic in tone and style as many US networks were."[46] In short, even though British troops were fighting in Iraq, news consumers in the United Kingdom were not solely exposed to rally-round-the-flag coverage as were their American counterparts, but had access to more critical voices as well. As a result, public support for the Iraq war and for Prime Minister Tony Blair in the UK was never as high as for the invasion and President Bush in the United States.

Major American news media web sites gave different reasons for the war than their counterparts abroad: "U.S. media cited more often freedom for the Iraqi people as justification for the war, which was rarely mentioned in foreign sites."[47] Communication research has established that news audiences pay special attention to pictures in television and in print and that visuals are more memorable than the spoken and written word. Thus, it is interesting that the American media differed in the selection of visuals from foreign news organizations. As one study established, American TV networks "rarely, if ever showed visuals of dead or wounded soldiers from the Allied forces but tended to mention such casualties verbally."[48] The opposite was true for dead, wounded, or captured Iraqi soldiers.

One can only guess why the reporting and framing patterns of the American media were different from those of foreign media: Given the American lead role in the "coalition of the willing" and the fact that opponents of the war assigned the bulk of the blame to the American superpower and not to coalition partners, news organizations in the United States seemed more inclined to "rally round the flag" than the news media elsewhere.

Notes

1. Brigitte L. Nacos, Yaeli Bloch-Elkon, and Robert Y. Shapiro, "The Threat of International Terrorism after 9/11: News Coverage and Public Perceptions," paper prepared for presentation at the annual meeting of the American Political Science Association in Philadelphia, August 31, 2006.

2. Judith Miller of the *New York Times*, for example, wrote some excellent articles on the danger of biological weapons. She and two of her colleagues published a book about this threat. See Judith Miller, Stephen Engelberg, and William Broad, *Germs: Biological Weapons and America's Secret War* (New York: Simon and Schuster, 2001).

3. National Commission on Terrorism, "Countering the Changing Threat of Terrorism," report, pursuant to Public Law 277, 105th Congress, 49.

4. Ibid., 6.

5. "Secure, Yes, but Also Free," *Omaha World-Herald*, June 12, 2000, 6.

6. Major acts of terrorism in the United States were feared for the New Year's celebrations marking the end of the twentieth and the beginning of the twenty-first centuries. The Y2K threats, which were believed to target the Internet and computer systems as well, were widely reported in the news.

7. Edward Alden, "Report Warned of Attack on American Soil," *Financial Times*, September 12, 2001, 5.

8. CNN, *The Point with Greta van Susteren*, January 31, 2001.

9. Richard Cohen, "The Terrorism Story—and How We Blew It," *Washington Post*, October 4, 2001, A31.

10. *NBC Nightly News*, December 8, 1997, according to transcript retrieved from the LexisNexis database.

11. Judith Miller, "Nation Lacks Plan to Deter Terrorism," *New York Times*, September 6, 1998, 30.

12. Joshua Green, "Weapons of Mass Confusion: How Pork Trumps Preparedness in the Fight against Terrorism," *Washington Monthly* (May 2001): 15–21.

13. Ibid.

14. Benjamin I. Page, *Who Deliberates? Mass Media in Modern Democracy* (Chicago: University of Chicago Press, 1996), 2.

15. The three letters appeared under "Dispatches from a Day of Terror and Shock," *New York Times*, September 12, 2001, A26.

16. William Safire, "New Day of Infamy," *New York Times*, September 12, 2001, A27.

17. Anthony Lewis, "A Different World," *New York Times*, September 12, 2001, A27.

18. "The National Defense," *New York Times*, September 12, 2001, A26.

19. "The Wrong Time to Fight Iraq," *New York Times*, November 26, 2001, A16.

20. Brigitte L. Nacos, *Terrorism and the Media* (New York: Columbia University Press, 1996), 38.

21. "The Terrorist and His Sentence," *New York Times*, April 15, 1986, A30.

22. From the transcript of ABC Breaking News, "U.S. Strikes against Iraq for Bush Attack," June 26, 1993.

23. Ibid.

24. "A Message for Saddam," *Washington Times*, June 28, 1993, E2.

25. "Strike on Baghdad," *Washington Post*, June 28, 1993, A18.

26. "Was This Strike Necessary?" *New York Times*, June 28, 1993, A16.

27. Ibid.

28. Ibid.

29. Statement by President Bill Clinton, Federal News Service, August 20, 1998, retrieved from LexisNexis.

30. News briefing by William Cohen, secretary of defense, August 20, 1998, according to FDCH Political Transcripts.

31. Vernon Loeb and Michael Grunwald, "Officials Won't Detail Evidence on bin Laden," *Washington Post*, August 21, 1998, A19.

32. "In Self-Defense," *Washington Post*, August 21, 1998, A22.

33. "Striking against Terrorism," *New York Times*, August 21, 1998, A22.

34. *NBC Nightly News*, August 21, 1998.

35. *CNN Late Edition with Wolf Blitzer*, August 23, 1998.

36. Daniel Benjamin and Steven Simon, "A Failure of Intelligence," *New York Review of Books*, December 20, 2001, 77.

37. From a statement by President George W. Bush, October 7, 2001, according to the Federal News Service transcript.

38. These numbers are mentioned by Fareed Zakaria, "Let's Spread the Good Cheer," *Newsweek*, November 26, 2001, 50.

39. Linda Wertheimer spoke of a "burgeoning" antiwar movement in the *All Things Considered* program of September 14, 2001, and her colleague Neil Cohen of a "fledgling" antiwar movement on the *Talk of the Nation* program of September 28, 2001.

40. Michael Kelly, "Immorality of the March," *Washington Post*, February 19, 2003, A29.

41. "White House: Americans Aren't Getting 'Full Story' on Iraq," www.CNN.com (retrieved October 13, 2003).

42. *NBC Nightly News*, December 14, 2006.

43. Ingrid A. Lehmann, "Exploring the Transatlantic Media Divide over Iraq," *Press/Politics* 10:1 (2005): 83.

44. Daniela V. Dimitrova et al., "War on the Web," *Press/Politics* 10:1 (2005): 38.

45. Kai Hafez, "The Iraq War 2003 in Western Media and Public Opinion," *Global Media Journal* 3:5 (Fall 2004), http://lass.calumet.purdue.edu/cca/gmj/fa04/gmj-fa04-hafez.htm

46. Ibid.

47. Dimitrova et al., 33.

48. The study was done by the German company Media Tenor and mentioned in Dimitrova et al., 27.

CHAPTER 17

Conclusion: Living with Terrorist Threats

THERE IS A GREAT DEAL OF DISAGREEMENT ABOUT THE CAUSES of terrorism and the most effective ways to respond to this sort of political violence. But there is agreement on one crucial point: Terrorism will not disappear as the weapon of choice in the hands of domestic and international groups and individuals who cannot fight their declared enemies in legitimate political arenas or in traditional wars. According to Walter Laqueur, "Even in the unlikely case that all global conflicts will be resolved—that all the political, social, and economic tensions of this world will vanish—this will not necessarily be the end of terrorism."[1] It is equally unlikely that terrorism that is rooted in the Arab and Muslim world would end if Israel were to disappear from the map of the Middle East, because a variety of other domestic and international conditions breed discontent and fuel terrorist ideas and deeds in the region. The same is true for other parts of the world and other countries. Moreover, there can be no doubt that the United States will remain the number-one target of international terrorism for the foreseeable future, because, as Paul Pillar concluded, "U.S. policies and the U.S. presence overseas can vary, but the United States' place as sole superpower, leader of the West, and principal exporter of modern culture do not seem likely to change."[2]

Although terrorist organizations come and go, those who represent today's greatest danger may prove more impervious than previous movements. The extremists, who were energized by Osama bin Laden's declaration of war against "Crusaders and Zionists" and by his terror attacks on the United States, emphasize patience as they pursue their long-term goals. Patience informs these terrorists' long-term strategy and their mode of operation. Al Qaeda and like-minded groups do not hastily plot their terror strikes, but prepare and rehearse for years. Their ideological fervor and their justification of unlimited violence are unequivocal. Omar Bakri Muhammad, the head of a radical Islamic group in London and a suspected follower of bin Laden, told an interviewer, "Terror is the language of the twenty-first century. If I want something, I terrorize you to achieve it."[3] This statement goes to the heart of the terrorist calculus and its assumption that terrorism triggers fear in target audiences that goes far beyond the damage inflicted. If you are patient enough, Omar Bakri Muhammad and like-minded people believe, violence will terrorize your targets enough so that you eventually get what you want. According to Muhammad, bin Laden and Al Qaeda have immediate and long-term goals: "They are engaged in a defensive jihad against those who attacked Islam. In the long run, they want to reestablish the Islamic state, the Caliphate. And to convert the whole world."[4] However preposterous such objectives may be, they motivate rank-and-file terrorists and produce a brand of terrorism that kills indiscriminately in order to inflict the greatest psychological damage on their target audiences. Laqueur has emphasized that the "believers in jihad are a minority, in most countries a tiny minority, but they can count on a substantial periphery of sympathizers, more than sufficient to sustain long campaigns of terrorism."[5] But there is also the threat of lone wolves and autonomous cells that lack the sophistication of the movement's leaders and followers but have the potential to inflict great harm.

A case in point was the arrest of a four-man team of would-be terrorists in May 2009 that planned to blow up two Jewish centers in New York City and shoot surface-to-air guided missiles at planes at an Air National Guard base in New York State. Reportedly, the four men met in prison and the ringleader had told a police informer that he was interested "to do jihad." Not known to be particularly devout Muslims among members of the mosque they attended, the men were charged with plotting three simultaneous strikes to retaliate against Jews and the American military for killing Muslims in Afghanistan and Pakistan.[6]

While the focus on the extremist Islamic movement is justified, it could be a costly mistake to ignore other movements, groups, and threats—not only of the international variety. The potential for devastating strikes by domestic terrorists is far from remote. Experts agree that the anthrax terrorist, who struck only weeks after 9/11, was a homegrown perpetrator and that he used a killer agent of domestic origin against fellow Americans. Yet years after the anthrax scare, the identity of the letter sender was still not known and the incident all but forgotten.

Fueling Our Fears

Unless there is clear evidence of an imminent attack, terror alerts issued by governments tend to raise the anxieties of the general public unnecessarily. After all, what is the average person to do in the face of such alerts? Stay home?

In August 2004, sixty-six-year-old Gale William Nettles was charged with plotting to blow up a federal building in downtown Chicago with a truck bomb similar to the one used by Oklahoma City bomber Timothy McVeigh. Nettles, a convicted felon, had bought 500 pounds of what he thought was explosive fertilizer from an undercover agent and rented a locker to store the bomb-making material. The would-be bomber had first told fellow inmates at a Mississippi prison that he was planning violent revenge against the federal government for convicting and imprisoning him for his counterfeiting activities. In this case, thanks to the involvement of undercover agents, the bomb-making fertilizer was in fact benign material.

Far more alarming was the accidental disruption of a terrorist plot in early 2003, when FBI agents were directed to a weapons arsenal in the Texas countryside that contained a large number of guns, pipe bombs, and a cyanide bomb "big enough to kill everyone in a 30,000-square-foot building."[7] Some observers charged that the case got little attention in Washington's antiterrorism agencies. As one critic wrote,

> The discovery of the Texas cyanide bomb should have served as a wake-up call: 9/11 has focused our attention on the threat from Islamic radicals, but murderous right-wing fanatics are still out there. The concern of the Justice Department, however, appears to lie elsewhere. Two weeks ago a representative of the FBI appealed to an industry group for help in combating what, he told the audience, the FBI regards the country's leading domestic terrorist threat: ecological and animal rights extremists.[8]

Nothing as dangerous as a chemical weapon—the mentioned cyanide bomb—was ever found in the possession of environmental and animal rights fanatics. But just as right-wing extremists may pose a serious threat, other extremists may move toward similar designs. Therefore, vigilance is needed on all fronts. Comparing the fight against terrorism with public health experts' struggle against communicable diseases, Pillar concluded,

> Some of the threats are waxing; some are waning. Some are old; others are new. Much of the challenge and the frustration comes from the fact that just as things are going well on one front—and occasionally even so well that a problem is eradicated altogether (small pox, the Red Army Faction)—a different and perhaps even more threatening problem emerges (AIDS, al-Qaida). Attention and resources get shifted around as threats evolve, but the effort as a whole can never stop.[9]

Such an analogy is helpful in understanding the nature of the terrorist threat in both the domestic and international arenas.

This book set out to explain the calculus of terrorism and trace its influence on the utility of political violence by weak non-state actors, the making of terrorists and terrorist organizations, and their strategies, tactics, and organizational structures. The idea was furthermore to describe and assess how targeted governments respond, how the media report, and how the public reacts to terrorist incidents. Most importantly, the question was whether and to what degree terrorist assumptions are borne out by the results of their violent deeds. The conclusion is unequivocal: Even small groups and lone wolves become political factors in strong nation-states, and at times in the international political arena as well, when they commit political violence—especially when their terror is of the spectacular kind. Terrorists force nation-states to react, and often they get their target societies to overreact at the expense of violating their most fundamental values.

The question, then, is how societies can cope with serious terrorist threats without being overwhelmed by the psychological warfare that terrorists wage. There are no silver bullets for this predicament. But the more people know about the dangers they face, the greater is the chance that they will not be consumed by fear before actual terrorist attacks occur and that they will not panic once terrorists strike. Public officials must provide and citizens must insist on realistic threat assessments that neither minimize nor maximize the dangers based on the best intelligence available.

Politicians must accept that partisan expedience should never enter anti- and counterterrorist discussions, measures, and policies. Terrorists aim at influencing politics and policies in their target countries. But neither politicians nor the public should play into their hands. If the architects of the train bombings in Madrid on March 11, 2004, struck in order to influence the outcome of Spain's national elections three days later, they were successful: Prime Minister José María Aznar and the Popular Party, supporters of the American invasion and occupation in Iraq, were defeated; and José Luis Rodríguez Zapatero and the Socialist Party, opponents of the Iraq war, won the election. Yet, it was far from clear that the Spanish electorate voted out Aznar because of the massive terror attack. Instead, observers believed that Spaniards punished Aznar because his government immediately blamed the bombings on Basque separatists and discounted Muslim extremists as possible perpetrators in spite of evidence to the contrary.

Regardless of the true reason for Aznar's defeat, administration officials in Washington warned in the summer of 2004 that Al Qaeda was likely to strike the United States again in order to influence the presidential election. In early 2005, similar claims were made in the United Kingdom with respect to upcoming elections. There was no doubt in both cases that terrorists could strike again at any time before or after the election. But to associate threat alerts with the upcoming elections validated bin Laden and his followers as powerful players for partisan politics' sake. Indeed, in early August 2004, after Secretary of Homeland Security Tom Ridge went public with a warning ahead of the November elections, 28% of Americans believed that this particular alert was "politically motivated," 50% thought it was based on "real intelligence," and 12% thought the alert was based on "some of both" factors.[10] Residents of New York City were even more skeptical in their assessment of the administration's motives, in that 46% believed "strongly" and 17% believed "somewhat" that this particular terrorism alert, supposed to last through Election Day, had political purposes.[11]

If public officials raise threat alerts in the absence of specific evidence, the news media must not scare the public by reporting prominently and frequently on vague information. Terror alerts play into the hands of terrorists because the mere threat of terrorism affects target audiences nearly as much as real strikes.

Public officials, experts, educators, and the news media have an obligation to educate and inform the public about the calculus of terrorism so that citizens understand the scheme of political violence in which the psychological impact on target societies surpasses the number of people killed and injured. Every person who is killed in a terrorist event means a tragic, utterly unnecessary loss. But we must also keep in mind that many more people die each year because of traffic accidents, crimes, cancer, heart attacks, and AIDS than in terrorist incidents. About 40,000 Americans are killed year in, year out in traffic accidents alone compared to the approximately 3,000 persons who perished on 9/11 in the World Trade Center and Pentagon and in Pennsylvania. Yet the deaths from diseases and accidents do not cause the widespread fear and depression that are common in the wake of major acts of terrorism. Target societies must become aware of these facts and realize that the psychological impact of terrorism is disproportionate to the likelihood that an individual will become a victim of terror strikes. Therefore, just as terrorists exploit the triangle of communication for their propaganda scheme (see Chapter 14), knowledgeable public and private sources must use the same communication vehicle to disseminate reliable and useful information that counters the fear tactics of terrorist foes.

The public has a right to know—even if the truth means learning about the likelihood that terrorists, sooner or later, will acquire and use weapons of mass destruction. But for the authorities to discuss possible horror scenarios makes sense only if they inform the public at the same time on the state of emergency preparedness in their communities. It is equally important that the public and private sectors tell the public what to do and what not to do in case of catastrophic terror.

A well-informed and well-prepared society is less likely to panic in the face of a terrorist crisis and more likely to opt for proportional anti- and counterterrorist responses at home and abroad than a clueless audience. It is necessary to act decisively in the area of prevention and preparedness, on efforts to apprehend terrorists and to disrupt terrorist operations, recruiting, training, indoctrination, and financing schemes. It is legitimate to use military force against state sponsors involved in or supportive of specific terrorist acts. The Al Qaeda–Taliban collaboration was such a case. But it is unwise to overreact at home or abroad. Overreaction undermines the moral fabric of a society that is victimized by terrorists and plays into the hands of terrorists and the assumptions central to their calculus of violence. As we know now, the invasion and occupation of Iraq did not decrease the terrorist threat but increased it, if only by driving more recruits into the arms of Al Qaeda and like-minded groups.

While terrorists can and do cause enormous harm and affect domestic and international politics and policies—at times significantly—few of them realize their ultimate objectives. Based on his comprehensive study of twenty-eight terrorist groups, Max Abrahams found that these groups "accomplished their forty-two policy objectives only 7 percent of the time." Just as important, those groups "whose attacks on civilian targets outnumbered attacks on military targets failed to achieve their policy objectives regardless of their nature."[12] In other words, terrorism does not work! This does not mean, however, that extremists will stop trying. Terrorist groups come and go. Some are more durable than others. Whenever Al Qaeda and similar organizations and cells cease to exist, other groups will emerge. Yet, given the poor success rate of terrorism, there is no reason for gloom and doom. The targets of terrorism will have to learn how to counter and contain the threat.

Notes

1. Walter Laqueur, *No End to War: Terrorism in the Twenty-first Century* (New York: Continuum, 2003), 231.
2. Paul R. Pillar, *Terrorism and Foreign Policy* (Washington, DC: Brookings Institution Press, 2001), 233.
3. From an interview conducted by the Portuguese reporter Paulo Moura, *Harper's Magazine*, July 2004, 23.
4. Ibid., 25.
5. Laqueur, 210.
6. For more on this case, see http://www.washingtonpost.com/wp-dyn/content/article/2009/05/21/AR2009052100424_pf.html (accessed May 21, 2009).
7. Paul Krugman, "Noonday in the Shade," *New York Times*, June 22, 2004, A19.
8. Ibid.
9. Pillar, 218.
10. According to a Fox News survey that was conducted August 3–4, 2004.
11. According to a Pace University survey of August 12–31, 2004.
12. Max Abrahams, "Why Terrorism Does Not Work." *International Security* 31:2 (Fall 2006): 43.

Major Terrorist Incidents Since the Early 1970s

I. Incidents That Deliberately Targeted Americans and/or American Interests

The Iranian Hostage Crisis (1979–1981)

On November 4, 1979, several hundred young Islamic militants, all self-proclaimed students and followers of Iran's supreme ruler, Ayatollah Ruhollah Khomeini, seized the American embassy in Tehran, burned the compound's U.S. flag, and took sixty-two Americans hostage. Initially, U.S. officials in Washington and in Tehran viewed the takeover as yet another annoying but manageable incident in the midst of the fundamental political and societal changes that followed the fall of the Shah Mohammed Reza Pahlavi regime, the triumph of the Islamic revolution, and the return of the Ayatollah Khomeini from exile in Paris. After all, a similar takeover of the embassy nine months earlier had ended quickly, after pro-Khomeini revolutionary guards had freed the American hostages and removed the militants from the embassy. But in this case, the three American officials who happened to be in Iran's foreign ministry at the time of the seizure pleaded in vain for the Iranian authorities to once again free the embassy staff.

The anti-American sentiment in Iran, especially among the supporters of the Islamic revolution and the establishment of an Islamic state, had markedly increased because the Carter administration had allowed the ailing shah to enter the United States to seek medical treatment a few days before the embassy seizure. What the White House considered a humanitarian gesture was seen by many Iranians as yet another sign of American support for the man who during his reign had brutally oppressed dissent. In this anti-American hysteria among militant Islamic elements, it did not matter that President Jimmy Carter, a strong advocate of human rights, had pressed the shah for reforms. The Ayatollah Khomeini recognized immediately the usefulness of the hostage crisis for his domestic purposes. The idea was to unite against a powerful and "evil" enemy, the United States, which he came to call "the

Great Satan." Thus, one day after the successful takeover, Khomeini and several of his highly placed supporters sided publicly with the hostage-holders; they supported their demands, primarily the return of the shah and his assets to Iran. Just like the militants who were in control of the U.S. embassy, the Ayatollah justified the predicament of the Americans by characterizing them as "spies" and the embassy as a "spy nest" (only a group of thirteen embassy staffers, predominantly women and African Americans, were not deemed spies and were released a few weeks after the takeover). Khomeini moved swiftly against possible opponents. According to Gary Sick, "Within a brief forty-eight hours [after the hostage taking], Khomeini had silenced the last important voice opposing his program, had diverted domestic attention away from internal disputes, and had launched a major confrontation with the United States that could be expected to galvanize public opinion behind him."[1] Given these constellations, the Iranian hostage situation turned into a major political crisis and a fourteen-month nightmare for the hostages, their loved ones at home, the American public, and, last but not least, President Carter.

In Iran, the Ayatollah Khomeini was able to exploit the hostage standoff to consolidate his power; in the United States, President Carter, after receiving an initial burst of public support, was increasingly blamed for allowing a gang of terrorists and a comparably weak country to hold the United States hostage—blamed by his political opponents in the Republican Party, by fellow Democrats, and by an increasing share of the American public. As criticism of Carter's "do-nothing" approach grew, the president ordered a highly complex and risky rescue mission by members of the counterterrorism unit Delta Force, who had trained for such an operation since shortly after the embassy takeover. Delta Force commandos were flown to a rendezvous place in the Iranian desert dubbed "Desert One," from where they were to fly aboard helicopters into the area of Tehran to stage a complicated attempt to rescue the hostages. But only five of the six helicopters needed for the operation (out of a total of eight) landed at Desert One in operational condition. Charles Beckwith, the mission commander, had no choice but to abort the rescue attempt. Tragically, during the refueling operations before takeoff, eight soldiers were killed when a transport plane and a helicopter collided. The failure of the mission and, even more so, the deadly disaster at Desert One weakened Carter's support further. While the president overcame challenges in his own party and again became the Democrats' candidate, Republican Ronald Reagan won the presidential election in November 1980. Nobody knows whether Carter would have won if the hostages had been released before election day, as some of his close advisors believed. Others doubted that the hostage crisis cost Carter the presidency and pointed to the increasingly severe economic downturn during Carter's term.

With the shah dead (he had succumbed to his illness during the summer in a Cairo hospital), Carter defeated, and the victory of the Islamic revolution sealed, the hostages in Iran had outlived their usefulness for Khomeini and his supporters. After negotiating the transfer of close to $8 billion of the shah's assets to Iran, the Iranian authorities released the hostages on January 20, 1981—only minutes after Jimmy Carter's presidency had ended and Ronald Reagan had been sworn in as president. For 444 days, as the media reminded the U.S. public day in and day out, the United States had been held hostage.

Shortly after he moved into the White House and shortly after the hostages had finally come home, President Reagan reinforced the tough message he had sent during the election campaign. "Let terrorists beware that when the rules of international behavior are violated, our policy will be one of swift and effective retribution," he said.[2] During his two terms as president, Reagan found out that it was far easier to speak tough than to act tough. He had relentlessly criticized his predecessor for the way Carter had handled the Iran hostage crisis. But with the exception of the servicemen who were killed during the ill-fated rescue mission, none of the immediate targets of the embassy seizure was killed or injured during the long ordeal. In stark contrast, Reagan's two terms as president were plagued by a multitude of anti-American terrorist spectaculars that resulted in hundreds of deaths and injuries.

Two Catastrophic Bombings in Beirut (1983)

On April 18, 1983, a delivery truck loaded with 400 pounds of explosives sped past the guards in front of the U.S. embassy in Beirut and, as it reached the front portico of the building, blew up in a powerful explosion that destroyed the central part of the building. Sixty-three people, among them 17 Americans, were killed, and 120 others were injured. General John Vessey, the chairman of the Joint Chiefs of Staff, called the most lethal attack on an American diplomatic facility "an inexplicable aberration."[3] As it turned out, the first anti-American suicide bombing was only the beginning of a sustained terror campaign against Americans by fundamental Lebanese Shi'ite groups, namely, the Hezbollah (Party of God) and the Lebanese Islamic Jihad, who were inspired by the Iranian revolution and actively supported by the Iranian Revolutionary Guards and thus by the Iranian leadership. What these circles resented most of all was the presence of U.S. Marines and other foreign forces on Lebanese territory even though the troops, together with their French and Italian counterparts, had come to restore law and order after Israel had invaded in the hunt for members of the Palestinian Liberation Organization (PLO) and had carried out the evacuation of PLO leader Yassir Arafat and his followers from Lebanon.

Far more devastating blows followed six months later, on October 23, 1983, when suicide bombers drove their explosive-laden trucks simultaneously into the U.S. Marine Corps' and the French forces' compounds outside Beirut. Two hundred and forty-one American Marines and fifty-eight French servicemen were killed. President Reagan called the terrorist attacks "despicable" and expressed his "outrage." But while the president emphasized his determination to keep a force in Lebanon immediately after he learned of the carnage, four months later his administration decided to withdraw all the Marines from Lebanon. The terrorists had achieved their goal.

TWA Hijacking and Hostage Situation (1985)

Nothing seemed out of the ordinary for the 8 crew members and the 145 passengers when TWA Flight 847 took off on June 6, 1985, from the airport in Athens, Greece. But once in the air, two heavily armed members of the Lebanese Hezbollah hijacked the Boeing 727, forcing the pilot to fly to Beirut and not, as scheduled, to Rome, Italy. En route, the hijackers brutally beat a young Navy diver, Robert Stethem, and searched for passengers with Israeli passports or Jewish names. After refueling in Beirut, the terrorists ordered the pilot to fly to Algiers, where some women and children were released, then return to Beirut airport, where they killed Stethem and dumped his body on the tarmac before ordering yet another stop in Algiers and a third flight to Beirut. Eventually, Nabih Berri, a lawyer, negotiated on behalf of the hijackers, who demanded the release of hundreds of Shi'ites from Israeli prisons. Seventeen days after the ordeal began and after intensive negotiations involving Berri, the United States, the Israeli government, the Red Cross, and, of course, the terrorists, the hostages were released—with the understanding that Israel would free the prisoners. Behind the scenes, the Reagan administration had pressed Israel to agree to this solution and violate its declared policy of making no concessions to terrorists, although President Reagan said otherwise when he addressed the nation. In Jeffrey Simon's words, "Terrorists worldwide could not have hoped for a better script. The message was clear: Hijack the right plane at the right moment, or perpetrate some other dramatic attack, and you can bring the president of the most powerful nation in the world to address you and take notice of you."[4]

The *Achille Lauro* Seizure (1985)

In April 2003, following the defeat of Saddam Hussein's Iraqi regime, members of the U.S. Special Operations Forces captured Muhammad Abbas—better known by his nom de guerre Abu Abbas, one of the more notorious terrorist leaders of the 1970s and 1980s—outside of Baghdad. Nearly eighteen years earlier, Abbas had masterminded, and four members of the Palestine Liberation Front (PLF) had carried out, one of the most brutal acts of terrorism. The ordeal began on October 7, 1985, when four heavily armed Palestinian men, seemingly passengers, seized the Italian cruise ship *Achille Lauro* off the Egyptian coast.[5] They demanded the release of 50 of their comrades from Israeli prisons. Because some 750 travelers had gone ashore at Alexandria for an excursion earlier in the day, less than 100 passengers and 344 crew members were aboard at the time. Singling out Americans and Jews, the Palestinians terrorized their hostages relentlessly. In an unspeakably cruel act, one of the terrorists killed 69-year-old Leon Klinghoffer, a New Yorker, who was partially paralyzed and confined to a wheelchair. After one of the terrorists shot Klinghoffer in the head and chest, he forced members of the crew to throw the body overboard. Soon thereafter, Egyptian officials convinced the terrorists to surrender by promising them free passage to a destination of their choice.

However, U.S. fighter planes intercepted the Egyptian airliner that carried Abu Abbas, one of his aides, and the four *Achille Lauro* hijackers, forcing the intercepted plane to land at a NATO base in Sigonella, Italy. There, Italian troops prevented U.S. Special Operation Forces from apprehending the Palestinians. Instead, the Italians took the four *Achille Lauro* terrorists into custody and allowed Abbas and his aide to leave the country. Pressured by the Reagan administration, Italy tried Abbas in 1986 in absentia and sentenced him to life in prison.

The Lebanon Hostages (1982–1991)

Foreigners were kidnapped in and around Beirut throughout the 1980s by members of radical Shi'ite groups that had close ties to Iran. Various groups claimed responsibility, but it was widely assumed that Hezbollah was behind most of these hostage-takings. Starting with the kidnapping of David Dodge, acting president of the American University in Beirut, a total of seventeen American men were held hostage by these circles. Of these hostages, three were killed brutally: William Buckley, the CIA station chief in Beirut; Peter Kilburn, a librarian at the American University in Beirut; and Marine Lieutenant Colonel William Higgins. One of the hostages was able to escape; the others were held under gruesome conditions for various lengths of time. When one or another captive was released, others were grabbed. Terry Anderson, an Associated Press correspondent, was by far the longest held of the "Lebanon hostages," spending 2,454 days (or close to seven years) in captivity.

The motives were not always clear. For example, at times the captors demanded the release of prisoners from Kuwait, Israel, and Germany; on other occasions, they seemed driven by the desire to gain publicity and attention at home and abroad. As the result of an arms-for-hostages deal between the Reagan administration and the Iranian government, several of the long-term U.S. hostages were released, but they were quickly replaced by others. The secret transactions between the White House and Iranian officials were a blatant violation of the official policy that President Reagan and his administration claimed to support, namely, not to give in to the demands of terrorists and not to make deals with terrorists.

The captives, among them Anderson, were finally freed in late 1991 after lengthy negotiations involving Iranian, Israeli, American, and United Nations officials. Although no side admitted to a quid pro quo, the Iranian authorities reportedly paid the hostage-holders between $1 and $2 million for each of the Western hostages released after July 1991. Israeli officials agreed to release Arab prisoners if they received information about the fate of some of their missing servicemen presumed to have fallen into Lebanese terrorists' hands. Last but not least, after protracted negotiations, the U.S. administration approved the transfer of $278 million to Iran as compensation for ordered military equipment that the United States had seized more than a decade earlier during the Iranian hostage crisis.[6] While nobody spoke of ransom, there was no doubt that once again terrorism had paid and that the White House had made deals—not with the terrorists themselves, but with their state sponsor.

The Bombing of Pan Am Flight 103 (1988)

On December 21, 1988, Pan Am Flight 103, which had originated in Frankfurt, Germany, was en route to New York after a stopover at Heathrow Airport when it was blown out of the sky over Lockerbie, Scotland. All 259 persons aboard, among them 35 undergraduate students at Syracuse University, and 11 persons on the ground were killed. Had it not been for a delay at Heathrow, the explosion would have occurred over the Atlantic and its cause never resolved. But with evidence on the ground in hand, the British authorities established that a small sheet of plastic explosives had been hidden in a radiocassette player inside a suitcase. Early on, there was the suspicion that the bombing was meant to avenge the accidental destruction of an Iranian civil airliner over the Persian Gulf by the USS Vincennes and that the Iranians had contracted with terrorists to do its dirty work. Bombing devices similar to the one used to destroy the Pan Am airliner were found in the possession of members of the Popular Front for the Liberation of Palestine–General Command (PFLP–GC) in Germany, but two Libyan agents were eventually identified as the perpetrators. This led to the suspicion that the downing of Pan Am Flight 103 was Libya's belated revenge for the 1986 bombing of Tripoli and Benghazi by the United States. It took years of sanctions by the United States and the United Nations and sustained pressure by the families of the Pan Am 103 victims before Libya's ruler, Muammar Qaddafi, handed over the two agents, Abdelbaset al-Megrahi and Al Amin Fhima, to the Netherlands in 1999, where they were tried by a Scottish court. In early 2001, al-Megrahi was found guilty and sentenced to a minimum of twenty years in prison, and Fhima was found not guilty and released.

Although the court established that the planning of the terrorist act had originated in Libya and that al-Megrahi was a Libyan intelligence officer, the judges did not implicate the highest level of the Libyan government. But the unyielding efforts by the families of the Pan Am 103 victims to get the U.S. government to pressure Qaddafi not only resulted in the trial of the two agents but also may have curbed Qaddafi's appetite for sponsoring more terrorism.

The First World Trade Center Bombing (1993)

The first bombing of the World Trade Center (WTC) in New York on February 26, 1993, marked the beginning of a new chapter in the history of anti-American terrorism. While the destruction of Pan Am Flight 103 in 1988 could be understood as a precursor to the catastrophic terrorism of the 1990s and thereafter, the 1993 bombing of the building in downtown Manhattan was the first major act of international terrorism inside the United States. Although the blast of more than 1,000 pounds of explosives in the parking garage beneath the Wall Street area's signature building did not, as the perpetrators had planned, topple at least one of the 110-story twin towers, its effects were far-reaching and transcended the immediate costs—6 persons killed, more than 1,000 injured, and massive damage to the WTC. The most severe consequences were to the American psyche, in that the "explosion in the bowels of the World Trade Center's twin towers dispelled for ever the myth that terrorists are simply not able to stage their violent spectaculars inside the United States."[7] The "Liberation Army Fifth Battalion" claimed responsibility for the bombing and warned that more targets inside the United States, among them nuclear facilities, would be attacked. Demanding that the United States sever its diplomatic ties to Israel and change its Middle East policy, the terrorists justified their deed in writing: "The American people must know that their civilians who got killed [in the WTC blast] are not better than those who are getting killed by American weapons and support."[8]

Several of the conspirators involved in the elaborate planning and execution of the WTC bombing were non-Afghan veterans of the fight against the Soviet invaders in Afghanistan, and in that role had received significant American support. But after the Soviet military was out of Afghanistan and no more assistance was forthcoming from the United States, these displaced mujahideen (holy warriors) had turned against their onetime American benefactor. Those who had settled in the New York and New Jersey area were followers of Sheik Omar Abdel-Rahman, an anti-Western, anti-American Muslim preacher. Before coming to the United States in the beginning of the 1990s, Sheik Abdel-Rahman was the leader of the extremist Islamic Group in Egypt and was allegedly involved in the assassination of Anwar Sadat, Egypt's president. Sheik Abdel-Rahman and four other men were accused of having plotted the WTC bombing in 1993, found guilty, and sentenced to lifelong prison terms.

But the hunt for the most important figure behind this bombing continued until Ramzi Ahmed Yousef was arrested in Pakistan and extradited to the United States in 1995. FBI investigators traced an early, if indirect, link between Yousef and Osama bin Laden. Yousef, born in Kuwait to a Palestinian mother and Pakistani father, was as vehemently opposed to what he believed was a corrupt Kuwaiti regime as bin Laden was to the Saudi rule in Saudi Arabia. In 1988, Yousef "spent several months in Peshawar in training camps funded by Osama bin Laden learning bomb-making skills and teaching electronics to other fighters."[9] However, as Simon Reeves found,

> The links between Yousef and bin Laden have always been shrouded in secrecy and confusion. Bin Laden himself has claimed that he never knew Yousef before the [first] World Trade Center explosion. "Unfortunately, I did not know him before the incident," he has said. Perhaps he did not know Yousef personally, but investigators believe that Yousef received support and funding from bin Laden via relatives and associates.[10]

Yousef had entered the United States in the fall of 1992 claiming to seek political and religious asylum. Instead, he found like-minded people among the followers of Sheik Abdel-Rahman and initiated the preparations for the bombing attack on the World Trade Center a few months later. In 1997, Yousef was found guilty by a jury in New York and sentenced to 240 years in prison.

Domestic Terrorism: The Oklahoma City Bombing (1995)

Shortly after 9:00 a.m. on April 19, 1995, a powerful truck bomb explosion destroyed the Alfred P. Murrah Federal Building in downtown Oklahoma City. One hundred and sixty-eight persons, among them nineteen children who had attended a day care center in the office building, were killed, and hundreds were injured. As the architect of the devastating terror who had personally ignited the bomb, Timothy McVeigh, a veteran of the Persian Gulf War, was eventually tried, convicted, and sentenced to death. His accomplice, Terry Nichols, was also brought to justice. Although neither McVeigh nor Nichols claimed responsibility following the catastrophic event, they left a powerful clue with respect to their grievances and motives: By striking on the second anniversary of the FBI's ill-fated raid on the Branch Davidian sect's compound in Waco, Texas, during which sect leader David Koresh and eighty of his followers died, the perpetrators revealed their roots in the radical-right milieu whose hatred of the federal government had been fueled by deadly encounters between, on the one hand, federal law enforcement agents and, on the other, individuals such as survivalist and white supremacist Randy Weaver and groups such as the Branch Davidian sect. The news media reported extensively on the sentiments of right-wing extremists. Thus, the *New York Times* quoted the leader of the notorious White Aryan Resistance, Tom Metzger, who seemed not surprised by the deadly blast in Oklahoma City when he stated,

> I have told people for years, at least since 1984, when the Order [another right-wing extremist group] declared war on the central Government of the United States that the Government of this country—what we call criminals—had better start listening to the dispossessed majority.
> Evidently these people [those responsible for the Oklahoma City bombing], who I don't know personally, saw the Federal building as a strategic military target and these are the things that happen at war."[11]

As soon as McVeigh was identified as a suspect, the media reported on his links to the extreme right, his visit to the site of the Branch Davidians' compound in Waco, and how this experience had magnified his hate of the federal government. The news revisited another incident that had intensified the antigovernment sentiments in the militia, patriot, and white supremacist movements: the deadly encounter between Randy Weaver and federal agents at Ruby Ridge, Idaho, in 1992, during which Weaver's wife and son and a deputy U.S. marshal were killed. Both incidents were on McVeigh's mind when he planned his act of terrorism. According to Lou Michel and Dan Herbeck, two reporters for the *Buffalo News* who interviewed McVeigh behind bars for some seventy-five hours,

> *McVeigh had considered targeting specific individuals, among them Lou Horiuchi, the FBI sharpshooter who had killed Randy Weaver's wife, Vicky, at Ruby Ridge. He considered going after a member of the sharpshooter's family, to inflict the same kind of pain the surviving Weavers had experienced. But ultimately he decided that he could make the loudest statement by bombing a federal building. By destroying people who compiled a complete cross-section of federal employees, McVeigh believed that he was showing federal agents how wrong they were to attack the entire Branch Davidian family. In McVeigh's opinion, every division of the federal government had, at one time or another, mistreated the public. Now, McVeigh decided, was the time to make them all pay.*[12]

McVeigh died with the conviction that the "statement" he had made by bombing the federal building in Oklahoma City was not simply heard around the world but was also heard by the federal government and federal law enforcement agencies in particular. He believed that the FBI and other agencies altered their rules of engagement during standoff situations similar to those at Waco and Ruby Ridge and, more importantly, that these changes were the direct result of his terrorist act.[13]

The Bombings of U.S. Embassies in Kenya and Tanzania (1998)

On August 7, 1998, two suicide bombers drove their explosive-laden cars close to the U.S. embassies in Nairobi, Kenya, and Dar es Salaam, Tanzania, before igniting their powerful bombs. The explosions killed 291 persons and injured more than 5,000 in Nairobi; an additional 10 persons were killed and 77 wounded in Dar es Salaam. The attacks were directed against U.S. facilities, but most of the casualties were Kenyans and Tanzanians. A group calling itself the Islamic Army for the Liberation of Holy Places claimed responsibility for the near-simultaneous blasts, but U.S. investigators suspected immediately that bin Laden's Al Qaeda organization was responsible. In response, President Bill Clinton ordered missile strikes against Al Qaeda training camps in Afghanistan and a pharmaceutical plant in the Sudan that the U.S. administration described as a chemical weapons–related facility. Bin Laden and his associates had lived in Sudan before they moved on to Afghanistan.

Within the next few months, the U.S. District Court for the Southern District of New York indicted a dozen individuals, among them Osama bin Laden; his chief of military operations, Muhammad Atef; and several members of Al Qaeda in the two east African bombings. According to the Department of State, "At the end of 2000, one suspect had pled guilty to conspiring in the attacks, five were in custody in New York awaiting trial, three were in the United Kingdom pending extradition to the United States, and 13 were fugitives, including Usama Bin Laden."[14] According to one account, the first trial in the case against four defendants revealed "al-Qaeda's planning sophistication, its ability to secretly transfer large sums of money to operational terrorist units in the field, the excellent military training and dedication of its leadership and operational personnel, and its marked ability to coordinate terrorist activities across locations."[15]

The Bombing of the USS *Cole* (2000)

On October 12, 2000, the crew of the USS *Cole* readied the mighty U.S. Navy destroyer to be docked and refueled in the Yemeni port of Aden, when a small boat with two men aboard moved straight toward the *Cole's* hull and exploded in a powerful blast. Seventeen sailors were killed, thirty-nine others were injured, and the ship was severely damaged. The suicide bombing was a stunning terrorist act and a success, in that a small fiberglass boat with some hundred pounds of explosives had taken on the most powerful of the United States' warships outfitted with an arsenal of guided missiles and a sophisticated radar system. The pictures of the massive hole in the *Cole's* hull and of the crew's desperate and ultimately successful fight to prevent their ship from sinking "added up to a stunning David and Goliath metaphor: A powerful symbol of the world's most formidable military superpower was incapacitated by members and/or agents of a comparatively weak group unable to fight the mighty United States in open warfare."[16]

Because of the boldness of the attack and bin Laden's family roots in Yemen, law enforcement authorities in Yemen and in the United States suspected immediately that Al Qaeda was behind the attack. Two suspects with alleged ties to the terrorist organization were arrested and jailed in Yemen, but more than two years after the attack on the *Cole*, no trial date had been set. Instead, in April 2003 the two men and eight other suspected followers of bin Laden managed to escape from prison. The following month, federal prosecutors in the United States indicted Jamal Ahmed al-Badawi and Fahd al-Quso for planning the terrorist strike against the *Cole*. According to the indictment, the men had been recruited by Al Qaeda, had attended training camps in Afghanistan, and had planned an earlier attack on another Navy destroyer, the *Sullivan*, that "was called off when their boat sank under the weight of its own explosives."[17]

While at the time not widely understood as a watershed event, in hindsight it is quite obvious that the bold strike against the USS *Cole* opened a new chapter in the history of anti-American terrorism and foreshadowed the far more lethal terror assaults on American soil less than one year later.

The Attacks of 9/11 (2001)

On September 11, 2001, after a long period of elaborate preparations abroad and inside the United States, nineteen male members of the Al Qaeda network set in motion what up to then seemed an unthinkable terrorist attack inside the United States. Hijacking nearly simultaneously four airliners shortly after takeoff from airports on the east coast by attacking crew members and passengers with box cutters and knives, the terrorists took command of the planes in order to fly them into predetermined buildings. The chain of events unfolded as follows:

1. Five of the terrorists hijacked American Airlines Flight 11 that departed Boston at 7:45 a.m. for a flight to Los Angeles. One hour later, the terrorists piloted the machine into the North Tower of the World Trade Center in New York.

2. Five of the terrorists hijacked United Airlines Flight 175, also taking off from Boston and bound for Los Angeles, at 7:58 a.m. An hour and seven minutes later, the aircraft was flown deliberately into the South Tower of the World Trade Center. When the two buildings collapsed soon thereafter, more than 2,800 persons, among them hundreds of firefighters and police officers, were killed, and many others were injured.[18]

3. Four terrorists took control of United Airlines Flight 93 after it left Newark at 8:01 a.m. on its scheduled trip to San Francisco. When passengers learned from cellular phone conversations with members of their families that two hijacked planes had been flown into the World Trade Center towers, they decided to fight the hijackers. Two hours after takeoff, Flight 93 crashed in Pennsylvania's Stony Creek Township. It is believed that the terrorists intended to fly the plane into a building in Washington, D.C., most likely the Capitol, and that the courageous action by passengers foiled this plan.

4. Five terrorists took control of American Airlines Flight 77 after it had departed Dulles Airport, Washington, D.C., at 8:10 a.m. en route to San Francisco. Twenty-nine minutes later, the aircraft was crashed into the Pentagon in Arlington, Virginia, just outside of the U.S. capital, killing 189 persons, injuring others, and destroying part of the building.[19]

Because they selected flights destined to fly nonstop across the United States and crashed them shortly after takeoff into the targeted buildings, the hijackers could be certain that the fuel tanks of their airplanes-turned-missiles were full and would cause the greatest possible explosions and devastation upon impact.

International terrorism against Americans had frequently shocked and intimidated the U.S. public and preoccupied several U.S. presidents during the closing decades of the twentieth century. The first World Trade Center bombing in particular had shattered the belief that serious terrorist acts occurred abroad, but not at home. Yet, when experts warned of catastrophic terror attacks on the United States and recommended tougher security measures, nobody—least of all decision-makers—paid attention. The events of 9/11 convinced American leaders and the American public that international terrorism represented the number-one threat to their national security and national interest.

Based on his pre– and post–9/11 communications, this was precisely the reaction that Osama bin Laden and his brain trust had intended and anticipated. The Al Qaeda leader hoped to shock the United States into a state of mind that would assure that its decision-makers would overreact in both domestic and foreign policies. Bin Laden left no doubt that the strikes against American symbols inside the United States on the heels of previous attacks against the United States were designed to rally support for his anti-American, anti-Israel, and anti-Western pan-Islamic vision and thus drive the Christian-Jewish "Crusaders" and their influence from the Middle East and other Muslim regions.

Additional Important Incidents Against American Targets

DECEMBER 17, 1972: Palestinian terrorists bombed the Pan Am office at the airport in Rome, Italy. Thirty-two persons were killed, and fifty were injured. The terrorists took seven Italian policemen hostage, killing one of them; hijacked an Athens-bound plane; and forced the pilot to fly to Kuwait, where they surrendered to Kuwaiti authorities.

JUNE 18, 1979: NATO's Supreme Allied Commander Europe, American General Alexander Haig, was the target of a terrorist bomb that exploded under a bridge immediately after his motorcade had crossed it. While no one claimed responsibility, the German Red Army Faction was the primary suspect.

DECEMBER 17, 1983: U.S. Army Brigadier General James Dozier, the senior American officer at the NATO facilities near Verona, Italy, was kidnapped from his home by members of the Italian Red Brigades. The terrorists held the general for forty-five days before Italian special commandos rescued Dozier. According to one account, "The Dozier case was a triumph for the Italians, who had delivered a body blow to the Red Brigades, and a miracle for Dozier, whom most Americans had given up for dead."[20]

APRIL 12, 1984: Eighteen U.S. servicemen were killed and eighty-three people injured as a result of a bomb attack on a restaurant near the U.S. Air Force Base in Torrejon, Spain. Obviously, the terrorists had been aware that members of the U.S. military frequented the targeted restaurant. The Lebanese Hezbollah claimed responsibility for the attack and made clear that Americans had been the targets.

APRIL 5, 1986: Two U.S. servicemen were killed and seventy American soldiers were injured when a bomb exploded in a restroom of the La Belle disco in Berlin that was, as usual, packed with members of the American military stationed in West Berlin. A Turkish woman was also killed. The Reagan administration retaliated by bombing targets in Tripoli and Benghazi, Libya, because an intercepted message from the Libyan mission in East Berlin to Tripoli, Libya, had revealed that the explosion was the work of terrorists working for Libya's ruler, Muammar Qaddafi.

JUNE 25, 1996: A potent truck bomb was exploded outside the U.S. military's Khobar Towers housing area in Dhahran, Saudi Arabia, killing 19 Americans and injuring 515 other persons, among them 240 U.S. citizens. The Dhahran facility housed at the time more than 3,000 members of the military involved in enforcing the no-fly zone over Iraq. Several groups claimed responsibility for the attack, but U.S. authorities were convinced that Iran had sponsored the perpetrators. It took five years before the United States indicted thirteen Saudis and one Lebanese for the bombing. Most of them had been apprehended at the time by the Saudi Arabian authorities. Strangely, however, "No mention of Iran was made in the United States indictment," although Washington believed that the plot's "purpose was apparently to support Iran in driving the United States from the Gulf region."[21]

FEBRUARY 23, 1997: A gunman opened fire on tourists at an observation deck on top of the Empire State Building, one of the highest skyscrapers in the world. After killing a tourist from Denmark and injuring sightseers from Argentina, France, Switzerland, and the United States, the Palestinian gunman killed himself. In a handwritten note that the shooter left behind, the deed was explained as a strike against the "enemies of Palestine."

MAY 12, 2003: In synchronized actions, terrorist groups shot their way into three gated housing compounds for Westerners, and especially Americans, in Riyadh, Saudi Arabia, and then suicide bombers set off several car explosions. Saudi and American authorities were certain that Americans were the primary targets of the attack. Of the three dozen persons killed, 7 were U.S. citizens. Nearly 194 persons were injured, 40 of them Americans. At least 9 suicide bombers died in the blasts. Several weeks later, the Associated Press obtained a videotape in which a masked Afghan militant claimed that Al Qaeda was responsible for the bombings in Riyadh and that future attacks would prove "our superiority over the Americans."[22]

II. Incidents That Involved U.S. Victims

SEPTEMBER 6, 1970: In the first quadruple hijacking in the history of terrorism, four New York–bound airliners operated by TWA, Swissair, BOAC, and El Al were seized by members of the Popular Front for the Liberation of Palestine (PFLP). While security guards aboard the Israeli plane overwhelmed and arrested the terrorists, among them a female terrorist named Leila Khaled, the pilots of the other airliners with hundreds of passengers aboard (most of them Europeans and Americans) were forced to land at a remote place in Jordan. Although the hostage situation dragged on for weeks, many of the captives were released in small groups. Finally, the last of the hostages were freed after the British, German, and Swiss governments agreed to release Palestinian terrorists from their prisons—among them Leila Khaled, who had been held in London.

MAY 30, 1972: Three members of the Japanese Red Army, who had been recruited by the PFLP, opened fire in the passenger terminal of Lod Airport in Israel. Twenty-six civilians were killed, among them eleven Christian pilgrims from Puerto Rico. Kozo Okamoto of the Japanese Red Army survived and was arrested by Israeli security personnel.

NOVEMBER 23, 1985: An EgyptAir airliner was hijacked by Palestinian terrorists belonging to the Abu Nidal group en route from Athens, Greece, to Luqa, Malta. Several U.S. citizens were among the passengers. The terrorists killed two and injured three of their hostages before Egyptian commandos, who had flown to Malta, stormed the plane in an effort to rescue the hostages. But the terrorists set off explosives and foiled the rescue attempt. Fifty-seven passengers were killed.

JULY 4, 1995: Members of the Al-Faran, a Kashmiri separatist group, took five foreigners hostage in Kashmir, among them two Americans. One of the non-American hostages was later found beheaded; the other four were never seen again.

DECEMBER 17, 1996: Twenty-three members of the leftist Tupac Amaru Revolutionary Movement (MRTA) took several hundred hostages at a reception in the residence of the Japanese ambassador in Lima, Peru. Many Peruvian government officials, Japanese business representatives, and foreign diplomats—among them several Americans—were held. The armed terrorists demanded the release of more than 400 of their comrades from Peruvian prisons. Peruvian President Albert Fujimori refused to give in to the demands. During the first few weeks of the standoff, most of the hostages—including all Americans—were released. The remaining seventy-one captives were freed on April 22, 1997, after commandos entered the compound and killed all of the hostage-holders.

October 12, 2002: A mighty truck bomb exploded in a popular section of Bali, Indonesia, in the midst of popular nightclubs, cafés, and bars that were mostly frequented by foreign tourists. Two hundred persons from more than twenty countries were killed, most of them Australians. Seven Americans died in the blast, which was perpetrated by terrorists with ties to the extremist Jemaah Islamic group and to Al Qaeda. Terrorism experts suspected that the perpetrators intended to harm Westerners and particularly Americans.

December 27–29, 2008: Ten heavily armed terrorists opened fire on civilians in ten different sites in Mumbai, India, and eventually held hostages in two hotels and one Jewish community center. When Indian security forces gained control, 173 persons were dead, five Americans among them, and hundreds were injured. All but one of the terrorists were killed in the incident that according to Indian authorities was planned, directed, and carried out by members of the Pakistani terrorist organization Lashka-e-Taiba.

III. Incidents That Did Not Involve Americans

September 5, 1972: Members of the Palestinian Black September group entered the living quarters of the Israeli team during the Olympic Games in Munich. In a bungled rescue attempt by German security forces, nine of the hostages and five of the terrorists were killed.

December 21, 1975: Carlos "the Jackal," at the time the best-known international terrorist, and members of the PFLP took eleven ministers of oil-rich states and fifty-nine additional persons hostage during an OPEC meeting at Vienna, Austria. After being flown to Algeria, where Carlos and his terrorist team collected a high ransom payment, the terrorists were allowed to escape.

June 27, 1976: In a joint terrorist venture, members of the PFLP and the German Baader–Meinhof group hijacked an Air France airliner with 258 passengers and crew members aboard, forcing the pilot to land in Entebbe, Uganda. The terrorists released all passengers except for Israeli nationals. On July 4, Israeli commandos flew to Entebbe, stormed the plane, and killed the hijackers. During the rescue mission, 3 passengers were also killed.

October 13, 1977: A group of Palestinian terrorists hijacked a Lufthansa Boeing 737 and forced the pilot to fly to several destinations in the Middle East before touching down in Mogadishu, Somalia, for good. The terrorists then killed the pilot. A commando of the German counterterrorism force Grenzschutzgruppe 9 (GSG9), assisted by the British Army's Special Air Service (SAS), stormed the plane, rescuing all of the ninety hostages and killing three of the four terrorists aboard.

April 30, 1980: A group of Iraqi-backed Iranians seized the Iranian Embassy in London, taking twenty hostages. The terrorists killed two of their hostages and injured two others. Six days after the hostage situation began, SAS commandos stormed the embassy, freed the hostages, and killed four of the five terrorists.

SEPTEMBER 19, 1989: All 170 passengers and crew members aboard a French UTA airliner were killed when the plane exploded in midair over Niger, Africa. The French government blamed and issued warrants for four Libyan terrorists.

MARCH 17, 1992: A bomb explosion devastated Israel's embassy in Buenos Aires, Argentina, killing 29 and injuring 242 persons. The Lebanese Hezbollah claimed responsibility for the blast.

MARCH 20, 1995: Twelve persons were killed and 5,700 were injured as a result of a sarin nerve gas attack in a crowded subway station in the heart of Tokyo, Japan. Nearly simultaneously, a similar release of nerve gas occurred in the subway system of Yokohama. The Aum Shinrikyo sect was blamed for the attack and its leader brought to justice. The same cult was responsible for another nerve gas attack in the Japanese city of Matsumoto the previous June. In this case, 7 persons died and 150 fell sick. The lethal incident in Tokyo's subway alarmed people around the world and magnified the fear that terrorists would increasingly resort to biological, chemical, and even nuclear weapons of mass destruction.

NOVEMBER 17, 1997: Members of the Egyptian Al-Gama'at al-Islamiyya (IG) opened fire on a group of foreign tourists at the Hatshepsut Temple in the Valley of the Kings near Luxor, Egypt. Thirty-four Swiss, eight Japanese, five Germans, four Britons, one French, one Colombian, one citizen with dual British and Bulgarian citizenship, and four unidentified persons were killed, and twenty-six others were wounded. Fanatically opposed to the Egyptian regime, the IG attacked foreigners in order to harm tourism and the economy in their homeland and thereby weaken Egyptian President Hosni Mubarak's power.

MAY 16, 2003: Suicide bombers struck simultaneously four targets in Casablanca, Morocco: a Jewish center, a Spanish restaurant, the Belgian consulate, and the Safir Hotel. In three cases, the terrorists detonated truck bombs; in the fourth case, a suicide bomber ignited his explosive belt. Thirty-one persons were killed and seventy were injured. In addition, twelve suicide bombers died. A month later, an Afghan militant claimed that Al Qaeda was responsible for the synchronized attacks.

MARCH 11, 2004: Within fifteen minutes and at the height of the morning rush hour, a total of at least eight backpack bombs exploded first on a commuter train inside Madrid's Atocha station, then on a crowded commuter train entering the Atocha railroad station, and finally on a third train entering the Santa Eugenia train station about nine miles from Atocha. One hundred and ninety-one persons were killed and 1,500 were injured. By exploding three additional booby-trapped backpack bombs under controlled conditions, the Spanish police prevented further harm but not the shock wave that swept through Spain and the whole Western world. Although the unknown Al-Quds al-Arabia group claimed responsibility for the attacks as punishment for Spain's participation in the "crusade alliance" in Iraq, Spanish officials were quick to name the Basque separatist group ETA as the primary suspect. Three days after the carnage in Madrid, José Luis Rodríguez Zapatero and his Socialist Party defeated Prime Minister José María Aznar and his conservative Popular Party. Aznar, a staunch supporter of the U.S.-led war against

Iraq, had contributed 1,300 Spanish troops to the invasion forces. While some observers concluded that the Spanish electorate had given in to terrorism and chosen Zapatero and his party because they had promised to withdraw the Spanish military contingent from Iraq, others argued that Spanish voters had punished Aznar and his government for denying the possibility that Al Qaeda–related terrorists had struck in order to punish Spain for backing and participating in the invasion and occupation of Iraq.

SEPTEMBER 1–3, 2004: A large group of heavily armed Chechen extremists took over a school in Beslan in south Russia and held more than 1,200 children, parents, and teachers hostage. On day 3 of the incident, the captors detonated explosives that they had rigged around the interior of the school—especially the gym, where many of the hostages were held. At least 330 hostages, about half of them children, were killed, and many more were injured.

JULY 7, 2005: Four nearly simultaneous suicide attacks on the London transit system killed 56 victims and injured over 700. Three of the bombs exploded in underground trains and the fourth in a double-decker bus. Two weeks later, another quadruple attack on a bus and three underground trains failed when the bombs failed to detonate. In both cases, Muslims who were British citizens or residents were identified as the terrorists or would-be terrorists.

JULY 23, 2005: Several car bombs exploded at tourist hotels in Sharm el-Sheik in Egypt killing 88 and wounding more than 100 persons.

NOVEMBER 9, 2005: Three explosions in three hotels in Amman, Jordan, killed 60 persons and injured more than 100 people. Within days, Jordanian authorities identified the three suicide bombers and connected them to an Al Qaeda–affiliated group led by Abu Musab al-Zarqawi who was also responsible for many terrorist attacks in post-invasion Iraq.

JUNE 15, 2006: Tamil Tigers in Sri Lanka targeted a crowded commuter bus. As two mines detonated, sixty-eight civilians, among them women and children, were killed and at least sixty persons injured.

JULY 11, 2006: Within ten minutes, terrorists detonated seven bombs on commuter trains in Mumbai, India, formerly known as Bombay. Two hundred and nine persons were killed and many hundreds injured. Nobody claimed responsibility for the attack. Although Indian police questioned and detained hundreds of people, the authorities did not come up with what they called "clinching evidence."

DECEMBER 27, 2007: Former Pakistani Prime Minister Benazir Bhutto was killed as she left a rally of the Pakistan Peoples Party (PPP) in the city of Rawalpindi. At the time, she was the chairperson and lead candidate of the PPP for the 2008 election. As Bhutto stood up through the sunroof of her bulletproof car, shots were fired at her and explosives ignited near her vehicle. In addition to Bhutto, two dozen or so people were killed and more injured.

Notes

1. Gary Sick, *All Fall Down: America's Tragic Encounter with Iran* (New York: Penguin Books, 1986), 240.
2. David C. Martin and John Walcott, *Best Laid Plans: The Inside Story of America's War on Terrorism* (New York: Harper & Row, 1988), 43.
3. Ibid., 105.
4. Jeffrey D. Simon, *The Terror Trap: America's Experience with Terrorism* (Bloomington: Indiana University Press, 1994), 193.
5. Originally, the quartet planned to take hostages once the ship reached one of the ports-of-call— Ashodod, Israel. But when a member of the crew happened upon the Palestinians as they cleaned their weapons in their cabin, they changed their plan and acted immediately.
6. For more information on the factors that led to the release of the hostages, see Don Oberdorfer, "Iran Paid for Release of Hostages; Tehran Gave Captors up to $2 Million for Each, Officials Say," *Washington Post*, January 19, 1992, A1; and Elaine Sciolino, "The Last U.S. Hostage: Tea in Tehran: How the Hostage Deal was Born," *New York Times*, December 5, 1991, 1.
7. Brigitte L. Nacos, *Terrorism and the Media: From the Iran Hostage Crisis to the Oklahoma City Bombing* (New York: Columbia University Press, 1996), 2.
8. Alison Mitchell, "Letter Explained Motive in Bombing, Officials Now Say," *New York Times*, March 28, 1993, 1.
9. Simon Reeve, *The New Jackals: Ramzi Yousef, Osama bin Laden and the Future of Terrorism* (Boston: Northeastern University Press, 1999), 120. This volume provides excellent accounts of the backgrounds and terrorist activities of Yousef and bin Laden.
10. Ibid., 47.
11. Peter Applebome, "Radical Right's Fury Boiling Over," *New York Times*, April 23, 1995, 33.
12. Lou Michel and Dan Herbeck, *American Terrorist: Timothy McVeigh and the Oklahoma City Bombing* (New York: Regan Books, 2001), 168.
13. Ibid., 378–80.
14. U.S. Department of State, "The Year in Review," in *Patterns of Global Terrorism 2001*, 2.
15. Michael J. Siler, "Kenya and Tanzania," in Frank Shanty, Raymond Piquet, and John Lalla, eds., *Encyclopedia of World Terrorism: 1996–2002* (Armonk, NY: Sharpe Reference, 2003), 416–20.
16. Brigitte L. Nacos, *Mass-Mediated Terrorism: The Central Role of the Media in Terrorism and Counterterrorism* (Lanham, MD: Rowman & Littlefield, 2002), 7.
17. Eric Lichtblau, "Aftereffects: The Cole Bombing; U.S. Indicts 2 Men for Attack on American Ship in Yemen," *New York Times*, May 16, 2003, A17.
18. Nearly a year after 9/11, the official number of victims killed in the World Trade Center stood at 8,823. As of August 2002, 2,726 death certificates related to the WTC attack had been filed, according to the Centers for Disease Control and Prevention and "Mortality Weekly Report," September 11, 2002, no. 51 (special issue), 16–18, www.cdc.gov/mmwr/preview/mmwrhtml/mm51SPa6.htm.
19. The timeline of the events on 9/11 is described in "September 11 and Review of Terrorism 2001," in U.S. Department of State, "Patterns of Global Terrorism, 2001," 1. See also Nacos, *Mass-Mediated Terrorism*, ch. 2.
20. Martin and Walcott, 63.
21. Martha Crenshaw, "Why America? The Globalization of Civil War." *Current History*, December 2001, 430.
22. Kathy Gannon, "Tape Says Al-Qaida behind Saudi Bombings," Associated Press, June 22, 2003, http://story.news.yahoo.com/news?tmpl=story&u=/ap/20030622/ap_on_re_as/al_qaida_video_16 (retrieved June 23, 2003).

bibliography

Abrahams, Max. "Why Terrorism Does Not Work." *International Security* 31:2 (Fall 2006): 42–78.

Adams, James. "Virtual Defense." *Foreign Affairs* 80:3 (May–June 2001): 98–112.

Adams, William C., ed. *Television Coverage of the Middle East*. Norwood, NJ: Ablex, 1981.

Adler, Freda. *Sisters in Crime*. Prospect Heights, IL: Waveland Press, 1985.

Alali, A. Odasuo, and Kenoye Kelvin Eke, eds. *Media Coverage of Terrorism: Methods of Diffusion*. Newbury Park, CA: Sage, 1991.

Allison, Graham T., et al. *Avoiding Nuclear Anarchy*. Cambridge, MA: MIT Press, 1996.

Altheide, David L. "Format and Symbols in TV Coverage of Terrorism in the United States and Great Britain." *International Studies Quarterly* 31 (1987): 161–76.

———. "Three-in-One News: Network Coverage of Iran." *Journalism Quarterly* 59 (1982): 482–86.

Arquilla, John, and Theodore Karasik. "Chechnya: A Glimpse of Future Conflict?" *Studies in Conflict and Terrorism* 22 (1999): 207–29.

Arquilla, John, and David Ronfeldt. "The Advent of Netwar: Analytical Background." *Studies in Conflict and Terrorism* 22 (1999): 193–206.

Ash, Timothy Garton. "Is There a Good Terrorist?" *New York Review of Books*, November 29, 2001, www.nybooks.com/articles/14860 (retrieved April 2, 2002).

Atta, Dale Van. "Carbombs and Cameras: The Need for Responsible Media Coverage of Terrorism." *Harvard International Review* (Fall 1998): 66–70.

Bagdikian, Benjamin. *The Media Monopoly*, 6th ed. Boston: Beacon Press, 2000.

Bacevich, Andrew J., "Rescinding the Bush Doctrine." *The Boston Globe*, March 1, 2007.

Baudrillard, Jean. *The Transparency of Evil*. London: Verso, 1993.

Bennett, Lance W., and David L. Paletz, eds. *Taken by Storm: The Media, Public Opinion, and U.S. Foreign Policy in the Gulf War*. Chicago: University of Chicago Press, 1994.

Bergen, Peter. "The Bin Laden Trial: What Did We Learn?" *Studies in Conflict and Terrorism* 24:6 (2001): 429–34.

Betts, Richard K. "The Soft Underbelly of American Primacy: Tactical Advantages of Terror." In Demetrios James Careley, ed. *September 11, Terrorist Attacks, and U.S. Foreign Policy*. New York: Academy of Political Science, 2002.

Biddle, Stephen D. "American Grand Strategy After 9/11: An Assessment." http://www.strategicstudiesinstitute.army.mil/pdffiles/PUB603.pdf

Bloom, Mia. *Dying to Kill: The Allure of Suicide Terror*. New York: Columbia University, 2005.

Bok, Sissela. *Mayhem: Violence as Public Entertainment*. Reading, MA: Perseus Books, 1998.

Bryant, Jennings, and Dolf Zillmann, eds. *Perspectives on Media Effects*. Hillsdale, NJ: Laurence Erlbaum, 1986.

Brzezinski, Zbigniew. *Power and Principle*. New York: Farrar, Strauss and Giroux, 1983.

Burdman, Daphne. "Education, Indoctrination, and Incitement: Palestinian Children on Their Way to Martyrdom." *Terrorism and Political Violence* 14:1 (2003): 96–123.

Byman, Daniel. *Deadly Connections: States that Sponsor Terrorism*. New York: Cambridge University Press, 2005.

———, "The Decision to Begin Talks with Terrorists: Lessons for Policymakers." *Studies in Conflict and Terrorism* 29 (2006): 403–14.

Catton, William R., Jr. "Militants and the Media: Partners in Terrorism?" *Indiana Law Journal* 53 (1978): 703–15.

Chase, Alston. "Harvard and the Unabomber." *Atlantic Monthly* 285:6 (June 2000): 41–65.

Chomsky, Noam. *The Culture of Terrorism*. Boston: South End Press, 1988.

Cole, David, and James X. Dempsey. *Terrorism and the Constitution: Sacrificing Civil Liberties in the Name of National Security*. New York: New Press, 2002.

Cook, Timothy E. "Domesticating a Crisis: Washington Newsbeats and Network News after the Iraqi Invasion of Kuwait." In W. Lance Bennett and David L. Paletz, eds., *Taken by Storm: The Media, Public Opinion, and U.S. Foreign Policy in the Gulf War*. Chicago: University of Chicago Press, 1994.

Cotter, John M. "Sounds of Hate: White Power, Rock and Roll and the Neo-Nazi Skinhead Subculture." *Terrorism and Political Violence* 11:2 (1999): 111–40.

Crelinsten, Ronald D. "Television and Terrorism: Implications for Crisis Management and Policy-Making." *Terrorism and Political Violence* 9:4 (1997): 8–32.

Crenshaw, Martha, ed. *Terrorism in Context*. University Park: Pennsylvania State University Press, 1995.

———, ed. *Terrorism, Legitimacy, and Power: The Consequences of Political Violence*. Middletown, CT: Wesleyan University Press, 1983.

———, "Terrorism, Strategies, and Grand Strategies." In Audrey Kurth Cronin and James M. Ludes, eds. *Attacking Terrorism: Elements of a Grand Strategy*. Washington: Georgetown University Press, 2004.

Crenshaw, Martha, and John Pomlitt, eds. *Encyclopedia of World Terrorism*. Armonk, NY: M. E. Sharpe. 1997.

Cronin, Audrey Kurth. "Behind the Curve: Globalization and International Terrorism." *International Security* 27:3 (Winter 2002/3): 30–58.

Cronin, Audrey Kurth, "How al-Qaida Ends." *International Security* 31:1 (Summer 2006): 7–48.

Dalby, Simon, "Geopolitics, Grand Strategy and the Bush Doctrine." IDSS Discussion Paper, October 2005.

Danitz, Tiffany, and Warren P. Strobel. "The Internet's Impact on Activism: The Case of Burma." *Studies in Conflict and Terrorism* 22 (1999): 257–69.

De Cataldo Neuberger, and Luisella Tiziana Valenti. *Women and Terrorism*. New York: St. Martin's, 1996.

Delli Carpini, Michael X., and Bruce A. Williams. "Television and Terrorism: Patterns of Presentation and Occurrence, 1969 to 1980." *Western Political Quarterly* 40:1 (1987): 45–64.

Dempsey, James X. "Counterterrorism and the Constitution." *Current History* (April 2000): 164–68.

Dershowitz, Alan. *Why Terrorism Works*. New Haven, CT: Yale University Press, 2002.

Drake, C. J. M. "The Role of Ideology in Terrorists' Target Selection." *Terrorism and Political Violence* 10:2 (1998): 53–85.

Edelman, Murray. *Constructing the Political Spectacle*. Chicago: University of Chicago Press, 1988.

———. *Political Language: Words That Succeed and Policies That Fail*. New York: Academic Press, 1977.

Egendorf, Laura K., ed. *Terrorism: Opposing Viewpoints*. San Diego, CA: Greenhaven Press, 2000, 77–80.

Esposito, John L., "Terrorism and the Rise of Political Islam." In Louise Richardson, ed., *The Roots of Terrorism*. New York: Routledge, 2006.

Eubank, William, and Leonard Weinberg. "Terrorism and Democracy: Perpetrators and Victims." *Terrorism and Political Violence* 13:1 (2001): 155–64.

Fanon, Frantz. *The Wretched of the Earth*. New York: Grove Weidenfeld, 1963.

Finkel, Michael. "The Child Martyrs of Karni Crossing." *New York Times Magazine,* December 24, 2000.

Freedman, Lawrence, ed. *Superterrorism: Policy Responses.* Malden, MA: Blackwell Publishing, 2002.

Gerbner, George, and L. Gross. "Living with Television: The Violence Profile." *Journal of Communication* 26:2 (1976): 173–99.

Gilboa, Eytan. *Media and Conflict: Framing Issues, Making Policy, Shaping Opinions.* Ardsley Park, NY: Transnational Publishers, 2002.

Gordon, Avishag. "Terrorism on the Internet: Discovering the Unsought." *Terrorism and Political Violence* 9:4 (1997): 159–65.

Gordon, Philip H. "The End of the Bush Revolution." *Foreign Affairs,* July/August 2006.

Graber, Doris. *Mass Media and American Politics.* Washington, DC: Congressional Quarterly Press, 1997.

Graham, Hugh, and Ted Gurr, eds. *Violence in America.* Beverly Hills, CA: Sage, 1979.

Guelke, Adrian. "Wars of Fear: Coming to Grips with Terrorism." *Harvard International Review* (Fall 1998): 44–47.

Hallin, Daniel L. *The "Uncensored War": The Media and Vietnam.* New York: Oxford University Press, 1986.

Harmon, Christopher C. *Terrorism Today.* London: Frank Cass, 2000.

Herman, Edward, and Gerry O'Sullivan. *The Terrorism Industry: The Experts and Institutions That Shape Our View of Terror.* New York: Pantheon Books, 1989.

Hershberg, Eric, and Kevin W. Moore, eds. *Critical Views of September 11: Analyses from around the World.* New York: New Press, 2002.

Hewitt, Christopher. "The Political Context of Terrorism in America: Ignoring Extremists or Pandering to Them?" *Terrorism and Political Violence* 12:3–4 (2000): 323–44.

Heyman, Philip B. *Terrorism, Freedom, and Security: Winning without War.* Cambridge, MA: MIT Press, 2003.

Hickey, Neil. "Money Lust: How Pressure for Profit Is Perverting Journalism." *Columbia Journalism Review* (July–August 1998): 28–36.

Hoffman, Bruce. " 'Holy Terror': The Implications of Terrorism Motivated by a Religious Imperative." *Studies in Conflict and Terrorism* 18:4 (1995): 271–84.

———. "Why Terrorists Don't Claim Credit." *Terrorism and Political Violence* 9:1 (1997): 1–6.

———. *Inside Terrorism.* New York: Columbia University Press, 1998.

Hollihan, Thomas A. *Uncivil Wars: Political Campaigns in the Mega Age.* Boston: Bedford/St. Martin's, 2001.

Houen, Alex. *Terrorism and Modern Literature: From Josef Conrad to Ciaran Carson.* New York: Oxford, 2002.

Israeli, Raphael. "A Manual of Islamic Fundamentalist Terrorism." *Terrorism and Political Violence* 14:4 (2002): 23–40.

Iyengar, Shanto. *Is Anyone Responsible? How Television Frames Political Issues.* Chicago: University of Chicago Press, 1991.

Iyengar Shanto, and Donald R. Kinder. *News That Matters.* Chicago: University of Chicago Press, 1987.

Jacobs, Lawrence R., and Robert Y. Shapiro. *Politicians Don't Pander: Political Manipulation and the Loss of Democratic Responsiveness.* Chicago: University of Chicago Press, 2000.

Jenkins, Brian M. "Der internationale Terrorismus." *Aus Politik und Zeitgeschichte* B5 (1987): 17–27.

Jenkins, Philip. *Images of Terror: What We Can and Can't Know about Terrorism.* New York: Aldine de Gruyter, 2003.

Jensen, Richard Bach. "The United States, International Policing and the War against Anarchist Terrorism, 1900–1914." *Terrorism and Political Violence* 13:1 (2001): 15–46.

Jervis, Robert, "Understanding the Bush Doctrine." In Demetrios James Careley, ed. *American Hegemony: Preventive War, Iraq, and Imposing Democracy.* New York: Academy of Political Science, 2004.

Juergensmeyer, Mark. *Terror in the Mind of God: The Global Rise of Religious Violence.* Berkeley: University of California Press, 2001.

Juergensmeyer, Mark, "Religion as a Cause of Terrorism." In Richardson, ed., *The Roots of Terrorism.*

Kaplan, Jeffrey. "Right Wing Violence in North America." *Terrorism and Political Violence* 7:1 (1995): 44–95.

Katz, Daniel, et al. *Public Opinion and Propaganda.* New York: Dryden Press, 1954.

Kegley, Charles, Jr., ed. *International Terrorism: Characteristics, Causes, Controls.* New York: St. Martin's, 1990.

Keohane, Robert O., and Joseph S. Nye, Jr. "Power and Interdependence in the Information Age." *Foreign Affairs* 77:5 (September–October 1998): 81–94.

Kernell, Samuel. *Going Public: New Strategies of Presidential Leadership,* 3rd ed. Washington, DC: Congressional Quarterly Press, 1997.

Kupperman, Robert, and Jeff Kamen. *Final Warning: Averting Disaster in the New Age of Terrorism.* New York: Doubleday, 1989.

Kupperman, Robert, and Darrel Trent. *Terrorism: Threat, Reality, Response.* Stanford, CA: Hoover Institution, 1979.

Kurth Cronin, Audrey and James M. Ludes, eds. *Attacking Terrorism: Elements of a Grand Strategy.* Washington, D.C.: Georgetown University Press, 2004.

Kuzma, Lynn M. "Trends: Terrorism in the United States." *Public Opinion Quarterly* 64:1 (Spring 2000): 90–105.

Laqueur, Walter. *The Age of Terrorism.* Boston: Little, Brown, 1987.

———. *The New Terrorism: Fanaticism and the Arms of Mass Destruction.* New York: Oxford University Press, 1999.

———. *A History of Terrorism.* New Brunswick, NJ: Transaction Publishers, 2002.

Laqueur, Walter, and Yonah Alexander, eds. *The Terrorism Reader.* New York: Penguin, 1987.

Lawrence, Bruce. *Messages to the World: The Statements of Osama bin Laden.* London: Verso, 2005.

Lia, Brynjar, "Doctrines for Jihadi Terrorist Training. " *Terrorism and Political Violence* 20 (4) (October – December 2008).

Lesser, Ian O., "Countering the New Terrorism: Implications for Strategy." In Ian O. Lesser et al., eds., *Countering the New Terrorism.* Santa Monica: Rand, 1999.

Lippmann, Walter. *Public Opinion.* New York: Free Press, 1949.

Livingston, Maurius H., ed. *International Terrorism in the Contemporary World.* Westport, CT: Greenwood Press, 1978.

Livingston, Stephen. *The Terrorism Spectacle.* Boulder, CO: Westview Press, 1994.

MacArthur, John R. *Second Front: Censorship and Propaganda in the Gulf War.* Berkeley: University of California Press, 1993.

Macdonald, Andrew. *The Turner Diaries,* 2nd ed. New York: Barricade Books, 1996.

Marighella, Carlos. "Handbook of Urban Guerrilla Warfare." In Walter Laqueur and Yonah Alexander, eds., *The Terrorism Reader.* New York: Penguin, 1987.

Martin, David C., and John Walcott. *Best Laid Plans: The Inside Story of America's War on Terrorism.* New York: Harper & Row, 1988.

McCant, William and Jarret Brachman, "Militant Ideology Atlas." Executive Report compiled and published by the Combating Terrorism Center at West Point.

McMullan, Ronald K. "Ethnic Conflict in Russia: Implications for the United States." *Studies in Conflict and Terrorism* 16:3 (1993): 201–18.

Morgan, Robin. *The Demon Lover: The Roots of Terrorism*. New York: Washington Square Press, 2001.

Nacos, Brigitte L. "Presidential Leadership during the Persian Gulf War." *Presidential Studies Quarterly* 24:3 (Summer 1994): 563–75.

———. *Terrorism and the Media: From the Iran Hostage Crisis to the World Trade Center Bombing*. New York: Columbia University Press, 1994.

———. "After the Cold War: Terrorism Looms Larger as a Weapon of Dissent and Warfare." *Current World Leaders* 39:4 (August 1996): 11–26.

———. *Terrorism and the Media: From the Iran Hostage Crisis to the Oklahoma City Bombing*, rev. ed. New York: Columbia University Press, 1996.

———. "Accomplice or Witness? The Mass Media's Role in Terrorism." *Current History* 99 (April 2000): 174–78.

Nacos, Brigitte L., Robert Y. Shapiro, and Pierangelo Isernia, eds. *Decision-making in a Glass House: Mass Media, Public Opinion, and American and European Foreign Policy in the 21st Century*. Lanham, MD: Rowman & Littlefield, 2000.

Nasr, Vali. *The Shia Revival: How Conflict within Islam will Shape the Future*. New York: Norton, 2006.

Nimmo, Dan, and James E. Combs. *Nightly Horrors: Crisis Coverage in Television Network News*. Knoxville: University of Tennessee Press, 1985.

Nye, Joseph S., Jr. *The Paradox of American Power*. New York: Oxford University Press, 2002.

Nye, Joseph S., Jr., and William A. Owens. "America's Information Edge." *Foreign Affairs* 75:2 (March–April 1996): 20–36.

Page, Benjamin I., and Robert Y. Shapiro. *The Rational Public*. Chicago: University of Chicago Press, 1992.

Paletz, David L., and Alex P. Schmid. *Terrorism and the Media*. Newbury Park, CA: Sage, 1992.

Picard, Robert G. "News Coverage as the Contagion." In A. Odasuo Alali and Kenoye Kelvin Eke, eds., *Media Coverage of Terrorism*. Newbury Park, CA: Sage, 1991.

Pillar, Paul R. *Terrorism and U.S. Foreign Policy*. Washington, DC: Brookings Institution Press, 2001.

Pluchinsky, Dennis A. "The Terrorism Puzzle: Missing Pieces and No Boxcover." *Terrorism and Political Violence* 9:1 (1997): 7–10.

Post, Jerrold M., Ehud Sprinzak, and Laurita M. Denny. "The Terrorists in Their Own Words: Interviews with 35 Incarcerated Middle Eastern Terrorists." *Terrorism and Political Violence* 15:1 (2003): 171–84.

Ranstorp, Magnus, and Gus Xhudo. "A Threat to Europe? Middle East Ties with the Balkans and Their Impact upon Terrorist Activity throughout the Region." *Terrorism and Political Violence* 6:2 (1994): 196–223.

Rapoport, David C. "To Claim or Not to Claim; That Is the Question—Always!" *Terrorism and Political Violence* 9:1 (1997): 11–17.

———. "The Fourth Wave: September 11 in the History of Terrorism." *Current History* (December 2001): 419–24.

———, ed. *Inside Terrorist Organizations*. London: Frank Cass, 2001.

Reeve, Simon. *The New Jackals: Ramzi Yousef, Osama bin Laden and the Future of Terrorism*. Boston: Northeastern University Press, 1999.

Reich, Walter, ed. *Origins of Terrorism: Psychologies, Ideologies, Theologies, States of Mind*. New York: Cambridge University Press, 1990.

Reuter, Christoph. *Mein Leben ist eine Waffe*. Munich: Bertelsmann, 2002.

Richardson, Louise. "Terrorists as Transnational Actors." *Terrorism and Political Violence* 11:4 (1999): 209–19.

Richardson, Louise, ed. *The Roots of Terrorism.* New York: Routledge, 2006.

———. *What Terrorists Want: Understanding the Enemy, Containing the Threat.* New York: Random House, 2006.

Ronfeldt, David. "Netwar across the Spectrum of Conflict: An Introductory Comment." *Studies in Conflict and Terrorism* 22 (1999): 189–92.

Rubenstein, Richard E. *Alchemists of Revolution: Terrorism in the Modern World.* New York: Basic Books, 1987.

Rubin, Bernard. *When Information Counts: Grading the Media.* Lexington, MA: Lexington Books, 1985.

Sageman, Marc. *Understanding Terror Networks.* Philadelphia: University of Pennsylvania Press, 2004.

Said, Edward W. *Covering Islam: How the Media and the Experts Determine How We See the Rest of the World.* New York: Pantheon, 1981.

Schbley, Ayla. "Defining Religious Terrorism: A Causal and Anthological Profile." *Studies in Conflict and Terrorism* 26:2 (2003): 105–34.

Scheuer, Jeffrey. *The Sound Bite Society: Television and the American Mind.* New York: Four Walls Eight Windows, 1999.

Schlagheck, Donna M. *International Terrorism.* Lexington, MA: Lexington Books, 1988.

Schlesinger, Philip, Graham Murdock, and Philip Elliott. *Televising "Terrorism": Political Violence in Popular Culture.* London: Comedia, 1983.

Schmid, Alex P., and Jenny de Graaf. *Violence as Communication: Insurgent Terrorism and the Western News Media.* Beverly Hills, CA: Sage, 1982.

Schmidt, Brian C., and Michael C. Williams. "The Bush Doctrine and the Iraq War: Neoconservatives vs. Realists." Paper presented at the Annual Conference of the British International Studies Association, Cambridge, YUK, December 17–19, 2007.

Sedgwick, Mark. "Al-Qaeda and the Nature of Religious Terrorism." *Terrorism and Political Violence* 16:4 (Winter 2004): 795–814.

Seib, Philip. *Going Live: Getting the News Right in a Real-Time, Online World.* Lanham, MD: Rowman & Littlefield, 2001.

Shanahan, James, and Michael Morgan. *Television and Its Viewers: Cultivation Theory and Research.* New York: Cambridge University Press, 1999.

Sick, Gary. *All Fall Down: America's Encounter with Iran.* New York: Penguin, 1986.

Simon, Jeffrey D. *The Terror Trap: America's Experience with Terrorism.* Bloomington: Indiana University Press, 1994.

Smith, Brent L., and Kathryn D. Morgan. "Terrorists Right and Left: Empirical Issues in Profiling American Terrorists." *Studies in Conflict and Terrorism* 17:1 (1994): 39–57.

Snow, Donald M. *National Security for a New Era: Globalization and Geopolitics.* New York: Pearson Longman, 2007.

Sprinzak, Ehud. "Extremism and Violence in Israel: The Crisis of Messianic Politics." *Annals of the American Academy of Political Science* 555 (January 1998): 114–26.

Sterling, Claire. *The Terror Network.* New York: Berkeley, 1982.

Stern, Jessica. *The Ultimate Terrorist.* Boston: Harvard University Press, 1999.

———. *Terror in the Name of God: Why Religious Militants Kill.* New York: HarperCollins, 2003.

———. "The Protean Enemy." *Foreign Affairs* (July–August 2003): 115–26.

Stern, Kenneth S. *A Force upon the Plain: The American Militia Movement and the Politics of Hate.* New York: Simon & Schuster, 1996.

Stohl, Michael. "Characteristics of Contemporary International Terrorism." In Charles W. Kegley, Jr., ed., *International Terrorism: Characteristics, Causes, Controls.* New York: St. Martin's, 1990.

Summers, Craig, and Erik Markusen. *Collective Violence*. Lanham, MD: Rowman & Littlefield, 1999.

Trager, Robert F. and Dessislava P. Zagorcheva. "Deterring Terrorism: It Can Be Done." *International Security* 30:3 (Winter 2005): 87–123.

Tulis, Jeffrey K. *The Rhetorical Presidency*. Princeton, NJ: Princeton University Press, 1987.

Weiman, Gabriel, and Conrad Winn. *The Theater of Terror: Mass Media and International Terrorism*. New York: Longman, 1994.

Whine, Michael. "Cyberspace: A New Medium for Communication, Command, and Control by Extremists." *Studies in Conflict and Terrorism* 22 (1999): 231–45.

———. "Islamist Organizations on the Internet." *Terrorism and Political Violence* 11:1 (1999): 123–32.

Wieviorka, Michel. *The Making of Terrorism*. Chicago: University of Chicago Press, 1993.

Wilkinson, Paul. "The Media and Terror: A Reassessment." *Terrorism and Political Violence* 9 (1997): 132–34.

———. *Terrorism versus Democracy*. London: Frank Cass, 2000.

Wolfsfeld, Gadi. "The News Media and the Second Intifada." *Harvard International Journal of Press/Politics* 6:4 (2001): 113–18.

Woodward, Bob. *Plan of Attack*. New York: Simon & Schuster, 2004.

Yankelovich, Daniel. *Coming to Public Judgment*. Syracuse, NY: Syracuse University Press, 1991.

Zanini, Michele. "Middle Eastern Terrorism and Netwar." *Studies in Conflict and Terrorism* 22 (1999): 247–56.

index